Don Pothier
Sept. 24, 2005

HISTORY OF TUSKET
NOVA SCOTIA

by

Don R. Pothier

Edited with an introduction
by
Peter Crowell, CG(C)

Library and Archives Canada Cataloguing in Publication

Pothier, Don R. (Don Richard), 1944-
    History of Tusket, Nova Scotia / by Don R. Pothier ; edited with an introduction by Peter Crowell.

ISBN 0-9737976-0-6

    1. Tusket (N.S.)--History. I. Crowell, Peter Matthew, 1954- II. Title.

FC2349.T88P68 2005   971.6'31   C2005-903611-7

Don R. Pothier
P.O. Box 68, Tusket, Nova Scotia
Canada B0W 3M0
dpothier@auracom.com

Cover: This portrait of Tusket, Nova Scotia is an oil painting by Jennie Morrow of Yarmouth, NS. My wife Barbara and I commissioned this painting in 1997-98. It depicts the village centre, circa 1890s. The John White Road (the main road during that time) is in the foreground. Lent's Corner is visible in the distance.

Printed by: Sentinel Printing Limited
1-800-565-3043
Yarmouth, N.S. B5A 1S7

I dedicate this book to my only grandchild, Keith Richard Green, whom I love so dearly, now an innocent young child only two years of age. As he matures and I grow older, the winds of time will surely separate us. I hope that this manuscript will leave with him lasting memories and a better understanding of the village where his grand-parents lived and where his mother grew up

Love, Papa

CONTENTS

PREFACE

I entered the world of work in 1961 in the village of Tusket, in the employment of my brother, Hubert Pothier, who had recently opened an auto body shop in the village. Gordon Wood, son of James and Bessie Wood of Tusket, lived near the auto body shop; he soon came to work in the body shop as well, and a lasting friendship soon developed. A few years later, (1962-63), my brother Hubert purchased the large lot of land to the north of his auto body shop. This lot was mostly grown up in spruce trees and a mixture of wild bushes and curiosity often brought us to explore the land during our noon-time lunch breaks. It wasn't long before we stumbled upon the remains of a large area of old red clay bricks that lay close to the shore of the river. In the centre of this area was a monstrous cement block with long and rusty steel rods protruding from its top. I was mystified until Gordon explained that "according to the old folks" this was the remains of a huge brick chimney that once stood here for a saw-mill and that many local residents had come here over the years to gather bricks to build chimneys for their own homes. By this time there were very few good bricks left – just a large area covered with small red fragments. Having always had an interest in "old stuff," I immediately wanted to know more. Gordon said they called this the McGrath Mill. This was my first introduction to Tusket's past … little did I realize at the time that it would eventually lead to the writing and publication of this book.

In 1965, newly married, I began the arduous task of trying to purchase land in Tusket to build my own home. This search for land soon made me even more aware of the historical richness that lay within the village. Everywhere I went asking about land availability, it seemed there was always a story to be told about things that once existed on these properties. I was overwhelmed with the stories I was hearing. As time went on, Gordon Wood and I often found ourselves discussing Tusket's past even more. As the stories unfolded, we became more curious as to what Tusket looked like during those earlier times. Eventually we decided to go around the village and ask people if they had old photographs and if we could borrow them to have copies made. The response that we received was overwhelming. We were welcomed into people's homes with open arms and it was gratifying to witness the expressions on the faces of the older people as they realized that someone had an interest in their "olden days" and that these memories might in some way be preserved.

Gordon and I soon became regular customers of Mr. Clyde Churchill at Rozee's Photo Studio Shop in Yarmouth. If we could bring in our photos by Friday night, we could have our copies back by the following Friday. That was the routine. (How times have changed.) It didn't matter what the size or condition of the pictures was, we each had an 8x10 print made. How the excitement would build as Friday would approach and we anxiously awaited to see what our next batch of pictures would look like! I gradually realized that what had started as a passing interest in Tusket's past had become something of a passion for me.

We also realized that the wonderful stories from the past that the older citizens were sharing with us were extremely valuable and needed to be documented. I began taking notes. Sometimes this meant going back to visit where we had already been. Of all the homes we visited in the village, only one refused us an interview. We were simply told that they had no photographs and no information to offer. We got to know the seniors of the village well, and afterwards it was a delight to meet some of them at the post office or at the country store. I often took out my note pad when they would say to me, "Oh, by the way, I forgot to tell you about ..." or "did I ever tell you the story of ..." By this time, several of them began to ask, "When are we going to be able to read this stuff?"

Gordon and I were both busy at our regular jobs and the thought of putting together a manuscript was beyond our means, and beyond the time at our disposal. Fearing that we might not be able to compile the information properly, I brought the matter up with a close personal friend, Mr. Edwin K. Ford, a well-known educator and writer, living in Yarmouth. He was keenly interested, and at once offered to do any necessary writing if we would supply the needed information.

The following summer, 1970, I received the appointment as Motor Vehicle Repair (Body) Instructor at Burridge Vocational School in Yarmouth, known in 2005 as the Nova Scotia Community College – Burridge Campus. This required that I take summer courses in Moncton, New Brunswick. During my absence, I received some shocking news; Mr. Ford had passed away suddenly while delivering a speech at the Yarmouth Historical Society. Consequently, we decided to put away our materials with the intention of resuming the project at some later date.

While taking courses as part of my teaching license structure, in 1973-74, an Acadian History course was offered at Collège Sainte-Anne, now Université Sainte-Anne. Although Tusket was not an Acadian village, my professor, J. Alphonse Deveau, granted me permission to work on a project on the history of my village based on the fact that Tusket was the administrative centre for the entire Municipality of Argyle and all its surrounding Acadian communities. This presented me with an ideal opportunity to resume the project that Gordon and I had embarked on a decade or so earlier. At this time I proceeded with the project alone. In doing so, I came to realize that what Gordon and I had originally gathered constituted only a small portion of the work required to put it all together.

It was during this winter of 1973-74 that I compiled the original manuscript that has become known and used at the Argyle Township Court House Archives as my "History of Tusket." Although it has served its original intended purpose of preserving the old photographs and the valuable information gathered, it was never intended to be a complete history of the village. Every effort was made during that winter to compile as much information as possible in a short period of time. I re-interviewed most of the people that Gordon and I had originally talked to.

It had been an idea of mine, that in my retirement, I would return to this history project, and attempt to have the manuscript published. When Peter Crowell finally convinced me to re-write the manuscript and I began to refresh my memory, it was with total awe that I realized that thirty years had slipped by since I wrote the original document. When I read my original preface, it was with a deep sense of sadness that I realized that only one of all the seniors that I had originally interviewed was still alive, and sadly, even she is no longer able to provide information … her name is Ruth Wood.

An Acknowledgement to Some of the Original Contributors to This History

Ruth Wood always welcomed us with her pleasant smile and shared a number of great photographs with us, including several by Tusket photographer, Gordon Hatfield, taken in front of her house and near the village square. This was a home that we visited many times and Ruth was one of those who frequently had more information to offer when I met her at the post office.

The late Mildred Hatfield had the most impressive collection of old photographs that we encountered during that time … we were simply overwhelmed! She had several of Gordon Hatfield's photographs and was very proud to show the pictures that had white horses in them; those were her father's horses and she was often the little girl sitting beside him in the carriage. She loaned us her entire collection and many of those photographs are included throughout this history. Her recollection of the past was remarkable and I wouldn't even dare to guess how many times I visited her for more information. It is she who provided me with the names on the 1912 photograph of the Tusket baseball team. She also continually tried to remember the names of the two unidentified persons on the team, insisting that she knew who they were. One day I met her at the post office (approximately two years later) and she said, "Don, I remember those two names." I took out my note pad, jotted the names down and filed them away. I can remember all these things as if they happened yesterday. I am sad to say however, that I have not been able to locate that piece of paper, with the two names.

Mildred's brother, William "Bill" Lent was a real gentleman. As curator at the Yarmouth County Museum, he was always cheerful and accommodating whenever we called upon him for help. He died much too young and we missed him greatly.

There was also the late Gertrude "Gertie" Wathen; how she enjoyed sharing the stories of her grandfather's stagecoach business! She related the stories in such a vivid way that you felt you were living in that time. All pictures relating to the stagecoach days and the fantastic picture of the Court House and stores looking south in the centre of the village, were compliments of Gertie Wathen.

Our oldest couple at the time was Alfred "Fred" Babin and his wife Elizabeth "Lizzie". Often, it seemed that when I was stuck for some piece of information, I would end up paying them another visit. Eventually they even gave me an entire photograph album with numerous family pictures which I have passed on to the Archives. It was indeed interesting to listen to Fred reminiscing, among other things, about when he and my grandfather operated the bicycle shop just south of the Court House and when he personally operated a garage repair shop in the old W.T. Lent store across from the Court House. This was also the location from which he served as postmaster of Tusket for many years. Alfred lived to be 102 years old.

And then there was Lent and Jessie Hatfield. Although they did not have many pictures to share, their stories were very special. The time shared with them was a unique experience and the memories of those times will remain with me forever. Jessie was always in charge while Lent was more quiet and "laid back", but always displayed his usual little grin. Elsewhere in this history I mention in more detail what those visits were like. They were charming people and eager to share their memories of Tusket's past.

I still remember the thrill when we visited the late Frank Hubbard on the John White Road and he produced the only picture that I have seen to this day of the men working **inside** the Dickie & McGrath lumber mill. Due to the problems with interior lighting during those days, photographs such as that one are rare indeed.

It was a similar experience when I visited with Arthur and Kathleen Woodruff of Pleasant Lake. They produced a photograph of Lent's Corner with the old Squire James Lent house on top of the hill. We had no idea previously how much this corner had changed over the years. It was a great thrill to have found such a photograph.

The late Dr. Percy McGrath from Kentville, originally of Tusket, was a joy to meet. It was after visiting with him in Kentville and sharing a special day together that he gave me all of his original pictures of the Dickie & McGrath Lumber Mill that had been managed by his father, Thomas N. McGrath. He will be mentioned again later in this text.

It is difficult to express the debt of gratitude that I owe to the late Robert Blauveldt. He was a well-known Yarmouth County historian who wrote regular columns for the Yarmouth newspapers over a period of some five decades. Although Gordon and I visited with him on a number of occasions, when I resumed my project in 1973-74, I spent even more time with him, and had the foresight to record some of those interviews on tape. Mr. Blauveldt had grown up in Tusket and he had a thorough knowledge of the village's early history. He is quoted a number of times throughout this history.

Several other people throughout the village were also very generous at offering pictures and information whenever it was asked of them. Arthur and Clara Marsters (who at the time lived in the oldest house in the village) couldn't do enough to accommodate us. I continued to visit them for several years afterwards. They were so proud of their historical house at "The Narrows."

The late Phyllis (Hatfield) Young, in a very special way, deserves to be mentioned. I first met Phyllis in 1972 when she joined the teaching staff in the Manpower Cooking Course at the Vocational School in Yarmouth. I got to know Phyllis well and it was a delight when she opened up her Hanging Oak Antique shop in the village. It was a pleasure to go there and we were soon sharing stories from the past. I remember when she phoned me that she had something important to show me. It was her first discovery of some of the Gordon Hatfield glass negatives; we were thrilled! Although my manuscript was already completed at this time, I often selected various pictures, as her own collection grew, and Phyllis would have copies made for me. In fact, I have a large framed 16x24 copy of my favourite Gordon Hatfield photo - a tall ship anchored at Lyons Hatfield's wharf that she had copied for me.

As an antique dealer, Phyllis played an unusual role in the preservation of village history. Although she was in business, and could have sold items to any prospective customer, when she acquired pieces that she felt were unique to the village she attempted to find them a new home with others in the village that might appreciate their unique history. This extended to furniture, ship's paintings and a variety of other items. When she purchased many old glass negatives from the former Gordon S. Hatfield property, she quickly understood their value, had prints made from them, and did her best to preserve them. Some of the finest images of the village from 1890-1910 were produced by this country photographer.

More Recent Village Contributors

With the loss of almost all the seniors who helped me at the beginning of this project so many years ago, I found when I came to revise and update this history, I had to rely on a new generation of seniors in the village for information. They have been equally supportive and equally knowledgeable on many of the historical details and dates that I needed to pin down. On the many occasions that I have had to knock on doors or make telephone calls for miniscule details, I have been treated with nothing but kindness and generosity. To all those people, I say a special "thank you." In this more recent wave of research I need to thank the following people: Margaret d'Entremont, Roland Bourque, Charlie Muise, Joan and Polly Patten, Laura (Blauveldt) Butler, and especially Cecilia "Sis" Crosby for coming through so many times with crucial information just when it seemed that it was nowhere to be found; and of course, a special thank you to Gordon Wood for his continued support whenever I asked him to research more detailed information for me.

An acknowledgement to Susan Young, for her permission to use some of her Gordon Hatfield photographs. They were part of the collection of her mother, the late Phyllis (Hatfield) Young. These particular photographs are images that for some reason I did not know about when my original manuscript was compiled.

A thank you to Earle Robbins of Ottawa who spent his youth growing up in Tusket; he supplied me with a wealth of old photographs and information. Included was a photograph of his grandparents, William and Jessie Robbins; thus, the name William Robbins Road.

A special acknowledgement to my brother-in-law, Robert "Bob" LeBlanc, of Moncton, New Brunswick, for his generosity and assistance in organizing the photographs and final text details. Also to his co-worker, Leo Blanchard, for his outstanding work on old photographs that in some cases would have been impossible to use without his expertise.

A credit to the Yarmouth County Museum for permission to use two photographs from their collection. While every effort was made to obtain "old" photographs of each house or property within the village, in some cases this was impossible to achieve. Consequently, more modern pictures have had to be used, showing alterations and modernizing that has occurred with many houses through the years. On rare occasions, I was unsuccessful in obtaining any photo of a certain house.

I also wish to take this opportunity to thank Jerry Titus who has been a tremendous source of information for me with regards to the lumber industry and shipbuilding. He has permitted me to quote from his numerous *Argus* articles on the shipbuilding industry of this village. Jerry was most supportive of my project and whenever I asked for information, I always received more than I dreamed possible. His careful and persistent research, especially through old Yarmouth newspapers, has turned up a wealth of information on this part of Yarmouth County.

Bill McLachlan has been very generous in sharing his information on the Tusket Radar Station during World War II.

Shirley (Prosser) Margeson was also most gracious in allowing me to reprint her article on her personal experiences while attending school in Tusket during the 1930s.

Finally, a thank you to my copy editor, Cathy d'Entremont. She did an outstanding job of editing this entire manuscript. Her scrutiny and advice have made this a much better book than it might otherwise have been.

The Argyle Township Court House Archives & Its Historical Society

As I embarked on this revised edition of my manuscript, it was with the knowledge that an incredible amount of information would be available to me that had not existed in the 1970s. This literal goldmine sits at the Argyle Township Court House Archives. Perhaps most important for my work was the fact that that institution had carried out a Heritage Property Inventory of the pre-1914 buildings throughout the Municipality of Argyle. This included in-depth research on every pre-1914 building still surviving in Tusket in 1985 and 1986. This inventory and the range of other work carried out at the archives has resulted in many people depositing historic photographs and manuscripts there. People know that these items will be properly preserved for future generations and made accessible to others. What is even more gratifying is the even-handed approach of this institution. What has been done for Tusket by this archive has been done for every community in this municipality. This has to be one of the finest research centres in Nova Scotia, and I hope the other residents of Argyle Municipality appreciate how lucky we are to have such a facility here.

The archives have given me a great deal of support over the years, but especially in the past year or two in bringing this project to a conclusion. I would like to thank Carol Jacquard, Roseanne Blades and Peter Crowell in particular for their support and their work on behalf of this history.

The Argyle Municipality Historical & Genealogical Society was founded in 1989 to support the work being carried out at the Court House and Archives in Tusket. More details on that organization are presented elsewhere in this history. The Society's quarterly newsletter, *The Argus*, has been very important in helping me put this history together. This newsletter, which was begun in 1989, has consistently published articles documenting the history of every community in the Municipality of Argyle. Some of those articles have found their way into this history in various forms. "The Bingay Letter" written in 1955 and published in *The Argus* with extensive explanatory footnotes has become a standard source of information on early Tusket - and one that I have relied on heavily. *The Argus* has also published many well-researched articles by Jerry Titus, who is acknowledged locally as the expert on anything connected with shipbuilding or shipping history for Yarmouth or Digby Counties. A number of other articles on Tusket excerpted from Yarmouth newspapers of the past have also been reprinted in *The Argus*. This newsletter is now entering its seventeenth year of publication and its contribution to the preservation of local history is immeasurable.

A Few Final Thank You's

I would be remiss if I did not mention the tremendous amount of work that my wife Barbara has done for me in relation to this project, especially in the very beginning, but more importantly, from beginning to end with this project. Throughout the winter of 1973-74, when we had a newborn child, and I was working hard on my manuscript, she spent countless hours helping with the project. It was she who hand-typed the entire manuscript. No computers back then! We had to both work on the manuscript in such a manner that she would type "around the pictures," as necessary, in order to make it all fit together. She has to be thanked as well for her patience in tolerating all the paperwork that was literally spread everywhere throughout the house during that long winter of 1973-74. I thank her as well for her patience again during the past two winters, 2004-5, as I continually monopolized the computer.

Finally, a heartfelt thank you to my editor, Peter Crowell, to whom I owe everything, for carrying me through to the end of this project. Since 1987 Peter had often tried to encourage me to embark upon this project. We both realized that the original manuscript required a number of corrections, but Peter always maintained that it was a pity not to publish something for the benefit of the public. Several years ago Peter agreed to be my editor, should I ever decide to undertake such a task. Looking back, one has to wonder if he would have made this offer had he fully realized the task ahead. Personally, I could never have made a better choice. On more than one occasion, Peter lifted me up when the project seemed like a never-ending task. I am at a loss for words to truly express how much I owe to Peter for the tremendous support that he has given in helping me see the publication of this book become a reality.

Although this revised edition of my original manuscript includes much more information than the original edition, it is still intended to be mainly a pictorial essay, a walking tour of the village combined with other facts I have been able to compile. Much more could be done, but one has to stop somewhere. It is my sincere hope that this manuscript will prove interesting to those who enjoy such things and helpful to those who might wish to use it as a basis for a deeper study into the matter. I trust that it will shed some new light on this old village I love so dearly.

Don R. Pothier

TUSKET,
Yarmouth County,
Nova Scotia
2005

INTRODUCTION

Don Pothier's *History of Tusket*

I first met Don Pothier when I started to work for the Municipality of Argyle in 1985, conducting the Heritage Property Inventory of pre-1914 buildings in the Municipality. I worked for, and with, the late Oscar F. Nauss, and was soon familiar with the roles Oscar, Don Pothier and Gordon Wood played in the restoration of Canada's oldest Court House. Eventually I became familiar with Don's history of the village, bound neatly between bright red covers, with each page inside carefully protected by plastic sheet protectors. From the beginning I was astounded with the rich history of the village, but even more surprised that no formal history of Tusket had ever been written or published.

Tusket's role in shipbuilding and in the lumbering industry alone makes it one of the most important communities in Yarmouth County. Initially the Argyle Township Court House Archives made a photocopy of Don's history, placed it in a three-ring binder and made it available for public use. It has been widely used over the years, not only by those interested in the history of the village, but by school students working on history projects. I always felt that the history needed to be published and made available to more people.

Don's initial manuscript, as he has indicated in his Preface, was completed in 1974. His life became hectic in the years following, making it impossible for him to return to the history in any serious way. In the early 1980s in addition to working his regular job as a teacher, his life was consumed with the restoration of the Court House in Tusket. A few years later, he took on the dismantling of the former Elmer Hatfield Store in the centre of the village, and reconstructing that building on his own property as a barn. He served a term as the first President of the Argyle Municipality Historical & Genealogical Society when it was founded in 1989, and in that position he actively and successfully lobbied Municipal Council to install a fulltime employee at the Court House and its Archives. Shortly after this he was elected to the Clare-Argyle School Board, and became its President, serving in that capacity for more than seven years. I am sure he was doing other things as well - but this short list gives the reader some idea of why his initial history lay dormant for 30 years.

Upon his retirement, I began quietly agitating for him to return to his history, with the goal of seeing his manuscript published in book form. Eventually he gave in and agreed to the undertaking, but only if I agreed to act as his editor. As they often say, "Be careful what you wish for!"

Finally, Don and I began serious work on his history in 2004. I realized at the time that Don thought the process would involve making a few minor corrections, tightening up the grammar a bit, and that would be it. I had slightly more subversive plans.

I knew that there was now literally "tons of information" available at the Archives in Tusket that had not been accessible to Don when he first worked on this history. I myself had researched every pre-1914 building in the village for the Heritage Property Inventory - and this information stood readily available for the use of anyone. *The Argus: the quarterly newsletter of the Argyle Municipality Historical & Genealogical Society* was also by that time into its sixteenth year of publication. Numerous well-researched articles on the village had been published in *The Argus* over that period of time. Included among those were the fabulous articles on shipbuilding in Tusket, researched and written by Jerry Titus. *The Argus* in 1991 and 1992 had also published the very lengthy "Bingay Letter" with extensive footnotes. James H. Bingay was a well-known educator and writer, and had at some point in time began a formal history of Tusket, which for some reason never extended much beyond five typed pages. His letter, written in 1955, is far more interesting and useful to historians of today. It was a letter written to friends in the west, and although it was clearly intended to preserve, in some part, his memories of the village, it was never intended for publication. James Bingay was a sharp-tongued observer of village life, his opinions were pointed, and could hardly be deemed "politically correct" by our standards today. Nevertheless, his letter has become a standard point of reference for information on the history of the village, and has been rightly used as a source throughout this history.

All these "new" sources, and many photographs received by the Archives in Tusket since 1989 have made this a richer and fuller history.

Those who read *The Argus* on a regular basis will have become familiar over the years with my own writing and editing style. Those with less charitable views have sometimes described that style as, "too long-winded." But I am plagued, as an historical researcher and genealogist myself, with so often wishing writers from the past had only told us a little bit more. Those familiar with *The Argus* will recognize the heavy hand of the editor in this manuscript. And yet – in spite of what readers may think, this remains very much Don Pothier's History. It could not, and would not, have been written by me.

It has also been of interest, and sometimes amusing, to see how we have influenced one another in the course of working on this manuscript. In the beginning, it sometimes seemed an effort to squeeze a new passage or two from the author. Towards the end of the project, imagine my consternation when the author delivers his new Preface and it was nine pages long. I was delighted! It remains for the reader and future critics to decide whether we have been a good, or a bad influence on one another.

There are one or two other things I would like to say in closing this Introduction to Don Pothier's history. When he came to me with his original manuscript, it contained a number of formal footnotes. For the most part they have been totally eliminated, and we have tried to make clear reference in the text to where various quotes and pieces of information have been taken. This has been done intentionally in order to make what we both feel is more pleasant reading for those who we feel will be most interested in this book. We hope that the bibliography at the end of the book, citing sources used in each chapter, will satisfy those more interested in the source.

This has sometimes seemed like an arduous task, but we were both determined to complete the project. So far we are still speaking to one another! It has been a privilege to be part of this project. I hope the readers of this history will take both pleasure and satisfaction from finally having a history of Tusket on their shelves.

Peter Crowell, CG(C)
Municipal Historian & Archivist
Municipality of Argyle
2005

CHAPTER 1

TUSKET'S BEGINNINGS

CHAPTER 1
TUSKET'S BEGINNINGS

The late Dr. James H. Bingay, a native of Tusket, was a well-known educator and the author of a *History of Canada for High Schools* (published in 1934). This book became a standard text in schools across the country in the 1930s and 1940s. After his retirement, he returned to Tusket and was able to purchase the old family home in which he had been raised. In his retirement, he made an attempt at writing a history of his native village. This would have been a great gift to the area, as no formal history of the village had ever been written. Unfortunately, his efforts, for whatever reason, never extended beyond five typed pages. Many of us with an interest in local history wish he had completed more. In acknowledgement of his efforts it seems appropriate here to let James Bingay's opening words stand as the beginning of this history.

"The name TUSKET is a variation of the older French name TOUSQUET (and other variations); which, in its turn, was one attempt to shorten the original Indian name of the river NIKETAOUKSIT, which means 'the broad forked, tidal river.' An excellent description: it is broad, considering its length, especially in its lower reaches; it is forked into many tributaries, whose sources lie in at least three or four different counties; and it is tidal for twenty miles, about a quarter of its whole length. Moreover, and, practically, more interesting, the name TUSKET is unique. There is none other in the world (New Tusket in Digby County, its only relative, has a distinguishing prefix) …"

"The village of Tusket takes its name from that of the river on whose left bank it lies, a mile or so below the head of the tide."

Mi'kmaq in Tusket

Before delving into the Loyalist history of Tusket, it seems appropriate to say something here about the fact that the original inhabitants of this land were the Mi'kmaq. The Mi'kmaq here, as in other parts of the province, were largely nomadic prior to European settlements. In summer they were inclined to establish their encampments near the ocean, taking advantage of the ready food source offered by the sea. In winter they often retreated along the river-ways to more inland areas. It is they, as stated above, who gave "Tusket" its name.

It is not known whether there were ever any established Mi'kmaq encampments within what is now known as the Village of Tusket. There were certainly many in the surrounding area. The late Wilbur Sollows, long acknowledged as one of Yarmouth County's most talented amateur archaeologists, uncovered numerous artifacts relating to Mi'kmaq culture from the area around Tusket Falls, to the north of the village. Much of his impressive collection is now housed at the Yarmouth County Museum.

Local Mi'kmaq affiliations with the European settlers were always stronger with the

Acadian population than with the English. This is shown through the fact that when they chose to make religious affiliations with the European settlers, they almost invariably became members of the Catholic Church. In the early decades of European settlement, marriage was quite common between the Acadian population and the Mi'kmaq.

It is common knowledge today that the original Mi'kmaq population was in many ways dispossessed of their way of life after Europeans and New Englanders arrived here. Prior to this time the concept of owning "private property" was unknown - the entire landscape and countryside was considered to belong to everyone and to no one in particular. This changed drastically with the arrival of the French, and then the English.

Early Mi'kmaq history is seldom a written history. The early English settlers to Tusket have left no written accounts on this subject either. As such, I am able to offer little information on the Mi'kmaq in the village during early times. In more modern times there have been Mi'kmaq families who have lived within the bounds of the village, and I will offer here what information I have been able to piece together from the records available and by talking to local residents. "A Summer-Day's Ramble," an article published in *The Argus,* vol.14 no.4, Winter 2002, deals with an 1859 excursion (in horse and buggy) from Yarmouth to the end of Sluice Point, and on to several islands. As the travellers made their way toward Tusket, they referred to one local Mi'kmaq who is certainly worthy of mention, and who was clearly an ancestor of some of the subsequent residents of the village. When passing through what we know today as Pleasant Lake, the travellers referred to a Mr. Bartlett who previous to 1859 had lived on the eastern banks of what is now known as the Annis River: "On the Eastern bank of this river formerly resided old Bartlett. He claimed to be the Governor or Chief of the Micmac tribe - whether legitimately or not I do not know, for I believe there was another claimant. He lived in a frame house, and cultivated some small fields."

It is believed that this man was the ancestor of other Bartletts who later lived in Tusket. The property known in recent times as the home of the late "Alec" and Helen (Paul) Daurie at Tusket had been occupied by Mi'kmaq families for some time before they were established on this land. In the 1920s, and probably earlier, two families lived at this location; the family of Steve Glode and that of Simon Bartlett. Simon Bartlett's name appears on the Tusket War Memorial as one of the local men who served overseas in World War I. Some time after the 1920s the Bartletts moved from this lot of land to Arcadia, it is believed to the reservation there. The Glode family remained in Tusket after this and are mentioned in Shirley Margeson's account of attending school in Tusket in the 1930s later in this history. By all accounts that have been related to me, Steve Glode was a highly respected and well-liked man by everyone. Sadly, he died of a most untimely death by burning in his home in Arcadia in 1957.

One of Steve Glode's daughters, Evangeline, married Charles Alexander "Alec" Daurie, and this is how the "Daurie" name came to the village. "Alec" Daurie was not Mi'kmaq himself, but was a native of Indian Lake, Lunenburg County. After the death of his first wife, he married a second time to Helen Paul, another Mi'kmaq woman who had been born at St. Bernard, Digby Co., NS, and who had also lived in Hectanooga, Digby Co., before settling at Tusket. They raised a family of seven daughters on their Tusket property. The majority of those daughters still live in Yarmouth County today. Over the years, the Daurie family have gradually dispersed from Tusket and today the house, located on the southern side of the 103 Highway intersection to the Raynardton Road, sits empty. "Alec" and Helen Daurie spent their last years in Arcadia and died there, Alec on 4 February 1990, and Helen on 30 June 1992.

The Loyalists: Tusket's First English Settlers

James Bingay, in his short beginning to a history of the village, writes, "Tusket is the child of Shelburne." This is very much the case. The area of Yarmouth and Chebogue, to the west of Tusket, was settled by New England Planters, mainly from the states of Massachusetts and Connecticut. The first settlers arrived there in 1761. Argyle situated on the other side of Tusket, was also settled around 1761, by New England Planters from Maine and New Hampshire. In Argyle as well, between 1763 and the settlement of Tusket in 1784, a substantial number of Acadian families established themselves. Many of these families were returning from exile in the New England states. The settlement of Tusket brought in a whole new group of settlers with an entirely different background.

The town of Shelburne, on the south shore of Nova Scotia, was founded exclusively by the United Empire Loyalists, former residents of the American Colonies who had fought on the side of the British during the American Revolution. At the end of the war, their properties were seized and they were forced into exile. When the treaty of peace between Great Britain and the new United States was about to be signed in 1783, the British Commander, Sir Guy Carleton, still held New York. A condition of the treaty was that he should evacuate New York only after the last Loyalist who wished to leave the country had done so. Because Nova Scotia was close to New York by sea, a large number came here, the first landing at Shelburne being in the spring of 1783. Within the course of the year, 8,000 Loyalist settlers had landed on the shores in Shelburne where formerly there had been little or no settlement at all. Later arrivals at Shelburne found much of the land in and around the town already taken up. Almost immediately, many of these settlers began to migrate towards outlying areas where land was still available. This is how Tusket received its first permanent residents.

In discussing the history of Tusket and its early settlers, it is important for the reader to keep in mind that it is the village proper, and the people who lived in that immediate vicinity, that are being dealt with in this history. Other areas that were settled at the same time, such as the communities of Gavelton, Raynardton, Tusket Falls, Canaan and Springhaven, all to the north of Tusket, will not be dealt with in this history except in a peripheral manner.

The majority of the original settlers at Tusket were Loyalists who had lived previously in the states of New York and New Jersey. Most were Dutch in origin, but had been established in the New World for several generations before their migration to Nova Scotia. In most cases they were probably no longer Dutch speaking by the time they arrived in Nova Scotia.

The following is a list of the early Loyalist settlers to the Tusket area, compiled from several different sources. In cases where these settlers are known to have established themselves outside of the bounds of Tusket, that has been indicated by the appropriate community name in brackets. Some settlers did not remain long, and we know little about them. In most instances where settlers remained and established themselves in Tusket, a brief biographical sketch will be found after the list.

It should be noted by the reader that the names of Loyalists for the Tusket area, many derived from good primary sources, contain the names of some people who appear never to have settled here. Often these names come from the lists of land grants given out by the provincial government. While many came and settled on their lands and developed them, others, for a variety of reasons did not, and often lost their rights to these lands. Consequently, these grants were later reissued to other people. Some early settlers also moved on after spending a short time in the area. Usually one can find evidence in Yarmouth County deeds of when these people sold their properties. The information given here is not comprehensive but will provide details on many of those who settled permanently, and clear up a few misconceptions.

Names of Original Settlers

Ackerman, Gilbert*
Ackerman, John*
Ackerson, Jacob
Ackerson, Richard*
Andrews, Samuel (Raynardton)
Babcock, David*
Banta, Simeon*
Berry, Anthony
Berry, William
Blanchard, Lewis
Blauvelt, Theunis
Brindley, Edward*
Byrn, Benedict
Byrn, Matthias
Colsworthy, William
Combauld, Richard*
Connor, Hugh
Daniells, Gilbert*
Decker, Isaac
Earle, Peter (Pleasant Lake)
Fisher, Peter*
Gavel, George (Gavelton)
Gavel, John (Gavelton)

Gismore, James*
Goddard, Daniel*
Gray, "Capt." Robert
Gray, Jesse (Morris Island)
Halstead, William
Hatfield, Abraham Marsh
Hatfield, Jacob Lyon
Hatfield, James (Tusket Falls)
Hatfield, Job
Horton, Jonathan (Little River)
Hurlburt, Titus (Raynardton)
King, Robert (Bell Neck)
Lawrence, Nicholas (Gavelton)
Lent, Abraham
Lent, James
Marling, Barnett (Raynardton)
Maybee, Isaac
Mires or Miries, Anthony
Mood, Jacob(?)
Morris, Robert*
Mullock, William*
Neall, Sebastian*
Nugent, Arthur B.*

Ogden, David
Ogden, Nicholas
Perry, Jacob*
Price, Abigail
Redman, Michael*
Richards, Nicholas
Richardson, Nathaniel
Ridgway, Thomas
Ruton, David*
Seers, Jonathan*
Servant, Abraham
Sloane, James*
Smith, Job
Taylor, Charles*
Tooker, Jacob
VanBlarcom, Peter*
VanBuskirk, Andrew*
VanBuskirk, Jacob*

VanBuskirk, William*
VanBuskirk, John*
VanCortlandt, Philip*
VanEmburgh, Adonijah
VanEmburgh, Gilbert
VanEmburgh, James
VanEmburgh, John
VanNorden, Cornelius
VanNorden, David
VanNorden, Gabriel
VanNorden, John
VanNorden, Stephen
VanTyle, Dennis
Williams, John
Withby, John
Wood, Jacob(?)
Wood, John (Gavelton)

*All these men are believed to have not settled in the Tusket area. They clearly received land grants, but this land was probably re-granted to other people at a later date.

Jacob Tooker, Dennis VanTyle and Their Families

First to arrive in Tusket, on May 11, 1784, was Jacob Tooker, his wife Margery (Hatfield), his daughter Deborah, and his son-in-law, Capt. Dennis VanTyle. There may have been other family members as well. They arrived on board VanTyle's ship the *CHERRY BOUNCE*. Of English descent, Jacob Tooker was born at Elizabeth Town, New Jersey, in 1740. He had served as a Master Shipbuilder in H.M. Dockyards at Philadelphia and later, as the war progressed, at New York. He married Margery Hatfield, daughter of John Hatfield, also of Elizabeth Town. Capt. VanTyle (not a sea captain) had served during the war with Tarleton's Light Horse, the cavalry commandos who, by having squadrons posted at various widely separated points, had made themselves thoroughly hated and feared by the rebel populace from Maine to Florida.

The following account written by Mrs. VanTyle, long afterwards known as "Aunt Deborah Smith," describes their long ordeal prior to settling at Tusket.

> We left New York on the last day of October, 1783, in the schooner 'Cherry Bounce', Captain John Gilchrist, master, and arrived at Port Roseway the 7th of November, so called then, now Shelburne. The snow was about two feet deep; went up to the town, there were a number of houses building, but none finished; plenty of marquees, tents and sheds for the people to shelter under, which they greatly needed at that season of the year. It looked dismal enough. Called on some of our friends in their tents, Col. VanBuskirk and his wife and two young

daughters in one; and his daughter Sarah, Lawyer Combauld's wife, and baby in another. I thought they did not look able to stand the coming winter, which proved a very hard one. The servants had sheds of boards to cook under. We heard the hammer and saw day and night. Fine times for carpenters. Three days after we sailed down to Robertson's Cove, and there remained frozen up all winter, and the whole harbour too until the 17th of March. During the winter, father and Mr. VanTyle built a log house on shore, having provisions on board the schooner, but when the spring came and we saw nothing but rocks and moss, they made up their minds to look for a more favourable place. They had orders from the Surveyors to take up land where they could find it unlocated. On the 20th of March they left the family, and with thirteen others set sail for Yarmouth, Joshua Trefry, pilot. There they found the land all taken up; were recommended to Tusket. Found the land there looked more favourable, returned to Shelburne, took the family on board, and arrived at Tusket 11th of May, 1784. At this time there was no one settled on the river, but the French. In the fall two families moved up, Mr. John Withby and Mr. John Williams. November 1st, Mr. Morris and Capt. Leonard came up to lay out the land about the lakes and at other places. In the course of the summer of 1785, Mr. James Hatfield and family came to Tusket; uncle Job Hatfield came up in the course of the summer, and others, vis. : - Mr. Lent, Mr. VanNorden, Mr. Maybee, and Mr. Sarvent. The river abounded with fish, salmon, and herring; and there was a large business carried on exporting them to the West Indies.

More settlers followed both during and after 1785. While at Tusket itself, many of the families came from the states of New York and New Jersey, in the surrounding areas along the river were Loyalists from all along the coast of New England, the Carolinas, and other Southern States.

Jacob Tooker and his family settled on a point of land on the west side of the Tusket River. A home was built and a large piece of land was cleared and cultivated throughout the summer of 1784. The Tookers' choice turned out to be unusual, because all of the other settlers chose the eastern side of the river, and this is where the village developed. Interesting to note that after the Tookers left Tusket no one else built on the west side of the river.

I have visited the Tooker site and the stonewall on the property (along the shore) serves as testimony to the family's hard labour in clearing the land for farming. Somewhat behind the stonewall the remains of the foundation of the Tooker home may still be traced. This is located more or less in line with the entrance to the village cemetery on the eastern side of the river. In recent times the cottage of the late Garth Hatfield on that side of the river is located fairly close to the Tooker site.

A year after arriving in Tusket, Jacob Tooker demonstrated his capabilities as a master shipbuilder by building the first ship to be constructed in Tusket. The vessel was launched in 1785, less than two years after his arrival here. Here he established the first of the many great shipyards that a century later were to make the village famous as one of the greatest shipbuilding centres of the province.

Jacob Tooker eventually removed from Tusket, and spent his last years in Yarmouth. He and his wife settled in the vicinity of Main Street in what is now known as Yarmouth

South. Their homestead was on the property owned and occupied in 2005 by Jonathan Rodney (son of Victor Rodney) at 12 Main Street. As well as being engaged in farming, Jacob Tooker became a very prominent shipbuilder and businessman. He died at Yarmouth in 1829 and his wife the following year. Both are buried in the Old Anglican Cemetery on Church Hill.

Dennis VanTyle was one of the other earliest settlers to Tusket. A Loyalist, he was also married to Jacob Tooker's daughter, Deborah. He died a very young man, and the name quickly disappeared from the area. In early December of 1784, Capt. VanTyle, in his ship the *CHERRY BOUNCE*, with Capt. Temple as master, set sail for the West Indies. The vessel, with her entire crew, was never heard from again. Captain VanTyle left a young widow and a young son. A few years later, Deborah remarried to Job Smith, and for a time lived in Tusket. Dennis VanTyle Junior was baptized under the surname of his step-father, "Smith." He died at the early age of nine years and was buried in the old Tusket cemetery.

Job Smith

Relatively little is known about this early settler, other than the fact that he married the widow, Deborah (Tooker) VanTyle. The couple lived in Tusket for several years. In 1795, Deborah and Job Smith moved to Yarmouth where they operated an inn. Deborah continued in the business after her husband's death. She died at the remarkable age, for that time, of ninety five years. She and her second husband are believed to be buried in the old Anglican Cemetery on Church Hill in Yarmouth, where her parents' graves are found.

"Squire" James Lent

"Squire" James Lent, of Tappan, New York, arrived in the summer of 1785, and like the other settlers, came by sea and up the river. Traditionally, he tied his boat to an oak tree, which still stands bravely at the "Corner." (We shall have more to say about this tree later.) There he disembarked his family and his goods, including his black slaves, and after a short time built a house on top of the hill across the road. This would have been one of the first houses built on the east side of the river. It has long since disappeared, though a photograph of this landmark does exist. This house was situated approximately where Terry and Karen Cottreau's house is located in 2005.

James (his name is sometimes given as "Cobus" (Jacobus) Lent became one of the most prominent and important men in this new settlement. He was born in Westchester County, New York, 17 February 1753, the son of Adolph and Cassie (Harring) Lent. *The History of the Lent (van Lent) Family* by Nelson Burton Lent (1903) has the following to say: "He was a fisherman by occupation, and caught herring, salmon and other fish for the market, and shipped large quantities to the West Indies, returning with cargoes of rum, molasses, & c. He took up land grants and became a very prominent citizen. He took with him from Nyack, N.Y, coloured servants then in slavery. He was influential with the Government at Halifax, was appointed a Justice of the Peace and ruled supreme, and had the authority of a Judge. The oldest inhabitant now living informs the writer that he remembers Judge Lent passing sentence upon several persons for stealing & c. They were fastened to a tree and whipped." James Lent was not only a Justice of the Peace, but also a Justice or Judge of what was then called the Inferior Court of Common Pleas.

When I was researching this book in 1974, the late Phyllis (Hatfield) Young informed me that she had been told when growing up that the old Lent house that sat high on the hill was known to have had shackles and chains anchored in the basement walls. Whether these shackles related to Squire Lent's role as judge before a jail was built, slavery, or both, remains open to speculation.

Nevertheless, by all accounts, Squire James Lent "was known as a man who maintained a good relationship with his black servants." One of them "was trusted by Lent to return to New York after the Revolution to bring back a valued family chest…" James Lent also secured grants of land for several of these black families, and their lots extended north from his own. These black settlers gradually dispersed, and helped to populate Greenville and Starr's Road.

James Lent was also one of the early Members to the Legislative Assembly in Halifax, Nova Scotia. He held his seat in the Assembly from 1806-1818.

James Lent's wife, Bridget, died at Tusket in 1825. He died at Tusket, 11 August 1839. Their gravestones, found in the Tusket Cemetery, are among the oldest inscribed stones in that burying ground.

Col. Job Hatfield

Col. Job Hatfield was born in Elizabeth Town, New Jersey, 2 January 1754, the son of John and Deborah (Smith) Hatfield. Margery (Hatfield), wife of Jacob Tooker, was an older sister. Col. Job married Jane VanNorden, daughter of Tusket pioneer Gabriel VanNorden. It is uncertain where Col. Job Hatfield lived, but it was probably on his lot (#14) in the centre of the village, shown on the confirmed grant of the village (1809). Job Hatfield was one of the leading citizens of the new community of Tusket. He was a merchant, and at the time of his death in 1825, his estate was appraised at a value of £1,010, a considerable sum for that time. His son, Capt. John V.N. Hatfield, was equally influential in the village during his lifetime.

James Hatfield, Jacob Lyon Hatfield and Abram Marsh Hatfield

These three men were brothers, and first cousins to Col. Job Hatfield. All three were sons of Jacob and Mary (Lyon) Hatfield of Elizabeth Town, N.J.

James Hatfield, the oldest of three brothers, was born in 1753. He and his wife, Mary, according to the late Robert B. Blauveldt, settled "near the iron bridge, Tusket Falls. His descendants are the Tusket Falls Hatfields." Although this couple only had one son, and one daughter, their descendants are numerous today.

Jacob Lyon Hatfield, the second brother, was born 9 December 1757. He married Mary VanNorden, a daughter of Tusket Loyalist, Gabriel VanNorden. They lived in Tusket proper, and their house still stands, one of the oldest three in the village. This house is located on the John White Road, and for many years was owned by one of their descendants, Christina ("Chrissie") Hatfield. Jacob Lyon Hatfield had a family of 12 children. His eldest son, known as "Capt." James Hatfield, married Elizabeth, the only daughter of Squire James Lent. While this couple settled in Gavelton to the north, many of their own children moved to Tusket as adults and played important and prominent roles in the village's history.

The third brother, **Abram Marsh Hatfield,** was born 15 January 1767. He married Constantina Jones, and they had a family of 11 children. He and his wife appear to have lived in a number of different places. They lived for a time in Tusket, but later lived in Central Argyle, and may ultimately have settled in the Kelley's Cove area.

The families of these three Hatfield brothers, plus the fourth family, that of their cousin, Col. Job Hatfield, present a complicated genealogical tangle. Intermarriage between all four families was common, with a number of first cousin marriages included. Several branches of the family that originated in Tusket moved to the Tusket Falls and Gavelton area, while other branches, born and raised in Gavelton and vicinity, settled in Tusket. It makes for a complicated family history. Many members of these families played important roles in the history of Tusket, and will be mentioned throughout this book.

Abraham Lent

This Loyalist settler did not remain in Tusket for many years. He did leave his mark however, and built what has long been acknowledged as the oldest house in Tusket. For some reason however, he chose to return to the United States. Some sources suggest he left Tusket as early as 1790. He was living in "Rockland, County of Orang[sic], New York," in 1804 when he sold all of his property at Tusket to his brother, "Squire" James Lent. The subsequent history of Abraham Lent's house will be touched on later in this history.

Theunis Blauvelt

Theunis ("Tunis") Blauvelt was born at Tappan, N.Y, 2 February 1747, the son of David Blauvelt of that place. He came with other Loyalist settlers to Tusket. He was twice married, and his first wife died before the end of the Revolutionary War. His two children by this marriage were raised by their maternal grandparents and remained in New York when their father emigrated to Nova Scotia. In Tusket he married a second time to Hannah VanNorden, a daughter of Loyalist Gabriel VanNorden. They had nine children. All of the Blauveldts or Blauvelts originating in Yarmouth County are descendants of this couple. Theunis and his wife lived in Tusket village proper.

Gabriel VanNorden

In his history, *Yarmouth, Nova Scotia: a sequel to Campbell's History,* George S. Brown has the following to say about this Loyalist settler to Tusket: "Gabriel VanNorden of New Jersey. At the beginning of the war, he removed to New York, where he opened a house of entertainment. At the peace, accompanied by his family of eleven persons and three servants, he went from New York to Shelburne, where the government granted him a town-lot. His losses were estimated at fifteen hundred pounds, for which the British Government made provision. He settled near Yarmouth (at Arcadia), and died, quite old, in 1810."

Gabriel VanNorden arrived first at Tusket and received land grants. He later purchased land in Arcadia and lived there. His family, mainly due to its sheer size, had an important influence on the development of Tusket. Gabriel VanNorden was born 25 October 1737, and married his first wife, Jane Westervelt, 19 May 1757. They had ten children before Jane's death in 1779. In 1780 Gabriel married a second time, to Magdalen Maine, a widow. There were eight more children by this marriage, for a total of 18.

Several of Gabriel's sons by his first marriage were old enough to have fought beside their father in the Revolutionary War. This may be the reason several of them are included on the list of original grantees. John VanNorden, Stephen VanNorden, Cornelius VanNorden and David VanNorden were all sons by his first wife. Most of these sons settled and remained in Tusket, while their father established himself in Arcadia.

Several of Gabriel's daughters also married into Tusket families and remained in the village. Although this surname has been gone from Yarmouth County for many decades the VanNorden influence in early Tusket was considerable.

Abraham Servant

Abraham Servant was of Dutch ancestry, and came from either New York state or New Jersey, as did most of the Tusket Loyalists. He was born on 22 May 1762, and came to Tusket with his wife, Penelope (Yarrow). They had eight children, several of whom married into other Tusket families. Abraham settled in Tusket proper, and the name remained in the village for several generations. The last person of this surname in Yarmouth County was the late Emerson Servant of Cheggogin, who died in 1985.

VanEmburgh Families

While well-documented genealogies exist for many of the families discussed here, the early history of the VanEmburghs remains obscure at present. Their Dutch surname suggests that they too came from New York state or New Jersey. Several men of this name appear among the early grantees, but I have not been able to document their relationship to one another. Adonijah, James, John and Gilbert VanEmburgh are all names found on the lists of original grantees. None of these men appear to have remained in the village very long. Their surname is found thereafter in such communities as Morris Island, Kemptville, Argyle and the Pubnicos. "VanAmburg" is the modern variation of this surname, and it is still found in Yarmouth County today.

William Halstead

This Loyalist settler, like many others at Tusket, came from New Jersey. He is supposed to have married Elizabeth Gavel, a daughter of Loyalist John Gavel. It seems uncertain as to whether he settled in Tusket or the Gavelton area. A number of his descendants certainly lived in Tusket in subsequent generations.

Ogden Families

There is some evidence to suggest that both Nicholas Ogden and David Ogden may have settled in the Tusket area, but it seems unlikely that they lived in the village proper. According to the late Robert B. Blauveldt, one of the Ogdens had land "approximately where Waldo Clayton lived, (in 2005, owned by his daughter Nancy and her husband Neil Wentzell) in the Raynardton area and this is where he is presumed to have died." Records from Yarmouth County deeds suggest that David Ogden sold his holdings and moved away.

Nicholas Ogden gained fame or notoriety by having been involved in a conspiracy to assassinate George Washington during the American Revolution. It seems less certain whether Nicholas spent much time in Yarmouth County, although he did receive a land grant.

Major Robert Gray

Major Robert Gray emigrated from the Carolinas or Virginia, and was granted some 700 acres of land, one of the largest Loyalist grants ever allotted in the local area. Major Robert Gray removed to Charlottetown, Prince Edward Island, where a friend of his by the name of Fanning was Governor. His son, Col. John Hamilton Gray became Premier of Prince Edward Island and a "Father of Confederation." In fact, he was Chairman of the Charlottetown Conference on Union. It seems unlikely that Major Robert Gray ever lived in the Tusket area and may have forfeited his grant.

Philip VanCortlandt

Philip VanCortlandt, whose name appears among the land grant recipients, has become something of an ironic character in terms of the history of Tusket. Primary records suggest that he never settled on his land grant, and may never have come to Tusket at all. His name, however, lives on in a small park in the centre of the village, known as "VanCortlandt Square." How this came about will be discussed later in this history.

Jacob Mood

The confirmed grant of Tusket Village shows a Jacob Mood living within the village. We are obliged to leave a question mark beside his name. Although the map of the grants shows him as "Mood", the relating documents give the surname as "Wood." Loyalist John Wood, who settled near Tusket Falls, had a son Jacob. There was however, also a Jacob Mood (or "Moodt"), of Dutch descent, who also settled in the area. He appears first among other Loyalists in the town of Shelburne. He was a single man, and later married Sarah Eldridge of Yarmouth County.

He and his wife, along with some other Loyalist families settled initially on Morris Island. However, they were never able to gain title to the lands they cultivated there. The entire island had been granted to the Provincial Surveyor, Charles Morris, and he chose not to sell. It is possible that Jacob and Sarah Mood also occupied the lot in Tusket for a time. Jacob Mood died before 1827, and it is believed his wife died a short time after that. Their sons settled in East Kemptville, Pleasant Lake (Mood's Mill Road) and also at Woods Harbour in Shelburne County. The Mood surname is still common in the county today.

Lewis Blanchard

We have no evidence to suggest that Lewis Blanchard, whose name appears on land grant documents, spent any length of time in Tusket. He did, however, remain in Yarmouth County, and appears to have established himself in the Yarmouth area.

Jacob Ackerson

This is a family about which little is known. No records have been found that show them selling their land and removing from the area. Yet the records of Christ Church Anglican Church at Shelburne tell us that they lived at Tusket for at least a few years. When missionaries visited the Tusket area in May 1790 they baptised "Katy" Ackerson, daughter of Jacob and Katy.

Thomas Ridgway

Thomas Ridgway is another early settler who does not appear to have remained in the Tusket area for many years. He may have lived in the village proper, or not. But in May 1790, Sarah and Hannah, both daughters of Thomas and Lydia Ridgway, were baptised by Anglican missionaries at Tusket.

Nathaniel Richards Esq.

Relatively little is known about this early settler, mainly due to the fact that there appears to have been no descendants. He did settle in Tusket, and may have spent the remainder of his life here. He was a Justice of the Peace and clearly a respected member of the community. The lot of land granted to him within the village was near that of Jacob Lyon Hatfield and is discussed under that topic. The following was written in regard to this settler around 1887, by Peter Lent Hatfield, of Tusket, "Nathaniel Richards was a Loyalist and came to Tusket with the Hatfields … from Shelburne in 1785 or shortly after. He was a single man but whether a bachelor or widower I cannot learn. He had some property when he came but died poor about 60 years ago at my father's (James Hatfield's) at Tusket Lakes and was buried at Tusket. He was a J.P. & was associated on the Bench with my Grandfather Jas Lent."

Other Settlers: John Williams, John Withby, Isaac Maybee, etc.

An account of early settlement by Deborah (Tooker) (VanTyle) Smith, quoted above, makes it clear that John Williams and John Withby were early arrivals. Like many others, they did not remain very long. Isaac Maybee also mentioned in this account clearly came to Tusket, but did not remain here. The same account suggests who the Richard Combauld is on the above list, but we find no evidence that he or his family came to Tusket.

Tusket's Early Blacks & "Mulatto" Settlers

Abigail Price, William Berry, Anthony Berry and Anthony Mires or Miries

It seems appropriate here to also offer what is known about the early black settlers to Tusket. Technically, they can probably not be termed "Loyalists," as they arrived here as slaves of the Loyalist settlers. Many blacks who arrived at Shelburne were free by virtue of the fact that they had fought with the British during the War. Since the Tusket blacks remained in slavery when they first arrived in Nova Scotia, they had probably not fought in the War in any official capacity. They had, no doubt, suffered as much as their masters.

Although it is possible that other families who arrived in the village brought black slaves with them, it is only the slaves of "Squire" James Lent that we have any record of. They were clearly not in Tusket for many years before they were granted their freedom. It is clear that James Lent, who was influential with the government in Halifax, obtained land grants for several of his freed slaves. Their lots of land, with houses on them, are shown on the confirmed grant of Tusket Village in 1809. One of these former slaves, Abigail Price, was the only woman to receive a grant of land in the village in her own name. She was a widow, and her husband may have been "Joseph" Price whose name appears on other land grant records.

William and Anthony Berry were also freed slaves of James Lent who received grants in 1809. One, or both of them, would be the ancestors of all the subsequent blacks of this surname in Yarmouth County. The Berry name is still common in the black community of Yarmouth County today.

Another name of a black connected with the James Lent family was Anthony Mires or Miries. He also received a grant in the village. His name either disappeared or was altered in some manner. It is not a surname known today.

In 1800 an Anglican priest or missionary from Christ Church Anglican Church in Shelburne baptized a number of people at Tusket. Included were "William Berry" and "Dinah", his wife, as well as daughters "Fillis", "Elizabeth", "Esther", "Eley" and "Margaret." At the same time baptisms are also listed for "Dinah Berry, adult" and her daughters, "Susannah" and "Margaret."

Since so little remains in terms of a written record of these early Tusket settlers, I offer here the few other items I have been able to find. A most interesting obituary taken from the *Yarmouth Light* of March 11, 1954, as reprinted from the *Yarmouth Times* files of 29 January, 1893, offers some important additional details on the Berry family.

YARMOUTH WOMAN LIVED TO THE AGE OF ONE HUNDRED AND
SIX

Days of Slavery recalled in death Sixty-One Years ago – One Hundred Dollars was price paid for a Wife.

There passed peacefully away today at her home on Starr's Road, Hester McKinnon, aged 106 years. Hester was the daughter of William and Dinah Berry, from whom sprang the entire race of Berry's who resided on the back road leading to Hebron. William Berry, Hester's father, was a slave belonging to James Lent Sr., who was one of the first settlers in Tusket Village and was known as Judge Lent as he administered the rights of justice in those olden times. Mr. Lent was one of the Loyalists who came here from Shelburne in the previous century and brought with him his slave, William Berry. William became discontented and induced Mr. Lent to buy him a wife, which he did. Her name was Dinah and he paid 100 (pounds) for her. Dinah married William Berry and Hester McKinnon was their daughter. She was born at Tusket in a small log cabin attached to the house in which Judge Lent lived. Although the Berry's were slaves they were always kindly treated. Hester was a true type of her race and lived as she died, a true, honest Christian woman. She had a kind word for everyone, and being an excellent nurse, her presence in times of tribulation and sickness was like a magic wand. She lived a good old age, and in departing left behind her footprints in the sands of time. (Hester McKinnon was named for the Lent housekeeper, who had charge of the slaves).

The main artifact that remains in the village today, of these early black settlers, is the house of Abigail Price, the second oldest dwelling in the village. This house will be dealt with in more detail in our tour of the village.

On October 28, 1813, and February 2, 1816, Abigail Price sold her property in Tusket, in two different deeds, to David VanNorden. On August 31, 1818 Anthony Miries sold his property to David VanNorden as well. No recorded deed exists for when the Berrys sold their properties, but William Berry was still living on his lot in Tusket as late as 1812-1816. It seems likely that these families all sold their properties around the same time and had probably all moved from Tusket by 1820.

As has been mentioned earlier, blacks who had clearly fought on the side of the British during the American Revolution were granted their freedom, provided with transport to Nova Scotia and other places, and many received grants of land. Many of these free blacks received land in Birchtown, outside of Shelburne, and founded that community. There does not appear to have been many, if any, free blacks in Tusket, although the slaves of James Lent were soon given their freedom and according to local tradition were well treated. This was not always the case with slaves owned by Loyalists from the southern states; the slaves owned by Samuel Andrews at Raynardton, and by Jesse Gray at Morris Island, both southerners, did not fare so well.

Free "Mulattoes"

The only reference we have had to date of free blacks, who might have lived in Tusket, is another record from Christ Church Anglican Church at Shelburne. In May of 1790 a priest or missionary visited the Tusket area, and among others baptized "Suby, Dinal and Peggy" – all children of Francis and "Suby" Sisco, "free mulattoes." The term "mulattoes" indicates that even in 1790 this family was considered to be of mixed race. Since the baptisms in 1790 included families that lived along the Tusket River, but not all in the village, we cannot be sure of exactly where the Sisco's were living. We have found no other reference to the family in the area. This surname still exists in Yarmouth County, but without further research we do not know if they are descendants of "Francis and Suby."

Land Grants - The Grant of Tusket Village

The lands granted in and around Tusket proper were exclusively grants given in order to compensate Loyalists for their losses in the American Revolution. The grants came with certain conditions, the main one being an obligation to clear and cultivate the land within a specified period of time. As has been indicated earlier, many grant recipients did not take up their lands for a variety of reasons, and usually forfeited these holdings which were later re-granted to other people. While most of the grants to the north of Tusket consisted of large homesteads measuring between 100 and 300 acres, there was obvious pressure for a different kind of land division in Tusket proper. These grants were smaller, and more closely resemble town lots with settlers establishing themselves along the Tusket River in close proximity to one another. The grant of the village was confirmed and surveyed by the Provincial Surveyor, Charles Morris, in 1809 although in some cases the settlers had been established on the lots for some 15 years.

The surveyed plan of the village grant is included here. It may be a useful exercise to say something of what is found on this plan, looking at the properties, from south to north.

The oldest house in Tusket, at the Narrows, is not shown here, as it was built on land not included in the grant. Although that property is considered part of the village proper today, it was not deemed as such in this early land division.

At the southernmost extreme of the plan one finds James Lent, Esq. owning two lots of land (#1 & #2) totalling some thirteen and a half acres. He is shown with three buildings on these lots as well as a wharf at the river's edge.

Next, north of James Lent, owning five and a half acres, with a house on the lot, is Anthony Berry (#3). He was one of James Lent's black slaves, but by this time was obviously a free man owning land in his own right. In fact, it seems certain that James Lent obtained several grants for his former slaves.

Next, north of Anthony Berry was a lot (#4) reserved for a "Burying Ground." It remains as such today.

Just north of the cemetery lot was William Berry, with three and a quarter acres, with a house on his lot (#5). He too had been a former slave. Today this is the property of Gordon & Evelyn Muise.

Moving north from William Berry's lot, one finds Thunis Blauvelt Esq. with a lot of four and a half acres (#6). No buildings are shown on it. Next north of Blauvelt is another lot of five acres (#7) owned by James Lent, with no buildings shown on it. Next north, with four acres, was Abigail Price, the only woman in the village to receive a grant in her own name (lot #8). As mentioned earlier, she too was a former slave of James Lent. Abigail Price's home still stands in Tusket today, the second oldest house in the village.

North of Abigail Price's home was Anthony Mires (#9), with four and a quarter acres and a house. He too was a former slave of James Lent. Little else is known about him, and his surname has either died out or been changed in some manner.

18

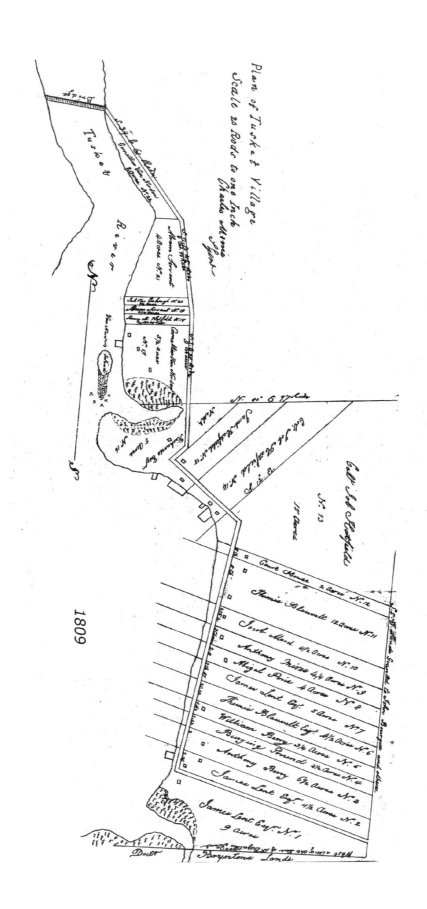

1809

Next, moving north is the lot of Jacob Mood (#10), with a house. There is some confusion regarding the person who owned this lot. The plan of division clearly shows the surname to be "Mood," while other documents associated with the grant spell it "Wood." There was a Jacob Wood who lived in the Tusket area, but it seems likely that it was Jacob Mood who owned and occupied this lot.

North of Jacob Mood is another lot owned by Thunis Blauvelt (#11). Two buildings are shown on this 12 acre lot, and it was from one of these houses that he and his wife operated an inn during the early days of the settlement.

The next lot moving north is a long narrow lot of two acres reserved for a Court House (#12). The Argyle Township Court House, Canada's oldest standing courthouse, still occupies this lot today.

The next two lots (#13 & 14), somewhat irregular in shape, and amounting to 15 acres belonged to Col. Job Hatfield. He was one of the earliest merchants in Tusket. His buildings are all shown to be on the river (or western) side of the main road. He is shown as having wharves as well.

The next lot (#15), moving north, was that of Jacob Lyon Hatfield. He is shown with a house. That house still stands today, and is one of the three oldest in the village. It is located on the present day John White Road.

The next lot (#16) belonged to Nathaniel Richards. He had buildings and wharves. His is a name that disappeared early from the village, but he was a leading citizen during Tusket's early years.

Cornelius VanNorden had five and a half acres and is shown having three different buildings on his lot (#17).

Next follows a series of three very narrow lots, belonging to Abram M. Hatfield (#18), Abram Servant (#19) and Jacob VanEmburgh (#20). Hatfield and Servant are both believed to have lived on these lots, and perhaps VanEmburgh did as well. No buildings are shown, but the scale of the map may have made it impossible to show buildings.

Next north is a larger lot (#21) of four acres owned by Abram Servant with no buildings shown.

The final lot (#22), on the river side, is one of two acres. It adjoins the approaches to the Tusket Bridge and was owned by Cornelius VanNorden. No buildings are shown on these last two lots.

All the other lands within the confines of the village were granted at a later date.

It should also be noted that most of the settlers shown on this plan also had other larger land holdings outside the village proper. These were used as woodlands and some were developed as farms. Some settlers, like Squire James Lent, had substantial land holdings throughout the county.

Early Aspirations of the Tusket Loyalists to Form Their Own "Township"

A short time after the Loyalist settlers established themselves at Tusket they exhibited a desire to form their own "Town" or "Township" within the existing County of Shelburne. J. R. Campbell in his *History of Yarmouth County* (1876), writes, "Before ten years, this new settlement had widely spread and clearly defined its position. It aimed at the erection of a new district, to be called FRANKLIN TOWNSHIP, with Tusket at its centre, lying mid-way between the Township of Yarmouth and the then distant settlement of Argyle."

According to the late historian, Robert B. Blauveldt, "The settlers' aim had been to form a new district, to be called Franklin Township, in honour of Benjamin Franklin's son, Sir William Franklin, who was the last royal Governor of New Jersey."

This was not to be. When the first Loyalists arrived in Tusket in 1784, the newly settled village was located in Argyle Township, which had been designated and established by the provincial government in 1771. The provincial government of the time deemed it judicious to allow the already established boundaries and names of the Townships (Yarmouth and Argyle) to remain.

That this sentiment on the part of Tusket's Loyalists lingered for some time is shown in a petition by the residents of the area to the Anglican Church in 1793, when they were requesting that denomination to build a church in the village.

> To the Right Rev. Father in God, Charles, Bishop of Nova Scotia, the memorial of the inhabitants of Franklin Township and its vicinity: Humbly sheweth, That your Memorialists, members of the Church of England, and Loyalists, being destitute of religious worship and desirous and willing to contribute to the building of a Church and support of a Missionary to the utmost of our abilities, most earnestly solicit your patronage and benevolent intercession with his Excellency the Governor, to appropriate one hundred pounds to our assistance, and we promise, Right Reverend Sir, as soon as the season will admit, to enter into contract with proper workmen, and to join our subscriptions and all necessary proceedings, to carry the same pious work into execution. And your Memorialists, etc.
> Franklin Town, April 6th, 1793.

The term "Franklin Town" did not persist for many years, and the Anglophone version, of the original Mi'kmaq name for the village, "Tusket," remained within Argyle Township.

CHAPTER 2

A VILLAGE WALKING TOUR

CHAPTER 2
A VILLAGE WALKING TOUR

Tusket Houses & Properties

At this point, I would like to turn the clock back, and take the reader on a walking tour of Tusket; Tusket as it was in times past, and Tusket as it was in 1974, when I first began this manuscript. The older buildings and landmarks will be pointed out, including a number of those that have disappeared from the landscape. In most cases I have been able to provide photographs of the older buildings on this tour. Short sketches of most of these older properties are offered. Some of these properties have had many owners and are often known in a number of different ways by local people. My naming of some of those properties reflects this fact. For example the "Thomas Phillips – Julien Doucette – Louie & Melanie Hubbard House" was built for Thomas Phillips and then owned for many years by Julien Doucette. People today know this house today as the Louie and Melanie Hubbard property.

Modern buildings (those built, for the most part after 1920), have their date of construction, original and present owners noted. The modern buildings, with a few exceptions, have not been photographed. Some residents of the village will notice that some properties are missing from this chapter. **Those properties that have been built after 1974 will be found in a later chapter, entitled "Tusket Thirty Years Later."**

***Aerial photo of Tusket village looking northwest from beyond the
Frank Doucette Road***

The following reference points in the village are identified. X indicates the approximate location where Jacob Tooker, Tusket's first pioneer and his family, settled on the west side of the Tusket River; #1 marks the location of the first house on the east side of the river, built by pioneer Abraham Lent; #2 Lent's Corner; #3 the site of J. Lyons Hatfield's wharf; #4 the Court House area and # 5 the Tusket River Bridge.

We will begin at the southern extremity of the village and proceed in a northerly direction in an attempt to describe what one would have witnessed in times past and what remains today.

We shall begin our journey at the oldest house in the village; the Abraham Lent house on the Point, commonly referred to as "the Narrows".

The Abraham Lent House – Tusket's Oldest

Abraham Lent, one of the original Loyalist settlers, chose one of the finest locations in the village on which to build his home. It is located on the east side of the river, at what is known as "The Narrows"; the point of land on which it is built being the narrowest point, from shore to shore, in this part of the Tusket River. Like all of the earliest homes, it was built facing the river, there being no roads at the time of its construction. This dwelling consists of two parts. The house built by Abraham Lent is the large two and a half storey main part of the house; and there is a one and a half storey kitchen ell with a history of its own.

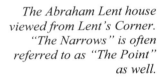

The Abraham Lent house viewed from Lent's Corner. "The Narrows" is often referred to as "The Point" as well.

Abraham Lent did not remain in Tusket for many years, and some sources state that he had returned to New York State as early as 1790. On 23 May 1804 he was living in the "Town of Orang[sic] in the County of Rockland", New York, when he sold all of his lands in Nova Scotia to his brother, "Squire" James Lent of Tusket. He never returned to Tusket.

The subsequent deeds associated with this property suggest that some complications arose in relation to this house. It seems likely that Abraham Lent had built this house, assuming that he would receive a grant to the land. This was obviously not the case, and any grants he received were located elsewhere. The land on which his house stood was obviously granted to others. "Squire" James Lent had purchased his brother's house, but did not own the land on which it sat. A short time after James Lent purchased his brother's property one finds him purchasing several lots of land from Acadian settlers in the vicinity of this house. It seems that several purchases of small lots of land were necessary in order to put together a homestead property around the house.

A rear view of the Abraham Lent house at the Narrows with the attached ell in the foreground.

The Abraham Lent house, as it stands today, and has existed for a very long time, also includes a one and a half storey kitchen ell attached to the rear of the main house. Tradition has it that this house was hauled here from nearby, and attached to the main house at a very early date. When viewed architecturally, this ell is clearly a small house unto itself, with its own central chimney.

Squire James Lent had his own home elsewhere in the village, so did not live in this house. This house served for many years as the Customs House, but not during the early years when it was owned by James Lent. Eventually, in 1835, James Lent deeded this property to his son, Abraham Lent, and that son (who had been named for his uncle who built the house) was already living on the property at the time. The 1835 deed describes the property as land that was bought in three different transactions and were lots "formerly occupied by Joseph Muse and Lawrence Muse" and another piece of land purchased from "Charlaman" Babin. The homestead was 60 acres at this time, all lots combined. This description suggests strongly that the kitchen ell of this house was the original home of either "Joseph Muise" or "Lawrence Muise." Quite likely being in close proximity, it was hauled and attached to the Lent house.

Abraham Lent, 1789 - 1873, son of "Squire" James Lent. He was named for his uncle who built the house at "the Narrows."

Abraham Lent (son of Squire James) lived in this house for the remainder of his life. He married Mary Hatfield, a daughter of Tusket Loyalist, Jacob Lyon Hatfield. Like his father, Abraham was prominent in local affairs and held a number of important positions. He was elected twice as a Member of the Legislative

Assembly and held his seat from 1818-1820 and again from 1832-1836. He was appointed a Justice of the Inferior Court of Common Pleas in 1836, a year after his father's death. He held the position of customs officer from 1857 until his death in 1873. Located where it was, his house made the ideal customs point for stopping ships moving up and down the river.

Abraham and Mary Lent had no children, and upon their deaths this property passed to their nephew, J. Adolphus Hatfield, who had already built a home of his own, nearby, on a portion of the homestead. Adolphus Hatfield deeded the "old house" on the point around 1874 to his son, George A. Hatfield, who occupied the house with his family. After George Hatfield's death in 1896, his widow, Annie (Churchill) Hatfield, continued to live here with her children. In 1907 her son, Norman B. Hatfield, became the owner of the property, and remained so until his death in 1954. He was best known as the "Tax Collector" for the Municipality of Argyle, a position he held for many years.

In 1954 the house was purchased by Arthur E. and Clara Marsters. This couple were natives of Kings County, Nova Scotia, who lived in New Jersey but always spent their summers in Nova Scotia. They valued the history and architecture of this old home and made many sympathetic improvements. They encountered serious controversy with this property in 1972 when the Department of Highways was in the process of constructing the 103 Highway. Plans called for the new highway to cross the river at this most convenient location, and would have meant the removal or demolition of this house. After months of debate the new highway was constructed north of the village.

The Marsters were wonderful people. I remember my first acquaintances with him. I was working for my brother Hubert in his recently opened auto body shop in Tusket. During their summer holidays Arthur Marsters would always have us do touch up work on his vehicle; a green International station wagon. Quite often he would visit while we did the necessary work and chat with us, always very friendly and pleasant.

On November 22, 1963 … my brother Hubert was working on Mr. Marsters vehicle and I was installing a moulding on Avite Burke's car in the paint shop. We had a tiny radio on a shelf, not far from where I was working. A news bulletin came over the airwaves … President Kennedy had been shot! I quickly went and told my brother and Mr. Marsters. He was visibly shaken up. Shortly afterwards the news came over the air that the President was dead; he broke down, sobbing and speechless. It was difficult to find words of comfort.

Later when I became interested in my history project, we spent many memorable hours together in their historical home at "the Narrows." How I remember the grand tour of the house. The huge open fireplace in the kitchen … I was so happy that they had left it intact; and the original self-closing door hinges … how they fascinated me! I still picture that magnificent Dutch door that opens to the river - how convenient for the shipmasters to pay their duties. Mr. Marsters was so proud of the numbers he had installed over the entrance door … 1784. It was very sad when they eventually had to sell the property.

Thanks to the current owners of this property (2005), John Terry and Andrea Doherty, this important house has been designated both a Municipal and a Provincial Heritage Property which protects it from future exterior alterations or demolition.

Leaving the Abraham Lent house, one climbs the rather steep driveway to the top of the hill. In doing so, we pass the barn which belongs to the property. Walking eastward along the road, now known as the Horatio Wood Road, we come to the home of the late Wilbur Wood.

Wilbur & Margaret Wood House

The home of the late Wilbur Wood is a moved building. This small hip-roofed house began its life on the Abraham Lent property that we have just left behind us. It was built on that property in 1907, by Stephen Doucette of Hubbard's Point, for Norman Hatfield. It remained on that property for the next 40 years. In 1947 Wilbur Wood purchased the "bungalow" from Norman Hatfield and had the cottage hauled onto a small lot nearby that he had also purchased from Norman Hatfield. Wilbur and his wife have lived here since then. Although Wilbur has since died, his widow, Margaret, still lives in the home in 2005.

It is probably worthy of note that when the "bungalow" sat on its original site, in the back yard of the Abraham Lent house, it had a concrete doorstep. This doorstep remains in the garden on its original location, a curiosity on that property. Some additional details on this building will be found in the chapter on "Hotels & Inns."

J. Adolphus Hatfield Homestead

Proceeding along the Horatio Wood Road a short distance east, on the south side of the road, we arrive at the homestead of James Adolphus Hatfield, who operated the largest shipbuilding yard in Tusket for several years.

This house was built around 1852-53 for James Adolphus Hatfield, who was later to become one of Tusket's most important shipbuilders. The house is built on a portion of the original Abraham Lent homestead. As has been indicated under that property, James Adolphus Hatfield was a nephew of Abraham Lent, and eventually inherited all of this property. Adolphus Hatfield's house overlooked his shipyards, located in the cove below and to the north. Here, some of the province's largest wooden ships were built and launched.

In 1916 the house was purchased by Horatio Wood who lived here for the remainder of his life. He lived beyond his hundredth year, and the naming of the road which passes in front of the house acknowledges his long tenure on this property. After his death, his widow, Beulah Wood continued to live here. It is owned in 2005 by Malcolm and Karen Sweeney. Karen is Horatio Wood's granddaughter.

Leaving the Adolphus Hatfield house, we arrive at the intersection of the Horatio Wood Road with the main road. The main road (Route 308 South) leads south to the village of Hubbard's Point, and north to the centre of Tusket. Just to the south along this road, and a short distance up the hill, is the last house in Tusket, according to current highway signs. This modern bungalow sits on the eastern side of the road and was built for Lester and Barbara Muise. They moved into this new home in the fall of 1969.

We will pause here for a moment and turn ourselves in a northerly direction. As we gaze down the long hill towards "Lent's Corner", on the eastern side of the highway, we see two buildings.

Roger Doucet House

The first, to our immediate right, is the home of the late Roger Doucet, built here in 1947. It is owned in 2005 by his son Abel Doucet. In the distance, facing north, on the same side of the road, stands a small building painted a pilgrim red which has served the village well.

This small building originally stood at the rear of the Court House in the centre of the village. It was built around 1884 as Mr. Evelyn Wood's blacksmith shop. After his death in the early 1890s, Evelyn's widow sold the lot and the blacksmith shop to the well-known blacksmith, Cyril Doucette, in October of 1893 for $200.00. Cyril Doucette was a highly skilled blacksmith and his work was in great demand throughout the community. He worked here in this blacksmith shop for several years while he lived just across the road. We shall discuss his homestead later in this history.

The Blacksmith Shop

In 1946, Roger Doucet purchased the blacksmith shop and hauled it to its present site on his property. Roger Doucet was a blacksmith with an excellent reputation and continued to operate his business here until the 1960s. He was also well known for his ability to make ox yokes, having carved out more than thirteen hundred in his lifetime. I remember Roger well; he was a robust man and was well known for his strength. He had a deep voice, chewed tobacco and talked rough; he also had a good sense of humour and a hearty laugh. When I first started landscaping around my property in the early 1970s, every spring Roger would bring me a load of manure with his team of oxen. (How I wish I had taken his picture!) On rare occasions, Roger continued to do work in his blacksmith shop until 1983. He died in 1984, leaving the property, including the blacksmith shop to his son, Abel Doucet.

Abel Doucet at age 11 with his father's team of oxen, 1952. The white ox on the left was named Lion; the black and white ox on the right was named Swan.

The Frank Doucette Road

We will cross the main road and proceed east on the Frank Doucette Road. This road forms a loop that leads east and then north to connect with Highway #3. There is only one old house on this road. As we continue in an easterly direction on the road, and down the hill, on our left we pass Roger Doucet's old country barn (now owned by Roger's son, Abel Doucet). This barn was originally owned by J. Adolphus Hatfield and was situated on his property. Just past the crest of the next hill, to our right, is the home of Louie and Melanie Hubbard. This house was built around 1872 for a blacksmith by the name of Thomas Phillips. Having purchased the land from Adolphus Hatfield, it is quite likely that he worked for Adolphus in his shipyard that was located a short distance from here. In 1880, Thomas Phillips moved away from Tusket, having lived here for only eight years. Nevertheless, this crossroad continued to be called "Phillips Road" for a long time afterwards.

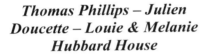

Thomas Phillips – Julien Doucette – Louie & Melanie Hubbard House

Thomas Phillips sold the house to Julien Doucette. Julien was a fisherman and was drowned at sea at a young age, leaving a widow and two young children, one of the children bearing his father's name, Julien Jr. His widow remarried two more times, the third marriage being to a Frank Doucette, after whom the road was later named.

During the time of her second and third marriages, Julien Doucette's two children continued to live in this house with their mother, and their step-fathers. The son, Julien Jr., remained a bachelor and after Frank Doucette's death the heirs signed over to Julien Jr. the property that his father had originally bought in 1880. He continued to live here and during his old age was looked after by his niece, Melanie Hubbard, who was also raised in this house from childhood. In 1971, Julien Jr. deeded the property to Melanie and her husband Louie Hubbard. Melanie and Louie had 17 children. Roy Hubbard, one of their sons, is well known in the village for his tremendous strength and as an excellent worker. Roy is a cousin of my wife (Melanie, Roy's mother, and my wife's mother are sisters). He and I have done numerous landscaping and other projects together over the years. Roy is well known as a rather shy but very witty person. His sense of humour always brings out a laugh when least expected.

*Roy Hubbard,
November 2003*

Lawrence "Barbe" LeFave House

On the opposite side of road and a short distance to the south of Melanie Hubbard's home, for some years stood the home of "Barbe" LeFave. His small house was built here in the early 1940s. Melanie Hubbard's husband, Louie, was hired to build this home for "Barbe." Lawrence LeFave lived here until his death in 1998. The house was demolished a short time later. A small shed is all that remains on the property in 2005.

As we continue on our journey, a short distance beyond the Frank Doucette homestead, we arrive at the intersection of the Frank Doucette Road with the main road, or Highway #3. Turning right here would take us to Sainte-Anne-du-Ruisseau. There is only one older house in this direction, within the bounds of Tusket. We shall proceed in this direction for about a half a mile, passing the road to Abram's River on the way.

The Pierre Melanson – Hilda Zellers House

Just beyond the curve after the Abrams River road, on the southern side of the highway is an older home, which is occupied in 2005 by Nathaniel Blauvelt. This house was built in 1864-1865 for a Pierre Melanson; he was a ship carpenter and had a large family. In 1912, Pierre, in his seventies, deeded the property to his son Joseph. It remained in the family until 1931 when it was sold to Jerry and Evelyn Saulnier. A few years later they sold the house to Mary Dukeshire.

On 8 October 1952 the property was purchased by two ladies from New Jersey who became well known in the area. Their names were Hilda Zellers and Mildred (commonly known as "Pat") Harper. They owned this house together until Pat's death in 1968. Afterwards Hilda continued to live here for a number of years. Their best known contribution to the village was their establishment of the HP Motel, Tusket's only modern motel across from their home. The story of that enterprise is found in the chapter on "Hotels & Inns."

Here, we turn around and walk back in a south-westerly direction for approximately half a mile. A short distance past the Frank Doucette road (already visited), to our left we arrive at the lovely home of John and Erite Frotten.

The Mission House –
John & Erite Frotten
House

The front entrance of this house is most appealing to the eye. The house was built in the 1850s and little is known about the original owner or builder. Records do show, however, that for a long time it was referred to as "The Mission House" and that a man by the name of Mitchell Normandy, a Protestant minister, was living in the house in the late 1860s. It is Mitchell Normandy that James Bingay refers to in his 1955 letter that was published in *The Argus* (vol.3 no.4 – vol.4 no.3). He writes that, "the builder of the house I don't know; but its name, The Mission House, originates with a French Protestant missionary who settled there with the avowed purpose of converting the Roman Catholic population of Eel Brook. He succeeded to the extent of one man …" This may have been an overstatement on the part of Bingay. However, when this proved to be an unsuccessful venture, Rev. Normandy moved on to Saulnierville, in the Clare region.

By 1889 this house had become the property of the Home Mission Board of the Baptist Convention. During this same year it was sold to Herbert and Emily F. Hatfield who lived here for the remainder of their lives. Their daughter, Ida C. Hatfield married in 1904 Robert Thornton Mack, a school teacher, and they afterwards lived here with her parents. "R. T." Mack, as he was known, taught school in Tusket for a number of years, and also taught in both Bridgewater and Yarmouth. It is not known whether he was related in any manner to "Andrew Mack" who owned a large sawmill in the village in the 1870s. R.T. Mack was living in Tusket at the time of his marriage in 1904, although he had been born in Londonderry. He and Ida Hatfield were married at Tusket by his father, Rev. R. Barry Mack, a clergyman. Ida Mack inherited her father's house in 1947 and continued to live here until her death in 1957. In 1960, the present owners, John and Erite Frotten bought the property; they have operated a very successful furniture upholstering business from the ell on the rear of the house. They have developed an excellent reputation for quality workmanship.

James Langille – May Stephenson – Joseph Blanchard House

Continuing in a westerly direction from the Mission House, as we walk around the curve in the road, to our left (south side of the main road) we arrive at what was once a beautiful two and a half storey, Greek Revival style home. Unfortunately, over the past twenty-five years or so, this house has fallen into a state of disrepair. This house was built in 1877 for James Langille and his wife, Sarah Harding. In fact, they purchased the land from Sarah's father, Israel Harding, who lived in the present day home of Susan Young, a short distance west from here. They lived in this house only a few years. It is interesting to note that in the census records of the time, while other residents of Tusket listed their religion as Baptist, Methodist or Church of England, the Langilles stated their religion as "Free Thinkers."

The Langilles moved to the American west and sold their home to a schoolteacher by the name of Abram S. Lent. He was a son of Rev. James Lent, and a brother to James M. Lent who will be mentioned later. Abram S. Lent married Eliza Gavel and spent the early years of his marriage living in Gavelton. They later moved to this house in Tusket, a short distance from the home where he had grown up. In 1909 the property passed on to Abram Lent's adopted daughter, May, who was married to a Capt. Robert Harding. He was a master mariner and travelled all over the world. Eventually he was lost at sea. May later remarried to a Mr. Stephenson and lived here the rest of her life. In the early 1950s the property was sold to Dan Armstrong who operated the former Elmer Hatfield store in the centre of the village. A few years later it was purchased by Dr. Milton O'Brien and his wife Audrey. In 1958 the O'Briens sold it to Joseph and Jacqueline Blanchard who lived here for many years. Having gradually deteriorated to its present condition, it is doubtful that this once grand home will remain standing for much longer. The house is unoccupied in 2005.

Almost directly across the road from this property was the home of Dr. Thomas Kirby.

Dr. Thomas Kirby House – Kilby Lodge

This house was the palatial home of Irish-born Dr. Thomas Kirby, who was one of the county's leading medical practitioners during his lifetime. This was his home, and of course his medical offices were also located here. His wife was Lydia Lent, a daughter of Rev. James Lent, and this house was built on Lent lands.

After the death of Dr. Thomas Kirby the family members sold this large rambling house to Mr. and Mrs. Ernest Hayes, who ran an inn from this property. The Hayes, by all reports, ran a highly successful business here. Their business was known as Kilby Lodge. For a number of years, after the Hayes, this property was owned by Capt. George P. Tuff, a native of Newfoundland. Many Tusket residents today will remember this house as the home of Alvin Trefry.

I remember when Alvin Trefry ran a canteen from a small addition he had built on the front of this house. My brother Hubert had opened a small auto body shop where we grew up in Belleville North. Every evening while working at my brother's body shop, we just had to have a couple of what we thought were the best hamburgers you could buy … and they only cost twenty-five cents! After the body shop was built in Tusket, our friend Gordon Wood joined us and we continued this tradition until Alvin finally closed his doors. This house was demolished several years ago and a modern bungalow style house has been built further
back on the property.

Peter Lent Hatfield – Elmer Hatfield House

On the south side of the highway and diagonally across the road from Kilby Lodge, and a short distance to the west of the Langille house, is the homestead of Peter Lent Hatfield. This house was built around 1862 and is a handsome property that has retained many of its original architectural features.

Peter Lent Hatfield was a well-known and highly trained land surveyor. He held many public positions and served as the Municipal Treasurer for the Municipality of Argyle for an extended period of time. Many people today remember this as the home of his grandson, Elmer Hatfield. Peter Lent Hatfield was a brother of James Adolphus Hatfield, whose home to the south has already been mentioned. Peter married Caroline Matilda Harding, a daughter of Tracy and Sarah (Cochran) Harding. Caroline had grown up a short distance to the west of

Peter Lent Hatfield
1835 – 1917

this property. The present owners of the Peter Lent Hatfield house, Michael and Kerry Lawson, deserve to be congratulated for the excellent job they have done to retain the original integrity of this beautiful home as well as having it declared a Provincial Heritage Property.

Alfred Crosby – Raymond
Z. Bourque – Edmund
Corporon House

The next house to the west of the Peter Lent Hatfield house, and still located on the southern side of Highway #3, was built for Alfred Crosby around 1860. Alfred Crosby married Mary Alice Lent, a daughter of Rev. James Lent. This was probably Lent land. The Crosbys lived here for several years. In 1879 Charles K. Hurlbert bought the property and owned it for the next 40 years, renting it out during much of this time.

In 1942 Raymond Z. Bourque of Sluice Point purchased the property and owned it for the next 30 years. In the early 1950s he was elected as the local Member of the Legislative Assembly for the Conservative Party of Nova Scotia. Through his travels, Raymond made contact with the well-known industrialist, Cyrus Eaton, and became his personal servant. Although Raymond moved his family to Cleveland, Ohio, where he was employed by Eaton, his family returned to spend the summers in Tusket for several years.

Since the house was unoccupied for most of the year, they often rented it out with the exception of the summer months. I remember well the first few winters that my brother Hubert was married, he and his wife Phyllis rented this home. This made it very practical for us to cross the road and go to Alvin Trefry's canteen to get our hamburgers! A few years later when my wife and I were married, we also spent our first winter together here. It was a comfortable home but very cold during the winter months. In 1973 the property was purchased by Edmund Corporon and his family lived here for several years. George and Jean (Doucette) Lunn purchased the house four years ago and are very happy to be living in Tusket.

"Squire" James Lent Property

Continuing in a westerly direction, the next property encountered in early days would have been the home of "Squire James Lent." It sat on the northern side of Highway #3, high on the hill, in the vicinity of where the modern bungalow of Karen and Terry Cottreau is situated in 2005. (This house is identified with an X in the photograph on page 48). As has been stated earlier, this would have been one of the first houses built on the east side of the river, shortly after the Lents landed here in 1785. "Squire" James Lent lived in this house until his death in 1839.

The house was afterwards owned and occupied by his son, James Lent, who was born on 3 February 1793. It is probably appropriate here to pause and offer a piece of genealogy for this family – for family relationships had a major impact on how this part of the village developed over time. James Lent (the second) was married first to Lydia Jeffery. By this wife he had two sons; one of whom, James M. Lent, will be dealt with shortly, and Abram S., who we have spoken of in relation to a previous property.

In 1828, as a widower, James Lent (the second) married a second time to Elizabeth Harding. They would have 10 more children. Elizabeth Harding was the daughter of Rev. Harris Harding of Yarmouth. He was the most prominent Baptist minister in Yarmouth County during his lifetime. It was clearly the influence of Harris Harding, and his daughter, that drew James Lent solidly into the Baptist fold. James Lent was ordained on December 25, 1836, as a Calvinist Baptist minister, and was afterwards known as Rev. James Lent. He presided as the resident minister for the Calvinist Baptist Church in Tusket until his death in 1850. His widow, Elizabeth, died in 1862. It is not known which family members might have occupied the old Lent home after 1862. It seems likely that the old home was eventually either rented out or sold. James H. Bingay, who would have remembered this property from the 1880's and 1890's wrote, "In my time, it was occupied by a shiftless family, the Henry Robbinses." The house appears to have been demolished a short time after 1900.

The Harding House –
John & Phyllis (Hatfield)
Young House

Continuing west, almost directly across the main road (on the southern side), the next property we arrive at is the house occupied in 2005 by Susan Young. The house was built between 1837-1840 for Tracy G. Harding. He was a son of Rev. Harris Harding, and his arrival in the village was surely connected with the fact that his older sister, Elizabeth, was married to James Lent, the minister. Tracy Harding married Sarah Cochrane of New York, and this house was built for them. In fact, two buildings were built here, side-by-side, one being their house, and the other being a commercial building in which they would establish a general store. The two buildings were very similar in design, and built very close to one another, as photographs shown here will illustrate.

Tracy Harding died a young man, in 1846. In settling her husband's estate it was necessary for Sarah (Cochrane) Harding to sell some of their property in order to discharge debts. The house was sold to her brother-in-law, Israel Harding, who moved onto the property a short time later. Sarah moved with her children into the store next-door, and a portion of the building was used as their home.

Israel Harding, the next owner of the house, was a shoemaker and tanner, a Justice of the Peace, and he and his wife also ran an inn from their home for many years. Further details on the Hardings' inn will be found in the chapter on "Tusket's Hotels & Inns." After the deaths of the Israel Harding and his wife, their son Smith Harding lived here for a number years. He eventually sold the property to Capt. Charles Hunter, and many seniors will recall when the Hunters, and afterwards their children lived on this property.

Although I remember the Hunters as elderly people, it is as the residence of John and Phyllis Young that I am most familiar with this historic home. John and Phyllis were the parents of Susan Young, who presently occupies the house.

The Harding - Hatfield Store at Lent's corner

Today this building sits in Hubbard's Point and is well known as the Harry Doucette house. To the far left in this photograph the Harding house is partially visible.

The next property immediately to the west of the Harding house was the store, which we have already referred to. The history of this property will be discussed in the chapter on "General Stores."

Lent's Corner – "Easy Corner"

We have now arrived on our walking tour to what has been called at different times both "Easy Corner" and "Lent's Corner." This corner is steeped in nostalgia, and over the years, life and business here have created many interesting stories. Although many people in modern times have assumed "Lent's Corner" referred to Lent Hatfield, it more likely refers to the "Lent family" who occupied land around this corner for several generations, and of course were the origins of "Lent" Hatfield's name.

The name "Easy Corner" is also highly appropriate. The road here takes a sharp ninety-degree turn, and also offers a breathtaking view of the Tusket River. Perhaps due to the sharp turn in the road and the steep embankment to the river below, travellers might have been cautioned to "take it easy going around the corner."

The James M. Lent house, including the Post Office & Customs Office.

Col. James M. Lent Property

Directly across the main road from the Harding-Hatfield store was the impressive property of Col. James M. Lent. He was the son of Rev. James Lent, and the grandson of the original Tusket pioneer, "Squire"James Lent. James M. had been born and brought up in the old Lent house on the top of the hill, to the rear and east of his own property. Family tradition states that as a young man he went to New York State for some of his education, and received training as a surveyor. Tracy G. Harding, his step-mother's brother, must have been a source of introduction to the Cochrane family of New York, for in 1845 James M. Lent married Theodosia P. Cochrane, a younger sister of Sarah (Cochrane) Harding. It was around this time that James M. Lent's home was built – and the two New York sisters lived directly across the road from one another.

"The Corner", looking south. The James M. Lent house is on the left. The road leading south towards Hubbard's Point fades into the distance.

This house was built into the side of the hill at road level for James M. Lent some time in the 1840s. The Lent house on the corner was a most interesting establishment, to say the least. It served as the village Post Office, the Customs House, and was tended by three generations of the Lent family. When this historic property was demolished by the Dept. of Highways in 1946, its destruction prompted at least two family members to write accounts of their memories of this property.

One of those accounts, written by "Jimmy" Lent, a grandson of Col. James M., was published in the local newspapers. Although "Jimmy" had grown up in the United States, he frequently visited his Tusket relatives and spent many summers here. He was obviously very fond of his grand-parents' home. It is rare that we are given such detailed account of a property, and because of that I quote his entire article on this Tusket landmark. This article is quoted verbatim and any grammatical or typographical errors are those of the original author.

The Corner – Tusket Nova Scotia
by
"Jimmy" [James W.] Lent

In this rambling account of my Grandparents' home in Tusket, and of a way of life in the past, I hope that the present generation of Tusket friends will enjoy a visit to the old landmark, "The Corner", which was recently torn down.

Geographically, Tusket Corner is the point where the South Shore highway, going south through the village, takes an abrupt turn to the east. To the large Lent family connection "the Corner" meant the homestead of Grandfather (Col. James M. Lent), and to the village it meant the Post Office through three generations of the Lent family.

Grandfather's building lot had been excavated from the side of the hill, where the original Lent house topped its crest.

The Home

The three story house was sturdily built of ship lumber by the ship carpenters of that era, with their accustomed precise craftsmanship. The style was of the Federal period, the exterior simple and austere. The western front faced a magnificent view … the broad sweep of the beautiful Tusket River, whose high bank hugged the highway passing the house. The house plan was unique throughout. The ground floor consisted of the house entrance and hall facing west, the Post Office facing south, backed by the stone walled dairy rooms and food storage space.

In front of the house entrance, opening out to the sidewalk, was a large grooved, cast iron Militia target, used as a door step, flanked on both sides by a narrow strip of lawn. The wide front door had glass side lights, and a polished silver door knob, no less, a little touch of elegance popular in those days.

On entering the door one faced a graceful staircase across the wide shallow hall; a door to the right was the private entrance to the Post Office. Hanging from the ceiling was a black wrought iron and red glass lamp; a chair and marble topped table completed the furnishing.

The winding staircase, the home's outstanding feature, had dark stained hardwood carpeted treads, and slender mahogany balustrade. Halfway up on the landing the stairs divided; to the left they curved up to the dining room door, and on the right the stairs led up to the upper front hall. The woodwork in the halls was painted in Colonial flat white, and the walls papered in dark red and gold design.

At the front of the upper hall, a window facing west, and overlooking the river, was flanked on the left by the parlour door, and on the right by the sitting room door. From this upper hall an enclosed stairway led to the third floor bedrooms.

The formal parlour was charming, and our pride and joy. The woodwork painted flat white, was of lovely Georgian design. The architrave of the two windows and door was very wide, carved with a narrow slashed ribbon of gold leaf running through the centre. The door knob of the two-panelled door was of glass, with a smooth surface, the reflection of a tiny star, etched at the back, showing through the centre. The bronze knobs throughout the rest of the house were old fashioned and small.

The large window facing south, and the "river window", facing west, each contained sixteen small panes of glass in the upper sash, and twelve in the lower. The window shades were quaint white cotton, rolled on a rod and tied through the centre, at correct height, by a narrow white tape. The wide Brussels net curtains were draped back at the window sill by exquisite tie-backs, gold metal, with large flower design medallions.

At the back of the room, in front of the high white mantle, stood a Franklin stove.

The narrow gold and blue striped wall paper extended up to the picture rail, the three foot space above being plastered with a beautiful bas-relief design in the four corners.A Brussels carpet of large pink roses and green leaves against a pale grey background covered the floor.

The furniture consisted of antique mahogany, and Victorian walnut, upholstered in black horsehair. The walls were hung with large mahogany framed steel engravings, a very dark old portrait in oils of Great grandfather Lent, and a portrait, in an ornate gold frame, of Grandfather, which dominated the room. Grandfather wore the dress uniform of a Colonel of the County Militia … a red tunic, blue trousers, and carried a sword … very colourful. (The photographic portrait of James M. Lent in full military dress is found on page 284).

A tall pair of Nile green Bristol Glass lustres, with a matching pair of Bristol glass vases, stood on the mantle. During the summer these vases, and a low bowl placed on the square centre table, were filled with white roses, moss roses, honeysuckle, mock orange, or pale yellow lilies, from the old fashioned garden.

The sitting room across the hall was pure Victorian, honey coloured grained woodwork, with wall paper and carpet in shades of tan and brown. The comfortable furniture was a mixture of wicker and walnut, with its accompanying whatnot holding fascinating small ornaments. An organ stood in the corner between the two windows, the latter treated in a conventional style, crisp lace curtains and yellow shades. The walls were hung with family photographs, steel engravings of the eighties, and water colours, the work of two of the daughters while at Mount St. Vincent Convent in Halifax. The marble topped centre table held the popular plush covered photograph album, and one of the handsome oil lamps used in the parlours. The lamps had a marble base, fluted brass column topped by a decorated bowl hung in sparkling prisms, the chimney of chased glass … collectors' items today. In winter the room was heated by another Franklin stove. In summer it was fragrant with garden flowers.

A door opened from the back wall to a small hall. Here was a narrow, locked closet, very mysterious to the children. This wine closet was filled with choice French wines, gifts of sea captains brought from Martinique and St. Pierre Miquelon. Cash and family valuables were also stored here in safety.

On the left side of the hall a door led into our Grandparents' bedroom, on the right another door opened into the long dining room which extended the width of the house on the east. This room was the heart and centre of the home. As in today's modern house plans, the room contained the dining area at one end and the living room area at the other end. A high wainscoting of varnished mellowed pine ran between the six doors and three windows which lent interest to the wall space. The floor was laid with wide oak boards and covered with braided rugs. The wide small-paned east window was filled with a half-moon shaped green flower stand, filled with potted plants; the window at the south overlooked the street. On the west wall a door opened on the front staircase, and was flanked on the right by a beautiful window, small-paned, with its graceful Gothic arched top, looking out towards the front hall entrance and stairwell. On the left a door led to a narrow, winding enclosed stairway, leading to a bedroom above.

At the back of the room was a deep built-in china closet, with Dutch double doors. This held the dinner set, with platters of all sizes, their pewter covers, soup tureens, etc. Everything for the use of a large family.

Near the front window a tall, many shelved closet held the finer "company" china and glass. The dining table and chairs were placed at the back of the room; the south window area was cosily furnished with rocking chairs, Windsor chairs, sofa, a high glass-doored bookcase set on its matching, slender-legged chest of drawers. A large base burner kept this room cheery and warm. An old clock ticked on a high shelf, under which hung a small, hand carved dog's head. Heavy brass candle sticks and small lustre jugs stood on the mantle.

Next to the back china closet was the door leading into the small entry of the kitchen ell, which was built on the bow of the hill. On the left of the kitchen was a long narrow pantry, on the north end of which, under the window, was a broad shelf, where cakes, cookies and pastry were prepared for cooking. The shelves, from floor to ceiling, running the length of the side walls, were filled with fascinating objects. A full set of pewter measuring pitchers, ranging from a gill to a gallon, brought from Holland by the family, was among them as well as canisters, scales, spice boxes, stone jars in various sizes. Here were stored the barrels of flour and sugar, also buckwheat, oatmeal, Jamaica molasses, highly decorated boxes of Spanish raisins, a large box of China tea, and coffee beans which were ground in the old black coffee grinder attached to the kitchen wall.

The sunny kitchen walls were wood panelled, the ceiling beamed, and high square casement windows opened out on three sides. The floor of broad pine, was painted battleship grey and covered with braided rugs. Directly in front of the huge old stone fireplace (boarded half way up and used as a wood box) was a large shiny black cook stove, mounted on four small red wood blocks. The right was a broad shelf and sink, with water pump. In season, herbs, in large bunches, hung from hooks on the wall to dry.

To the left of the fireplace was a steep enclosed stairway to the maid's room above. It was mostly used for rug making equipment, etc., as the maids in my childhood slept at their homes (French Hill).The large table pushed against the wall, scrubbed until white, was often set for the overflow of grandchildren during their parents' visits, and for the farm hands during harvest season.

On the third floor of the main house were three bedrooms tucked in under the eaves, two to the south, and a large room on the north side. Along one side of the hall a built-in linen closet contained quantities of bedding for the family and guests.The walls were papered in a small flower sprig design, the floors painted and covered with braided rugs. The small windows were curtained in dotted muslin, tied back with coloured ribbon. Dotted muslin (full skirted) also covered the small dressing tables, with their framed mirrors above. High chests of drawers and small, reed seated ladder back chairs, made up the furnishings. The four-poster and spool beds were made up with high feather beds, linen, blankets and topped by gay patch work quilts. Heated and wrapped stones were placed between the sheets in winter to take the chill off. There were also folding cots kept in readiness in storage for the visiting grandchildren. Those were the days! The rooms were lighted by small hand lamps (oil) and heavy antique brass candlesticks.

The Post Office

The Post Office, which occupied the southern half of the ground floor, was divided into two parts. The main office consisted of a front lobby, backed by the private office; the public office on the right, containing the mail boxes, stamp and mail delivery window. The business of the Canadian Customs was also conducted by the Postmaster. Over the narrow small paned front door, stood the Canada Customs sign, with the Canadian coat of arms, while over the other door was placed the Post Office sign. The high windows on two sides were closed at night with large wooden shutters, kept in place by heavy wooden bars; Government property, well protected.

Customs Canada, 1914

Left to right: Thomas K. Lent (Post Master); Abram Lent, both sons of Col. James; Frank Andrew Doucette; James M. Lent, son of James W. (a nephew of Thomas K. and Abram); and Mary Doucette, "the store girl" is seen with the horn used to talk to the ships approaching to declare their supplies. James M. ("Jimmy") Lent, standing next to Mary Doucette, was the author of the sketch quoted here.

Looking back I realize how Colonial in feeling was the Post Office—a treasure chest of antiques. Long Windsor benches occupied two walls of the lobby, Windsor chairs and Captain's chairs. A 4 ft. by 3 ft. oil painting of the British Coat of Arms, dark with age, hung high on one wall. This rare and cherished possession had been brought by the family from New York in Loyalist days.

Two high black desks, with their high stools, divided the front and private offices. In the back was the priceless Governor Winthrop mahogany desk, with its beautiful fittings, old maps on the walls, and a gun rack holding antique guns and "horse pistols", deer antlers, duck decoys, etc., decorated the walls. A West Indian water jug of black clay, in its little rack, stood on a small shelf near the desk, filled with cold spring water. A large letter press, pewter ink wells, brass letter scales, etc., made up the necessary office equipment.

The Cellar

A door from the back office, or the east, opened into the cool cellar behind. Here the walls were of rock. A dairy room contained shelves holding the large shallow earthenware bowls of rich milk set for cream, the churn and other butter making equipment.

In another small room shelves held the result of summer canning … pickles, jelly and jams, not forgetting tall bottles of delicious homemade blackberry wine.

A larger storage space, across the hall, held the winter's food supply … barrels of apples, corned beef, salt pork, salt fish, bins of vegetables, hams, sausages, bacon and head cheese, etc., the results of a plentiful harvest and plenty of hard work.

Huge flat stones, carried from the shore, formed the winding steps in the covered entry, leading up to the back yard through a heavy wooden door, cleated and bound with bolts, long hand-wrought iron hinges, and heavy latch.

The Yard

The large enclosed yard was a wonderful place for children's games. Save for the wide gate opening on the southeast, it was completely enclosed and private.

The kitchen door opened on a narrow railed stoop which ran the length of the ell. Story high steps led down to the yard level. As the yard had been excavated, a high stone wall supported it on two sides. On the higher level towards the east, stood a beautiful orchard of apple, pear and cherry trees. Shady chestnut trees spread their branches above the stone wall and along the street side of the orchard ran a stone wall topped with a tall hedge of Irish black thorn. During the blossoming season these trees and hedges provided a lovely background.

By the east side wall stood a long chicken house. On the street side a 7 ft. board fence contained the wide entrance gate in the form of double sliding doors, the same height as the fence. A long, open doored shed covered the deep well, and fire wood storage.

Flower gardens lined the yard; high hollyhocks, climbing roses ran riot. Every spring the hen and well houses were freshly whitewashed, and when flowers were in bloom this was a lovely spot.

The Farm

In 1785 Cobus (James) Lent and family arrived in Tusket via Shelburne, from New York (Dutch Loyalists). In 1788 he was one of the grantees in the Van Cortlandt Grant, receiving 175 acres, later acquiring, by purchase, other considerable areas in Argyle township" (Great grandfather Lent). Across the highway to the south east stood the barns housing a horse, cows, oxen and swine, also carriages, sleighs, farm wagons, etc. Hay from the many fields and salt marshlands was stored in the hay lofts for winter. Along with pasturelands, woodlots, etc., this farm property took in a large area.

The Old Store

Across the highway from the west side of the house stood the "Old Store", a small wooden building, two stories high, built on a rock foundation on the edge of the river bank. A hand bridge from the level of the highway, extended to the store's entrance. In early days it was used as a "meeting house;" later as a store house it contained fishing equipment, kegs of nails, ladders, tools for carpentry and repair jobs, etc; … a storage space necessary to the upkeep of a house and farm. In those early days men had to be versatile, knowing how, and having the means to meet every emergency. A knowledge of how to treat sick animals was very necessary, as no veterinarian was on call.

* * * *

This house, after the death of James M. Lent and his wife, continued to be owned and occupied by several of his children, all of whom remained single. They were Adolphus Lent, who served as postmaster for a number of years; Abram J. Lent, who tended to the farm operations; Arabella ("Belle") Lent; Thomas K. Lent (who had been married briefly but was either widowed or divorced); and Polly Lent. Other siblings lived in homes nearby. James M. Lent's eldest daughter, Adelaide Lent, had married Stephen Gillis, a shipwright, and they eventually moved to Somerville, Massachusetts. Two of their children, Henry F. ("Harry") Gillis, and Helen ("Nell") Gillis, moved to Tusket in the early 1900s. They lived in the James M. Lent house and took care of their uncles and aunts in their last years. Adolphus Lent died in 1913 of Bright's Disease. Polly Lent died in 1920. Belle Lent died in 1923, and Abram Lent and his brother Thomas K. Lent both died in 1924.

"Nell" Gillis and her brother, "Harry", who was mentally ill, were the last to occupy the old James M. Lent home. Dr. Bingay in his 1955 letter writes, "Nell Gillis, spinster daughter of Stephen Gillis and his wife, Adelaide nee Lent, fell into possession of the Corner (P.O.) house, where with the 'help' of her brother Harry, she established the 'Tousquet' tourist lunch tables - and very nice they were. But Nell died, Harry went foolish and died a few months later." Nell Gillis died 25 November 1943 of heart disease, and Harry Gillis died at the Waterville Hospital on 30 December 1943. Unfortunately, after the deaths of their aunts and uncles, little remained financially of the former Lent estate. Nell Gillis had little means of support other than the small income from her "tea room." Unfortunately there seems to have been no family left interested in taking on the old property.

Sadly, in the end, the Lent home suffered the fate that so many graceful old homes too often do. In 1946 the Department of Highways expropriated this house with the intention of altering the sharpness of the corner. The house was afterwards demolished, but no real road alteration was made. All that remains of this once beautiful homestead is an empty hole in the side of a hill and a well constructed stonewall which served as part of the foundation to the Lent home at "Easy Corner."

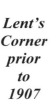

Lent's Corner prior to 1907

The house shown high on the hill, marked with an "X", was the original home of Squire James Lent, mentioned earlier, and one of the first houses built on the east side of the river. The other buildings shown; left to right, are: the "fish house" of Squire James Lent; the Col. James M. Lent house (Post Office & Customs) and the Issac S. Hatfield house and store combined.

The two old buildings on the riverbank, one of which was "Squire" Lent's "Fish House," were used until around 1965. These buildings over the years had become the property of Lent and Jessie Hatfield and were used for storage in connection with their store across the road. Between 1965 and 1970 these buildings were demolished, and Lent Hatfield had Augustin Surette of Lower Eel Brook construct a new building on the old stone foundations. This modern building can be seen in the photograph on page 31.

Evening on the Tusket

To the left is a small shed probably belonging to the Lents, then, moving right, Squire James Lent's "fish shed". A close look reveals the hand rail bridge leading from the main road to this building entrance (second storey) that "Jimmie" Lent refers to in his description of the "old store." In the centre is the Lent Hatfield store. To the right is the rear of the Harding house (the present home of Susan Young). A glimpse of the James M. Lent house (Post Office) is visible between these two buildings with the towering Baptist Church steeple in the background.

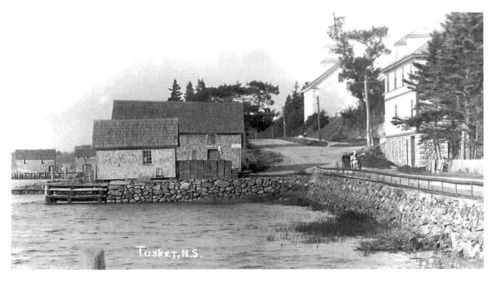

"Lent's Corner" from the waterfront

A closer look at some of the same buildings shown in the previous photograph. In this photograph a different view of the Baptist Church is shown. Also shown in the background, beyond Squire James Lent's "fish house," are two other buildings. These are located just to the north, on the wharf of J. Lyons Hatfield. That property will be discussed shortly. The great masonry foundation work, clearly visible on the Lent Hatfield store, was the work of Thomas Doucette from Quinan. The man with the horse and carriage is William H. Lent.

The Hanging Oak

Rounding Easy Corner and walking north, to our left along the main road stands the intriguing old oak tree which is one of Tusket's oldest landmarks. Dating back to the first settlers, this weathered old oak tree has withstood the test of time, and from one generation to another, it has been referred to as "the hanging oak." Several stories have circulated over the years regarding this tree. I remember during my youth that whenever the hanging tree in Tusket was mentioned it was usually with an air of eeriness about it; supposedly this was the tree where criminals had been hung. I have not, however, been able to find one piece of evidence to substantiate such stories. Others believe that Squire James Lent tied his boat to this tree when he first reached the shores of the Tusket River in 1785. A more likely story related to me by some older citizens of the village is that this tree was used in the early days for butchering livestock and to hang sides of beef and pork from this tree for curing purposes. Under the biographical sketch for "Squire" James Lent, earlier in this history, mention is made of "Judge" Lent (as he was also known) having felons tied to a tree and whipped as punishment for their misdemeanours. Could this have been the tree?

Today, it is obvious that time has taken its toll on this once magnificent oak tree along the riverbank. Only a few main branches remain intact and I cannot help but wonder how much longer it will continue to exist.

Baptist Church

Proceeding north up the knoll a short distance, we arrive at the former site of the impressive Baptist church, uniquely positioned on the east side of the main road. The view must have been magnificent overlooking the river from this lovely building. Erected on common land, the village cemetery, the church was built around 1813 and served the community Baptists until it was eventually torn down more than one hundred years later. A more detailed account of the village churches will be discussed separately in this history.

The following photograph gives an overview of the area we are currently proceeding past as we continue along on our journey in a northerly direction.

Looking north from the Adolphus Hatfield property

Tusket at one time had four churches, three of which can be seen here: the Baptist Church # 1, in the south of the village; the Methodist Church # 2, at the centre of the village; and the Free Baptist Church # 3, located beyond the railroad tracks, at the top of Parade Hill, visible in the distance. The large wharves along the waterfront in the southern and central part of the village are clearly visible.

To the north of the Baptist church, along the hillside, is the land originally designated as the village cemetery. Very early after the settlement, a fairly large area was set off as a cemetery for the use of all residents, without distinction of race, colour or creed. On the wooded slope just inside the gates rest many of the early settlers. With one or two exceptions, their graves are now unmarked. Among the earliest burials here was that of Dennis VanTyle Jr., the small son of Capt. Dennis and Deborah (Tooker) Van Tyle. The more modern part of the cemetery is at the top of the hill.

John V.N. Hatfield – Nettie Reed – Gordon and Evelyn Muise Property

51

Immediately north of the village cemetery we arrive at another lovely old property, owned, when I began this history, by Mrs. Nettie Reed. This large property was one of the oldest in the village, and consisted of the house, a large barn and several other smaller buildings. (The photograph on page 53, identifies this entire property. It is the first homestead located on the right). The house was probably originally built around 1823 for Capt. John V. N. Hatfield, son of pioneer Col. Job Hatfield, one of Tusket's early settlers. Capt. John V. N. lived here all his married life and was one of the most influential men in the village during his lifetime. As well as being a merchant, he also held many shares in some of the largest ships ever built in Tusket. As the old Tusket map on page 141 reveals, he also owned very large parcels of land, particularly in the vicinity of the village centre.

In 1919 the John V.N. property was sold to Tusket's well known photographer, Gordon S. Hatfield and his wife, Nettie. Many of Gordon's photographs are seen throughout this history. After Gordon's death, Nettie remarried to a Mr. Reed. A widow for the second time, she continued to live here by herself until her death in 1975. Nettie was well known for her lovely gardens and even in her later years, she still managed to keep her property most appealing to the eye.

Gordon & Nettie (Gavel) Hatfield

In 1985, Gordon and Evelyn Muise purchased this property. They demolished the old house and built a new colonial style brick house on top of the hill, directly behind where the old house stood. Fortunately, they have kept the unique curved roof outbuilding next to the road and have restored the large barn.

J. Lyons Hatfield Property

Directly across the road from the John V.N. Hatfield property, and on the bank of the river, his son J. Lyons Hatfield (commonly referred to as Lyons), built his home. It is clear from early maps that John V.N. Hatfield himself had developed wharves and other structures here. His son, Lyons, not only built a large house but also operated a store and sawmill from the property. (This wharf is well identified in the photograph on page 253). For a period of time Lyons was a very successful businessman in the village. His wharf served as a major commercial point of activity in the village during the days of shipbuilding & shipping. In addition to all the structures located here, the property also boasted a large well that served to load the ships with fresh water prior to heading out on the open seas. Later in life, Lyons sold his Tusket properties and spent his last years living in Yarmouth.

Decayed Lyons wharf ... 1940s photo

This aerial photograph of the southern portion of Tusket was taken during the 1940s. Outlined in this picture, we see the remains of the once extensive wharf of Lyons Hatfield. The house burned, then the mill and shop and the wharves decayed through the years, though remnants can still be seen today. Only the well remains. Properties on the opposite side of the highway are described here from right to left, or south to north. The first house shown is that of Capt John V.N. Hatfield (son of Col. Job.) Just to the north are the barns associated with the house; this property is now owned by Gordon and Evelyn Muise. Immediately next to the left is the Mildred Hatfield house, followed by the Dr. H. J. Fulde and the Fred Babin houses.

Abigail Price – Mildred Hatfield House

The next property to the north of the John V.N. Hatfield homestead, and still on the eastern side of the road is the second oldest house in the village, built in the 1790s. As mentioned earlier in this text, the first owner was a woman by the name of Abigail Price. Abigail Price was a black woman and had formerly been one of "Squire" James Lent's slaves. She was a widow, and her husband may have been the "Joseph" Price listed on one of the land grant documents for the Tusket area. This house was restored with a number of tasteful exterior additions in the 1930s-40s by Allan and Mildred Hatfield. Until the renovations by the Hatfields, this house had amazingly retained its original architectural details as seen in the photographs on the following page.

Tuskets's second oldest house, 1930s.

The same house in 1985.

Abigail Price sold her land here in two deeds to David VanNorden in 1813 and 1816. In one deed she is referred to as "widow woman" and in the other as "black woman." The house remained in the VanNorden family until 1895 when it was purchased by a Samuel Robbins. Even to this day, the house is sometimes referred to as the old Robbins house. In 1896 it was sold to Alfred Servant who had been living further north in the village. The Servants occupied the house until 1932. Allan and Mildred Hatfield purchased it in 1933. Allan died quite young and Mildred continued to live here the rest of her life, dying in 1993. I have extremely fond memories of time spent with Mildred. She provided me with a wealth of excellent old photographs of Tusket, many of which are included in this history. She was very knowledgeable about the history of the village and it was always a pleasure to visit with her. In 2005 Mildred's granddaughter, Woody Esterwood, continues to live in the house. It is interesting to note that although this home is the second oldest in the village, only five families have occupied the house – the Prices, the VanNordens, the Robbins, the Servants and the Hatfields.

***Rev. Charles Knowles –
Dr. H. J. Fulde House***

The next house, proceeding north, was built around 1857, and was the original home of Rev. Charles Knowles. Charles Knowles was one of the pioneers and staunch promoters of the Free Baptist Church in the southwestern part of the province. He was often referred to as the "Free Baptist Bishop." He also became influential as far away as the province of New Brunswick, where the settlement of Knowlesville was named after him. More will be said about this remarkable man under the section on churches. After his first wife died, he remarried in 1847 to Caroline Hatfield, daughter of Capt. James Hatfield of Gavelton. Quite likely this is what brought him to the village. Caroline was a sister to Adolphus Hatfield who owned the large shipyard to the south of the village, and also had several other siblings living in the village. Charles Knowles's daughter, Ann, married Capt. John R. Blauvelt and after the death of her mother in 1920, the Blauvelts inherited this property. They lived here the rest of their married lives. During their tenure here, before they were the formal owners, they made major renovations to the house. Being a sea captain, John R. Blauvelt added the two dormers and the central tower, making the house look more like those belonging to sea captains in Yarmouth. To my knowledge, this is the only house ever built in Tusket with the resemblance of what one might refer to as a "widows-walk." The small windows in the tower are certainly well situated to catch a bird's eye view as the ships came through the Narrows and up the river.

Various owners have occupied this property since then. In 1961 it was purchased by Dr. Milton O'Brien and his wife Audrey. For a long period of time after 1961 the house was owned and occupied by medical doctors. Most recently it served as the home and medical office of Dr. H.J. Fulde. In September 2002, the property was purchased by Edwin and Carmen Coffin who continue to live here today.

Capt. Alfred VanNorden –
Alfred Babin House

The next house, proceeding north, was built in the mid-1860s for a master mariner, Capt. Alfred VanNorden, a son of Loyalist pioneer, Gabriel VanNorden. In 1890 his widow sold the property to Capt. John Crosby who remained the owner for some 20 years. On May 1, 1920, the property was purchased by Alfred Babin of Belleville North. Alfred and his wife became very well-liked citizens of the community. Alfred first operated the "Tusket Cycle Company" with my grandfather, Albanie Pottier. Later, during the early days of the automobile, Alfred operated a car garage in the former W.T. Lent store. When the Lent family gave up the Post Office at "The Corner", Alfred Babin became Post Master in Tusket and served in this capacity until his retirement. Some of my fondest memories during my early research for this book, nearly thirty years ago, are my visits with Alfred and his wife. They were a pleasure to spend time with. Fortunately, they never altered this lovely old home and the village has been even further blessed with the present owners of this property, Scott and Lisa Hurlburt. They have done a fantastic job at preserving and enhancing the original architectural details of this beautiful house. They deserve to be complimented for their efforts.

The Enos Gardner – Tracy G. Hatfield – Hubert & Margaret d'Entremont House

The next house to the north of the Alfred Babin house is the attractive Cape Cod style house built for Enos Gardner, around 1850. He and his brother Nathaniel were major shipbuilders and operated a very profitable business during the golden era of shipbuilding in Tusket. Although the business eventually struck misfortune and declared bankruptcy, Enos Gardner remained a prominent and valued member of the community. He was a highly respected and well-liked man. Besides being a Justice of the Peace, Enos Gardner became the Town Clerk for the old General Sessions of the Peace for Argyle. After municipal incorporation in 1880, he became the new Municipal Clerk for the Municipality of Argyle and served in this capacity from 1880 until his death in 1898. Mrs. Gardner continued to occupy this house until 1901 when she passed away. The property was then purchased by Tracy G. Hatfield, a leading merchant in Tusket during his lifetime. He has been mentioned earlier, as having built the new store at "The Corner," in 1907. Tracy Hatfield lived in the Gardner house from 1901 until his death in 1943, and his widow remained here until her death in 1952. In 1953, this well-maintained property was purchased by Hubert and Margaret d'Entremont. Hubert was a very meticulous and neat person. I can still remember him using a heat gun and scrapers to completely remove the old paint from the clap-boards, a most time consuming task. Hubert and Margaret have done an excellent job of preserving the original architectural integrity of this lovely house. Hubert died in 1990, and Margaret has continued to live here. The manner in which she has maintained this property is a credit to her and the community.

The Village Centre

We have now arrived to the part of the village that may best be described as the "centre" of Tusket; the Court House area.

Shown here, right to left (south to north), the Methodist Church; the second home of William T. Lent (later owned by Dan Armstrong); and a barn shown in the background.

Immediately north of the Enos Gardner house is the Methodist Church, nicely surrounded by trees, with its pleasing façade overlooking the Tusket River. It was first opened for worship on February 3, 1878. Still in good condition, in 1973 it was sold to the Seventh Day Adventists, the only church of that religious denomination in the county. Additional details on this property will be given in the section devoted to churches in this history.

James Bingay – W.T. Lent House

W.T. Lent & his wife Matilda, in front of their first home on this lot.

The large house, which once sat just north of the Methodist Church, was probably originally built for James Bingay, an early settler who operated a general store on the opposite side of the road. The house was later sold to William T. Lent, commonly known as W. T. Lent. Mr. Lent and his second wife, Matilda Brown, are shown in a photograph here, in front of their large, two-storey home during the latter part of their lives. This

57

beautiful home was consumed by fire around 1900. Shortly afterward, Mr. Lent had another house moved from Court Street and placed on the same foundation. This latter house is shown in the previous photograph, with the Methodist Church. It is believed that this house was originally situated on the site where Charles and Barbara Britain reside in 2005 prior to being moved onto this lot. After William T. Lent died in 1911, his wife Matilda continued to live here until her death in 1916. At this time the homestead was purchased by LeBaron "Barney" Floyd, who later deeded it to his son Harold Floyd. Harold operated a lumber mill a short distance from here along the shores of the Tusket River for several years. The Floyds, first Barney and then Harold, together lived in this house for forty years.

In 1955, Dan Armstrong purchased the homestead and this is when I remember it best. At this time Dan Armstrong had also purchased and was operating the Elmer Hatfield store across the road. After a succession of various owners this property gradually fell into a state of disrepair and in March 1990, the Argyle Municipal Council purchased the property and had the house demolished, in an effort to protect their own property, the historical Court House.

Just north of the W.T. Lent house, very close to the Court House, was a small but attractive store that appears in several photographs during the period 1890-1920. This building has a complicated history, and began its life on the opposite side of road. We will discuss its history along with other general stores and commercial buildings.

General view: Court House, churches and stores, looking south.

The next property moving north is the site of the Argyle Township Court House. First opened in 1805, this building has been documented by Parks Canada as being the oldest standing courthouse in Canada. Since this building is the most important heritage property in the village, and I had a personal role in its restoration in the 1980s, it will be discussed more fully in a chapter of its own in this history.

Tusket's Old Centre of Commerce

At this point in our tour, we will leave the Court House and cross the main road. We will only briefly discuss the buildings on the western side of the highway. All of the older buildings which sat in this location along the banks of the river were general stores or similar businesses. Many of those old commercial properties had complicated histories, and are discussed in detail in the chapter on "Tusket's General Stores."

Tusket's "Village Centre" ca. 1900. Gordon Hatfield photo.

The above photograph, by Gordon S. Hatfield, taken around 1900, shows many of the old general stores in the centre of the village, as well as a number of other landmarks. The three large buildings to the right, and leading into the picture, all played major roles in the development of the village centre. Around the turn of the century they were known as, #1 Bernard Hurlbert store, #2 W. T. Lent store, and #3 Elmer Hatfield store. The warehouse extensions on two of these stores extended all the way to the waterfront, providing loading and unloading facilities for the ships directly to the stores. A fourth building, just beyond the Elmer Hatfield store is not visible in this picture. Seniors will recall that building as one that was used for storage by Elmer Hatfield, and later by Dan Armstrong.

There are two buildings shown in the photograph on the lot at the rear of the Court House. The building closest to the Court House was the "Mayflower Engine House" for Tusket's Fire Department of the time. The other building is Cyrille Doucette's blacksmith shop. Note the free-standing bell-tower for the fire bell at the rear of the Engine House. The entire area shown in the foreground of this photograph, between the roadway and the Bernard Hurlbert store was at different times from the 1850s to the late 1880s occupied by some of Tusket's most important shipbuilding yards. Tusket's last tall ship, the *SUSAN CAMERON,* was launched from this same property in 1919.

Photo dated May 24, 1907. W.T. Lent owned a very successful general store in the centre of the village from 1897 to 1916. This photograph shows Mr. Lent's horse and carriage picnic trip around Tusket Falls. This was his annual treat to the local children in commemoration of Queen Victoria's birthday. W. T. Lent and his wife Matilda are shown behind the carriage, exiting the store. The driver is W.T. Lent's son, William H. Lent. Sitting next to him, (with a child) is his wife. The children identified are: # 1 Lent Hatfield; # 2 Allan Hatfield and # 3 Bernard Hurlbert. Notice the heavy wool blankets used during the cool springtime period. The waving Union Jacks on the four corners of the canopied wagon give an added touch for the occasion.

This part of the village remained the centre of commerce in Tusket for several years. Today it remains the geographical centre, although much of the village's commerce, with the exception of Carl's Store, is located in the northern part of Tusket.

Continuing on our walking tour of the village we will proceed along Highway #3 to the northwest toward Yarmouth. The original old highway followed the course of the river. In 1936-37, when Highway #3 was being paved, a newer, shorter section of highway was cut over the hill. The old section of the highway in this area became a loop of unpaved road that was afterwards named the "John White Road."

The "new road" under construction in 1936-37

The house on the right was the home of Bernard Hurlbert. The lumber mill on the left, at the entrance to the John White Road, was owned and operated by Harold Floyd for many years. The arrow identifies the Frank Hubbard house.

This aerial view, taken in 1975, illustrates the "loop" (John White Road) and the new highway over the hill. Five landmarks have been marked on this photo: #1 Jacob Lyon Hatfield house, #2 Raymond "Peege" Hubbard house, #3 Tusket Community Hall, #4 short strip of road between both highways often referred to as "Clip Street" and #5 the road formerly known as Parade Street, now Route 308 North.

61

Jacob Lyon Hatfield House

Third oldest house in the village.

A short distance along the John White Road, and on its northern side, is another of Tusket's most historic homes. This house, in Cape Cod style, was built in the 1790s by Jacob Lyon Hatfield. Jacob Lyon Hatfield was among the very early Loyalist settlers to arrive at Tusket in 1785. He was a farmer and a fisherman and played a leading role in the early development of Tusket during its pioneer days. During early times there were many other buildings on this property, such as barns, outbuildings and wharves. The property stretched down to the banks of the Tusket River, and would have been built before there were any roads.

From one generation to another, this house remained in the Hatfield family for a very long time. In 1903, Tusket photographer, Gordon Hatfield, purchased the house, although he only kept it for a short period of time. Gordon Hatfield practiced photography during this period. His photographic shop, or studio, was situated almost directly across the road from this house, on the same site where Cecilia Crosby has her home in 2005. He probably maintained his shop here, even after he sold the house to his sister, Christina. The *Yarmouth Light,* 25 June 1903, reported that, "Mrs. Chase Hatfield has opened an ice cream parlour in Mr. Gordon Hatfield's studio."

The Jacob Lyon Hatfield house is still best known today as the Christina "Chrissie" Hatfield house. She was a great-granddaughter of Jacob Lyon Hatfield. She operated the telephone office and switchboard from her home in this house for many years, until 1959. In addition to her job as the local telephone operator, she also served as the organist for the Methodist Church in the village. Chrissie remained single and in 1946 she sold this property, subject to her right to live in the house for the remainder of her natural life. At her death in 1964, the Hatfield family's long connection with this house ended. This house remained relatively unchanged until a few years ago. Some windows have now been altered and vinyl siding has been installed on the exterior. Nevertheless, its original shape and structure are the same and it remains one of Tusket's most important landmarks. It is owned in 2005 by Bradford and Paula Jacquard.

*The Frank Hubbard house ...
a building "on the move"*

Almost immediately next door to the north is a very small house on a neatly kept property, overlooking the Tusket River. This is another building that has an interesting history of having been moved around. It was built around the 1860s or 1870s and was either used as a small store or storage shed. It stood on one of the properties presently owned by either Norma and Jeff Muise or my mother, Josephine Pottier. From 1851 until 1877 these two properties were owned by William S. Robbins and Phillip Hilton who were partners in business and had several outbuildings on those adjoining lots. (The property was later divided between the two of them). This small house was one of the buildings on that property. Sometime in the early 1900s it was sold to a gentleman from Hubbard's Point by the name of "Frankie" Doucette who had it hauled to that village and placed on a lot on what is known as the Back Road.

The moving of a building from Tusket to the community of Hubbard's Point. The photographer has captured the ox teams and the men going south past Lent Hatfield's Store. This building very much resembles the Frankie Doucette/Frank Hubbard house.

Ironically, in the early 1920s the house was purchased by a Mr. Mark "Maco" Hubbard who had it hauled all the way back to its present site in Tusket; only a few hundred yards south from its original location in the village. In the 1970s the house passed on to their son Frank Hubbard, whom I had the pleasure of visiting while I was working on this manuscript during that time. Frank Hubbard was a very likeable gentleman; he passed away shortly afterwards. In 2005, the house is owned by Marie Octavie Babin, Municipal Councillor Bruce Hubbard's mother.

On the opposite side of the road from the Frank Hubbard house is the home of Cecelia "Sis" and the late Carl Crosby. They first moved onto this property in 1945, and for the first 11 years lived in a building that had formerly been the photographic studio of Gordon S. Hatfield. Around 1956 they built a new home just to the south on the same lot; "Sis" continues to live here in 2005. The former building was demolished.

The Staley Hatfield – Peter "Eddie" LeBlanc House

Continuing north, a very short distance around the corner, back on the northern side of the road, was another large, two story house. Information on this house has been difficult to find, and unfortunately I was not able to locate a photograph of it. Capt. Staley & Hannah (Robbins) Hatfield apparently built the house. He was not closely connected to the Hatfields who lived in this vicinity, so must have purchased this lot of land to build on. Staley and his family moved to Massachusetts. The next owner was Jackson "Jack" Hatfield. He was a son of Jacob & Eleanor Jane (MacKinnon) Hatfield, and would have grown up in the Jacob Lyon Hatfield house nearby. Sometime in the early 1920s, Peter Edward LeBlanc, originally from Abram's River, and his wife, Annie Louise (Doucette) purchased the house from Jack Hatfield and moved here. Prior to this they had been living for a time in the present James Pottier house. They had six children; Cecelia "Sis" Crosby was a daughter. She was three years old when they moved here. She will be eighty five in June 2005. She has lived in this area her entire life and it is to her that I owe much of the information on properties in this area. Of the former Staley Hatfield house she says, "It was a big, beautiful, lovely house … it was a warm home … we were never cold. It had a gorgeous staircase and a large hallway upstairs. It had two chimneys and four bedrooms upstairs; most had walk-in closets. The windows in the front were tall and the wood trim was beautiful." Her father was a fisherman, mostly fishing out of Boston. When the depression arrived, he came home only occasionally and "times got tough." The house began to deteriorate. For a period of time, another family rented part of the house. Later, Peter Edward LeBlanc and his wife purchased the house directly across the road, formerly known as the Riverside Inn. Peter sold (or gave) the old Staley Hatfield homestead to Franklyn Muise who had married their daughter Emma. In the early 1960s, Franklyn tore down the old house and in 1962 built a bungalow on the same foundation. Franklyn died in 1989; Emma continued to live here until December 2004.

Directly across the road was the very large homestead known as the John and Fannie White property.

Chase Hatfield – John & Fannie White – Fred & Barb LeBlanc House

This was a large house stretching out a considerable distance with various sheds and a huge barn all attached to the main house shown above. The four large trees in front of this house still stand today.

According to James H. Bingay, the main part of the house that belonged to this property was erected here by William Hatfield (1806-1881), a son of Tusket Loyalist, Jacob Lyon Hatfield. According to oral tradition this house began its life somewhere in the Cape Island area, was dismantled, brought up the Tusket River, and reassembled here by William Hatfield. Clearly, he and subsequent owners made many additions to the property after this. Eventually the house had a number of extensions and also was connected with outbuildings and the barn. After William Hatfield's death, his third wife and widow, Lydia (Jeffery) Hatfield remained on the property. Eventually the property passed to their son, W. Chase Hatfield, and his wife Florence. Chase and Florence sold this property after the closure of the Dickie & McGrath mills in 1912. It was purchased in the 1930s by John and Fannie White. They developed an inn known as the "Riverside Inn" that is discussed in the chapter on "Tusket's Hotels & Inns." After John White's death, a succession of people owned this property. Freddie LeBlanc became the final owner in the late 1960s. He demolished the old building in 1969-70 and built a new home slightly north of where the old house stood. Freddie and his wife Barbara still live there in 2005. Freddie is a brother to Cecelia "Sis" Crosby.

The Urbain "Reuben" Doucette – Felix Muise House

This photograph was taken a short time before Albert Muise, son of Felix, did extensive alterations to the house. It was unoccupied when the photograph was taken in 1986.

Leaving the John White Road, on the left as we turn onto Highway #3, in what is commonly referred to as "the Cove." The first older house we encounter sits on the western side of the road, down in the cove area. Most people in the village know this as the Felix Muise house. This small house was built for Urbain (the English called him Reuben) Doucette. His brother, Peter, who lived nearby, will be discussed later. Little is known about the early dates of Reuben's house. It is situated close to the road and on very low land. As far as I can discover, Reuben and his wife lived here most of their lives. In 1936, he sold the property to Felix and Louise Muise who had previously lived in Central Argyle. Felix and Louise had a large family; Franklyn Muise, whom we recently mentioned, was a son. The house has remained in the family since then. It is presently owned by Albert Muise, another son of Felix. Albert was thirteen years old when the family moved here from Argyle; he is now eighty-two years old and he informs me that his mother, Louise, paid $40.00 to Reuben Doucette for the property. Shortly after Albert came into possession of the house he built additions around the existing house and made considerable architectural changes to its style. Although Albert still plants a garden on the property every summer, the house is presently unoccupied.

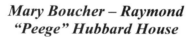
Mary Boucher – Raymond "Peege" Hubbard House

The larger building in the centre is the Mary Boucher – Raymond "Peege" Hubbard house. Part of the Felix Muise house and sheds are visible in the forefront. St. Stephen's Anglican Church is to the left in the background.

Immediately to the north of the Felix Muise property, and still on the west side of the highway, was the Mary Boucher house. This was a large house and quite well kept in its early years. The front of the house sat only a few feet from the road; the southern side of the house was extremely close to the brook which runs under the highway and empties into the cove and the Tusket River. There was very limited space between this house and the Felix Muise property. The origin of this house is not known, but it is said that the people who owned it previous to Mary Boucher, abandoned the house and "moved out west."

A woman by the name of Mary Boucher, originally from Sluice Point (Muise's Point), lived in the house for several years. James Bingay writes that "Mary spent a goodly portion of her time sitting on her doorstep and chatting with the passers-by." Eventually she was able to purchase the property. Mary was not small, she was very dark and had a fierce temper. She had a daughter, Lena Bourque, who was a widow with five children; they all moved in with Mary. Lena was a hard worker and she was always employed as a housemaid throughout the village while her mother, Mary, looked after the children. With Lena's income, they lived quite comfortably. Difficulties arose between the mother and daughter and for a number of years Lena moved with her children to a nearby property where they rented. When Mary Boucher could no longer look after herself, she was cared for by Millie Doucette (à Théophile) in Hubbard's Point. After Mary's death, her daughter Lena, with some of her children moved back into her mother's home. After Lena's family had grown and left home, the house sat empty. Around 1941-42 Oscar Blauvelt occupied the house for a short period of time, and the next occupant was Raymond "Peege" Hubbard, from Hubbard's Point. I remember "Peege" well. He was a carefree, jolly old man, very likeable and always had a smile.

"Peege" was married to Felix Muise's daughter, Barbara. Since she grew up next door, this is perhaps why they ended up in the Mary Boucher house. In 1975, "Peege" and his wife moved into a new mobile home, elsewhere in the village. The old Mary Boucher house was demolished a short time later.

The New Road

As has been mentioned earlier in the tour, in 1936-37, when Highway #3 was being paved, the Department of Highways cut a new shorter road over the crest of the hill in this area. All of the houses along this "new" stretch of road have been built or moved here after that date. We retrace our steps back to the centre of the village at this point, and then proceed northwest over the hill, toward Yarmouth again, in order to give a brief history of these "newer" homes.

Daniel & Patsy Amstrong house – The first house, also on the western side of the road, is a modern bungalow, built in 1964 for Daniel and Patsy Armstrong. In 2005 this house is owned by Esther (White) Frail.

Elisha & Eva Gavel – John & Regina Muise house – This house was moved onto this lot for Elisha and Eva Gavel, by their son Harris "Pat" Gavel around 1946-47. The house came from Central Argyle. In Central Argyle, it had at one time been the home of Felix Muise. Felix Muise (who has been mentioned earlier on the John White Road) had moved his family to Tusket around 1936. After Elisha and Eva Gavel, John and Regina Muise lived here for many years. The house is owned in 2005 by Reya Doucette.

Harry & Velma Hamilton house – Across the road from the Elisha Gavel house is the home built in 1948 by Harry and Velma Hamilton. Velma, a widow, still lives there in 2005.

Robert Jeffery house – The next house, travelling toward Yarmouth and on the same side as Velma Hamilton's was built in 1946-47 for Robert Jeffery, son of Andrew Jeffery. The house is owned in 2005 by Mrs. Joseph Dukeshire.

Michael Rymer house – The next house, on the same side of the road, was built for Michael Rymer around 1945-46. Around 1949 he moved to Little Egypt and sold this house to Frederick and Fannie Bourque. Frederick still owns the property in 2005.

There are two more houses here that were built during the same era as those built on the "new" section of road, over the hill. Both, however, are located on the original Highway #3.

Harris Gavel - Wallace & Helen Hurlburt House – On the western side of Highway #3 is a small hip-roofed house built around 1946-47 for and by Harris "Pat" and "Nan" Gavel. The windows and doors for this house came from the old John Bullerwell house, on the end of the "point" in Little Egypt. Pat and Nan Gavel sold this house around 1949-50 and moved to Pleasant Lake. Wallace Hurlburt and his family, the next owners, lived here for many years. In 2005 the house is owned by George and Susan Muise.

"Andy" Jeffery house – This house, on the eastern side of the road, was built for "Andy" and Margaret Jeffery, son of Andrew, in 1946-47. This house is owned in 2005 by Bernard "Bernie"and Geneva d'Entremont.

Proceeding north along Highway #3, and on the same side as the Andy Jeffery house, is another of Tusket's older homes.

Peter Doucette –
Remi LeFave House

This house was probably built around the 1860s and is similar in style to several other houses built in the village during this time. It was built for Capt. John Murphy who came here from the Pubnico area. Capt. Murphy appears to have built two houses on this property. The house that he occupied as his own residence was moved from Tusket to Yarmouth when he moved to town in the 1880s. His barn was moved as well. After Murphy moved to Yarmouth he appears to have rented this property to the family of Peter Doucette. Peter was a brother to Urbain "Reuben" Doucette recently mentioned. Peter Doucette became the owner of this house in 1906, and continued to live here until 1941, when he sold it to Remi LeFave. Remi and his wife, Benedicte, a granddaughter of Mary Boucher, lived here for many years. This house remained very original until a few years ago when the wide corner boards were removed and vinyl siding was installed. What I remember best about this property is that every fall Remi and some friends would get together and have a pig-butchering bee. To my knowledge this is the only local property where this rural tradition continued beyond the 1960s. Remi died a few years ago, and a very close friend of his, Bernie Doucette, continued this tradition on the property until the fall of 2003. In 2003 this property was sold to Renee Muise and Joseph Bishara, who are making impressive improvements to the interior of the house.

William S. Robbins – Thomas N. McGrath – John Deveau House

The William Robbins house, located almost directly across the road from the Remi LeFave house, is built on what was a portion of the homestead of Loyalist Cornelius VanNorden. This lot of land was purchased from Phoebe VanNorden, Cornelius VanNorden's widow in 1851 by William S. Robbins and Philip Hilton. A house existed on the property in 1851, but whether or not it forms a part of the present day house is impossible to say. William S. Robbins would certainly have been responsible for the appearance of this house as it was known from the 1860s onward.

After they purchased this property, a division took place, and William S. Robbins lived in this house, while Philip Hilton owned, and probably built the next house on the same side of the road.

Front view
North view
The "Gingerbread house" with its original ornamentation.

William Robbins was a very successful businessman and was highly esteemed in the village. After his death the property was purchased by his son-in-law, Ephraim Simonson, the well-known blacksmith, who will be mentioned later in this history. In 1903 the property was purchased by Thomas N. McGrath and was used for several years as a boarding house and cook house for the Dickie & McGrath Lumber Company. After the disastrous fire and loss of Thomas McGrath's first home, immediately next door to the north, his family moved into this dwelling. Freda McGrath, one of Thomas McGrath's daughters, was the last of the McGrath family to live in the house; she died in 1957.

From 1958 to 1963, this house was owned by Hilda Zellers and Mildred "Pat" Harper, who were operating the HP Motel that we discuss elsewhere in this history, at the extreme eastern part of the village. In 1958 when they purchased the old William S. Robbins house, it still retained all of its original architectural features. For a time Hilda and Pat intended to open a bed & breakfast style establishment in this large rambling house, in addition to their already successful HP Motel. The house sported some attractive trim, and Hilda decided she would call it the "Gingerbread House." This plan never materialized, and she later sold this property. Although the original trim on this house was handsome, it was not nearly as ornate as the trim usually described as "gingerbread." Nevertheless, her name for the property stuck, and some people still refer to the house in this manner today.

The property has had several owners since then. Most residents today remember it as the John "Bull" Deveau house. This house has gone through a number of exterior alterations and no sign of the original ornamentation remains. In 2005 the property is owned by Norma and Jeff Muise.

Philip Hilton – Thomas N. McGrath House

Thomas N. McGrath and his wife, Alice Maud in front of their home in Tusket.

The next house, immediately next to the William Robbins house, and still on the western side of the street, was the original home of Philip Hilton. It was probably built on this site shortly after 1851, when he and William S. Robbins purchased, and then divided the property. Philip Hilton lived in the village for several years, and appears to have maintained ownership even after he removed from the village. In the *Yarmouth Light*, 24 December 1896, the Tusket columnist reported that, "It is rumoured that Mr. McGrath has purchased the homestead property of the late Philip Hilton, Esq."

Thomas N. McGrath came to Tusket in order to operate the Dickie & McGrath sawmill enterprises. In 1896 he and Ira Dickie, an industrialist from Stewiacke, purchased the large and impressive sawmill operations of the Tusket River Lumber Company. Although the Philip Hilton house was obviously a very nice home when it was purchased by Thomas N. McGrath, he made many improvements to both the house and the grounds. This was at a time when wooden shipbuilding, as an industry, was finished in the village. The Dickie & McGrath sawmill provided significant employment to the area. The home that Thomas McGrath developed in the old Hilton house befitted his position as one of the leading industrialists in the county. Although we do not have the same kind of account of life in this house as we do of the James M. Lent House at "The Corner," we are left with a number of exterior and interior photographs. The photographs of the inside of the house in particular, are a rare treat from an era when lighting made interior photography of any kind very difficult.

The dining room.

The reading room.

The parlour.(The wicker chair next to the piano is now in my possession.)

The grounds of this property were also beautifully landscaped, and hedges were planted along the edge of the road. In 2005, this is the site of the modern home of my mother Josephine Pottier. The McGraths also had a tennis court built on part of the property, situated roughly where the home of Norman and Betty Anne Pottier is situated in 2005.

Thomas N.
McGrath's
Residence,
Tusket, N.S.

Thomas McGrath, his wife and children photographed in front of their beautifully landscaped property. Mr. and Mrs. McGrath are sitting on each side of the doorway. Dr. Percy McGrath, with whom I became acquainted, is the boy sitting on a bench to the far left. The two large cast iron flower pots that adorn both sides of the front steps are now used in front of my own home.

The McGraths were clearly a wealthy and prosperous family during this period. They were well-liked within the community, and highly regarded for their generosity. Not only were they the main employer in the village, they were public-minded people as well. In 1903 Mr. McGrath donated the bell for the new Amirault's Hill Church, Sainte Famille. Three years previously he had also donated a significant amount of the lumber needed to build Sainte Anne's Catholic Church at Eel Brook. He also donated the two large religious statues still situated today on each side of the altar.

Sadly, the McGrath's beautiful home was lost to fire in October 1912. The following is the account of that fire as reported in a Yarmouth newspaper on October 22:

> Oct. 22 – For the benefit of many of your readers who only take the *"Light"*, it will not be amiss to write a brief description of the disastrous fire that occurred here last Thursday morning whereby the beautiful home of Mr. T. N. McGrath was totally destroyed.
> For some time past the acetylene lights had not been giving satisfaction and that morning Mr. Maurice Turpin, the man in charge, was working in the storehouse where the gas plant was, where the explosion occurred. Mr. Turpin was badly burned about the head and face by the explosion. Mr. Arthur McGrath, knowing there were nine hundred pounds of carbide in the storehouse, hastily got the men from the mill yard and had it carried to a place of safety, or the consequences might have been more serious.
> A fire was started by the explosion in some way, which quickly spread to the barn where a large amount of hay was stored. As the barn was immediately in the rear of the house nothing could be done to save the house, as the wind was blowing the flames right on it. Willing hands soon cleared the house of the furniture, bedding etc., and everything of value was saved. Mrs. McGrath, who

was ill at the time, was taken to a friend's house and Dr. Melanson attended her.

Mr. McGrath and Miss Freida were in Halifax and the news of the loss of their home was a great shock to them.

The fire engine was absolutely useless and we think it is time the Municipality took the matter in hand and provided better equipment for fires for the protection of the property in the village.

After this the McGrath family moved in the large house next door to the south, which they purchased in 1903. Since all of their furniture and possessions had been saved, they were able to set themselves up comfortably in this house.

I would like to pause here, and relate some cherished personal memories connected with the McGrath family, from the time when I first began to work on this history. At that time there were no McGraths living in the Tusket area, although a granddaughter, Freda (McGrath) Bullerwell lived in nearby Brooklyn. My interest in the family, and their impact on Tusket, was common knowledge around the area. A gentleman by the name of Alfred Pottier from Belleville told me he had bought some items at an auction in Tusket at "The Gingerbread House," formerly owned by the McGrath family. He realized my interest, and wanted me to have something that had originally belonged to the family. What he presented me with was a beautiful and intricately designed antique wicker chair, and a large framed professional portrait of the entire McGrath family. I was thrilled to have both of these items.

In the late 1960s, I was told that one of the McGrath sons, Percy, who was a medical Doctor, lived in Kentville. I decided to get in touch with Dr. McGrath, who was retired at the time. He was more than willing to see me and we set a date for getting together. As I was getting ready to leave for Kentville, I decided to bring the McGrath family portrait with me. Our acquaintance was an immediate success. He was thrilled that something was being done to preserve Tusket's past. He soon had his photo albums out and I stood there in awe, as I saw the fantastic pictures he had relating to the lumber mill.

I told him I had brought a picture he might like to see. I can't forget the tears in his eyes when he saw the family portrait. He had always wondered what had become of it. As we looked at his own photographs, his eyes kept returning to the family picture. It was at this time that I offered to give it to him. To me this seemed the most natural thing to do, but he was deeply moved by the gift. I later asked him for permission to make copies of some of his photographs, to which he replied he was giving them all to me in return for the family picture. You can imagine my surprise. This was a most generous gift, not only to me, but to the village of Tusket. An important part of the village's past travelled home with me that day. My only regret is that I never made a copy of the McGrath family picture before I gave it to him.

Dr. Percy McGrath
1893-1988

Although Gordon Wood and I had originally managed to locate some pictures of the mill, Dr. McGrath's collection was a treasure trove. There were many photographs of the mill, but also included in the collection were the exterior and interior photographs of the

McGrath home. It was only upon my return home and after a careful scrutiny of the photographs that I realized the wicker chair that Alfred Pottier had given me was shown in one of the interior photographs. I still own the chair today and we use it for special family occasions. Most of the pictures inherited on that day are included in this history. I owe this pictorial record to the generosity of Dr. Percy McGrath.

More information on the mill operation will be offered in the section on industries in this history.

Gordon and Evelyn Muise – Josephine Pottier House

On the former McGrath property there are now two modern homes. The first is a home built by Gordon and Evelyn Muise in 1972-73. They sold this property in 1986 to my mother Josephine Pottier. She still lives in the house in 2005.

Norman and Betty Anne Pottier House

Just to the north of this house, still on the former McGrath property; is another house, built for and by Norman and Betty Anne Pottier in 1970-71. They continue to live here in 2005.

To continue our tour we will proceed a bit further along Highway #3. On the eastern side of the road in this area is the Public Well. Just how long it has been situated here is not known, but it may have been dug here by Tusket's early fire department, the Mayflower Engine Company, or earlier, as a means of supplying the ships with fresh water prior to setting sail on the high seas.

Here, we find the intersection of Highway #3 with the VanNorden Road; the well is located in the middle of VanNorden Road. Traffic passes to the north and south of the well.

Maurice Prosser – Benoit Pottier – Carl & Audrey Pottier House

Almost directly across the highway from the Public Well on a small raised knoll is the home owned in 2005 by Carl and Audrey Pottier. Early documentation on this property is somewhat vague and complex. In 1872, Gabriel Servant, a shipwright, sold a portion of this land to a farmer from Plymouth by the name of John Purdy. In 1901, John Purdy sold it again to the lumber firm of Dickie & McGrath for $500. In 1904, Dickie & McGrath sold a very small piece of this lot (1/4 of an acre; 53 feet wide at road frontage) to a labourer by the name of Sidney H. Taylor for $100.00. Only three months later, on October 14, 1904, Sidney Taylor sold it again to a merchant from Wolfville by the name of Alexander Bleakney for $800.00. It appears that a house or building of some sort was established on this small lot by this time. Judging by the size of the lot however, one can assume that this would have been a rather small dwelling.

In August, 1925, Maurice Prosser, of the lumber firm Boutilier & Prosser from Yarmouth purchased this property from Alexander Bleakney, and also purchased the Samuel Kelley lot, which bordered it to the south. Maurice Prosser then built the present house, now occupied by Carl and Audrey Pottier. It appears that Maurice Prosser built his new home just a bit north of the site of the old Samuel Kelley house, which by this time was probably gone. Although Maurice had combined two separate properties, this was still a relatively small lot. In 1933 he purchased a large parcel of land to the north of his property from the Nova Scotia Timber Lands Company. This entire lot today is the property that is located between the Norman & Betty Anne Pottier property to the south and Hubert Pothier's former body shop on the north.

Some members of the Prosser family maintain that Maurice Prosser made substantial changes to an existing house on the property. If this is the case, the house was clearly not a very old one, and may have been built for Alexander Bleakney.

Maurice Prosser's wife died and he remarried to Dora Killam. Dora was the daughter of Jennie Killam who operated the Killam Hotel in the present Geraldine "Gerry" Rhyno house. In August 1949, Maurice Prosser and his wife Dora sold the property to The Acadia Trust Company of Truro and they removed to Yarmouth. A few months later my Uncle Benoit Pottier purchased the property and lived there for the next fifty years.

In 1964 Uncle Ben sold a small cottage that existed on this property to Adolphe Doucet's son, Basil, from Quinan. Basil had the house hauled near the entrance to the tower road in Quinan where he used it as his home. Uncle Ben used part of the space on his property where the cottage had been to build the large building which still exists on the property today. This building will be discussed elsewhere in this history.

Benoit Pottier (Uncle Ben, my father's brother) was a son of Albanie Pottier. Carl Pottier who operates the general store at the center of the village is Benoit's son. Carl inherited this home upon his father's death in 2000.

John Calvin Hatfield House – James "Jim" & Bessie Wood House

Another of Tusket's older homes is located just across the main road, somewhat to the north of the VanNorden Road intersection. This Cape Cod style house was built for John Calvin Hatfield on this lot some time in the 1820s or 1830s. He was born in 1795, and was a son of Loyalist Jacob Lyon Hatfield. He and his wife, Jane (Gavel), lived here for their entire married lives. John Calvin Hatfield died in 1881, and his widow continued to live here until her own death around 1906. They left the property to a young man they had brought up, Abram L. Crosby, and he sold the property in 1907. There were a series of owners after this, with the Nova Scotia Timberlands Company owning it from 1925 to 1944. In 1944 the property was purchased by James and Bessie Wood, the parents of Gordon Wood. Jim and Bessie operated their store here until 1965 and lived in the house until 1969. The additions to the front of this house were done by Jim Wood around 1949-50 when he opened his general store. In 2001, this house was purchased by Michael and Jackie Jacquard.

The Asa Robbins – Harold Allen House

The next house, proceeding along Highway #3, and still on the eastern side of the road, is what is best known as the Asa Robbins house. The house was built between 1843 and

1846 by James A. Sterritt. He was a tanner and shoemaker. In 1846 James Sterritt sold his house and business to Asa Robbins who was also a tanner and shoemaker. Asa became a prominent local businessman and was also active in many community affairs. He and his brother, William S. Robbins, were also involved in shipbuilding. Asa was an important member of the Free Baptist Church where he served as a Deacon for fifty years. Asa Robbins lived here until his death in 1896; he will be discussed further in the section on Tusket's Industries.

Near the Van Norden Road at the public well

The Asa Robbins house was located just north of the two large buildings in the centre; it is not visible here because of the proximity of the buildings to the road. These two large buildings were utilized in his tannery and shoemaking business. The previously mentioned Remi LeFave house is on the right in the foreground; St. Stephen's Anglican Church stands in the background.

A few years after Asa Robbins' death, this property was purchased by the Dickie & McGrath Lumber Company. After the demise of the Dickie & McGrath Company, the property continued to be the property of various large lumber companies for several years. The buildings associated with this house were gradually all demolished and today only the house still stands. Harold Allen purchased the property in 1959. He built a small country store by the roadside (just south of the house … where the shoe factory had been) and operated it until he sold the property in 1974. Today this property is owned by my brother Norman Pottier. He makes use of the former Harold Allen store as a woodworking shop for his carpentry business and uses the house as a rental property.

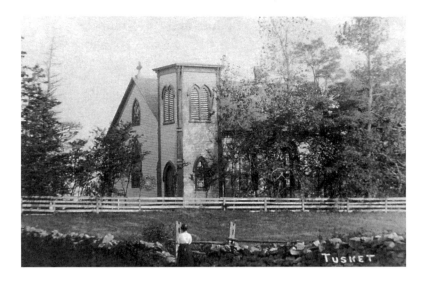

St. Stephen's Anglican Church

The next building on our journey, a short distance north of the Asa Robbins homestead, is St. Stephen's Anglican Church. This was the third church built in the village, officially opening its doors in September of 1845. It is the only church left in the village still offering services to its parishioners. Malcolm Patterson of Tusket, a member of this church, has been instrumental over the years in seeing that this attractive building and the surrounding cemetery are kept in good order. As with the other churches in the village, St. Stephen's Anglican Church will be discussed in greater detail under "Churches."

Dickie & McGrath Mill Properties

At this point on our walking tour we have arrived at the properties of the once-dominant Dickie & McGrath Lumber Company. Along the north side of the highway their property extended from St. Stephen's Anglican Church as far as the property of the late Henry Muise, owned in 2005 by Doug and Joyce Sisco.

On the opposite side of the main road, where the main mill was located, their property covered practically the entire north end of the village along the shores of the Tusket River. Along the road this would have extended approximately from where the Benoit Pottier property is to the former Nathaniel Blauvelt house, near the Tusket Bridge. The lumber mill itself was located almost exactly where the home of Hubert and Phyllis Pothier is presently located. The large 80-foot high chimney would have been approximately where Hubert's hobby machine shop is located. The Dickie & McGrath Lumber Company was by far the largest employer that ever existed in the history of the village and will be discussed more fully under industries.

Hubert and Phyllis Pothier House

The home of Hubert and Phyllis Pothier, mentioned above, was built here in 1963. Between 1991 and 1993 they carried out major improvements to this property. The attractive stonewall along the road was built by Hubert Pothier and Roy Hubbard in 1987-89. Hubert and Phyllis still own this house in 2005.

Don and Barbara Pothier Property

The next property, directly across the road from the Hubert and Phyllis Pothier homestead, is the property that has been owned and occupied since 1966 by my wife, Barbara and me. The home that we live in is a bungalow, built in 1966-67. In 1978, I built the "salt box" style carriage shed on my property. It is located on the exact foundation site of a former Dickie & McGrath cookhouse, just north of St. Stephen's Anglican Church property line and near the road. The barn on our property, however, has a most interesting history, and one that I will pause to tell here.

The Former Elmer Hatfield Store – Don Pothier Barn

This building began its life as a general store in connection with the shipyard of J. Adolphus Hatfield at the southernmost point in the village. It sat originally on the corner of where the main road intersects with the Frank Doucette Road, on the lot of land now occupied by the home of the late Roger Doucet.

In 1896, some years after the shipyard had closed, this building was sold to Smith Harding who had the building moved to the centre of the village, diagonally across the road from the Court House. In 1904 he sold his two buildings to Tracy G. Hatfield, who established a highly successful general store in the building in question. In 1917 this business was passed on, or sold, to his son Elmer Hatfield. Elmer ran the general store and most of the older people in the community today remember that business well. Elmer remained in business here for thirty five years; selling it to Daniel "Dan" Armstrong in 1952. Dan operated the business for the next fifteen years.

After a succession of owners this store eventually closed its doors, and in 1983 the property was purchased by Carl and Audrey Pottier, who by this time were operating a general store in the former Bernard Hurlbert store, situated just to the north. The decision was made to demolish the Elmer Hatfield store.

One of the things I had missed on my own property and longed to have was the kind of barn I had grown up with on my parents' property in North Belleville. I had been looking for an old barn to tear down and rebuild on my own property for some time. This seemed like the perfect opportunity. I bought the old Elmer Hatfield store from Carl Pottier (my first cousin), and with great enthusiasm, immediately started dismantling the building. It was exactly twenty-one years ago this month, February 1984, that I started tearing down the old store.

My initial intentions were to salvage enough lumber to rebuild a small barn. I quickly realized, however, that the lumber was in such good condition that it was possible to

Dismantling the "old store." Some boards were 36 feet long. The small addition in the foreground was the former Post Office.

Transforming the store into a barn. Roy Hubbard is the man working on the roof.

The completed project. The cupola originates from an old barn in Yarmouth where the present town hall is situated.

salvage all of it; the decision was made to rebuild it exactly the same size as it was. From this point on, I took on the arduous task of labelling and marking boards, wall studs, wooden pegs, documenting and writing details, etc; so as to be able to put it back together as it had been. In order to give the building a "barn look", it was necessary to change the window and door openings. Otherwise, the building has exactly the same proportions and dimensions, measuring 26 feet wide by 40 feet in length. It turned out to be a three-year project, the results of which can be seen in the photographs here.

The cupola on the roof is not from the original store, but from an old barn that stood on the site where the new Yarmouth Town Hall building stands today (2005). In 1991, it was on its way to the landfill, when I was able to rescue it, in a considerably damaged condition. My good friend Gordon Wood and I restored it to its present condition.

This old building, having been moved for a second time, from one end of the village to the other, has found a new use and new life. It has brought me a great deal of pleasure. I hope that future owners will appreciate it as much, and that it will survive for future generations to enjoy it as much as I do.

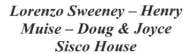

Lorenzo Sweeney – Henry Muise – Doug & Joyce Sisco House

The next homestead to the north; not far from my barn, was built in the early 1890s. In 1889, Nathaniel Blauvelt, who lived just across the road, purchased this lot of land from Ralph Blauvelt. It was purchased in order to build a home here for his daughter Maud, and her husband, Lorenzo Sweeney. The Sweeneys lived here for the remainder of their lives, for over 30 years. Maud died in 1934, and Lorenzo Sweeney continued to live here until his death in 1947. The property was left to their daughter, Guytha (Sweeney) Marlyn. She sold the property shortly afterward, in 1947, to Henry Muise. Henry Muise, who was a native of Amirault's Hill, and his wife, Antoinette, raised a large family and lived in the house the rest of their lives. In the 1960s my wife and I bought the land bordering on the south side of Henry and Antoinette (formerly part of the Dickie & McGrath property) and built a home here. One could not have asked for better neighbours. Antoinette was a lovely and kind person and it was always a pleasure to talk to her. A few years before Antoinette died (February 14, 2002), her daughter, Joyce, and Joyce's husband, Doug Sisco, bought the property. We have again been blessed with excellent neighbours. This is the last of the older homesteads on the north side of the main road on our journey through this part of the village.

Golden Pheasant Restaurant

Directly across Highway #3 from the property of Doug and Joyce Sisco, was a restaurant, which opened in the early 1960s and was located where the Dickie & McGrath general store was formerly situated. This business had been built and originally owned by Fred and Mary Phillips of Marblehead, Massachusetts. They called this the "The Marblehead Light Restaurant." Later the business was sold to Ernest McGowan and Bernard and Ruth Pothier of Sainte-Anne-du-Ruisseau who renamed it the "The Golden Pheasant." Ernest eventually sold his share to Bernard and Ruth who continued to operate the business. Bernard died in the early 1970s and shortly afterward his widow Ruth sold the business to my brother, Hubert Pothier, and Edgar Smith, with the understanding that Edgar and his wife Ida would operate the business. The restaurant caught fire and burned on a Sunday afternoon in the spring of 1972.

Nathaniel Blauvelt – Colby Marlyn House

Just across the road from the Sweeney house is another old Tusket property. This land was originally granted to Cornelius VanNorden in the early 1800s. Cornelius VanNorden was one of the leading members of the Tusket community during his lifetime. For several years he served as a Magistrate at the Court of General Sessions. He was a farmer and also made his living as a merchant. It is difficult to ascertain when the house was built on this property. It appears that it was during the 1830s or 1840s, although there is no record of who occupied the house during this time. Cornelius VanNorden and his wife Phoebe were living further south in the village, and he never occupied this house himself. Records show, however, that in 1847, Asa Robbins purchased this property from the estate of the late Cornelius VanNorden with the stipulation that VanNorden's widow, Phoebe, could live in this house for the remainder of her life. It appears likely that in settling her late husband's affairs, the decision was made to sell their larger home in which they lived, for this smaller, more manageable house. After her death, Asa Robbins owned the place until 1880 when he sold the property to Nathanial Blauvelt. In his letter of 1955, James Bingay, who was born in 1878, has the following to say about this house, "It is one of the older Tusket houses …. In my youth, this house was owned by Nathanial Blauvelt …. He was a kindly gentleman." He was a farmer and involved in the civil affairs of the village. Nathanial and his wife lived here for the rest of their lives. After their deaths, their daughter Maud and her husband, Lorenzo Sweeney, who lived across the road, came into possession of the property. In 1929 they sold it to their daughter, Guytha and her husband, Colby Marlyn. The Marlyn family lived in this house the rest of their lives. Colby died here in 1967. After the Marlyns, the property changed ownership a few more times and in July 1992, it was purchased by Gordon Wood with the intentions of someday restoring this old Tusket home.

Gordon and Marlene Wood Property

A short distance further, to the north of the Doug and Joyce Sisco property, and on the same side of the road, is the colonial style home of Gordon and MarleneWood. This land was once the homestead property of Ralph Blauvelt. Unfortunately, according to J. Murray Lawson, Ralph Blauvevelt's home and barn on this porperty were totally consumed by an early morning fire on November 17, 1891. Gordon and Marlene built their house on this property in 1974-75. The large, two story "salt box" style carriage shed was built in 1990.

The George A. Clements House

Continuing in a northerly direction, just prior to the Tusket Bridge, and again on the north side of the main road, tucked into the trees along the river bank is the well known property of George Clements. This house was originally built as a cottage, probably in 1943, by Sheriff Jack Baker of Yarmouth, NS. On 15 October 1956 Jack Baker sold the property to Dennis DeViller and his wife. Dennis was originally from Comeau's Hill, but had been living in New York and wanted to retire here. My first recollection of Mr. Deviller was in the 1960s when he would come to his cottage in Tusket during the summer months and every summer he would have us touch up his car at my brother's auto body shop. He drove a 1955 black Buick at the time. He was a real character and we always enjoyed him. He was George Clements' uncle and in 1967 George inherited the property from him. In December 1967, George and his wife, Frances (LeBlanc) moved into their newly acquired home in Tusket. In 1968-69, George made a substantial addition to the original building, consisting of a kitchen and a complete upstairs. In 2001, George had Harry Doucette construct a new "pitched" roof on the house, giving it its present appearance.

George Clements was a good neighbour and I wish to pause here and say a few words about this extraordinary man with very strong personal convictions. George began his career as a schoolteacher in 1941 in Morris Island and taught in various local communities for the next 17 years. In 1959, he made a career change; he began working at Huskilson's Funeral Home in Yarmouth and became a registered embalmer and funeral director. George continued to work at Huskilson's Funeral home until his death in March, 2003, at the age of eighty years old.

Undoubtedly, one of the things that George will be mostly remembered for was his lifelong service to the Boy Scout movement. One can literally say that George gave most of his life to the Boy Scouts. He was a member of the Scout movement for fifty seven years and in 1995 he was awarded the highest honour possible … the Silver Wolf award, presented to him by the Governor General of Canada. I am proud to say that I personally served some of my youth years in the Boy Scout movement under the direction of George Clements. I remember fondly the times spent at the far end of "la Pointe à Rocco" with George as leader.

George was also very much involved in our local Credit Union, having served as Past President for nineteen years. He played a major role in the evolution of this thriving local business in our community. Unfortunately, George's list of accomplishments are too numerous to list here. For those wishing further information regarding this extraordinary man's personal accomplishments, I refer them to the local Tusket Archives. Most of his life, George went far beyond the normal call of duty to help others. His obituary says it all: "George was a kind man who helped many people in his life." George was a "young" eighty years of age, and unfortunately, he left us much too soon.

In August 2004, George Clements' property was sold to Robert MacLeod, an employee at the Bank of Montreal in Yarmouth; he hails from New Minas.

Dr. Willard O'Brien – Walter Murphy – Fred Churchill Cottage

After crossing the Tusket Bridge and proceeding a few hundred yards, a road to the right leads across the 103 Highway and north to Tusket Falls and Raynardton. Between Highway #3 and the 103 Highway and on the eastern side of the road is small house located near the banks of the Tusket River. This building was hauled to this location sometime around 1955 to serve as a cottage for the late Dr. Willard O'Brien. The original site of this building was the "East Camp" military base at the Yarmouth airport.

For several years it was owned by Walter Murphy. The property is owned in 2005 by Fred Churchill and is used as a rental property.

Alec and Helen Daurie Homestead

A bit further along the road, on the western side, at the 103 intersection, is the former "Alec" and Helen Daurie property. The buildings on the property are not particularly old. The present house was hauled onto this site from it original location approximately across the road from Trafton White's house in the northern part of Tusket. It was formerly the home of Angela Crosby. The Dauries' previous home had been lost to fire. This occurred in the mid 1960s. The Dauries lived here for many years but do not occupy the house today.

Back on Highway #3 about a quarter of a mile to west, towards Pleasant Lake, is the Tusket Combustion Turbine Generating Plant. This was built in 1971, and is discussed in more detail in the chapter "Odds & Ends."

Returning to the Centre of the Village

We will now retrace our steps to the centre of the village. Although we have earlier sketched in the history of the commercial buildings in the centre of the village, there are a number of properties on the eastern side of the main road that we have not looked at.

Heading Up Court Street

On the eastern side of the main road, and on the northern side of the Argyle Township Court House is Court Street. This is a road that was constructed in the 1840s or 1850s. It leads eastward, and has several interesting properties. We will travel east along this street, and visit the properties located on the northern or left hand side, of the street until we reach its easternmost end. We will look at the properties on the south side of the street as we make our way back to the main road.

On the north eastern corner of Court Street is a curious lot. Today it forms part of the Post Office property in the village. The lot is a curious one, as it should be a very desirable piece of real estate, and yet nothing of any substance or duration has ever been built on it. One early map notes a carriage factory on this lot. It must have had a very short life indeed. From the early days of settlement until today, this parcel of land remains vacant.

Travelling east along Court Street the next property is the modern Post Office. This small brick-faced building was built in 1968-69.

The house in the foreground was, for many years, the home of the well known blacksmith, Cyril Doucette, and more recently, the home of Toussaint & Exilda Muise. The graceful building in the centre is the old Tusket schoolhouse. The Patterson house is visible in the background.

Cyril Doucette – Toussaint Muise House

Proceeding east along Court Street, the first house on the north side of the street, after the Post Office, is the house occupied in recent times by Toussaint and Exilda Muise. This house was built in the mid-1860s and had several owners until it was purchased by Cyril Doucette in 1878. Cyril Doucette was a well-known blacksmith. He was regarded by many as one of the best in the county. His blacksmith shop, formerly owned by Mr. Evelyn Wood, another well-known blacksmith in the village, was situated across the road from his home, at the rear of the Court House lot. This is the same blacksmith shop that was hauled in 1946 to the south of the village for Roger Doucet, as mentioned earlier on page 31 in this history. The house remained in the Doucette family until the 1940s and many senior citizens in the village still refer to this homestead as the Cyril Doucette home. Toussaint and Exilda Muise bought the property in 1944 and they lived here for the remainder of their lives. Toussaint Muise's wife, Exilda, died recently at the grand old age of 91.

The Tusket School – Argyle's Municipal Office

On the northeast corner of School Street, just to the east of the Toussaint Muise house, where it intersects with Court Street, stood the old Tusket School. This institution will be dealt with in more detail in the chapter on schools in this history. This was a large and impressive two-storey building, with a cupola on its roof. Because of this architectural feature, old photographs of the building are sometimes confused with the Court House. This old school building was demolished in 1950 and replaced with a more modern building. The school was closed in 1969. The building sat empty for a few years, only being used occasionally for such things as the polling station during elections.

In 1976, the Argyle Municipal Council, who owned the building, decided to abandon their offices in the old Court House in favour of this more modern building. Many renovations and alterations have taken place since, especially to the interior. The Municipal Offices are still located here in 2005.

School Street

Just between the Toussaint Muise property and the schoolhouse, another road leads to the north. This was known for many years as School Street, and is still the name of choice for this lane. Several years ago this road extended all the way to the main road (Parade Street … see map of 1862), exiting near the present home of Bernie Doucette.

There were probably plans to develop this street in the early days, but this did not materialize. There were never more than two houses situated along this road during early times, and today only one remains.

Evelyn Wood – Richard and Emma Bourque House

On the eastern side of School Street, behind the present day Municipal Offices, is an older property. This house arrived on this lot around 1872 and was owned by Mr. Evelyn Wood, a blacksmith. He was a highly respected man in the village of Tusket. He died around 1898 and his widow remarried to Capt. John Crosby. In 1915 the property was bought by one of Evelyn Wood's sons, Louis E. Wood and the property remained in the Wood family until 1953. I have indicated above that this house "arrived on this lot" around 1872. Ruth Wood, who was connected to the Evelyn Wood family, indicated some years ago that she had been told that the house was originally moved onto this site from Eel Brook. This would make the original structure an Acadian home, rather than one with Loyalist connections. Who its original owner was, or where it was situated in Eel Brook, is not known.

One of the interesting anecdotes about this house involves its proximity to the old Tusket School. The school had no well of its own in early times, and whoever was the owner of this house expected regular knocks at the door from the students and teachers whenever they were in need of fresh water, which was always willingly supplied. Some other neighbours may have supplied similar services from time to time.

Richard and Emma Bourque owned and lived in this house from the early 1950s until January 1969. Hubert Muise, son of John and Regina Muise, and his wife Nancy, purchased the property in 1976 and lived here until 1983. In 2005, the house is occupied by Steven Berryman and Heather MacNeil.

Further north on School Street, at one time, was another house. We know nothing of its history on its original site. Tradition has it that the building was moved at an early date, a short distance into the centre of the village. It eventually became the home of the late Andrew Jeffery, and will be discussed later.

Since we know of no other older buildings having been located on this street, we will return to Court Street.

Proceeding east along Court Street, the next property we arrive at is an exceptional one. Although this is by no means the largest house in Yarmouth County, it may well be one of the most elegant.

Job Lyons Hatfield - Patterson House

The house is unique with its curved gables and the curved base of the large front dormer with its balustrade. These unique features make the house extremely interesting to students of architectural design. This magnificent home was built around 1863 for Job Lyons Hatfield (son of Capt. John V.N.).

Job Lyons Hatfield was a prosperous man at the time he built this lovely home. He was involved in shipbuilding and other business enterprises. This is the same Lyons Hatfield who owned and operated the huge wharf complex that was discussed earlier to the south in the village. After building this home, probably due to the extreme ups and downs of the shipbuilding industry, he ran into financial difficulties, and by the year 1873 he had to sell the home. It was at this time that he returned to some of his father's land on the banks of the Tusket River, built another home, a store and sawmill.

Job Lyons Hatfield
1832 – 1916

His home on Court Street was purchased by a gentleman from the village of Kemptville by the name of Calvin Hurlbert. For a short period of time during his tenure, it was operated as the "Pine Grove Hotel." It eventually passed on to their son, Charles K. Hurlbert. Charles Hurlbert became a prominent businessman in Tusket and his general store in the centre of the village has already been discussed. In 1897 he was appointed Municipal Clerk for the Municipality of Argyle; a position he held for many years.

Mrs. Alta Patterson was the daughter of Charles K. Hurlbert, and she and her husband Sheridan (better known as "Pat") became the next owners of this property. Their son, Malcolm Patterson, is the current owner. This house has been appropriately featured in such books as *Seasoned Timbers, vol.1* (1972) and *Atlantic Hearth* (1994) for its outstanding architecture. The elaborate spiral stairway was constructed by Lezin Pottier of Belleville. The house has always been beautifully maintained.

John and Linda Conrad House

The next property also on the northern side of the road is owned by John and Linda Conrad in 2005. They began their home here in 1967 with a mobile home that has been added to and transformed into an attractive property.

Joe Thibeau House

Our journey continues in an easterly direction along Court Street for a fair distance before we arrive at the next house, again on the northern side of the road. This is the homestead of Joseph "Joe" and Elizabeth Thibeau. This house was hauled here from Eel Brook. It sat somewhere in the general vicinity of where Roy Doucette's auto body shop is located in 2005. It may have belonged to a member of the Lorgéré family on its original site. The house was hauled here in 1926 for Lawrence Thibeau of Tusket. "A large set of wheels, a makeshift rudder and twenty-two teams of oxen were used for the operation," according to the Heritage Property Inventory research on this property. The fact that this house was at least partly constructed with mortise-and-tenon joints suggests that it is quite old. Lawrence was Joe Thibeau's father; thus this house has only had three owners since being moved on this location in 1926. Joe Thibeau is best remembered as a long time clerk at the Bernard Hurlbert store. Today the house is owned by Joe and Elizabeth's son, Kenneth "Ken" Thibeau and his wife Carmen.

Moïse ["Moses"] Muise – Tommy Muise House

A short distance further east on our journey, still on the northern side of the road, is the property of Thomas "Tommy" Muise. The new home that sits on this lot today was built for Tommy Muise in 1987. A very old house sat here previous to that. That house was built sometime in the 1870s as the home of Moses (English pronunciation) or Moïse (French pronunciation) Muise. Moses had a large family and in the early 1900s, he abandoned his wife and children. His wife continued to live here and eventually one of their sons, Vincent, came into possession of the property. In 1966 Vincent's wife deeded the property to their son "Tommy" Muise, who still lives on the property today.

Edmund LeFave House

This brings us to the end of the houses on the north side of the Court House Road. We shall now turn around and proceed in a westerly direction, back to the main road, and visit the houses on the south side of Court Street. Proceeding westward, we soon arrive at the Edmund LeFave property. Although this house is not as old as most others in this area, it is worth mentioning that the lumber used to build this house came from the rear extension of the Methodist Church in the village, when a portion of that structure was demolished. This took place in the 1930s. In 2005, the house is occupied by Edmund's granddaughter, Carrie Tatton and Gabriel Dussault.

Louise Doucette – Erlin Lowe –
Harold and Eileen Tatton House

Continuing on our journey in a westerly direction, we again walk a fair distance before arriving at the next older house, located almost directly across the road from the Patterson homestead. This is a small, neatly kept property, nicely tucked into the trees. Originally, this land was part of the Bingay estate; however, deeds show that in 1906 this lot of land was purchased by Louise Doucette from Lloyd Hatfield. Louise Doucette was an outstanding seamstress and dressmaker. She was a sister to Fanny (Doucette) White who operated the Riverside Inn that was mentioned earlier in the text. Louise Doucette lived in this house until the 1960s when it passed on to her heirs, James Doucet and others. There have been several owners to this property since that time. In 1974, the property was purchased by Erlin Lowe and Pauline Tatton. Pauline became our baby-sitter who took good care of our young daughter during those years. In 2005, the house is occupied by Pauline's son, Harold Tatton and his wife Eileen. Eileen is Edmund LeFave's daughter.

Dr. John M. Bingay – Charles R. K. Allen House

The next property, located to the west, is the beautifully landscaped and secluded property known as the Bingay homestead. This lovely home was built by the Bingays in the early 1860s and for the most part remained in the family until the late 1950s. The Bingay family became very prominent citizens in the village, being businessmen, doctors, lawyers and educators. Readers may recall that James Bingay Sr., the patriarch of this family in Tusket, lived in the large two storey house situated immediately to the south of the Court House on the main road. His store was situated across the road from his house on the banks of the river. In his elderly years he obviously played a part in financing the construction of this house, although it appears to have been built built for his son, Dr. John M. Bingay. After its construction, his old home next to the Court House was sold, and James Bingay spent his last years living with his son's family in this new house. After James Bingay Sr.'s death in 1877, the house eventually became the sole property of his son, Dr. John M. Bingay, a physician. John Bingay's son, Dr. James H.Bingay (Dr. of Education) was a schoolteacher and historian, and wrote the remarkable letter in 1955, that I have quoted throughout this history. Dr. James H. Bingay retired from the teaching profession in the late 1940s and purchased this house where he had grown up. He lived here with his wife and sister until his death in 1957.

A school teacher and historian, he wrote a **History of Canada for High Schools** (1934) that was used in our schools for several years. His 1955 letter, recording his memories of the village, has been quoted many times throughout this text.

Dr. James H. Bingay
1878 – 1957

In 1958 the property was sold to Charles R. K. Allen. Mr. Allen and his wife moved here from Halifax upon his retirement; both he and his wife were avid antique and glass collectors. Being glass collectors ourselves, my wife and I became good friends of the Allens and spent countless memorable evenings together at their home talking antiques and glass collecting. In fact, it was they who taught us most of what we know about glass. Charlie was also known throughout the province as an outstanding amateur naturalist. His book, *A Naturalist's Notebook* (1987) is an intelligent and charming look at natural history in this corner of Nova Scotia. In 1995 a very important commemorative event took place in honour of Charlie Allen and his contribution to the knowledge of local natural history. In that year the Bowater-Mersey Paper Company sold its forestry holdings in Yarmouth and Digby Counties to J. D. Irving Ltd. At the same time it donated a 26-acre parcel of land in the Gillfillan Lake area to the Tusket River Environmental Protection Association. TREPA chose to have this parcel of land designated a nature reserve and named it the "C. R. K. Allen Nature Reserve." Charlie was very moved by this tribute. Following the official ceremony for this event a reception was held for Charlie at "The Narrows" in Tusket's oldest home, which has been spoken of elsewhere in this history.

I would like to mention here that Charlie Allen's working years had been spent as the Superintendent of the School for the Blind in Halifax. Charles Allen spent the last few years of his life living in Cape Forchu and Port Maitland. He died in 1998.

In 2005 the old Bingay property is owned by Abel Warner. He has made many improvements to this already beautiful property.

Maritime Tel & Tel Switching Centre

The next building, also on the southern side of the road, is the MT&T telephone Switching Centre. These facilities were originally located in a trailer that was placed on this site in 1969. The more substantial building has been built since that time.

Augustin"Gus" and Ethel Moulaison – Linda and Raymie Morris House

Just to the west of the MT&T lot is a modern bungalow that was built on this lot in 1970 for a Newfoundland native, whose surname was LaPierre. James Pottier, a local contractor built the house. The contractor held a mortgage on the property and later became the owner. James Pottier sold the property in September 1971 to John Augustin "Gus" and Ethel Moulaison, who moved here from the US and lived here for several years. He died in 1987. The house has been owned since 1989 by Linda and Raymie Morris. Linda is a niece of Augustin Moulasion.

The Harvey Roddick House - An Abram's River House in Tusket

Continuing a short distance further, still in a westerly direction, (almost directly across from the Argyle Municipal Office) is the home of Charlie and Barbara Brittain. This home is remembered by most Tusket residents as the property of Harvey and Rosalind Roddick.

The history of this house, and this lot of land, remains somewhat confusing. From a number of sources, it is clear that a house has existed on this lot from at least the 1880s. The house on this lot of land today was moved here, probably around 1925-1930, from Abram's River. In that community this was the home of Robert called "Tobert" Muise. It was moved here, renovated, and turned into a very attractive residence.

There was an older house on this lot, and it seems likely that this was the house that was moved onto the lot south of the Court House, to replace the home of William T. Lent that had been lost to fire.

In 1934, Harvey and Rosalind Roddick purchased this house and property on Court Street. Mr. Roddick worked for the railroad. Both he and his wife were well-liked people in the community. The owners in 2005, Charles and Barbara Brittain, have made a very attractive property of this house and its surrounding grounds.

Lorraine Amirault's Beauty Shop – Lawrence LeBlanc House

Just to the west of the Roddick house, and to the rear of the Court House, is a small building that has served as a dwelling for a number of years now. This building was originally built here around 1963 by Steve Muise of Hubbard's Point for his daughter, Lorraine (Muise) Amirault. She set up a beauty parlour in the building around that time. She operated her business here for a few years. By 1970 the building had become a rental property. Many people will remember this as the home of Lawrence LeBlanc throughout much of the 1970s and 1980s. There have been several owners since his death. In 2005 the property was sold to Gilles Muise.

On the southeast corner, where Court Street meets the main road, sits the Argyle Township Court House. This building and its history will be dealt with in a chapter of its own in this history.

Back on the Main Road

Arriving at the main road, we turn right and proceed north. Most of the houses in this area of the village appear to have been built around 1845-1865, during a very prosperous time for the shipbuilding industry in Tusket. Many people came to Tusket seeking employment, as well as land on which to build homes. Shipbuilders, carpenters, blacksmiths, skilled tradesmen and labourers were in high demand. John V.N. Hatfield owned all the land on the east side of the main road in this area of the village, as the old Tusket map of 1862 on page 141 indicates. He sold several house lots along this stretch and the new owners built homes here.

Looking north from the Court House

The Forman Hatfield house is to the right, followed by another prominent homestead during those times, the Nathaniel Churchill Jr. house which later became well known as the Killam Hotel. The huge elm tree in front of the Killam home stood here for more than a century. The Nathaniel Churchill Jr. store (Andy Jeffrey's garage during my time), sits to the left, on the corner of "Clip Street."

John Daniels – Forman Hatfield House

Proceeding north along the main road the first house, on the east side of the road, is best known at the Forman Hatfield house. It was built around 1850 for John Daniels. He was a tailor, married a local girl, Ellen Prout, and they lived in this house for at least a few years. In 1859 the house was sold to Forman Hatfield. He was born in 1828 and raised in the Gavelton area. He was a brother to several other prominent Tusket citizens who have already been discussed in this history, namely: J. Adolphus Hatfield, Peter Lent Hatfield, Isaac Hatfield and Caroline (Hatfield) Knowles, wife of Rev. Charles Knowles. After 1859 Forman Hatfield made Tusket his home. He was a very successful merchant and became a prominent man in local community affairs. For several years he owned and operated the store across the road from his home (later known as the Bernard Hurlbert store).

He was also elected a Member of the Legislative Assembly and held his seat from 1890 to 1894. He was Warden of the Municipality of Argyle from 1908 to 1910. After his death in 1910, the property remained in the Hatfield family until 1943. Several owners have lived here since then; although many of the older residents of the village still refer to this home as the Forman Hatfield house. I personally have fond memories of eating lunches here "with the boys" when it was owned by Doug and Doris

Forman Hatf
1828 – 19

Trefry. Doris operated a diner in the front part of the house. Doug Trefry sold the property to a Mr. Forsythe who operated a Denture Clinic from the house for a few years. Afterwards the property changed ownership several times until it was purchased in 1990 by Roger Devine of Yarmouth; he continues to use it as rental property in 2005.

Nathaniel Churchill Jr. House – Killam Hotel – Geraldine "Gerry" Rhyno House

The next house on the eastern side of the main road, proceeding north from Forman Hatfield's home, was built in the mid-1850s by Benjamin Richards. He was a master shipwright who turned his hand at building and selling houses as well. Benjamin Richards bought the land from John V.N. Hatfield. He purchased this lot in 1853, and sold the house in 1858 to Nathaniel Churchill Jr. who had come here from the village of Kemptville. Churchill established himself as one of Tusket's foremost shipbuilders. He lived here until the decline of the shipbuilding industry; he then moved to Caledonia, in Queens County and in 1912 the property was purchased by Mr. Luther Killam.

The Killam Hotel – Geraldine "Gerry" Rhyno House

His wife, Jennie (Fairweather) Killam owned and operated this property as an inn for many years. Details of that business will be found in the chapter on "Tusket's Hotels & Inns." The Killams eventually moved to Yarmouth. Scott Killam, a son, and Dora Killam, who married Maurice Prosser, were the only two members of this family who remained permanently in Yarmouth County. Since 1960, this property has been owned by Geraldine "Gerry" Rhyno.

To the right is the home owned until recently by Ruth Wood. On the left was the Kilby Lodge, operated by W.H. Lent (P'tit Willie), presently the home of Murray & Cecile Doucette. William H. Lent (with his white horse) and young daughter, Mildred, are sitting in the horse carriage in their driveway. Barely visible, to the immediate left, was the Nathanial Churchill Jr. store on the corner of Clip Street. It was known in my time as Andy Jeffery's garage and was demolished in 1973.

Henry Tedford Goudey – Ruth Wood House

The third house along this stretch of the main road was built around 1844-45, for Henry T. Goudey. He had married a daughter of John V.N. Hatfield of Tusket. Mr. Goudey clearly "married into" this house lot. In 1865 the Goudeys sold this house to Benjamin Richards, mentioned above, and Thomas B. Crosby. They kept the house only for a year or two before selling it to Nathaniel Churchill, Sr. He probably moved to Tusket from Kemptville to be near his son, who had opened shipyards here. Nathaniel Churchill Sr. was a reasonably well-to-do man, and he may well have helped finance some of his son's first shipbuilding efforts.

It appears that after the death of Mr. Churchill Senior, the house was rented for some time. In 1891 the property was purchased by the well-known Tusket blacksmith, Mr. Evelyn Wood and it has remained in the Wood family until recently. Since the early 1950s the house was owned by Roy and Ruth Wood, both highly respected citizens in the community. In January 2004 the property was sold to Jeremy Boudreau and Elaine Doull. Jeremy is a relative of Ruth Wood.

It is worth mentioning that among the renters of this house was a Ross family who were involved in shipbuilding. One of their sons, Charles Sarsfield Ross, lived here with hi parents. An article in the *Yarmouth Light* referred to this house as the "Old Ross H during this time although no Ross appears to have owned it. Local historian Robf

Blauveldt says the following about Mr. Ross: "Charles Sarsfield Ross - although not a direct pioneer's descendant, was born at Tusket on December 10th, 1868, the son of Donald Ross. Gifted with a very fine intellect, with a bend toward journalism, he entered the employ of the *Yarmouth Times*, later going to the United States, where he was engaged in newspaper work and 'freelance' writing for some 25 years. In 1906, having secured employment in San Francisco, he proceeded there. Arriving the morning after the great earthquake and fire, he found that his prospective employers' offices and business had been completely destroyed in the disaster. Mr. Ross decided to remain in San Francisco, and there he wrote the poem, due to which Mother's Day, now observed throughout English-speaking America was instituted. Mr. Ross died very suddenly at his home in San Francisco on February 3rd, 1920, at slightly more than 58 years of age."

Charles Sarsfield Ross
1868 - 1920

Benjamin Richards – William H. Lent – Murray & Cecile Doucette House

Like two of the previous three houses, the next house to the north was also built by the master shipwright, Benjamin Richards, this one around 1867. This was his own home. Sadly, he died in 1869, less than two years after building the house. His widow, Bethia Richards, ran a popular and prosperous hotel from this house for many years. She sold the property in 1891. In 1894 the house was purchased by William H. and Mary E. Lent and they may have bought the property because of its established reputation, for they too ran a hotel here. For at least a portion of the time that they ran an inn here, they called it "Kilby Lodge."

William H. Lent was the son of William T. Lent, who has been mentioned earlier. William H. (le P'tit Willie), according to his daughter, the late Mildred (Lent) Hatfield, was very fond of white horses. The Lents remained on this property for the rest of their lives. After Mary E. Lent's death in 1941 the house became the property of their son, William E. Lent. "Bill" Lent was first a teacher, then florist in Yarmouth, and is also well-known as the first curator of the Yarmouth County Museum. He sold this house in 1944 to Walter and Myrtle Nickerson. I remember the house best as the home of Ken Durkee during the early 1960s. In 1969 it was sold to Murray and Cecile Doucette and they still live here today.

Before proceeding northward to the subsequent houses along the main road, we will pause and deal with a few other properties located in the centre of the village.

VanCortlandt Square and the Properties to the north of it

To the west and in front of the properties that have just been described is a small triangular park which is known today as VanCortlandt Square. To the north of this piece of land is a short street that connects the main road with Highway #3. On some deeds this is referred to as "Clip Street."

Nathaniel Churchill Jr. Store – Andy Jeffery's Garage

Three properties were located on the north side of "Clip Street" facing south into the village. Of the three buildings, the one that was located to the eastward, I knew best as Andy Jeffery's garage. The history of this building is given in the chapter on "Tusket's General Stores."

Andrew Jeffery's "unique" blacksmith shop, circa 1973.

The quaint little blacksmith shop was built in the early 1850s. It was a jewel; unique in style, with its small arched roof on top of the other existing roof. Sitting in an ideal location, with the shipyards just across the road along the riverbank during the height of the shipbuilding industry in the 1850s – 1880s, this blacksmith shop was a small but prosperous business. During that time it was owned and operated by a David MacDonald who lived in the house just across the main road where James and Barbara Pottier live in 2005. After a succession of owners, in 1917 the property was sold to Andrew Jeffrey Sr., as part of his overall homestead. I remember him well; he was always at his son Andy's garage. Andrew was a jolly old man.

Andrew Jeffery Sr. at work in his blacksmith shop during his senior years.

Mr. Jeffrey was a highly skilled blacksmith, and he operated this tiny shop until he was an old man. The Heritage Property site form for the blacksmith shop states of Andrew Jeffery, "He is well remembered by local residents for his good humour and his fine craftsmanship. The Jeffrey family has boasted some of the finest blacksmiths in Yarmouth County in every generation of their family, from the first settler, John Jeffrey, who arrived in Yarmouth County in the 1780s. Andrew C. Jeffery was the last of this long family tradition in Tusket, and one of the last working blacksmiths in the village."

The late Tracy Hatfield, who was born and raised in Tusket, shared the following, rather humorous story relating to Mr. Jeffery's fine craftsmanship. It is a story worth sharing with the reader. When Tracy was a young lad, approximately fifteen years old, he loved to hunt. He didn't own a gun of his own and his father (Elmer Hatfield) was strict about no one using his guns. Occasionally however, when his father was not around, Tracy would quietly take his father's double-barrelled shotgun and go out hunting and simply put it back upon returning home from the hunt. One day he took the double barrelled shotgun and went hunting towards Eel Brook. When he returned home and went to put the gun away, he realized that one of the two cocking "hammers" was missing … it was lost! Tracy panicked … what to do now so his father wouldn't find out! He hurried over to "Old Man" Andrew Jeffery and told him exactly what had happened and asked him not to tell. Old Mr. Jeffery chuckled and said: "leave it with me for two days." When Tracy returned two days later, Mr. Jeffery held out two identical pieces in his hand. Tracy said "You found the piece … where was it?" Mr. Jeffery had made it by hand in his blacksmith shop. Tracy says it looked exactly like the original piece; he had duplicated it to perfection … even the colour tone was an exact match! Mr. Jeffery wouldn't accept anything for payment. The gun was quietly put away and Tracy's father never found out. But Tracy says Mr. Jeffery frequently had a chuckle about it all. Later when Mr. Jeffery started servicing automobiles and selling gas, Tracy always made a special effort to purchase his gas there. "I always felt I owed him that," he said.

Unfortunately, in 1990, the old blacksmith shop, no longer in use, was demolished.

Andrew Jeffery House

Although this house has had some alterations over the years, it still retains its original shape and structure.

Just to the west of the above mentioned building, was Andrew Jeffery's house. His family owned this building as well from 1917 to 1973. This house had a number of previous owners – but its origins remain somewhat obscure. Deeds suggest that the house probably first appeared on this lot in the 1860s. One of the early owners of this lot was Thomas B. Crosby who purchased the property in 1865. There is some oral tradition in the village of this house having been moved onto the property. It is said to have began its life on School Street, north of the Evelyn Wood house. If that is the case, its original owner is not known. It has certainly sat on its present location for a long time. The house is presently owned by Billy and Pam Crosby.

Nathaniel Gardner - Bernard Hurlbert - Oscar Nauss House

The third and final property on the north side of "Clip Street" is best known as the Nathaniel Gardner and Bernard Hurlbert house. It has had more owners over the years than any other house in the village. The house was originally built for a blacksmith by the name of John Grant around 1853. Shipbuilder Nathaniel Gardner bought the property in 1862. The location would have been ideal for him, as it overlooked his shipyards on the shores of the Tusket River. He lived in this house only four years before his shipbuilding enterprise failed financially. There were a series of owners before Bernard Hulbert, who owned a general store in the centre of the village, purchased this home in 1927. His family remained in possession until 1968. Bernard was also the Municipal Clerk for the Municipality of Argyle from 1924 to 1953. The house has undergone a good many alterations over the years, with some additions having been built by the Hurlberts.

The Bernard Hurlbert – Oscar Nauss house

In 1973, Oscar Nauss and his wife Barbara bought the property and it was shortly after this that Gordon Wood and I became acquainted with Oscar. He worked diligently with Gordon Wood and I towards the restoration of the Court House in the village. He was responsible for salvaging the old municipal records which had been left unattended and scattered in the building. Unfortunately Oscar died in 1987, much too young. His wife Barbara sold the house and removed to Yarmouth.

It should probably also be mentioned that a number of physicians have lived in this house as well, and in some cases conducted their practices from the building. Some of those doctors have been John W. Pennington (1892-1906); Vernon L. Miller (1906-1914); Roderick O. Bethune (1914-1922); Lewis M. Morton (1922-1923); Harold Trefry (1923-1925); and Donald R. Sutherland (1925-1927).

Oddly enough the present owner is also a doctor, Dr. Renier van Aardt, who established a medical clinic here in 1997.

VanCortlandt Square, looking north

The buildings along Clip Street in 1986, left to right, are: the Bernard Hurlbert – Oscar Nauss homestead; the large barn in the rear was built by Bernard Hurlbert as storage space for his store; and Andrew Jeffery's house and blacksmith shop. By this time Andy Jeffery's garage had been demolished. Both the Loyalist Monument and the War Memorial Monument are visible in the foreground.

VanCortlandt Square and the War Memorial Monument

VanCortlandt Square, as it is now known, is a triangular park in the centre of the village. This piece of public land was first used as a small park around 1923 by the Tusket War Memorial Association. Additional details on their activities will be found in the chapter entitled "The Military."

The War Memorial is on the left; the Loyalist monument is in the background.

In the 1930s, local historian, Robert B. Blauveldt, wished to erect a second monument in this park to commemorate and honour the United Empire Loyalist settlers who had founded the village. He and other interested persons formed themselves into an organization to bring this about. In 1938 by an Act of the Nova Scotia Legislature "The Association of VanCortlandt Grantees" was officially incorporated with its purpose being "To collect and preserve the records and history of Tusket and surrounding district, and of its early settlers and their descendants; and more particularly, by the establishment of a Public Park, the erection of monuments, and by other appropriate means, to perpetuate the memory of those United Empire Loyalists of Dutch origin, who were participants in the Royal Grant of the district to Major Phillip VanCortlandt and his associates on May 19, 1788." This Act of the Nova Scotia Legislature also granted a portion of land in this park to the Association. It is clear from the description of the land given in the Act, that the "Association of VanCortlandt Grantees" did not own the entire park, as their property bordered on land of the Tusket War Memorial Association to the north. The Minute Book of the War Memorial Association does record a joint meeting of the two groups on May 10, 1945. But this is where their records end.

It seems likely that by the 1960s both groups had ceased to operate as organized or official bodies. On March 9, 1964, the Association of VanCortlandt Grantees deeded this park to the Yarmouth County Historical Society, who maintains ownership to the present day. The Loyalist Memorial was dedicated in 1964.

The inscription on the Loyalist Monument reads as follows:

**IN PROUD MEMORY OF THOSE
UNITED EMPIRE LOYALISTS
The Majority of them of Dutch origin
Who
Defeated and despoiled, were compelled to find refuge here following the American
Revolution. Arriving here, the first in 1784, they established new homes in the
wilderness and have made a most noteworthy contribution to progress and
development of the Province and nation.
"They sacrificed all – Save honour."**

Local historian Robert Blauveldt reads the inscription on the Loyalist Monument.

Although the erection of this monument was a highly appropriate manner in which to
honour the founders of the village, the choice of name for the Association and for the
park remains somewhat puzzling. The naming of the park "VanCortlandt Square" was
clearly the result of some major misinterpretation of the early records. Phillip
VanCortlandt's name is the first of many that appears on a large grant of land to the
Loyalists at Tusket. He may have been considered something of a leader within this
group of people, but it seems more likely that his name being mentioned first is
completely random. In this grant he received 300 acres of land. There were others on the
list, including Nicholas Ogden, Jonathan Seers, David Ogden and Capt. Robert Gray who
received much larger tracts of land. Subsequent records offer no indication that Philip
VanCortlandt ever settled in Tusket or the surrounding area. It is somewhat ironic
therefore, that his surname became attached to this park. The late James H. Bingay, who
has been much quoted in this history, in 1955, wrote, "The Loyalist monument was also
not completely without controversy when it was first built. The large millstone which
makes up part of the monument was brought here from Tusket Falls. Some of the
residents of that community were not happy to see this artefact leave their village."

The setting aside of this area in the centre of the village, has greatly enhanced the appearance the centre of Tusket.

Leaving VanCortlandt Square, we will return to our walking tour of those houses found on the eastern side of the main road.

David McDonald – James & Barbara Pottier House

The David McDonald house in the early 1920s. Shown on the doorstep is Marion Doucette, with her nephew, Johnnie LeBlanc (on her lap), a son of Nicholas & Ada (Doucette) LeBlanc, and her niece, Cecilia "Sis" LeBlanc, a daughter of Peter Edward & Annie Louise (Doucette) LeBlanc.

The next house, proceeding north from the Benjamin Richards house was built around 1860 for David McDonald, a blacksmith. For a time he operated his business out of the blacksmith shop that was later known as Andrew Jeffery's. This would have been located directly across the road from his house. David McDonald died before 1870, and sometime after that the property was sold by his widow. From 1902 until 1909 this home was owned by the Tusket Baptist Church and served as their parsonage, although they rented it for several years prior to this.

In 1919 this house was purchased by John Doucette ("Tiga") and his brother Charles Doucette. They were sons of Reuben and Maria Doucette of Hubbard's Point. The two brothers had served overseas in World War I, and during that time had forwarded the majority of their wages home to their mother. At the end of the War this money used to purchase this house. Due to a complicated series of events, this eventually became the property of their widowed sister, Lena (Doucette) Moulaison, in 1927. Various members of the Doucette family lived in this house from 1919 until 1969.

A well proportioned two-posted front door entrance with side-lights and an elaborate roof railing surrounding an open porch roof-top adorned the front of this house at one time. Although the basic shape and size of this house have not been altered, the original exterior architectural details have all been removed to give it a more "modern look."

This house was purchased by the present owners, James and Barbara Pottier, in 1972.

Bob & Polly Patten "A Frame" – Glen & Rhonda Flemming House

To the north of the James Pottier house is a lane that leads a short distance to the east. There are two modern houses here. The oldest of the two, built in 1969-70, is Tusket's only A-frame. This was built for and by Bob Patten. This property is owned in 2005 by Glen and Rhonda Flemming.

Mac & Joan Patten – Marcel & Tina LeBlanc House

A bit further east on the lane is the home built for Mac and Joan Patten in 1970. In 2005 this house is owned by Marcel and Tina LeBlanc. Both of these houses are built on land that used to be the Tusket ball field.

The Anglican Rectory – Ralph Blauvelt - Bernie & Linda Doucette House

The girl in front of the tree is Clarisey Sweeney, sister to Roy Sweeney. Although the veranda no longer exists, the original "gingerbread" style wood trim still decorates the front gable of this house.

Returning to the main road, Route 308 North, the next house, still on the eastern side of the road, was built in the late 1850s to serve as the rectory for St. Stephen's Anglican Church in Tusket. It served in this capacity for nearly fifty years, until the parish was no longer capable of sustaining a resident priest. It has been a private dwelling since that time. In 1906 this property was sold to Ralph Blauvelt and it remained in the family until 1946, a period of 40 years. Ralph Blauvelt was well known throughout the community. He served as Stipendiary Magistrate in Tusket for many years, until 1929. He also owned several properties, and was obviously heavily involved in real estate. He was the father of Robert Blauveldt whom I have quoted so often throughout this history. Laura (Blauveldt) Butler, who now lives in Yarmouth, is Ralph Blauvelt's granddaughter. She has kindly supplied the fine picture above of this home where she grew up. Her parents, Robert Blauveldt and Muriel (Bishop) owned the home from 1929 to 1946. In 1946 the property was sold to Anthony LeBlanc and he lived here with his family for the next twenty-five years. In 1971 he sold the property to his daughter and son-in-law, Bernie Doucette; they continue to live in the house in 2005.

Capt. Charles W. Hatfield – Kenneth & Margaret Wood House

Immediately north of the former Anglican rectory is the home built for Capt. Charles W. Hatfield, in the 1860s. It is the last of the string of houses here that were built during the shipbuilding years, on land owned by John V.N. Hatfield. Charles W. Hatfield was a master mariner and owned this house until his death sometime in the 1870s or 1880s. Various members of the Hatfield family continued to own the house until 1886. Zacharie Doucette, and afterwards his family, owned this property from 1901 to 1957. Many people remember this as the Ken and Margaret Wood property. They purchased this property in 1957 and remained the owners until around 1983. William and Sharon Muise became the owners of this property in 1983. Several owners have occupied the house since. In April 2004 it was purchased by Cleve and Lisa Muise.

Gilman's – The American House

A short distance further along this stretch of road, known for many decades as Parade Street, still on the eastern side of the road, once stood by far the largest and most glamorous of all Tusket's hotels, "Gilmans", also known as "The American House." This establishment was opened in 1870 and luxury, gaiety, and gentility reigned there for many years. The history of "Gilmans" will be found in the chapter on Tusket's Inns & Hotels.

Gilman's, also known as "The American House."

In 1976 Nova Apartments, a Seniors Apartment building was constructed on the former Gilman lot.

St. Stephens Parish Hall – Tusket Community Hall

Returning to the west side of the road, a short distance north from Andrew Jeffrey's blacksmith shop, was the Tusket Community Hall. In the aerial photograph on page 61, the Tusket Community Hall is indicated to the right, with the #3 on the west side of "Parade Street." This building was originally St. Stephen's Parish Hall and stood beside the rectory, the present home of Bernie Doucette, on the east side of the road, which has already been discussed. Eventually the Parish sold this building to the community and it was moved from its original site to this lot on the opposite side of the road. The picture below shows Horatio Wood with his team of oxen that was used in the moving of this building to its new location. The hall eventually became the property of the Tusket Women's Institute. For a number of years, it was here that the local Friday night dances were held. Not too long after I completed the first draft of this manuscript, in 1974, it was with sadness that I drove by one morning and found that the building had burned through the night.

*Horatio Wood
with his team of oxen
November 6, 1939.
Mr. Wood used these oxen to help
in the moving of the Tusket
Community Hall.*

Nathaniel E. Butler – Roy and Vivian Sweeney House

An older picture of the house. Notice the three posted open front porch on the house which has long since been removed and the large barn to the right with a steep cupola on top.

A short distance further north, still on the western side of the road, is the tall, weathered home of Roy and Vivian Sweeney. This weathered home is unique to the village. It remains unpainted and it is well worth noting how well the exterior wood has stood the test of time, it is a great example of how much better the quality of wood was at that time

111

than the wood currently available. This large home was built in the mid-1890s for a gentleman from Weymouth by the name of Nathanial E. Butler. It was he, along with others who formed the Tusket River Lumber Company in Tusket. They built the large mill that would later become the property of Dickie & McGrath. A few years after this house was built, in 1896, N.E. Butler sold his mill interests, and also his home, and moved back to Weymouth. He sold the house to the Tusket Free Baptist Church (located further north) and they used it as their parsonage for several years. When it was no longer feasible to retain a resident minister, they rented the house to Roy and Vivian Sweeney who eventually purchased it. Vivian had a deep voice and a most hearty laugh. She was a cheerful person and it was always a pleasure to meet her on the street. After Vivian's death this house belonged to her son, Murray Sweeney for a number of years. It is currently owned by her son Rodney Sweeney.

Mayflower Engine House – Joe Gaudet House

The original "Mayflower Engine House" is the taller section to the right in the photograph. This part of the house was moved to this location in 1934. The lower, front section was an addition made several years later.

A short distance north, and on the eastern side of the main road is a relatively small dwelling. This building began its life to the rear of the Court House in the centre of the village around 1867. It served as the Mayflower Engine House, and belonged to Tusket's early fire department which was still in operation during the era of the Dickie & McGrath sawmill in the village. The organization was disbanded in the 1930s. It was moved north at this time to the lot it occupies today, where it became a private dwelling. Simon and Lizzie Muise lived here for several years; he was a well-known fishing guide. In recent times it has been the home of Joe Gaudet. Through the years, several additions and alterations have been made to the original small building. It is owned in 2005 by Danny Dukeshire, and is used as a rental property.

In this vicinity, a road now known as the VanNorden Road intersects with the main road. It leads west and connects with Highway #3. Where it intersects with Highway #3 one finds the Public Well situated in the middle of the VanNorden Road. This has been mentioned earlier. There are three older homes on this road. We will turn left (west) and proceed down the road to look at these three properties.

Looking south from the steeple of the Free Baptist Church

The straight stretch of road (Parade Street) fades into the distance toward the centre of the village. Sidewalks are visible the entire length of this road. The Roy & Vivian Sweeney property is barely visible on the right along this road. The four properties along the VanNorden Road are: #1 - Esther Hubbard #2 - the Arthur and Gertrude Wathen property with its huge barns #3 - Roland Bourque property and #4 - the home of Ruth Hatfield.

Rowland VanNorden – Arthur and Gertrude Wathen Homestead

In the above photograph, the first property, on the northern side of the VanNorden road is the home of the late Arthur and Gertrude Wathen. The older residents of the community still refer to this homestead as the Rowland "Rollie" VanNorden property. Originally the property consisted of the house, a substantial ell, and quite large barns.

Gertrude Wathen was a granddaughter of Rowland VanNorden, and the last person born with that old Loyalist surname to live in Tusket. Records indicate that Rowland VanNorden purchased this property in various lots between the early 1860s and 1883 with buildings on the property. He had formerly lived in a house on what is now known as Lent's Hill across the river, to the west of the village. This property is presently the home of Dr. Milton and Audrey O'Brien. Rowland VanNorden's home in that location burned to the ground on December 8, 1875. After the fire, he moved to this property. Mr. VanNorden was a prosperous farmer and he also operated a hotel from his house known as the "Scotia House." But it is his prosperous stagecoach business, which he operated between Yarmouth and Pubnico for several years that he is best remembered for. VanNorden began running a daily stage on the route between Yarmouth and Tusket on July 11th, 1866 and continued to operate this business until the late 1890s. The business was eventually expanded to Pubnico. When I began this history in the early 1970s, Gertrude Wathen was still living in this home, and was a great source of information. She has died since that time, and there have been several subsequent owners of the property. Over the years, the property had seen many changes. The barns and outbuildings on the property and the large ell on the house were gone before the 1960s. Recently the house itself was demolished and in 2005 the new Coastal Financial Credit Union, Tusket Branch, has their new building on this site. It was built in 2004. The stagecoach business will be discussed in greater detail in the chapter on transportation in this history.

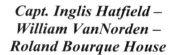

Capt. Inglis Hatfield –
William VanNorden –
Roland Bourque House

The next house, to the west of the VanNorden property, and still on the northern side of the road, has been owned for many years by Roland Bourque, a native of Sluice Point. This house was built around 1860 by master mariner, Capt. Inglis Hatfield. His father, William Hatfield, deeded him the land in 1860, and Inglis was married in the same year. Inglis died at the young age of twenty eight years. Mary, his widow, remarried twice. The last time was to a John Halstead, and they lived here for many years. John Halstead had a reputation as being one of the best road builders in Yarmouth County. Mary Halstead died suddenly in 1914 and the property was sold to William "Willie" VanNorden, son of Rowland VanNorden who lived on the property that we just discussed next door. William VanNorden worked with his father in the stagecoach business and continued to operate it until the automobile forced him out of business. In 1950, William VanNorden's widow, Della VanNorden sold the property to Roland and Janet Bourque and they have lived here since. The small ell extension on the rear of this house has been removed. Roland and Janet, and now Pauline, his second wife, have been wonderful neighbours. A cleared path through the woods on an old abandoned railroad joins our properties together and it is always a pleasure to meet Roland here for casual chats.

Rear view, 1941   *Front view, 2005*

Simon Doucette – Roger and Ruth Hatfield House

A short distance further, on the south side of the road is the present home of Ruth Hatfield. This house first appeared on this lot some time in the 1880s. On this location it was originally the home of an Acadian, Simon Doucette. He and his wife Fannie lived here their entire lives. It was they who raised my father's brother, Uncle Alphonse Pottier. My grandfather, Albanie Pottier, died a young man and to help out the family, Uncle Alphonse came here to live, supposedly for a short period of time and ended up being raised by Simon and Fannie Doucette. They had no children of their own. Simon Doucette told my Uncle Alphonse that the main part of this house had been moved here. Its original location was the area between where the homes of Carl Pottier and Norman Pottier sit in 2005. Its previous history in that location is not known, although it is possible that it may have been the old Kelly house that was located between Uncle Ben's house and Norman Pottier's house, mentioned by James Bingay in his 1955 letter.

The living room in this house has a tin ceiling with oval and circle indentations in the tin that are spaced out evenly around the perimeter of the ceiling. These ovals in the ceiling are identical to the ones in the Ambroise Pottier house in Belleville North where I grew up, and both of these tin ceilings were hand-painted with various country scenes by Melbourne Surette of Sainte-Anne-du-Ruisseau. The paintings in my grandfather's house (Ambroise Pottier) are mostly representative of Acadian scenes while the ones in the Simon Doucette house are more of a general nature. Melbourne Surette was the son of well known master shipbuilder, Denis Surette of Eel Brook (now Sainte-Anne-du-Ruisseau), of whom we shall hear more later with regards to shipbuilding. We may recall that this was the same Melbourne Surette who was the "decorator painter" of the Tracy G. Hatfield Store (now Hanging Oak Antique Store), at the Corner in 1907.

Fannie Doucette outlived her husband, Simon, by 25 years and she lived here as an aged woman until 1962. Roger and Ruth Hatfield have owned the property since 1976. Roger died around 1980 and Ruth continues to live here. Ruth is from Germany and met Roger in Montreal shortly after World War II. She is a wonderful person, always cheerful, and loves to have a chat. She will be remembered as the nice elderly lady with a strong accent who always walked to the store and the Post Office, preferring to walk when offered a ride, saying it was better for her arthritis.

This completes the older properties on VanNorden Road. We will now turn around and retrace our steps to the main road (Route 308 North) and continue to proceed north through the remainder of the village.

Intersection at Parade Hill, looking north

This view shows that no houses had been built along this part of the road during this period of time (circa 1890s). The work crew is in the process of widening the road. Since the railroad later was constructed exactly where the men are working in the photograph, it has often been thought that they are working on preparation for it. A close look, however, reveals that they are actually cutting down the banks along this stretch of road. The Free Baptist Church on the hill was built around 1840.

The Old Parade Ground

Back on the main road, proceeding north, on the eastern side of the road is a parcel of land that was used as the Parade Ground for the local militia. The railroad passed through this area in the 1890s and altered the appearance of the land here considerably. This portion of the road was at one time referred to as Parade Street and the hill, Parade Hill. Tusket had its own unit in the local militia during the 1800s.

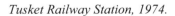

Tusket Railway Station, 1974.

On this same property, the railway station was built in 1895-1896. The *Yarmouth Light* reported on 21 November 1895 that, "The material for the station house of the Coastal Railroad is on the spot – on ground formerly owned by W.H. Gilman."

This Gordon Hatfield photograph, produced as a commercial postcard is entitled "Late for the train at Tusket, N.S."

As in every such community, this area of the village became an important focal point with the establishment of the railroad. Today the railroad is gone, as is the old station. Nothing remains here but the abandoned railway bed. The history of the railroad, and this site, will be covered in more detail elsewhere.

The VanNorden Road corner, several years later than the photograph shown on page 116. The buildings in the picture are, left to right: the William Halstead - John & Esther Hubbard house; the Thomas Coleman - Charlie Muise house and barn; the Free Baptist Church; and the Zebulon Servant – Job Raynard - Larry & Jill Trask house.

William Halstead – John and Esther Hubbard House

The large house on the western side of the main road, across from the railway station, and just slightly north of the VanNorden Road corner is quite unique in style with three large bay windows projecting out from the main part of the house and extending from the ground floor level to the second story roof. It was built around 1900-1906 for William Halstead. He was a master mariner and the son of John Halstead who lived a short distance from here in the house presently owned by Roland Bourque. These Halsteads were direct descendants from the William Halstead who arrived with the first Loyalist settlers at Tusket. William Halstead's wife was Bertha Earle, a descendant of Peter Earle, another original Loyalist settler in the area who lived at Pleasant Lake. It appears that William Halstead spent most of his time working in the Boston area, and consequently, in 1923 he sold the property. Afterwards, it changed ownership a number of times. Several of our senior citizens remember this as the home of Harold Floyd and later Hannah Spates (mother of Lester Spates). He was a school teacher and purchased the property in 1949. In the same year he deeded the property to his mother who continued to live in the house until the early 1960s. During the 1960s John and Esther Hubbard rented the house and eventually purchased the property; John died in 1979 at the age of fifty-six. His widow, Esther, still owns the property in 2005.

Thomas Coleman – Charlie & Annie Muise House

The next property, proceeding north along the road and still on the western side, is the original home of Thomas Coleman. He was born in England and came to Tusket as a "Home Child." Much has been written about the thousands of orphans and other children who were brought to Canada in the 1800s by various British agencies, one of the most famous being the "Bernardo" organization. We do not know which organization was responsible for Thomas Coleman's arrival. He grew to adulthood in the village, having been taken by the family of William T. Lent, and he married here. This house and a barn were built for him around 1898. As well as operating a small stable himself, for a time, Mr. Coleman also worked for Rowland VanNorden who lived a short distance from here. He married Marion Earle, a sister of Bertha Earle who was married to William Halstead and owned the house next door to the south. Thomas Coleman died in 1909, still quite a young man. His widow continued to live here until 1922 when she remarried and moved elsewhere, selling the property to well-known Tusket resident, Charles K. Hurlbert. A year later he sold it again to a William Raynard who lived here until 1945. He was a butcher and meat-cutter and operated his slaughterhouse from the barn on this property. In 1946 the property was purchased by Charlie and Annie Muise who have lived in the house since. The well proportioned front veranda which has been added in recent years has enhanced the appearance of this home.

Free Baptist Church

Just north from the Thomas Coleman house, and still on the western side of the road, stood the Free Baptist Church. Some sources state that the church was built around 1840, and this may be the case. It is shown on this site on the A.F. Church Map (1866). This church burned down on a Sunday afternoon in 1934, and the congregation did not rebuild in the village. The history of the church will be discussed in more detail elsewhere in this history.

Mac & Karen Sweeney – Blaine & Cindy McCall House

In 1966 Malcolm and Karen Sweeney built a modern bungalow on the site of the old Free Baptist Church. That home is owned in 2005 by Blaine & Cindy McCall.

Servant – Blauvelt - Raynard – Trask House

This older photograph illustrates what a remarkable job the owners of this property have done to retain the original integrity of this house through the years. Very little has changed except the fencing along the road and the "small" trees (seen in the photograph) that now tower above the house after more than a century of growth.

Proceeding north, up past Parade Hill, the next property, still on the western side of the road, is a large, attractive and well-maintained home. This house was originally built around 1860 as the home of Zebulon Servant. The Servants were among the early settlers of Tusket and it appears that they established themselves in this area of the village early on. Zebulon Servant kept this house only a short time, selling it in 1861 to Nathanial

119

Churchill Jr., one of Tusket's most prosperous shipbuilders during those years. Nathaniel sold it again a year later to Master Mariner and ship owner, Capt. Aaron Webb Blauvelt, son of Job Blauvelt. Capt. Aaron Blauvelt lived in the house until his death in 1910. The property was then sold to his brother Jacob L. Blauvelt who was a well-known local artist and musician. The beautiful ceiling paintings that surround the altar in the Sainte-Anne-du-Ruisseau Church are among his masterpieces. In 1912, Jacob L. Blauvelt sold the property to a local merchant by the name of Job Raynard who lived here until his death in 1947. Even today, the property is often referred to as the Job Raynard property. Several owners have lived here since. I remember it best as the Alfred Sweeney property and since the early 1980s it is the well-kept homestead of Jill and Larry Trask. Jill is a descendant of the Tusket Hatfield family. In recent years they have operated a popular bed and breakfast from this home called "The Plum Tree."

Robert S. Eakins – Foster Stewart House

The original front entrance to this house was most attractive. It had artistic mutton bars on both sides as well as across the top. It has been replaced in recent years with a modern steel door.

The next property proceeding north is on the opposite or eastern side of the main road. It is one of Tusket's older homes. The house was built in 1846 for Robert S. Eakins Senior, a native from the north of Ireland. The Heritage Property Inventory for this dwelling states, "He was a prosperous merchant in Tusket, and two of his sons, Arthur Eakins and Robert S. Eakins Jr. became prosperous and well-known merchants in Yarmouth. Arthur Eakins was one of the founders of the dry-goods firm of Parker & Eakins of Yarmouth, N.S. as well as one of the founders of the Grand Hotel Company. Robert S. Eakins Junior was one of the founders of the Yarmouth Building and Loan Society, one of Yarmouth's first formal lending and mortgage companies". Robert Eakins Senior lived in this house for the rest of his life; he died in 1905. For the next decade or so, the house was used as rental property until it was purchased in 1918 by Basil Stewart. In 1945 the property passed on to Basil's son, Foster Stewart and his wife Grace. Foster worked most of his life in the lumbering industry, being employed for several years at the Boutillier & Prosser Lumber Mill in Yarmouth. Foster Stewart died in the mid 1970s and his wife Grace continued to live here for the remainder of her life. The property has since had several owners. It is presently occupied by Melvin d'Eon of Pubnico and Donna Thorburne.

Proceeding north, still on the eastern side of the road, the next property is not visible from the main road. At the end of a long driveway that leads eastward, is the well known property of Charles and Jean Goldring.

Alfred Servant – Charles & Jean Goldring Property

The house shown to the left was built for Alfred Servant around 1863. The white house to the right and rear is the older structure. It was built in the 1820s or 1830s for Abraham Servant. It was moved from its original location on this property to its present site many years ago.

There are actually two old houses on this property. The original, smaller house was built during the 1820s or 1830s by Abraham Servant Jr., a son of Tusket pioneer Abraham Servant. In 1863, Alfred Servant, a son of Abraham Jr., and grandson of pioneer Abraham Servant, built his home here on part of his father's homestead. This is the house that Charles and Jean Goldring owned and occupied for many years. The smaller, original, house now serves a storage shed directly behind the main house. Alfred Servant was a ship's carpenter and he worked in the various shipyards throughout the village. In 1907 he sold this house and moved into a house further south in the village, afterward owned and occupied by Allan and Mildred Hatfield. The old Servant property changed ownership several times during the next fifty years or so, until the Goldrings purchased it in 1960. The Goldrings were well known and highly respected in the community, and Charlie was well known for his historical research work. In 1989 they sold this property and moved to Yarmouth. The property is presently owned by Doug, Samantha and Shannon Nickerson.

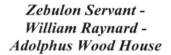

Zebulon Servant -
William Raynard -
Adolphus Wood House

The next property, still on the east side of the road, and directly north of the driveway leading to the former Goldring property, is the large home known to my generation as the Adolphus Wood property. This once beautiful homestead was built in the early 1850s, for and by, Zebulon Servant. He later built another home on the western side of the main road that has been discussed previously. He sold this house in 1861 to shipbuilder, Nathaniel Churchill Jr., who sold the house in 1863 to Joseph Jeffery. Joseph Jeffery, who was a ship's carpenter, lived here with his family until 1898 when the house was sold to William Raynard who operated a butcher shop from this property. He sold this property in 1923 and purchased the Thomas Coleman house nearby, which has been discussed previously. In 1923, the property was purchased by Adolphus Wood, also known as "Long Dolph," to distinguish him from another man of the same name who lived in the village. Adolphus was a brother of Horatio Wood, who was shown earlier with his team of oxen. Adolphus and Sadie Wood were the grandparents of my good friend Gordon Wood, whom I have mentioned several times in this manuscript. After the death of Mr. and Mrs. Adolphus Wood, the property was inherited by their son, Whitfield Wood. Whitfield lived here and farmed the land until poor health forced him to move out of the house several years ago. Although the house is still standing, sadly, it has fallen into a state of disrepair. Whitfield passed away on January 28, 2003, at the age of eighty; he was a very well liked and missed by everyone.

The Barney Little -Trafton White House

Barney Little's wife, Emma (Wood) is shown here next to their home.

Continuing in a northerly direction on our journey, the next home, still to our right, is best remembered as the Barney Little property. From 1879 to 1902 the property was owned by Frank Little. He was a farmer and a sawyer. In 1902 his house burned to the ground and shortly afterwards the present house was built for his son, Barney Little. Barney was a farmer and labourer and he lived here for the rest of his life. He served overseas in World War I and he was a member of the Tusket Fire Department. Barney Little was considered a real village character and is humorously, and most importantly, fondly remembered by many of Tusket's residents. He died in 1955. The property had always remained in the Little family until Barney's son, Elmer Little, sold it to Trafton White in 1957. Trafton has lived here since and still occupies the property in 2005. The property has been well maintained.

Almost directly across the road from the Barney Little homestead (on the western side of the road) stood a house which sat some 150 yards back from the road. This house was built around 1860 for Job Sterns Blauvelt. He was known as "Stern" and lived here his entire life. James Bingay, in his 1955 letter, remembered him "as a man with a long beard, and (because of a rupture) a much longer coat reaching to his knees. For many years he was Secretary to the Board of School Trustees. He did a little farming and much more fishing in the river nearby..." He died around 1913 and shortly afterwards his

*Job Sterns Blauvelt –
Norman Kuhn House*

widow sold the property to William Halstead who used it as rental property until he sold it in 1936. Mr. and Mrs. Harvey Roddick rented this house from William Halstead from 1928 until 1931. During the next thirty years or so, the property changed ownership several times until Norman Kuhn purchased it in 1962. Later, in 1976 the Kuhns built a new bungalow near the highway, almost in line with the old house. Since 1987 the entire property has been purchased by Tusket Sales & Service, and the house, which had sat abandoned for a number of years, was demolished.

*Tunis Blauvelt – Henry
Gaudet – Russell
d'Entremont House*

A very short distance to the north, and back on the eastern side of the main road, was the home of Tunis Blauvelt. He was a grandson of the original Loyalist settler of this name. Tunis and his wife Sarah were living on this lot in a house that was destroyed by fire on April 9, 1889. James Brayne, a local carpenter, was hired to build a new home for this couple. Tunis Blauvelt and his wife owned this house until 1901. There have been numerous owners since that time. Many people today recall owner Budd Gavel, who owned the house from 1928 to 1935, although he is perhaps even more strongly associated with a neighbouring property. He was followed on this property by Henry Gaudet, who owned the property for nearly three decades, from 1935 to 1964. Russell d'Entremont purchased the property in 1968 and made several alterations to give the house a more modern appearance, which can be seen in the above photograph. He lived here until he sold it to N.A. Pottier Building Supplies who demolished the house for further development of its construction business.

James Brayne – Gerald Wood House

James Brayne's wife, Lahlia, is shown above with their three children in front of their home in 1896. Left to right: Gerald, whom I remember well as an old man in the village, Violet and Claude.

A short distance further, and on the western side of the road is the house that was built for and by James Brayne around 1870. He was a carpenter, and as has been mentioned above, around 1890, built the "new" Tunis Blauvelt house across the road. The houses were very similar in style. James Brayne built at least one other home in this part of the village and lived on this property with his family until his death by drowning in 1901. His body was found under the railway bridge in the Tusket River. His widow continued to live here until her own death in 1941. Earle Robbins, who was born in the Budd Gavel house across the road and spent his early childhood years in Tusket, remembers Mrs. Brayne as a very loving and caring person, "she was like a mother to all the kids around." In 1946, Gerald and Mildred Wood purchased the property and lived here until 1984 when they sold it to Tusket Sales & Service. The house was renovated and rented as the Riverside Restaurant until it was eventually demolished to make room for further business expansion.

The James Brayne – Gerald Wood house as the Riverside Restaurant. It was demolished a short time later.

Peter LeBlanc – Budd Gavel - Elmer Little – Tommy Robicheau House

The next property proceeding north, back on the east side of the road was a smaller house, built around 1896 for a Peter LeBlanc. In 1906 it was purchased by William T. Lent and used for a time as a rental property. In 1928 it was sold to Budd Gavel, a farmer from Gavelton, who lived in the house until 1940 when it was sold to his son-in-law, Elmer Little. The Peter LeBlanc house was owned by Elmer Little from 1940 to 1969. Tommy and Carol Ann Robicheau purchased the house in 1975. A few years later it was sold to my brother Norman Pottier, who owned N. A. Pottier Building Supplies. In order to make room for expansion, the house was hauled to the rear of the lot, and was used for a few years as a storage-shed for his lumber business. It has since been demolished.

The Budd Gavel – Arnold Gavel house, 1986

When Budd Gavel sold the "Peter LeBlanc house" to Elmer Little in 1940, he built a very small house for himself, a short distance to the north. He lived there for several years. Later the house was owned and occupied by his son, Arnold Gavel. Arnold lived here until his death in 1987. The property was afterwards purchased by Hubert Pothier and Gordon Wood. The house was demolished around 1999.

At this point in our walking tour we will proceed north over the overpass that crosses above the 103 Highway, and visit the homes that remain in this area within the bounds of the community of Tusket.

Eddie & Irene Thibeau House

Just beyond the overpass, on the western side of the road, is the home built for Eddie and Irene Thibeau just after the end of the Second World War. The materials used to build much of this house came from and old ell that had been removed from the old Rowland VanNorden house further south in the village. The Thibeau family sold this property to Hubert Pothier in 2004.

John Doucette – Norman Dulong - Lawrence Dukeshire House

The first older home encountered in this part of the village is on the west side of the road, and has been owned for many years by Lawrence Dukeshire. This house was built in the early 1890s for John Doucette. It appears that prior to his death in 1923, John Doucette deeded the property to his wife Pauline Doucette who continued to live here until the early 1940s. Norman Dulong purchased the property in 1942. He had grown up approximately half a mile north of here, very near the sharp corner where the road leads to Belleville and Quinan. Norman married an Italian woman from the Boston area and they eventually removed to the U.S. They rented out the house for several years and in 1966 the property was sold to Lawrence Dukeshire. The Dukeshires have occupied the house since then.

Luke Doucette House

This house, directly across the road from the Dukeshire house, was the home of the late Luke Doucette, better known throughout the Acadian communities as Luc à Robert. The house was moved onto this lot from Bell Neck in 1953, and Luke hired Peter L. Muise of Quinan to move the house for him. It was moved here because of an ongoing feud he had with his neighbours in Bell Neck. The house had been built in Springhaven around 1883-1890, and had been moved once before. Luke remained the owner of this house until 1972. There was a succession of owners after this. The house was demolished around the year 2000 to make way for the construction of the new École Secondaire de Par-en-Bas.

The William Robbins Road

A few hundred yards north of the Lawrence Dukeshire house mentioned above, is a road that leads west from the main road towards the Tusket River. This road has been known for many years as the William Robbins Road. There used to be several old homes on this road, but only two remain today.

Paul & Marion Doucette House

A short distance along this road, and on the northern side, is the home built for Paul and Marion Doucette around 1971. The house is owned in 2005 by Lezin Doucet and Nicole MacNeil.

The Martin Amirault –
Dave Mason House

The first older homestead on the William Robbins road sits on the northern side, and is the property known in my generation as the home of Martin Amirault. Although this house was originally built during the mid-1860s for Joseph Spates, it appears that he first made use of it as rental property for a number of years. Records show that in 1871 he was living in Raynardton. Ten years later however, he was living in this house. In 1914 the property was sold to Arthur Blauvelt. After Arthur's death, his widow continued to live here until 1942 when she sold the homestead to Martin Amirault for $300.00. Martin lived here with his family for the next thirty-six years, until he passed away in 1978. Shortly afterward, his widow Mary Jane sold the house to Dave Mason who continues to live here to this day. It is most likely that this house had an ell hauled here and attached to the original house. I cannot ascertain which section is the original building, but the fact that one roof intersects the opposing roof at a different height is a clear indication that these were two separately constructed buildings. Although the house is now clad in vinyl siding and the windows have been changed over the years, this is a very neatly kept property and the house has retained much of its original appeal.

The Fanny Daugherty House

This photograph was taken in June, 1921. Fanny Daugherty is seen in the white dress. Her mother is sitting on the bench, to the right.

Continuing on the William Robbins Road, a short distance beyond the Martin Amirault house, also on the northern side of the road, there was at one time a driveway leading to a property many today recall as the home of Nathaniel Blauvelt. This house no longer exists and unfortunately, very little of its early history is known. I offer what little I do know about this property here, mostly due to the fact that I have been successful in obtaining an excellent photograph of this once-beautiful homestead that is now all but forgotten. This may have been the original home of Lemuel Crosby, a very early settler in this part of the village. He is also mentioned in relation to the next property. In the late 1800s and early 1900s, this property was owned by Harvey and Fanny Daugherty. Harvey died a young man (52) and Fanny continued to live here with her mother for several years afterwards. It was a very private and well kept property with a beautiful home. The Daughertys occupied the "old" house until 1929. In that year the original house burned; another house was built on the same location, but only about half the size. Sometime afterward, the property was purchased by J. Phillip Hurlburt of Yarmouth. I knew Phil Hurlburt well and often visited him at his home in Yarmouth. He was a dignified gentleman in every sense of the word. Phil Hurlburt was married to Jean MacKinley of Yarmouth and Judge Vincent Pottier of Belleville had married her sister, Lena. Phil bought this property as a summer cottage and Vincent Pottier purchased the next property to the north, as we shall see momentarily. Obviously, the intention here was to be next door to each other, each enjoying their summer homes in this very secluded part of the village. Eventually, Nathaniel Blauvelt moved onto the property and lived here for several years. The house fell into a state of disrepair and has since been demolished.

The Old Crosby (or William Robbins) Homestead – Vincent Pottier Cottage – Dr. Roland Muise House

At the end of the William Robbins Road we arrive at the Dr. Roland Muise homestead. This house may have been built in the late 1850s. Although records suggest that this was the original home of John Crosby, it is possible that it may have been built by his father,

Lemuel Crosby. Lemuel Crosby did live somewhere on this property. It is also possible that the house previously mentioned, Fanny Daugherty's, may have been the old Lemuel Crosby house. John Crosby however, lived in this house for over forty years. In 1903 the large lumbering firm of Dickie & McGrath purchased the property but owned it for only one year when they sold it again to Mr. William J. Robbins; thus the name William Robbins Road.

William J. Robbins and his wife Jessie on their property in Tusket, at the end of the William Robbins Road. The dog's name was Ted.

The property remained in the William Robbins family until 1941when it was sold to Judge Vincent Pottier of Belleville. During Vincent Pottier's twenty-year tenure, the house was mostly used as a cottage or summer home. In 1961 it was sold to Fred and Mary Phillips from Marblehead, Massachusetts. The Phillips came to Tusket and built the Marblehead Light Restaurant, later known as the Golden Pheasant Restaurant, located just north of the present home of Hubert and Phyllis Pothier. After the Phillips ownership, the old Crosby property was sold to Dr. Frank Ozvesgy, and in1973, was sold again to Kennard and Bruni Fletcher. In 1978, Dr. Roland Muise purchased this homestead. He and his wife Suzanne continue to live here today. The exterior of this house has been greatly altered and the original architectural details have been absorbed in the newly restyled exterior designs.

Norman Pottier Rental Home

Returning to the main road, (308 North) we will proceed north. On the left hand side of the main road, on the corner of the William Robbins Road, is a modern bungalow, built as a two-unit apartment building. It was built on this lot by Norman Pottier in 1972. He still owns the property in 2005.

George Muise – William & Rose Emma LeFave House

The George Muise house being moved in the mid-1960s.

A bit further along the main road, on the left, and situated at the sharp turn to Belleville, is a house owned in 2005 by Billy and Rose Emma LeFave. This house was moved onto this lot in the mid-1960s by George Muise. The house was previously situated north in the community of Gavelton and sat on the same spot where George and Dale Duncanson's home is found in 2005. George Muise had purchased this house from "Bobbie" Allen. Alfred Sweeney and Martin Amirault moved the building with two large bulldozers.

A few hundred yards to the north of Billy LeFave's home is the last older home found in this part of the village.

Capt. Robert R. Blauvelt –
Arthur Bowering House

This home is located on the west side of the main road, a short distance north of the William Robbins Road. It was built in 1865 as the original homestead of Robert R. Blauvelt who lived here until 1901, at which time it was deeded to his son-in-law, Ralph Blauvelt. Ralph was a Stipendiary Magistrate in Tusket for a number of years. In 1952, Ralph Blauvelt's son, lawyer and local historian, Robert Blauveldt came into possession of the house. The property remained in the Blauvelt family until 1959. Arthur Bowering and his wife Dorothy purchased the property in 1962 and have lived here since then.

Conclusion of Tour

This concludes our walk through the village. It is hoped that the tour has shed some light on the history of many of the properties in Tusket, and provides some idea of how the community has developed over the years. Some of the properties included in this tour will be dealt with in greater detail in the later chapters in this book.

CHAPTER 3

GENERAL STORES

CHAPTER 3
GENERAL STORES

Tusket has had many general stores since it was settled in the 1780s. Little is known about the earliest general stores in the village. We do know from probate records that Col. Job Hatfield, one of the original settlers, was also one of the first merchants in the place. According to *The Descendants of Matthias Hatfield* (1954), he had two schooners, one brigantine and one brig. The confirmed land grant of Tusket Village dated 1809 shows Job Hatfield having several buildings as well as a wharf on the shores of the river, in the centre of the village, more or less across from the Court House. He was involved in the West Indies trade and it seems safe to assume that at least one of his buildings in 1809 would have been a general store. From here he would have sold West Indies goods such as sugar, molasses and rum, and probably other imported goods needed by the early settlers.

In the southern end of the village, at Lent's Corner, lived Squire James Lent. His "Fish House" is sometimes also referred to as a "store." He too was in the West Indies trade and exported fish. One assumes his vessels returned carrying goods similar to those of Col. Job Hatfield, and that he too carried on some type of mercantile establishment here for a number of years. Squire Lent's Fish House remained a landmark in the community for well over 100 years, but does not appear to have been used as a general store by any of his children or grandchildren.

Cornelius VanNorden, in the northern part of the village, possibly in the area Josephine Pottier lives today, is also believed to have had some type of general store, but of what size, or during exactly what period is not known.

Col. Job Hatfield died in 1825. Afterwards, his son John V.N. Hatfield may well have continued to operate his father's businesses for a time. He was certainly one of the leading businessmen in the community during his lifetime, but he does not appear to have operated a general store as such for long. He was more heavily involved in business as a ship owner and in real estate.

In the early 1830s the Bingay family arrived in Tusket, and shortly afterward established a general store in the centre of the village. The sketches that follow attempt to present what is known about Tusket's general stores from 1832 onward. We will start in the southern part of the village and proceed north to the centre and beyond.

The James Adolphus Hatfield Store

James Adolphus Hatfield was born 24 February 1821. He was the son of James and Elizabeth (Lent) Hatfield of Gavelton. His paternal grandfather was Jacob Lyons Hatfield, one of Tusket's original Loyalist settlers. His maternal grandfather was "Squire" James Lent, another Tusket Loyalist. In 1860, he established one of Tusket's most important shipyards in the southern part of the village. His general store, which was established in connection with his shipyard, probably opened shortly afterward. General merchandise of all sorts would have been sold here. He did a substantial business. Although he certainly would have sold to any customers, a large part of the business centred on labourers in the shipyards taking a good part of their pay in goods from the store. Most shipyards during this period set up such establishments.

His shipyard, which is discussed at more length in the chapter "Industries", flourished here until the year 1888. During much of this time his brother, Peter Lent Hatfield, managed the store for him. In 1888 the shipbuilding firm failed, and the store was closed. It was located very near to the shipyards, on the lot of land occupied in more recent times by the home of the late Roger Doucet.

It seems likely that the building sat empty and unused for about eight years, from 1888 until 1896, when it was moved north into the centre of the village, where it once again became a store. We will pick up its history, after the move, later in this chapter.

The Harding - Hatfield Store

The Corner, before and after. On the left we see the original store of Isaac S. Hatfield. On the right we see the new Tracy Hatfield store, built in 1907.

In our walking tour of the village we have discussed the home in the southern part of the village built between 1837 and 1840 for Tracy G. Harding. This house was owned and occupied in recent years by the late John and Phyllis (Hatfield) Young. Immediately to the west of the house, and very close to it, Tracy Harding had another building constructed in which he established his general store. Unfortunately he died in 1846, quite a young man, leaving his wife a widow, with children. In settling her husband's estate it was necessary for her to sell off some of their property in order to discharge the debts. His widow, Sarah (Cochrane) Harding, a native of New York, sold her home to her brother-in-law, and moved with her children into the store. She continued to run this general store as a means to support herself and her children. Not many years after the death of her first husband, she remarried Isaac S. Hatfield, a brother of J. Adolphus Hatfield and Peter Lent Hatfield. Isaac and Sarah Hatfield had children of their own, and continued to run their business here. Isaac was also elected as a Member of the Legislative Assembly of Nova Scotia, and held his seat from 1863-1867. Isaac Hatfield died in 1872, when he was drowned in the river near their property. Afterwards Sarah (Cochrane) (Harding) Hatfield continued to live in the store and run her business. Store ledgers for this business held at the Argyle Township Court House Archives reveals that they dealt in a wide range of goods.

Sarah Hatfield died in 1891, and at some time between then and 1900 the store was sold to her grandson, Tracy G. Hatfield. It is possible that it was run for a few years by one of her children before being sold to Tracy Hatfield. Tracy had spent several years working in the U.S. before returning to Tusket to establish himself in business.

Tracy Hatfield (son of Peter Lent Hatfield) was one of the leading merchants in the village during his lifetime. He made improvements to the property and expanded the business. He was doing so well here financially that around 1905-1907, he decided to expand his business and build a new store on this property. The *Yarmouth Light,* 30 May 1907, reported, "Mr. Tracy Hatfield has moved his lower store across the road and has laid the foundation for a much larger shop on the site of his old one."

The old building (which had been built for Tracy Harding between 1837-1840) was sold and moved south to Hubbard's Point. It still exists, and for many years, was the home of Harry Doucette. In 1907 the new store was opened. It was an impressive building and its opening, which was a major event in the village, received the following coverage in the local press:

NEW STORE AT TUSKET
An article which originally appeared
in the *Yarmouth Light* [newspaper],Thurs. 14 Nov. 1907,
reprinted in *The Argus*, vol.6 nos.3 & 4, Fall & Winter 1994

The attractive little town of Tusket shows many signs of a wave of prosperity, one of the principal being a new general store, recently erected on the corner opposite the post office, for Mr. Tracey G. Hatfield. This store which is pronounced by commercial travellers and others in a position to know, to be the best general store in the country districts of Nova Scotia, and is an ornament to the community, and an earnest confidence of the faith of one of her citizens in the future of Tusket.

The building occupies the site used as a business stand for 65 years, the house and shop of the grandparents of the present owner having been removed to make room. The new store is a two-story frame building 65 x 31 feet, with a hip roof. It rests upon a foundation of field stone with cut granite trimmings. Engraved fluted columns support the front which is lighted by two plate glass windows, 8x8 feet. Well proportioned dormer windows and a belt of fancy shingling between the first and second stories give the exterior an attractive appearance.

The basement may be entered through a single door on the west side, or double doors large enough to admit a loaded express with horses attached. The floor is of cement, and there is 9 feet 6 inches 'in the clear'. The walls are 20 inches thick and frost proof. A valuable feature is a never failing well of water in the basement. A force pump and tank system will provide the whole building with running water. A sewage pipe leads directly to the Tusket river. Among the fittings in the basement are an oil tank with patent pump and a freight elevator leading to the first floor.

A flight of stairs lead to the back shop in the southeast corner, first floor. In the southwest corner is the office, beautifully finished with metal walls and ceiling, daintily tinted, and hardwood floor. It is lighted by windows looking south and west, and by an art glass in the partition back of the main store. The office is to be fitted with inside shutters on the Venetian system.

The shop itself is about 50 x 31 feet. It has metal ceilings and walls, metal coated and capped pillars, hardwood floor, and woodwork of mahogany finish. Teak wood rails surround the show windows which are plate glass of ample size as before mentioned. In addition there is a bevelled glass panel in the front door and a transom light. There is also a single window looking west.

The fittings of the shop are in keeping. Patent Walker bins in quartered oak and cabinets of the same wood are in evidence, and there is a multitude of drawers, shelves and all conveniences for doing a large trade. The counters represent the best workmanship of the Canadian Wood Working Co.

The second and third stories are entered either by stairs from the shop or by separate doors from the street. These apartments are used for storage. They are amply lighted with windows, the view from which is magnificent.

The building reflects credit alike on the owner and the builders. The boss carpenter was Ambrose Potier of Belleville, his able assistant having been Jos. Babine, both mechanics of the first rank, having had wide experience in the United States. Thomas Doucet was the mason, and Melbourne Surette of Eel Brook the decorator. The workmanship in each department could scarcely be excelled. *The Light* congratulates all concerned.

An interesting point: Ambroise Potier was my great-grandfather. Thomas Doucet, from Quinan was certainly one of the best stone masons to have lived locally; Melbourne Surette of Eel Brook was a very talented artist.

The Tracy Hatfield Store prospered here and was eventually passed on to his son and daughter-in-law, Lent and Jessie Hatfield. They ran a very successful business here, which concentrated on the wholesaling of dry goods such as flour, animal feeds, fertilizers, shingles, etc. in addition to other general merchandise.

Shirley Margeson, in an article in the *Argus,* vol.7 no. 1 (Spring 1995) says: "Lent and Jesse lived in an apartment above the store – an apartment equipped with electricity and flush toilets, whose large windows must surely have been washed by all the gold and blue light that flowed down the splendid river." When I first began research for this history, Gordon Wood and I first visited Lent and Jessie in their upstairs apartment, but generally we had more spare time during the winter months and it was these winter visits that bring back more vivid memories.

Somehow it always seemed that we chose the coldest evenings to go visit. Often, upon arrival, one could see the large windows in the storefront frozen over with a glaze of ice. Toward the rear of the store stood an old upright oil burner stove; obviously with the control valve turned on "low" to conserve on fuel. Huddled next to this stove were both Lent and Jessie wrapped up in well worn dark coloured blankets, sitting on an old dark upholstered couch. Lying down next to them was their shiny, jet-black dog, "J.D." Occasionally, J.D. would get up and try to curl up closer to the stove, surely trying to capture some of that heat. However, J.D. would soon be called back to sit on the old couch with them, while they stroked his shiny black fur. I remember the chair that I usually ended up sitting in; it was not upholstered, and it was like sitting on a block of ice. I always had my notepad and pen and occasionally had to blow into my clutched hands to warm them, trying to make it a bit easier to write. I tried to do this as inconspicuously as possible. Jessie and Lent were famous for

Lent Hatfield as I remember him in his store in the early 1970s.

their frugal ways and this clearly extended to heat. These visits were experiences to cherish. They were both always so pleased to see us and it was wonderful to see the gleam in their eyes as they recounted the past as they remembered it. When I resumed the project alone a few years later, I wondered if things might have improved. Nothing had changed. The room was just as cold; but warmth of a different kind was always offered by Lent and Jessie.

Job Lyons Hatfield Store

A short distance north along the main road, leading toward the centre of the village, was the general store of J. Lyons Hatfield. I have not been able to obtain a great deal of information on this establishment, but it was a general store, and apparently a thriving one. This store was located on the banks of the Tusket River across from the present-day home of Gordon and Evelyn Muise. The remnants of the extensive wharves connected with this property can still be seen. "Lyons" first built a home on Court Street further north in the village, and did not really establish himself on the banks of the river until he sold that property in 1873. He built a new home at the river's edge, a barn, and also a general store and a sawmill. After being here for about 15 years, his sawmill burned in 1890. He rebuilt the sawmill. Only three years later, in 1893, he suffered another fire, and this time he lost everything. Lyons Hatfield and his wife were no longer young people. They chose not to rebuild after this fire, but moved to Yarmouth and spent their last years in the town.

Moving north from the Lyons Hatfield property we proceed towards the centre of the village where the most of Tusket's general stores have been located.

Tusket's Centre of Commerce

It seems likely that this area in the centre of the village of Tusket, on the river's bank, became a commercial centre very early in the history of the settlement. As has been mentioned earlier, Col. Job Hatfield, one of Tusket's earliest settlers is believed to have had his general store this vicinity. Around the time of Col. Job Hatfield's death in 1825, the Bingay family arrived in Tusket. James Bingay, who had been born in Shelburne on 15 September 1797, was the first of this family to settle in Tusket. A short time after he moved to the village with his family, James Bingay established a general store across the road from the Argyle Township Court House.

One thing that has become clear through research on this part of the village – this commercial centre has always been subject to change. Not only have buildings and businesses been frequently bought and sold – they have also been moved and recycled in a variety of different ways. So unless information on particular buildings and businesses has been documented in some way, I have avoided speculation. What is known, however, makes for a very interesting account.

James Bingay had established his general store in Tusket as early as 1832. This can be documented from one old store ledger that has survived and is held at the Argyle Township Court House Archives. This store was definitely situated on the western side of the main road, on the opposite side of the road from the Court House.

With the advent of shipbuilding as a major industry in Tusket, especially in the 1850s, other stores began to spring up. Often these stores were established in conjunction with the various shipbuilding yards. Labourers in these yards would be able to obtain goods from these stores "on credit" or "account." According to tradition, these businesses were often run quite ruthlessly, and if the workers did not act prudently, they could end a working season in debt, rather than having any cash to show for their labours.

On an 1862 surveyed plan of Tusket, on the following page, directly across from the Argyle Township Court House, one finds the N. & E. Gardner Store.

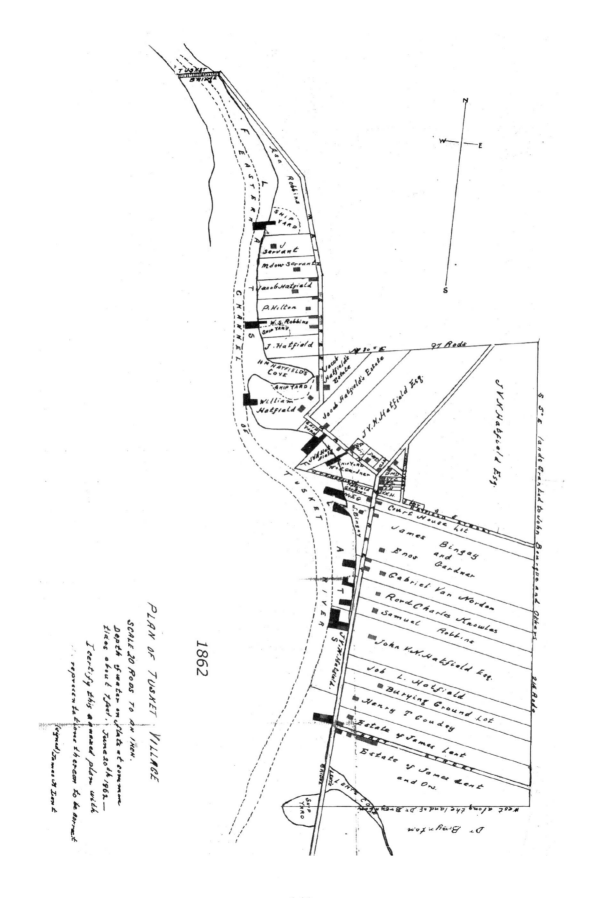

PLAN OF TUSKET VILLAGE

1862

SCALE 20 RODS TO AN INCH.

Depth of water on flats at common tides about 7 feet. June 20th 1862.—

I certify this annexed plan with representations thereon to be correct.

(signed) James H. Lent

This general store would have belonged to the shipyard firm of Nathaniel and Enos Gardner. Somewhat to the south of this store, on the same (western) side of the road was the store of "J. Bingay." Whether or not this is the same building and location that James Bingay had occupied since the 1830s is impossible to say. In 1862 these were the only two buildings in this area.

By 1866, four years later, the A.F. Church Map shows an additional property. The "E. Gardner" Store (now owned by Enos Gardner alone) still sits directly across the road from the Court House. Just to the south of this store one still finds James Bingay's Store. Somewhat to the south of his store one finds a building not shown in 1862 – and this building is shown as being Dr. J. M. Bingay's medical offices.

J. M. Bingay Medical Offices – a Building of Many Uses - And For Short Periods of Time a General Store

The building which housed the medical offices has a complicated history. James H. Bingay, (grandson of James Bingay) in his 1955 letter, says the following of this property: "As I first remember it … it was about opposite the Methodist Church … It was then (say about 1883-4) occupied as a medical office by my father. The office part was in the rear …"

In 1886 William T. Lent, a native of Tusket, who had lived for a time in the U.S., returned to Tusket with his family. In this year he purchased the former James Bingay house on the eastern side of the road and to the south of the Court House, and he and his family moved onto the property. James H. Bingay explains that, "When Wm. Lent bought the old Bingay house (my grandfather's), the 'office' went with it. Uncle Billy [William T. Lent] moved it [the former medical office] across the street to a position between his house and the Court House and opened a shop there." (In the picture on page 59, Tusket's "Village Centre" ca. 1900, this small shop is clearly visible, just south of the courthouse). Bingay indicates that a number of years later W.T. Lent opened yet another store on the western side of the street. This transaction took place in 1897. After this date the former medical offices served a variety of purposes. James H. Bingay indicates that for a time W.T. Lent used the building for storage purposes, probably in connection with his new business across the road. It had, however, operated as general a store from about 1897 to 1902.

The *Yarmouth Light* newspaper of 7 May 1903, in their Tusket column, reported, "W.T. Lent Esq. has converted the store next to his residence to a reading room where men of the village, as well as strangers, can meet and find wholesome recreation in reading." How long the reading room lasted, or whether it was a success, is not known. We do know that about three years later, W.T. Lent rented out this building to other businessmen. For a period of time, starting in 1906, a bicycle shop occupied the building.

W.T. Lent died in 1911, and James H. Bingay indicates that after that date, Lent's son, William H. Lent, "ran it as a shop (again a general store) for a while, but soon gave it up."

In 1916, after the death of W.T. Lent's widow Matilda, the small "shop" and the W.T. Lent home were sold to LeBaron ("Barney") Floyd. His family owned this property from that time until 1955. During some of this time Barney Floyd's wife, and his son Harold's wife, ran an ice cream parlour from the building.

A number of years before 1955 the Floyds sold this small shop to Magloire LeBlanc of Abram's River, while they continued to own the house on the property. Magloire had the building hauled from the centre of the village to a spot near the Abram's River Road on Highway #3 where it was converted to a private dwelling. His family lived here for several years before moving to Yarmouth. This old store building, abandoned, fell into a state of disrepair and was eventually demolished after 1955.

Due to the fact that we have had to move back and forth across the road, I should re-establish that in our tour of the commercial centre of the village, we are talking about the stores on the western side of the main road, on the bank of the Tusket River. The medical offices of the late Dr. John M. Bingay, whose history has just been sketched in, originally was the most southerly building in the string of buildings found in this part of the village.

From here we will proceed north to the next commercial building. Many of these general stores had complicated pasts, and I hope that the following visual key will assist the reader in following the history of these buildings as presented here.

Aerial view of Tusket's "Village Centre" during the 1970s

Key to numbers on photograph:

1. W.T. Lent – LeBaron "Barney" & Harold Floyd – Dan Armstrong house.
2. Original site of Dr. James Bingay medical office, a vacant lot in the 1970s.
3. Location of Dr. Bingay's medical office after purchased and moved by W. T. Lent to the opposite side of the road.
4. Approximate original site of James Bingay's store; later sold to Smith Harding.
5. Location of Smith Harding store after having been moved slightly south to create space for his new store, the Adolphus Hatfield store that was hauled here from the southern end of the village.
6. Smith Harding's new store … later the Tracy G. Hatfield – Elmer Hatfield store.
7. Site of N. & E. (Nathaniel & Enos) Gardner – W. T. Lent store.
8. The Forman Hatfield – Charles & Bernard Hurlbert – Carl's store.
9. Wharf remains that once extended to the stores for loading and unloading ships.
10. Remains of N. & E. Gardner shipyard.
11. VanCortlandt Square.
12. Tusket school house – the present Argyle Municipal Offices.

The James Bingay – Smith Harding – Tracy G. & Elmer Hatfield Store Site

As we have mentioned previously, James Bingay came to Tusket and established a general store in this area in the 1830s. On the surveyed plan of the village, dated 1862, his store is shown as being located on the western side of the main road, just to the south of the Argyle Township Court House, and almost directly across the road from his own house. Although we cannot be certain, it is possible that he had occupied this same site from the 1830s to 1862. The store is still shown here on the A.F. Church Map (about 1866). It seems likely that James Bingay, after many years in business, retired a few years after this. The Bingay store was sold on 19 July 1870 to Thomas B. Crosby, a businessman at that time quite involved with various enterprises in the village. In 1873 Crosby sold the property to Enos Gardner. Gardner sold the property on 6 March 1876, to the firm of Parker-Eakins of Yarmouth for $1200.

In 1884 Parker-Eakins sold the property to Smith Harding of Tusket. Although Harding owned the property, he had close links with Parker-Eakins, and in some ways may have been working for them.

It should be stated that although Smith Harding, in 1884, became the owner of the former James Bingay store property, we cannot be certain that the old Bingay store continued to be used, or whether it was replaced by a new building. The surviving photographs which show Smith Harding's building suggest it did not date from the 1830s, or if it did, it had probably undergone major alterations over the years. In 1896, twelve years after coming into possession of this business, Smith Harding made another major change to the property.

The *Yarmouth Light* of 29 October 1896, reports, "Mr. Smith Harding has purchased the store formerly occupied by James A. Hatfield Esq. and moved it near his store."

The reader will recall that the James Adolphus Hatfield store is the first one mentioned in this chapter. According to James H. Bingay, Smith Harding had his existing store building moved a short distance to the south on its lot, in order to make room for the Adolphus Hatfield store. His original store was afterwards used for warehouse purposes for his business. The addition of this building to his lot suggests an expansion of his business interests with Parker-Eakins. This was probably the case, for only two months later the *Yarmouth Light*, 10 December 1896, reported that, "Mr. Smith Harding is in his new store. He is shipping fish in quite large quantities."

A few years after this, Smith Harding received the appointment of Customs Agent in Yarmouth and sold his Tusket properties and moved there. On 21 May 1904, his two commercial buildings in the centre of the village were sold to Tracy G. Hatfield. Tracy Hatfield operated a prosperous general store from Smith Harding's "new" building, and like the previous owner, used the older and larger building as a warehouse. Eventually, in 1917, these two buildings were passed on, or sold, to his son Elmer Hatfield. Many seniors will still remember these properties as the Elmer Hatfield Store and the building next door that he used for storage. Elmer operated his business here for thirty-five years.

Daniel Armstrong, the next owner, owned it from 1952 until 1967. These buildings changed hands several times before being purchased in 1984 by Carl and Audrey Pottier. Their intentions in developing this property commercially was to demolish both of the Elmer Hatfield buildings in order to create more parking space. At this time, I offered to buy the Elmer Hatfield Store (the original store of J. Adolphus Hatfield), dismantle it, and remove it from the property. This has been related previously in more detail in the Walking Tour. After I dismantled and removed the store, the older building that had been used for so long as a warehouse was also demolished.

Three stores in the village centre, left to right: The James Bingay - Smith Harding store (and warehouse) after having been moved "slightly to the south"; the Tracy & Elmer Hatfield store; and the William T. Lent store. The third person from the right in this photograph is Arthur McGrath, son of Thomas N. McGrath.

The N. & E. Gardner - William T. Lent Store

As the reader will be aware by now – the history of Tusket's stores in the centre of the village is complicated. We will proceed north. The next store building, to the north of the buildings just discussed, was the original N. & E. Gardner Store, established in connection with their shipyard property. On 3 May 1855, John V.N. Hatfield sold this lot of land, and some additional land to the north, to Nathaniel and Enos Gardner, and to J. Lyons Hatfield, his son.

Nathaniel & Enos Gardner operated a major shipbuilding yard, and their store would have been built in connection with that property. The store is clearly shown on the 1862 plan of the village and on the A.F. Church Map of 1866. A few years after 1866, the firm of N. & E. Gardner, after building some very impressive ships, ran into financial difficulties. A judgement filed against them by Samuel Killam of Yarmouth resulted in their losing their business establishments. By 1873 the former N. & E. Gardner Store, located directly across the road from the Argyle Township Court House, was the property of Samuel Killam, as were the former Gardner shipyards.

Finally, on 22 December 1888, the executors of the estate of the late Samuel Killam sold this store, and another to the north, to Forman Hatfield of Tusket. Forman Hatfield was a well-known Tusket businessman during his time. In 1893 the property was sold or deeded to Forman Hatfield's son, Lloyd Hatfield and to Charles K. Hurlbert. James H. Bingay indicates that Lloyd Hatfield and Charles K. Hurlbert did establish some kind of business in the old N. & E. Gardner Store, but for some reason it was short-lived. On 14 April 1897 the store was sold to William T. Lent.

William T. Lent, who has been discussed previously, had his smaller store on the eastern side of the road, and to the south of the Court House. At this time, he moved his business across the road, into the old N. & E. Gardner Store. He prospered here, and his former "small" store next to the courthouse, as has been mentioned earlier, was afterwards used for storage or rented out.

William T. Lent was born in 1840 and was the grandson of pioneer "Squire" James Lent who settled on top of the hill by Lent's Corner in 1784. He grew up and married in Tusket and later moved to the U.S. with his wife. During that time they had a son, William H. Lent, whom we have seen in the previous photographs and will hear more about later. By 1875 they had returned to live in Tusket. He was a well-liked man and became very active in community affairs; he was elected and served several terms as a Councillor and was the Warden for the Municipality of Argyle at the time of his death. He died of cancer on July 25, 1911. His widow died in 1916; afterwards the store passed into other hands.

W. T. Lent
1840 - 1911

After W.T. Lent's death in 1911 the ownership history of this store becomes somewhat vague. For a time, Fred Babin operated a business from the former W.T. Lent Store, servicing automobiles. A few senior citizens can still remember a garage in this building. The name Waldo Clayton is often mentioned as having worked here when it was a garage. Some photographs show a lengthy extension on this building – and for a period of time, a bowling alley existed in the building. Various people who remember the property describe it as being run-down and in very poor condition as early as the 1930s. The Post Office from 1925 to 1953 was located in a small addition on the building. That small space appears to have been kept up, while the remainder of the building was allowed to deteriorate.

James H. Bingay in 1955 has the following to say about the demise of this building: "Quite a change was made last year, across the road from the Court House. The old building which once housed "The Robbery" (afterwards Barry Coleman's bowling alley in the mill days), and the Post Office (when Tom Lent died, and Fred Babin got the job), was torn down, leaving a fine view of the river to anyone walking down Court St." From the information that I have been able to gather, it seems likely that more than one year had passed since the building was demolished when Dr. Bingay was writing in 1955.

The Forman Hatfield – Charles & Bernard Hurlbert – Carl's Store

The Bernard Hurlbert Store in 1978. The store owner, Del Surette stands waving by the gasoline pump. The person about to cross the road is the late Jerry P. Doucet, Municipal Clerk at the time.

The final store building to be discussed here is the only commercial building in this area, a piece of which still survives today. The exact beginnings of this store remain somewhat obscure. It is situated on what would have been a portion of the N. & E. Gardner property in the 1860s. On the surveyed plan of the village dated 1862, there is no building on this lot. Four years later, in 1866, on the A.F. Church Map, this lot still remains empty. The Gardners lost their properties in the late 1860s. Whether this store was built by them, before they went into receivership, or was built by Samuel Killam who next owned this property is not known. There was also a great deal of recycling of buildings during this period, and it is not out of the question that some other store or building may have been moved onto the lot after 1866.

What is clear is that when Forman Hatfield purchased this property from the estate of Samuel Killam in 1888, there was a store on this lot of land. Forman Hatfield established his own general store in this building and according to reports of the time did very well here. On 7 June 1909, Forman Hatfield and his wife sold this store to Charles K. Hurlbert of Tusket. Charles Hurlbert's general store operated from this building and was a highly successful enterprise. Eventually, it became the business of his son, Bernard Hurlbert, and is remembered by many seniors as the "Bernard Hurlbert Store." It is worth noting here that Charles K. Hurlbert, and later his son, Bernard Hurlbert, both served as Municipal Clerks for the Municipality of Argyle. Prior to 1945 there was no formal Municipal Office, and a great deal of municipal business was transacted in this store. Subsequent owners of the store have donated many municipal records found in the building to the Argyle Township Court House Archives.

In 1961 the store passed from the Hurlberts to Ernest and Willetta Raynard, and Vernon and Lillian Raynard of Glenwood, Nova Scotia. They operated the business successfully until they sold the store in 1973. In 1973 the store was purchased by Delbert Surette. He owned the store until 1980. It was during this period that he purchased a considerable amount of land to the north of the store. The land had been owned by Harold Floyd. From 1980 to 1983, the store was owned by Nathan Crosby. In that year the property was sold to Carl and Audrey Pottier.

As has been mentioned above, Carl and Audrey Pottier sold the former Elmer Hatfield store to me and I removed it from the property. The old Elmer Hatfield warehouse building was also demolished at this time. They retained the former Bernard Hurlbert store, and it still forms part of their business today. They have developed a highly successful and unique business here.

Nathaniel Churchill Jr. Store – Andy Jeffery's Garage

Ox team with two unidentified men in front of the old Nathaniel Churchill store.

There is one other general store located in this part of the village that we will discuss here. It too was established in connection with one of Tusket's early shipyards. In the late 1860s Nathaniel Churchill Jr. of Kemptville moved to Tusket and established a shipyard in this part of the village. Like other shipyard owners, he also established a general store in connection with his business. This store was built on land that now faces south onto VanCortlandt Square in the centre of the village. Most seniors in the village today will remember this building as Andy Jeffery's Garage. When I first moved to Tusket this is where I purchased my gasoline.

149

As previously stated, Nathaniel Churchill Jr. had this store built in connection with his shipyard, and it operated for about 10 years under his ownership, or until the mid to late 1870s. Afterwards the store was purchased by Ephraim C. Simonson. He did not have a shipyard, but continued to operate the general store for at least a time. It seems that there may have been a number of enterprises in this building over the years. The *Yarmouth Light,* 13 September 1894, reported, "Miss B. Laskie and Miss F. Shaw of Brooklyn, Yarmouth Co., have opened a millinery and dressmaking shop in Mr. E. C. Simonson's shop." Since I have never heard anyone mention this business, it seems likely that it closed after a season or two.

There were a series of owners of this property before Andrew Jeffery Sr. purchased this property in 1917. It would eventually become a garage operated by the Jeffery family. That family would own the property until 1973. The old Nathaniel Churchill Jr. Store (Andy Jeffery's garage) was demolished in 1973, shortly after the property was sold. Andrew Jeffery Sr. was a blacksmith and operated his blacksmith shop out of another building that sat behind the building being discussed here.

Andy Jeffery was the son of "Old Man" Andrew Jeffery; he closed his garage in the late 1960s when he received the appointment of small gas engine repair instructor at the Burridge Vocational School in Yarmouth. This store can be seen in the photograph on page 149. Another excellent view of this building is shown during the unveiling of the war memorial monument on page 286.

I am not aware of any general store ever having been located on the road that leads north out of the village toward Gavelton (Route 308 North). But there have been two general stores located on Highway #3, out of the centre of the village and travelling towards the Tusket Bridge.

James & Bessie Wood General Store

In 1944 the old John Calvin Hatfield property on Highway #3 was purchased by James and Bessie Wood, the parents of Gordon Wood. This is the same house shown on page 77 in our Walking Tour of Tusket. "Jim" had been a clerk in the Bernard Hurlbert Store, and obviously felt he had acquired enough knowledge of the business to set up his own store by the late 1940s. He built an addition onto the front of their home around 1949-50 and opened his own general store at that time. It was here, and at work, during the early 1960s that Gordon Wood and I became close friends. Jim and Bessie operated their general store until 1965, when Jim went to work as a custodian at the Post Office in Yarmouth. His work there saw him transferred to Kentville in 1969. Jim and Bessie were wonderful people. At times, Jim was somewhat pessimistic and it was rather hilarious sometimes to listen to his "doom and gloom" predictions. He was an avid hunter and fisherman and lived for the outdoors. Bessie had a heart of gold, and never, ever had a bad word to say about anything or anybody. I was always made to feel most welcome whenever I went to their home with Gordon.

Harold Allen Store

*The former Harold Allen store in 2005. New siding, windows
and a short extension were added on at the rear in the late 1980s
by the present owner. Only the right side (where the windows
are) was used as a general store by Mr. Allen. The left half of
the building was used for storage.*

Just beyond Jim and Bessie Wood's store, and on the same side of Highway #3, was
another general store that operated for a few years. The Harold Allen Store was opened
sometime around the mid 1960s and operated until about 1974. This was a rather small
store but did sell general merchandise here for the years that it was in operation. The
building still survives and since 1987 has been owned by my brother, Norman Pottier, on
Highway #3. He uses the building as a workshop for his carpentry business. The
building can be recognized by the western style false front on the building.

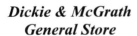

*Dickie & McGrath
General Store*

*This large group photo was taken in front of Thomas McGrath's general store.
According to Dr. Percy McGrath, the young boys sitting in the front row were "water
boys" who went around the mill-yards offering drinking water to the workers.
Women workers (perhaps cooks) can also be seen in this photo. Thomas McGrath
and his son Arthur are standing in the store entrance to the left. Standing in the
window, right of centre, are Chase Hatfield and Jack McCarthy, both book keepers
for the Dickie and McGrath firm.*

151

In 1892 when the Tusket River Lumber Company established their large sawmill in Tusket, one of the partners in this business, Nathaniel E. Butler, established a general store in connection with the mill property. This store probably operated in a similar manner to those that had been established in earlier decades by the shipbuilding yards in Tusket. Mill workers were able to draw on accounts at the store for various provisions. In 1896 the mill property was purchased by the firm of "Dickie & McGrath." Thomas N. McGrath, the mill manager, continued to operate this general store in conjunction with the mill. A short time after the Dickie & McGrath mills closed in 1912 Thomas N. McGrath was able to purchase the store. He continued to run his own general store from this building for about ten years, or until his death in 1923. By all reports this was a very popular gathering place in this end of the village during this period.

A Final Word on General Stores

For those readers who do not live in Tusket, I should state that today "Carl's Store", is the only general store remaining in the village. Most general stores throughout Yarmouth County have been reduced to "convenience stores" where one can pick up a few of the bare essentials when supplies run low. Most people shop for groceries and similar items in the Town of Yarmouth. Carl's Store has been unique in the entire county in maintaining a market share of this business. This has been because of the development of a good hardware and paint business as well as general merchandise. Gardeners throughout Yarmouth County come here every spring to buy their Vesey's Seeds. It is a unique business and we hope it will survive for many years to come.

CHAPTER 4

THE JEWEL OF TUSKET
The Court House

CHAPTER 4
THE JEWEL OF TUSKET
The Court House

The historic Tusket Courthouse

*From the original painting by Frank Boudreau commissioned by the Burridge
Community College staff as my retirement gift ... June 1998.*

The Construction and Establishment of the Court House

The Argyle Township Court House, located in the centre of the village, is without
question, the most important heritage property in Tusket, even though there still remain
three private dwellings that were built at an earlier date. Research carried out by Parks
Canada has determined that this is the oldest surviving courthouse in all of Canada. The
Court of General Sessions of the Peace for the Townships of Yarmouth & Argyle, then in
the County of Shelburne, decided to build the Court House in 1801. This location was
chosen, obviously as being a central one that would serve people from all parts of the two
townships.

Plans for the courthouse were adopted in 1801. An examination of the Records of the
General Sessions of the Peace for the October term of 1801 reveals the following:

held at Tusket village on the first Tuesday (the 6th), it was ordered that the sum of 75 pounds be raised for building a goal [sic] in the district of Yarmouth and Argyle. At the latter sitting it was ordered that a goal [sic] shall be built on public land near the burying ground at Tusket village; that said goal [sic] shall consist of the following dimensions: on the floor twenty feet by twenty-five feet; height of posts to be 13 feet; the lower story to be 6 feet 6 inches in the clear between the floor and beams; the lower room to be made in two separate apartments, the one to contain eight feet by nineteen feet for criminals, and the other to contain twelve feet by nineteen feet, for debtors, with an entry across one end of six feet wide. The wall of the lower story to be made with squared timber, to the thickness of nine inches, exclusive of the covering. The building to be framed; posts to be 9 inches thick; the floors and walls for criminals to be 9 inches thick, made of plank or timber. The floor for debtors to be made of plank 2 inches thick. The outside to be clapboarded, shingled and well served from the weather. For criminals, one window of 6 panes, with a grate of iron (inch bars); for debtors, one window of 12 panes, with iron grates; for the upper story to be four windows with 22 panes each.

Capt. Theunis Blauvelt, of Tusket, and James Kelley, of Yarmouth Township, were appointed to oversee the construction of the building.

Work proceeded on the building over the next three or four years. In October 1805, the first meeting of the Court of General Sessions took place in the new building. Prior to the construction of the building, sessions had been held in churches, meeting houses, schoolhouses, Richan's Tavern, and in other buildings in Yarmouth, Chebogue, Tusket (James Lent's fish shed), and Abuptic, now called Argyle. In 1819, 7 pounds, 11 shillings and 8 pence were voted to sustain the repair costs for the building. It was extended 20 feet in length on two separate occasions - 1833 and 1870.

COURT

The Court of General Session

The earliest form of civil court held in the Argyle Township Court House was, as has been mentioned above, the Court of General Sessions of the Peace for the Districts of Yarmouth and Argyle. The Court of General Sessions were presided over by the local Justices of the Peace, who were appointed by the provincial government in Halifax. This level of court heard petty criminal and civil cases and rendered verdicts, but their larger role was that of what we know today as "municipal government." While at any given session there may have been cases of petty theft, assault and battery, and similar matters dealt with, by far the larger portion of the Court's time was spent in dealing with governmental matters such as the building and repair of roads, control of the river fishery, issuing of licenses and the appointment of tax collectors and other local officials.

The Court of General Sessions met twice yearly during these early years, once in the Township of Yarmouth and once in the Township of Argyle. The Yarmouth sessions were held in taverns and other public buildings until they constructed their own courthouse in the 1830s. All the Argyle sessions after 1805 were held in the Court House at Tusket. Special sessions as needed were also held from time to time, in addition to the two yearly sittings.

Inferior Court of Common Pleas

Another level of court that would have presided here during early years was the Inferior Court of Common Pleas. This was a level of court that ran simultaneously with the Court of General Sessions, and was established to deal with cases that were deemed not to require the attention of Supreme Court. The Nova Scotia Archives describes this level of court and its history in the following manner:

> The Inferior Court of Common Pleas, County of Annapolis, commenced on 22 August 1761 with commissions appointing judges and instructing them to follow the procedure used by the Inferior Court at Halifax. Cases were to be heard by a bench of three or more judges, who were not required to have legal training and who were generally the senior justices of the peace for the county. The court's jurisdiction was civil and cases were often heard in connection with the Court of General Sessions meetings at Annapolis. In 1800 legislation allowed the Inferior Court to divide its sittings between Digby and Annapolis. The court's structure was adjusted in 1823 and 1824 to require a legally trained first judge, who would receive an annual stipend, to attend each case and sit as part of the bench. To facilitate this, the province was divided into districts, with Annapolis and Shelburne Counties sharing a stipendiary judge and forming the court's western district. In 1837 Digby became a separate county with its own Inferior Court. The gradual expansion of the court's jurisdiction and the increased circuit presence of the Supreme Court made it appear as if there were two courts with the same jurisdiction. In 1841 the Inferior Court was abolished and the remaining cases were transferred to the Supreme Court.

In reality the Inferior Court of Common Pleas, because of the above-mentioned legislation, operated out of the Court House at Tusket for a relatively short period of time. As indicated above, this level of court was abolished throughout the province in 1841.

During early times in Tusket it was "Squire" James Lent, and afterward his son, Abraham Lent, who appear to have presided over this level of court in Tusket.

Supreme Court

During the earliest years of the Court House's history at Tusket, Supreme Court did not sit in this building. The judges of the Supreme Court, three in number, were a circuit court, and travelled throughout the province. They held court only at county seats. As the Townships of Yarmouth and Argyle were part of Shelburne County until 1836, all sittings of the Supreme Court for the area were held in Shelburne up until that time.

In 1836 the Townships of Yarmouth and Argyle were set aside to constitute the new County of Yarmouth. Shortly afterwards, a sitting of the Supreme Court was established for the County. It appears that for the first year or two these sessions were held at Yarmouth, but by 1840 Supreme Court was sitting at the Argyle Township Court House as well. From that time until 1924, two sittings of Supreme Court were held annually for the County of Yarmouth, one taking place in the Town of Yarmouth, and the other at Tusket.

A number of famous judges presided here, including Justice Thomas Chandler Haliburton, who is even better known as an early Canadian author and humourist.

The last sitting of Supreme Court took place in Tusket in 1924. It was decided at that time that due to the changes brought about by the automobile, it was no longer necessary to hold sittings of Supreme Court in two locations in the county, and that thereafter all sittings of Supreme Court would be held in Yarmouth. Although it is clear the automobile and ease of travel was an influence, other circumstances also factored into this decision. Supreme Court judges had always found their accommodations in Tusket at the elegant American House or "Gilmans" as it was also known. This establishment had closed at this time, and provided a further incentive for the judges to hold court only in Yarmouth.

Magistrate's Court

From 1924 to 1944, Magistrates Court continued to preside at the Argyle Township Court House. This was to be the last form of court held in this building. Magistrates Court was a lower level of court that was established at the time of Confederation in 1867. In some ways it replaced the old Inferior Court of Common Pleas that had been abolished in 1841. It dealt with civil and criminal matters that were deemed not to require the attention of Supreme Court judges. The Magistrates who presided over this level of court were not required to be lawyers or to have formal legal training. In 1938 new legislation changed the requirements for legal training, but existing magistrates were allowed to continue in their positions until they chose to retire. At this time Gordon S. Hatfield was the local magistrate who held sittings of court in Tusket. He continued to hold his position until his death, in October 1944. This was the last year the Argyle Township Court House served as a working courthouse in any way.

Most Famous Trial

By far the most famous trial that was held in the Argyle Township Court House was the murder trial of Omar P. Roberts in 1922. Omar P. Roberts, a highly respected man from the community of North Kemptville, in a passionate outburst, had murdered his house-keeper, Miss Flora Gray, of East Kemptville. He had smashed a kerosene lantern on the floor of her bedroom, and she was horribly burned. Although she died, she lived long enough to tell what had happened. Mr. Roberts pled guilty to the charges and was sentenced to hang. The execution took place in the Town of Yarmouth at the jail there. He was the last person to be executed in Yarmouth County. The judge who presided at this trial was Judge J.A. Chisholm.

The Gaol (Jail) – Crime & Punishment in Argyle Township

Like many early Canadian courthouses, the Argyle Township Court House housed both a jail and court facilities. In fact, the original specifications for the building make it clear that the need for a "gaol" (jail) was considered more pressing than the need for court facilities. The jail has always been located on the ground floor of this building, while the courtroom, judge's chamber and Grand Jury room were located on the second storey.

From the beginning, the gaol (jail) served to house both criminals and debtors. During the very early years there was also a set of stocks located on the property. A few typical early sentences found in the records of the Court of General Sessions are as follows:-
1808 – Assault & Battery – Thomas Andrews found guilty and fined 2 pounds, or to do time in the jail
1810 – John Trefry Jr. did time in the gaol, and also escaped and was afterwards charged with that.
1811 – A young woman named "Harritt" a mulatto served 11 weeks in the gaol, on a charge of "felony."

During early times it is clear that the gaol was used extensively for debtors. The original specifications for the building make it clear that this was an expectation for the building as well.

The gaol continued to be used officially until about 1924, the same time that Supreme Court ceased to be held in the building.

Other uses of the Court House

Like any public building of this nature, the Court House has been used for a number of purposes over the years. Tradition has it that the courtroom was used at different times for church services, before the various denominations built their churches in the village.

Elections were held in this building for all three levels of government at different times, and these were "rough and ready" affairs according to many accounts. Pie socials were held here, and various community groups made use of the Court House.

At one point a portion of the ground floor at the rear served to house the village fire engine, owned by the Mayflower Engine Company.

After municipal incorporation in 1879-80 all meetings of Argyle Municipal Council and their committees were held in this building. This included meetings of School Commissioners for the District of Argyle, and later, the School Board.

Court House as Municipal Office

After the death of Gordon S. Hatfield in 1944, the Municipal Council moved to establish a Municipal Office in the building. Prior to this time it seems that most daily business conducted by the Municipal Clerk took place from his home or his place of business in the village. The first Clerk, Enos Gardner, lived a couple of houses away from the Court House. Subsequent Municipal Clerks, Charles Hurlbert, and then his son, Bernard Hurlbert, also lived close by. Charles Hurlbert and Bernard Hurlbert also had a general store in the centre of the village, and much municipal business appears to have transpired from those places.

In 1945 renovations took place and the Municipal Offices, with a staff, were established on the ground floor of the Court House at the rear. This official use of the building continued until 1976, when it was decided to move the Municipal Offices to more modern premises nearby. The new offices were moved to the former Tusket School building, and are still located there in 2005.

The Restoration

After the Argyle Municipal Offices moved from the premises of the old Court House in 1976, the building remained empty and soon started to deteriorate. The roof began to leak in the courtroom; plaster was cracking and falling down in some areas. Rumours began to circulate that a growing number of local residents thought that the building was "an eye-sore, it's no good there, and it should be torn down".

Most local people are now grateful that this did not take place. It was around this time that I and my good friend Gordon Wood, became very interested in older buildings. We had travelled in the New England area of the United States and also to the Williamsburg, Virginia area, often referred to as the Colonial Capital of North America. Over time we had acquired an appreciation for the gracefulness of older buildings. We came to realize that although many of these buildings had been around for a long time, their appeal was timeless. We soon began to appreciate the many old homes and buildings that we had locally, and most particularly, the Court House. We didn't know much about the history of the building at the time, but we realized that we had a jewel right here in our own village.

As the rumours of demolition intensified, Gordon and I became deeply concerned. We discovered that a gentleman living in the village, by the name of Oscar Nauss, also shared these same concerns. For some time, he had been particularly interested in the old records and documents that were literally scattered everywhere in the upstairs courtroom area. Gordon and I were more interested in the building itself. As it turned out, the three of us worked very well together. Oscar took care of the paperwork and we took care of

160

the building restoration. We discovered that since the Municipal Offices had moved from the Court House in 1976, Oscar had taken it upon himself to try and sort out as many of the valuable old documents as possible. He was deeply concerned about these records. He would go to the Court House alone and sit next to an oil-stove in the same small area that is still used today for the Archives. As is still the case today, it was cold in this room but he always sat there in the winter time perusing old documents, wearing a heavy beige coloured jacket with black barrel type buttons down the front. It was during these times that I took the picture of him that hangs in the same office today.

Oscar was also concerned about vandalism and kept a close eye on the building. He lived in the former Bernard Hurlbert house and could see the courthouse from his home. He had never been formally asked to do this; he simply took on these custodial duties as a volunteer and a good neighbour. A very close friendship quickly developed between the three of us and serious discussions began regarding a possible restoration of the building.

As is always the case, it required money. In 1981, we filed an application through the federal government Winter Works Program and also approached the Argyle Municipal Council for funding. We were unsuccessful this first time, but we didn't give up. The following year, 1982, we reapplied and were successful in receiving a federal government grant. Our local Member of Parliament at the time, Colleen Campbell, was most helpful and a pleasure to deal with. The Argyle Municipal Council also made a modest contribution. We were thrilled, and immediately went to work. The total cost of the restoration was approximately $80,000.

After a series of interviews, we hired Arthur LeBlanc from Abram's River as job superintendent; it turned out to be an excellent choice. Arthur was tough, he wanted good workers. He hired, and fired, until he was satisfied with his crew. He took good care of his workers and had great respect for what we wanted to achieve in this old building.

Oscar took care of the paperwork connected with the project, and Gordon and I supervised the construction work. Our main objective was to keep the appearance of the building as close to the original as possible. Two priorities for the exterior of the building were the windows and the roof. We knew that the large window panes had to be replaced with the original small panes. We had to have wooden shingles on the roof! Both of these objectives were met, as well as various other challenges. The front door entrance went through major improvements, and the cupola was brought down by crane and completely restored. Windows were closed in where necessary and others were reinstalled where they had been originally. How excited we were when the dark green trim was finally painted white and the graceful details of the dentil blocks boldly stood out again. Many people would ask "Did you have all those made?" We hadn't, but quite simply, they had just disappeared in the dark green trim colours.

Restoration Project Manager, Arthur LeBlanc of Abram's River and his workers standing next to the restored cupola. Left to right, front row: Fred Surette; Percy Bourque; Arthur LeBlanc; Albert "Kinky" Landry; Nancy Amirault; Monica Sweeney. Left to right, back row: Ernie Doucette and Richard Thibeau.

The interior proved to be equally challenging and rewarding. I remember when Gordon and I first started assessing what had to be done to the interior. From 1945 to 1976 when the Municipal Offices were in the building, Municipal Council had covered a lot of the walls with sheet-rock. We discovered a "mystery corner" in one of the hallways in the jail-cell block. For some unknown reason, there was a completely boxed in section (approximately three feet square) located in the corner of this corridor. We were mystified and had to find out why that was boxed in. With hammers and pry bars, we went to work. After removing most of the sheet rock we could see nothing but a solid brick wall on one side. On the other wall, however, we could see a very narrow wooden door. We pried with all our might, but we couldn't get it open! We discovered that the floor in this area had been cemented over, perhaps to make it more level. This prevented the door from opening. We absolutely had to see what was in there! We finally decided to saw the bottom of the door off - just high enough so it would open. What a surprise! It was the indoor toilet for the prison inmates! It was so small that the door would have had to remain open when in use. (Prisoner's rights were obviously not an issue at this time!) The removable metal pan that slid out from underneath for cleaning was still there, although quite rusted away! A new one had to be made. Later, in provincial inspection reports of the jail we learned the politically correct term for the box was the "cess trough."

Another exciting time was when we removed the wall that had been installed at the base of the spiral stairway leading to the courtroom. What a thrill when we discovered that this was an open stairwell, completely open underneath with all the original plaster, still in excellent condition. We also discovered that the newel post for the bottom of the hand-rail had been removed and thrown under the winding stairway prior to closing in this section. How fortunate we were to have the original newel post to reinstall again!

All the old documents in the building were boxed and stored while the construction got underway.

The sheet rock was removed and countless hours were spent scraping and removing the old whitewash paint from the bricked walls as well as the wooden beamed walls and ceilings in the front entrance and cell block areas. Fred Surette, an excellent painter from Sluice Point was our hired painter. Fred is a skilled craftsman and did an excellent job. So much so, that it was more than twenty years before the interior required painting again.

All this was accomplished during the winter of 1982 and spring of 1983. Although Oscar continued to keep an eye on the building as he had in the past, it became obvious that a new level of care and maintenance was required for the building – especially to make sure that records held here would survive. The Argyle Municipal Council was most helpful in this regard.

A few years later, in 1987, sadly, Oscar passed away.

The Argyle Municipality Historical & Genealogical Society

It was fortunate that in 1985 Peter Crowell had been hired to work on the Heritage Property Inventory for the Municipality of Argyle. He had worked with Oscar and understood instinctively the importance of what had been accomplished in the building, and much of what would be needed to ensure the future of this facility. He was soon recruited and hired as full time historian and archivist at the Court House.

As events unfolded, it soon became obvious that a good choice had been made. Peter held fast to the belief that had been shared by Oscar Nauss that a historical society needed to be formed that would act as an ongoing organization of support for the Court House and the Archives. In 1989 the Argyle Municipality Historical & Genealogical Society was incorporated. The founding Directors were: Gordon Wood, Peter Crowell, Michael and Rose Rymer, Kenneth and Doris Peters, and me.

It is truly amazing to have witnessed what a healthy and vibrant institution the Court House and its Archives has become since 1989. The Municipal Council, who still owns this building, has been dedicated to providing the core funding for this facility year after year. The historical society, which has been placed in charge of the administration of the building, has taken its responsibilities very seriously. In any given year they have brought in revenues that equal the contribution of Municipal Council. This has had a huge impact not only on the success of the facility but in economic benefits to the community.

Some benchmarks should be noted here which demonstrate the Society's positive impact on the Court House:

In 1998 the wooden shingled roof that had been installed on the Court House during the restoration failed. It quite simply had deteriorated and was leaking. We had assumed that its life would be much longer than 15 years. We had not realized how the quality of shingles had deteriorated since 1982. The Society, believing in the importance of maintaining the wooden roof, hired an architect to come up with better specifications for wooden roofing, purchased the highest quality of shingles brought in from Quebec, and took many other precautions to ensure a new roof with a longer life. More important, they fundraised for this initiative. In spite of high costs, the new roof was installed, with a surplus.

In 1997, the Argyle Township Court House lined up with other museums across the province, was professionally assessed, and became part of the Nova Scotia Museum Assistance Program. They have continued to be assessed every three years, and in the most recent round of assessments, emerged with the highest score of any museum in the province. The Court House receives annual funding for its operation through this important program.

In 2000 the Society took the bold step of purchasing the former Seventh-Day Adventist Church, on the property immediately to the south of the Court House. They are currently engaged in the ambitious project of saving that important heritage building and transforming it into a modern archival facility. This will not only enable the operation of the Archives to improve, but will allow the Court House itself to be further developed as a museum and historic site.

In 2005 the Society is still awaiting word from Ottawa on whether the Historic Sites and Monuments Board of Canada will designate the Court House as a National Historic Site.

It should also be noted here, that in 2004, the Argyle Municipality Historical & Genealogical Society, with 655 members, became the largest local historical society in Nova Scotia. This has happened in large part because of the success of *The Argus*, the quarterly newsletter of the Society. It is an outstanding publication, publishing articles of historical interest that pertain to every part of the Municipality of Argyle. It is an amazing publication, and makes countless people with Argyle connections, regardless of where they live today, want to remain connected to the place.

Some Final Court House Notes

When the Argyle Municipality Historical & Genealogical Society was incorporated in 1989, I was given the honour of becoming the first President. Gordon Wood as well has served a term as President of the Society. There have been a number of Presidents since

1989. The current President, Roseanne Blades, is particularly dedicated to the development of the Society and its properties. The information given in this history on the old Methodist Church will make it clear that in 2005, some of the most ambitious aspirations for the "Court House Complex" are just now underway.

I would like to acknowledge some of the behind the scenes contributions that have been made to the Court House over the years that are easy to overlook. In 1979, a few years before Gordon Wood and I began work on the Court House restoration, Gordon was elected to Municipal Council for the Municipality of Argyle. Gordon served as the Councillor for the Tusket district from 1979-1988, and as Warden for the Municipality from 1988-1991. During all his years on Council, in his own quiet way, he played an important role in raising the appreciation for this historic landmark in Tusket. He was instrumental in leading Council to purchase and demolish a house situated between the Court House and the Church, which had become a threat to both properties.

Today Municipal Council is a strong supporter of the Court House, and demonstrates a real pride in this most important property that they own. Much of that appreciation and pride can be attributed to the quiet and steady work of Gordon Wood.

It might be appropriate here to quote James Bingay from his 1955 letter. This is what he had to say about the Court House as he remembered it from his childhood. "The finest, and by far the largest building in the village is the Courthouse. It was not so in my youth; for even then, it was approaching what men call old age; and it looked as if nothing had been done to it for years. An uninterrupted line of barn-swallows' nests adorned the north eaves, and their droppings garnished the windows below. I don't believe that the Court Room was ever cleaned, and was only swept when the judges were about to sit (usually once a year). Yet the Municipal, Provincial, and Federal elections were held in it – and elections, especially in the olden times, were not exactly prayer-meetings."

These rare views of this important building during earlier times are precious. They also serve to confirm the idea that the Court House today, in it's restored and carefully cared for state may indeed be in its finest hour. May it prosper in its present form for countless generations to come!

CHAPTER 5

CHURCHES

CHAPTER 5
CHURCHES

The Baptist Church

This old church or "meeting house", built in 1813, was Tusket's first church. It was built in the southern part of the village on a portion of the lot reserved in the original grant of Tusket for a public burying ground. It is likely that prior to its construction, the residents of the area would have gathered to worship in other buildings such as the Court House or private homes. This church was originally built as a "Proprietor's Meeting House." A Proprietor's Meeting House was built in shares by different members of a community and was subsequently owned in shares by them as well. As a rule the early meeting houses built in this manner did not affiliate themselves with any one denomination, although they did tend to be Protestant. Baptists, Congregationalists, Methodists, or any other ministers were allowed to preach there.

The Baptist Church, Tusket's first church, was built in 1813.

The Tusket Meeting house remained a "Proprietor's Meeting House" for many years before finally aligning itself with the Baptist denomination and becoming a branch of the First Baptist Church of Yarmouth, now known as "Zion."

The photograph shown here was taken around 1900-1915. The large tower and steeple were probably additions made to the building after 1839. It was a huge building, as the photograph indicates, and it sat on an elevated lot near the main road.

Early problems with the maintenance of this meeting house have left us with some valuable information on the building. In 1839 the proprietors of the Tusket Meeting House petitioned the Provincial Government concerning problems they were encountering in maintaining the church. The petition reads as follows:

> To the Honourable the House of Assembly of the Province of Nova Scotia
>
> The petition of the undersigned inhabitants of Tusket Village in the County of Yarmouth
> Respectfully sheweth
> That your petitioners are proprietors in a Meeting House in Tusket Village in which the Revd James Lent officiates stately and other ministers occasionally, that your petitioners own 22 out of the 27 pews which the said Meeting House contains, that it was built, except the ceiling and a small gallery in the year 1813 by a number of persons who were mutually interested therein, several of which

persons are since dead, and the property in such pews in said Meeting House has now become vested in the Heirs of families of such deceased original proprietors and the interest of the several owners of the said pews has now become so inconsiderable that great difficulty is experienced in procuring funds to finish or keep the said Meeting House in repair owing to the neglect or refusal of many of the owners of the said pews to pay their proportion of the expense necessary to repair, finish and ornament the said Meeting House in consequence of which the said Meeting House is in great danger of going to decay. Wherefore your petitioners respectfully solicit your Honourable House to pass an Act to authorise and impower certain persons to be chose according to the provision of the said Act to be passed, to the value thereof a proportion of the expenses which may be found necessary to repair, furnish and ornament the same, and to let or sell according to circumstances such pews for which no person shall come forward to pay the expense which the said pew shall be assessed aforesaid. And your petitioners as in duty bound, will ever pray

Argyle,
December 24th, 1839

Abram Lent
Archd Jeffrey
James Lent
David VanNorden
William Hurlburt
John Gavel Senr
Andrew Gavel
William Hatfield
James Blauvelt
Abraham Blauvelt
Gabriel VanNorden
Peter VanNorden
Edward Raynard
James Servant
John Gavel 3rd [2nd?]
Titus Hurlburt
William _____ [may be "Halstead"] Sr.
James Hatfield

The House of Assembly did indeed pass an act that allowed the proprietors of the Meeting House to assess the pews for the funds needed, and to put up for sale those pews owned by people who would not pay their share for the upkeep of the building. The list of above proprietors indicates that they came from a number of areas around Tusket as well as the village itself. Archibald Jeffrey lived in Hubbard's Point; the Gavel men in Gavelton; Edward Raynard and James Hatfield in the Tusket Falls area; and others from Raynardton. It is difficult to say how smoothly affairs progressed for the Tusket Meeting House after 1839. Perhaps not all that smoothly, for only two years, later a number of the above proprietors were involved in the building of the Gavelton Meeting House.

From the mid-1800s this was a "Calvinist" or "Regular" Baptist Meeting House or Church. Its membership declined gradually over the years, probably largely due to increased competition. In the 1840s both a Free Baptist and an Anglican Church had been built in Tusket. In 1877 a Methodist Church was built. In addition to these, several nearby communities whose residents travelled to Tusket to worship during early times built their own churches. Hence Tusket's oldest meeting house declined. In 1905, the Calvinist Baptist churches and the Free Baptist churches joined to form the United Baptist Church. When this took place, the Free Baptist Church building in the village was the one that became the home of the newly united congregation. The old Meeting House fell into disuse, and was finally taken down some time prior to 1934. A few people yet living can still remember the old building.

In a letter written around 1887, Peter Lent Hatfield gave the following details on some of the early ministers who he recalled serving the old Meeting House. During early times there was clearly no resident Baptist minister in the village. He indicates that Rev. Harris Harding of Yarmouth presided here on a fairly regular basis until about 1834, and that during some of this period Rev. Enoch Towner of Argyle also preached here. In 1834 James Lent, the son of "Squire" James Lent was ordained as a Baptist minister. He presided at this church, and lived in the community, until his death on 14 November 1850. Peter Lent Hatfield then gives the following names and dates for those Baptist ministers who followed Rev. James Lent at this church from 1850 to 1887.

Rev. James Lent, son of "Squire" James Lent.

Rev. Wm. C. Rideout from November 1850 to September 1851.
Rev. Jas. Spencer from August. 1853 to August 1854.
Anthony Martell from January 1855 to August 1856.
Jas. B. Tabor from February 1857 to February 1858.
Jos. F. Sanders three months.
Anthony Martell again from September 1858 to April 1866.
P. R. Foster from November 1869 to June 1874.
Augustus Shields from January 1875 to January 1876.
Rev. P. R. Foster again part of the time from January 1876 to September 1879.
Rev. Wm. Richan from September 1879 to January 1880.
P. S. MacGregor from June 1880 to August 1882.
"Dr. Crandall" 3 months first part of 1884.
Geo. H. Goudy from January 1885 to July 1885.
Jas. W. Tingly from July 1885 to October 1885
Jas. A. Stubbert from November 1885 and is now [1887] pastor.

The Calvinist Baptist Church owned and maintained a parsonage in the village for their ministers for a brief time, from about 1902 to 1909, in the house owned in 2005 by James and Barbara Pottier in the centre of the village.

Free Baptist Church

The meeting house for the Free Baptist Church in Tusket is said to have been built in 1840. I have been unable to document this from the records of the time. The Free Baptist Church is clearly shown on the A.F. Church map which dates from about 1866. This was the second church built in Tusket. Both it and the Calvinist Baptist Church mentioned above had their own resident ministers in the village and many of the adherents of one church would not enter the doors of the other under any circumstance.

One of the key differences in doctrine between these two Baptist denominations centred around the issue of open or closed communion. The Regular or Calvinist Baptist Church practiced closed communion, where only baptized members of the church could take communion. The Free Baptists practiced open communion where both members and non-members were able to receive communion. There were other differences between the two denominations, but this was the major bone of contention.

The Free Baptist Church, Parade Hill, the second church in Tusket, said to have been built in 1840.

One of the main organizers and establishers of Free Baptist churches in Yarmouth County was the Rev. Charles Knowles. He lived in the Arcadia area with his first wife. After her death in 1845, he married a second time to Caroline Hatfield. She was a daughter of Capt. James and Elizabeth (Lent) Hatfield of Gavelton. Several of Caroline's brothers who settled in Tusket have been mentioned elsewhere in this history – i.e. J. Adolphus, Peter Lent, Forman and Isaac S. Hatfield. It is not known what year Rev. Charles Knowles moved to Tusket, but in 1857 he purchased a lot of land and built a house in the village. For the remainder of his life he lived here, and served the Tusket Free Baptist Church as well as several others in outlying area. There were a few occasions before his death when other ministers served the Tusket church. Charles Knowles died on 18 May 1877 at the age of 69.

There was, of course, a succession of Free Baptist ministers and preachers who served this church after 1877. I have not been able to compile a very comprehensive list. Although Rev. Charles Knowles lived in Tusket, not all the ministers who followed him did, as these preachers often served a series of churches in different local communities.

A few Free Baptist ministers who served Tusket are given below. I have not been able to determine their years of service here, so have provided their birth and death dates (when available) so that readers can at least have some idea of the time in which they might have worked in the village.

Rev. William Downey (b.1834-d.1893)
Rev. Edward Sullivan – served the Tusket Free Baptist Church circa 1863-1870
Rev. William Mortimer Knollin (b.1828-d.1914)
Rev. Edwin Crowell (b.1853-d.1926)
Rev. T. H. Siddall
Rev. Joseph E. Wilson – lived at Tusket and preached there in 1905

Eventually a parsonage was acquired for the church in the village. This was the former Nathaniel E. Butler residence. The Free Baptist Church acquired this property on 20 March, 1897. After church union the United Baptist Church continued to own this property until 25 March, 1965 when it was sold to Roy and Vivian Sweeney. The property was rented out for a number of years before it was sold.

The Free Baptist Church was a handsome and imposing building built on Parade Hill. It had a large central tower with a very tall steeple. In several photographs of this church, the steeple appears to be leaning slightly backwards. This is not an illusion; it was built that way intentionally to protect the steeple from toppling over onto the firefighters should a fire ever strike the building.

In 1905 when the Free Baptist churches and Calvinist Baptist churches merged to form the United Baptist Church, it was the Free Baptist Meeting House that became the home of the newly united congregation. Fire completely destroyed the Free Baptist Church on a Sunday afternoon in 1934. The late historian, Robert B. Blauveldt, writes in 1974 that, "A magnificent mural, 'The Ascension', by the well-known artist, Jacob Lyon Blauvelt, was destroyed in the fire."

Unfortunately, the old Calvinist Baptist Meeting House had been demolished by this time, and the Baptist congregation was without a home. It seems odd that the Baptists never rebuilt in the village. In most villages around the county, when a Baptist church burned or was damaged, the congregation rallied to build anew. There may have been several reasons why this did not happen in Tusket. The enrolment of the Church was in decline at this time, and as the fire happened in the midst of the Depression, it may have been impossible for the smaller congregation to finance a new building. Some accounts state that for a time the Baptists made use of the Methodist Church building when they were able, but this seems not to have gone on for very long. There were Baptist churches in many nearby communities, such as Pleasant Lake, Gavelton and Raynardton, and perhaps some of the church members transferred to those churches.

St. Stephen's Anglican Church

St. Stephen's Anglican Church, the third church in Tusket, was built in 1843.

A number of the Loyalist settlers who arrived in Tusket at the end of the Revolutionary War were members of the Anglican Church or Church of England. In 1793 they petitioned the Anglican Bishop, requesting that a church be built in Tusket. A copy of that petition can be seen on page 21. The names of those who signed this petition, and who considered themselves Anglican in 1793 are given below.

Gabriel VanNorden	Benedict Byrn	Lewis Blanchard
James VanEmburgh	Matthias Byrn	Jacob Tooker
Nathaniel Richardson	David VanNorden	Daniel Godard
Job Hatfield	Peter Earl	Abraham M. Hatfield
Nicholas Lawrence	Abraham Sarvant	John Wood
James Blauvelt	Job Smith	John Gavel
William Colsworthy	James Hatfield	John Purdy
James Lent	Jacob Hatfield Jr.	Robert Symes
Thomas Ridgway	Isaac Decker	Jesse Gray
Jonathan Horton	Titus Hurlburt	Hugh Conner
William Halstead	John VanEmburgh	Robert King
Jacob Hatfield	Samuel Andrews	John Ackerman
David Ogden	Stephen VanNorden	James Gisnone
Cornelius VanNorden	James Sloane	George Gavel
Gilbert VanEmburgh	Gilbert Daniells	Sebastian Neall

This petition carries the names of the majority of Tusket's early settlers, and also contains the names of settlers on both sides of the Tusket River as far south as Plymouth and Morris Island and as far north as Raynardton.

Unfortunately the Anglican Church did not see fit to build a church in Tusket for some 50 years after this petition was submitted. During that long period of time some Anglicans traveled to Yarmouth, when they were able, to worship at Holy Trinity, the Anglican Church in that place. In many cases the Baptist church absorbed these families, and by the time an Anglican church was built here those families who counted themselves as Anglicans had diminished substantially.

On January 30, 1843, the lands where St. Stephen's Parish Church and the surrounding churchyard are located were conveyed by Captain Abraham L. Blauvelt and his wife to Fitz William Redding and Greggs Joseph Farish, who were Wardens of Holy Trinity Anglican Church in Yarmouth. They received the lands as representing the "Society for the Propagation of the Gospel in Foreign Parts," the Missionary body of the Church of England. St. Stephen's was always a separate Parish.

On Wednesday, June 7, 1843, the Church's cornerstone was laid with all the conventional ceremonial proceedings. The Church was consecrated on Monday, September 22, 1845, by the Rt. Rev. John Inglis, son of the first, and he himself the third Lord Bishop of Nova Scotia.

Reverend Richard Avery became the first Rector of the new parish. St. Stephen's had its own resident rectors for almost half a century. Peter Lent Hatfield of Tusket, in an 1887 document lists some of the early resident Anglican clergymen as follows:
Rev. H.M. Spike, summer of 1851 until 1853
Rev. Philip Tocque - "He moved to Barrington in 1855 and preached at Tusket and then moved to Tusket. He left in 1862," according to Peter Lent Hatfield.
Rev. J. T.T. Moody - 1862 until his death October 1864.
Rev. J. P. Sargent - 15 October 1864 - 17 October 1867.
Rev. Frederick M. M. Young - August 1868-1873
Rev. Mr. Padfield - 1874-1877
Rev. Henry Sterns - 1877-1884

In 1857 St. Stephen's Parish purchased a house lot from John V.N. Hatfield and built a rectory. The parish maintained and owned the rectory for about fifty years, or for as long as they were able to maintain a parish priest. The rectory was sold in 1906, and has since been owned by a succession of owners as a private dwelling. A parish hall was also built on the rectory property, but was afterwards sold and removed from the property. Its history and that of the rectory is dealt with elsewhere in this history.

It was economic conditions and a small congregation that made is impossible after 1906 for the parish to sustain its own resident rector, and the parishioners were forced to rely upon the somewhat irregular services of the successive rectors of Holy Trinity in Yarmouth.

In 1916, Reverend Richard Avery, priest and scholar, became Priest-in-charge and gave able and faithful service to the Parish for a period of almost 30 years; this was the longest incumbency in the history of St. Stephen's. Incidentally, he was a direct descendant of Jacob Tooker, who had been Tusket's very first pioneer.

In the history of any church, there are people who stand out as exceptional supporters of these sacred institutions. One of the most outstanding past supporters was Jacob Blauvelt of Tusket. He was a single man, and an artist, who lived and worked in the village for most of his life. For a substantial period of time he single-handedly kept St. Stephen's going when there was no permanent rector. He acted as lay reader, choir director and organist. He also spearheaded various fundraising events for the parish. At the Argyle Township Court House Archives there are copies of some of the sheet music he composed, published and then sold in order to raise funds for St. Stephen's. Jacob Blauvelt died on January 23, 1917, at the age of 70.

Rev. Gordon T. Lewis
priest-in-charge
1916 -1945

In recent decades it has been Mr. Malcolm Patterson of Tusket who has overseen the physical care of this church. He is a Church Warden and although there are very few remaining members of St. Stephen's Church, he attended faithfully to the grounds and the upkeep of the building for many years. He was instrumental as well in ensuring that this church was designated both a Municipal Heritage Property and a Provincial Heritage Property. This protects the building in some measure from future demolition or substantial exterior alteration.

This is a charming gothic style church. Services continue to be held here at least once a month during the summers, with the rector from Holy Trinity in Yarmouth conducting the services. Occasionally a concert will be held here.

The church has been altered very little over the years. Only recently has it been learned that the church originally had a spire or steeple. It was clearly taken down within the first twenty years of the building's life. With luck, the church, as it stands today, will continue for a long time. It is a charming building, and a real heritage landmark within Tusket.

The Methodist Church

The Methodist Church, the fourth Church in Tusket, was built in 1878.

The Methodist Church at Tusket was the village's fourth place of worship. The Methodist congregation was a relatively small one, even in the 1870s, and one of its leaders was Peter Lent Hatfield, a local surveyor and merchant, who would later become the Municipal Treasurer for the Municipality of Argyle. Local tradition has it that he mortgaged his own fine home in the village in order to raise some of the funds needed to construct the Methodist Church. J. Murray Lawson in his book, *Yarmouth Past and Present – A book of Reminiscences*, reports on the opening of the church in the following manner:

> The new Methodist Church at Tusket was opened for Divine worship on Sunday, February 3rd, 1878, the dedication services being conducted by Rev. James Taylor, of Shelburne, assisted by Rev. Robert Tweedie, of Arcadia, and Messrs. T. M. Lewis and R. W. Woodworth taking part. Rev. Mr. Taylor preached in the morning and Rev. John Read in the afternoon.

It was not until after the official opening that the deed for the land on which the church was built was drawn up, for it is dated 22 February 1878. The land was deeded by John M. Bingay and his wife, Mary N. The people who received the land on behalf of the church were James Langille (Tusket), R.W. Woodworth (a church official), William T. Lent (Tusket), Charles Brown (Tusket), John Benham (Tusket), Ansel Robbins and A.H. Poole (both of Arcadia) and Thomas M. Lewis and Augustus F. Stoneman (Yarmouth), all of them listed as Trustees of the church. It is curious that some of the Tusket people listed on the deed do not list themselves as Methodist in the subsequent census returns of 1881 and 1891.

In the 1891 census of the Tusket area the following families are shown as members of this church:

> Charlotte Blauvelt (wife of Sterns Blauvelt)
> Staley Crosby (son of Capt. John)
> Annie B. Blauvelt (wife of Fred) and her son Byron.
> Maria VanNorden
> Peter Lent Hatfield, his wife and children
> Dora Hatfield, wife of Lloyd
> Forman Hatfield (brother to Peter Lent) and his family
> William & Julia Hatfield

This Methodist Church, though it did grow somewhat in later years, served a relatively small congregation from its beginnings. It is interesting to note that the original church building, which was opened in 1878, probably did not much resemble the building we see today. Underneath the present roof of the building is another complete and intact roof, still covered with its wooden shingles, which do not look unduly weather-beaten. The original roof style is somewhat unusual and it is possible that the church members felt the original building did not look "church-like" enough. Regardless of the reasons, the church underwent a major refurbishment less than twenty years after its original opening. The newspaper reports of the time offer more details on that renovation than they do on the original construction.

The *Yarmouth Light* newspaper of Thursday 31 May 1894 reported on the church as follows:

> CHURCH DEDICATION AT TUSKET - The Methodist church at Tusket was formally dedicated to the service of God on Sunday the 20th inst. Rev Mr. Strothard preached in the morning and evening. The dedicatory service was conducted by Rev. W. H. Langille, chairman of the district, in the afternoon. Mr. P. L. Hatfield, one of the trustees – the others being Messrs. Forman Hatfield and William Hatfield – presented the building to the Conference on behalf of the congregation. The whole service was interesting and impressive. The church was well filled throughout the day, many of the brethren from neighbouring villages being present, Mr. Boyd, of Arcadia, took the lead in the singing, and the music was exceptionally good. The collections amounted to $40.
>
> The church is 25 x 45 feet on the ground, and is of pleasing appearance, having a spire at the north-west corner and a vestry 22 x 40 feet on the rear. The church building was commenced some twenty years ago, but the Methodist denomination being sparsely represented in the village, it was left for another generation to finish. Services have been held in the church for many years, however. About nine years ago the spire was added and a new roof put on. The vestry was added later. Recently the interior was completed, nice pews with hardwood arms and top mouldings having been built, the walls covered with a plain paper of mild tint and with a heavy border, a handsome desk placed for the preacher, two splendid chandeliers hung, the aisles and platform carpeted and the woodwork all newly painted and varnished, altogether making it an ideal village church, a credit to the denomination and an ornament to the place.

Mr. Benjamin Wyman, of Brooklyn, built the pews, etc. and Mr. Alvin Earle did the paperhanging and painting. This church is the Rev. J.E. Donkin's circuit.

Even before 1894, some improvements had been made to this building. The *Yarmouth Light,* 16 December 1890, reported that, "The Methodists have enlarged their church by the addition of a vestry at the rear. Messrs. A. Kinney, David Lamoreaux and William Hatfield doing the work." Much of this addition to the building was dismantled or demolished some 40 years later in the 1930s.

In 1925 this church became "United Church of Canada" in name, after the union of many Presbyterian, Congregational and Methodist churches, which joined to form the United Church. The Methodist and then United Church at Tusket continued to operate over the years. It was never a church with a resident pastor in the village, but was serviced by Methodist ministers from neighbouring communities.

Peter Lent Hatfield, in a document written around 1887 lists the first four ministers who served this church as follows:
> Rev. Robert Tweedy - July 1876 - July 1878
> Rev. Jas. Taylor - July 1878 - July 1880
> Rev. Byron C. Borden - July 1880 - July 1883
> Rev. P. Robinson - July 1883 - July 1886

There are still a number of former members of the old Methodist Church living in the village. Gordon Wood and Karen Sweeney both attended church and Sunday school here when they were growing up the 1940s and 1950s. Some of the families that attended during those years were Harry Hamilton's children, Grace Stewart and her children and Harvey and Rose Roddick and children, Ruth Wood, Christina (Chrissie) Hatfield (long time organist), Jessie Hatfield, Wallace and Helen Hurlburt, Andrew and Margaret Jeffery and a few others.

In 1960s the local United Church of Canada undertook the construction of Beacon United Church in the town of Yarmouth. It was a large modern church, with modern facilities including meeting rooms, an auditorium, a modern kitchen, administrative offices and more. It was designed as a church to serve as much of the County of Yarmouth as possible, and enabled the congregation to close down many of the smaller village churches. The dedication of Beacon United Church took place in June 1967. It was after this that the Tusket church was closed. At the time of its closure there were about nine regular members remaining. The building sat empty and unused for some years between 1967 and 1973. On 13 April 1973 the Maritime Conference Corporation of the Seventh-Day Adventist Church became the new owners of the Tusket building.

The Seventh Day Adventist congregation used the church building for a number of years, sometimes choosing to meet elsewhere during the winter months. Some of the people from the area who attended or were members of the Seventh-Day congregation were Vivien Sweeney, her son Murray Sweeney (both of Tusket), Leta Dukeshire and her family (Gavelton), Winona Pierce and family (Gavelton), Doug and Hazel Hicks, Gladys Goudey, Peter Muise, Margaret Nickerson, Geneva Jarvis, Beulah Farmer, Wilfred and

Helen Michaels, Mr. and Mrs. Jack Sands and others. The church was declared a Municipal Heritage Property within the Municipality of Argyle in 1991, mainly through the efforts of Wilfred and Helen Michaels, members from Yarmouth. Wilfred Michaels served the church as a lay preacher at different times. Mrs. Winona Pierce was the church member most closely involved with the sale of the church building in 2000.

A New Life for the Old Methodist Church

In 2000 the old Methodist Church building was purchased by the Argyle Municipality Historical & Genealogical Society. This organization, which was incorporated in 1989, is in charge of the administration and operation of the Argyle Township Court House, for the Municipality of Argyle. The Archives, which had operated out of the Court House since its partial restoration in 1982, had outgrown its space within the Court House, and any alterations or additions to the building were deemed inappropriate for Canada's oldest standing courthouse. The Society realized that the former church building provided them with an opportunity to preserve another important heritage building in the centre of Tusket - and to create a new home for the Archives. That this building was located immediately to the south of the Court House placed it in the ideal location.

There are not many appropriate re-uses for church buildings. Establishing the Archives in the building ensured a future use for the church and one that would not offend members of the community.

The overall plans for this project call for enhancing, while preserving, the exterior appearance of the old church building, and transforming the interior into a modern archival facility. The interior of the main body of the church building will serve as a large public research room and library. The extension on the rear of the main church, which is in poor condition, will be demolished and replaced with new construction. The present extension is only a portion of the original vestry. Much of that was demolished in the 1930s and the materials from it were used to build the home of the late Edmund LeFave on Court Street. The new extension will more closely resemble the original one which can be seen in photographs of the church taken around 1900. The ground floor of this extension will be taken up almost entirely by a fire-proof, climate-controlled vault for archival documents, photographs, maps, etc. A full basement under the extension will accommodate such things as kitchen, mechanical room, photographic darkroom, a large multi-purpose area and more. The second floor of the extension will house two offices, an area for project workers and volunteers and storage.

When the New Archives is completed, Phase II of this project calls for the development of the property between the Court House and the church into a small park with walkways connecting the two properties, benches, gardens, etc. Further restoration will be carried out in the Court House, and the space currently occupied by the Archive's office will be turned into a gift shop that can generate income for the complex.

Much of the needed funding is in place for the construction of the New Archives and restoration of the church building. Although the Society is engaged in fundraising the remainder of the funds needed, construction is expected to move forward in 2005.

This is an important and exciting project that will result in a major improvement to the centre of this most historic village, and ensure the appropriate development of the land around Canada's oldest Court House.

Sainte Anne's Catholic Church at Sainte-Anne-du-Ruisseau

Although not closely affiliated with the early history of Tusket, Sainte Anne's Catholic Church in nearby Sainte-Anne-du-Ruisseau plays an important role in the religious life of this village today. While the original settlers of Tusket were almost entirely Protestant, and the village is still often viewed by many as an Anglophone community, this is really no longer the case. Tusket today is populated largely by Acadians, and with their Catholic roots, they attend church at Sainte Anne's. This parish was founded by Rev. Father Jean Mandé Sigogne in 1799. Sainte Anne's is a massive and impressive building, built in 1900 to replace their previous church that had burned. My great-grandfather, Ambroise Pottier, mentioned earlier in this text, was master builder of this church. Jacob Blauvelt, the artist mentioned with regards to St. Stephen's Anglican Church and the Free Baptist Church in Tusket, also painted the magnificent religious pictures above the altar in this church, the "Gethsemane." The church is a major tourist attraction. Like most churches today, Sainte Anne's has experienced a decline in church attendance.

CHAPTER 6

SCHOOLS

CHAPTER 6
SCHOOLS

The history of education during the earliest decades of the 1800s in all of the communities of Yarmouth County remains somewhat obscure, mainly due to a lack of records. It is quite possible that the earliest schools in Tusket, like many other communities, were held in private homes.

A provincial government report, however, done on the state of education in the province in 1824-25 shows that there were no public schools anywhere in the Municipality of Argyle, and only two in the entire county. This report seems to have resulted in some action being taken on the part of the government, for in the late 1820s and early 1830s a number of public schools began to appear throughout Yarmouth County, including in the Municipality of Argyle.

Tusket's first public school appears to have been established around this time. In school records found at the Nova Scotia Archives, a return of various schools in the Municipality is found, usually listing the teacher's name, and the names and ages of the students. Such a list exists for 1831. The school in "Tusket Village" was known as "No. 9" and in that year Smith R. Harding taught at the school for 11 weeks and Mary VanNorden taught for 12 weeks. The students enrolled were as follows:

Jane VanNorden - 18
Stephen VanNorden - 12
P. VanNorden - 9
H. VanNorden - 4
J. Harding - 5
Phoebe Harding - 3
James Lent - 8
S. or T. Lent - 5
Jas. Jeffery - 14
M. Jeffery - 11
B. Jeffery - 8
R. Jeffery - 7
Lus? Jeffery - 7
A. Jeffery - 5

Job Williams - 10
A. Hetfield - 10
J. VanBeuren - 17
Prince Robbins - 15
Samuel Robbins - 10
Alex Black - 12
P. Amero - 12
Luis Bourque - 20
Gab. VanNorden - 5
W. Hetfield - 5
L.A. Hatfield - 7
Thos.[?] Jeffery - 7
W. or H. Earle - 14

Tusket had a public school continuously from this time until 1959.

It has been difficult to gather many details about the exact locations of the early schools in the village, although the information may exist somewhere in private hands. Dr. James H. Bingay in his 1955 letter states that he had been told that at one time there was "a small school building on Main Street, somewhere near the brook near Capt. J. V. N. Hatfield's." This would be the property owned in 2005 by Gordon and Evelyn Muise. The school in this location obviously predated Bingay's recollection.

The late Robert B. Blauveldt, historian, stated that an early school was also located on "Parade Street" in Tusket, "in the field to the south of the community hall."

J. Murray Lawson's *Yarmouth Past and Present: a Book of Reminiscences* states that in 1853, "The schoolhouse at Tusket was burned to the ground on the evening of 6 October. Incendiary." It is not known whether or not the arsonist was ever apprehended.

There was a period of some eight or nine years between this fire and the construction of the new two story substantial school that was built on Court Street. The students of Tusket may have attended school for those years in some smaller building, perhaps at one of the two locations listed above.

A brief history of Tusket written by the Women's Institute states that the large two story school on Court Street was built in the year 1861. This is probably fairly close to the year of construction. A surveyed plan of the village dated 1862 shows this lot of land as a school lot but does not indicate any building on it. However, the A.F. Church map of 1866 clearly shows the building on the lot.

This new school, built during a prosperous decade of shipbuilding in the community, was a handsome two-story building, with a cupola or belltower. It is sometimes mistaken in old photographs as the Court House, because of a similarity in style. The building was well built and served the community for some eighty years.

The "old" Tusket School served the community from the 1860s to 1949.

Every person who ever attended a village school like the old Tusket School has countless and indeed "timeless" memories of early years spent in these institutions. Many of memories are cherished – others perhaps would be better forgotten. It is impossible, of course, in a history such as this one, to tell all those stories. A very good account of "life at the Tusket School" was written by Shirley (Prosser) Margeson and published in the Winter 1993 issue of *The Argus*. She has kindly given me permission to reprint that article here. I hope that those readers who subscribe to *The Argus* will enjoy reading this account again. I know first-time readers will be as pleased as I was when I first had the pleasure to read this article. During the years that Shirley Prosser's family lived in Tusket their dwelling was the residence at the corner by the Public Well that I knew as the home of Jim and Bessie Wood.

"My Little Red School House": an article on the Tusket School in the 1930s
by Shirley (Prosser) Margeson

A unique fragment of my past is attendance at the small country school in Tusket. There, dedicated teachers opened the eyes of innumerable rural children to the world around them for the first time; and, there, the problems that were met with routine dignity and propriety, introduced us to a healthy association with village neighbours.

The school was a two-storey building, centred on a large square of land. The yard was denuded by the scampering feet of the children who had played there for countless years. Baseball, Red Light, Tag – all had taken their toll, and the west school yard was essentially hard sun-baked gravel,with an occasional tuft of dandelion or clover to break the monotony.

On the second storey were housed the students from Grade VI upward, who would be instructed by the teacher/principal. Downstairs, the younger group was taught by a second teacher. A small bell tower rose above the door, and one of the older pupils would be entrusted with the sacred duty of the ringing, at the appropriate times, and this job was coveted by just about everyone.

Recess was the most popular activity on the daily schedule, and its length was predicated on the current ambition of the teacher. When the weather was favourable the children flushed out through the double doors to pursue some vigourous activity on the "grounds." The girls enjoyed the east side where there were swings and tilting boards, while the boys usually opted to chase a ball or play horseshoes in the graveled west yard. Once everyone took skates and spent the morning skating on Roy Wood's pond, while a huge crackling outdoor fire warmed cold hands and toes.

On very stormy days all had to remain inside. If there were projects to claim our attention, we would work in the classrooms, but if our spirits were extra high, we would be ushered up to the "attic." This was considered a great privilege. The attic had one small window, no heat, and a brick chimney around which the students crowded. The space could barely contain the press of small bodies vying for a place. By the time a pupil had stood in line to go up the stairs, had made the passage, and had circled the chimney once, greeting friends, the bell would be summoning all back to the books.

The walk to school was a big part of the education experience. We were never allowed to take the shorter, "Main Road" route because of the excessive speed of the motorists who traveled there (30 mph). Instead, we trudged along the other two sides of the village triangle. Often, in the winter, only a horse and sleigh would have made a path through the snow. In the spring we walked on the side walk, which was an unusual feature for a small village. I still remember the little side trips into deep ditches and over garden walls.

When we reached the end of the first edge of the triangle, we would meet the children who were coming from Parade Hill, and all would walk along together.

My sister always wanted to tag along with me, and I wanted my freedom. Therefore, I would scoot ahead of her. This would make her cry very loudly. We called her "the radio" because I could "turn her on" merely by walking faster than she walked. Nasty child that I was! She remembers another incident that should give me shame.

For some unknown reason, our parents provided us with only one schoolbag. Into this we put our scribblers, crayons, pencils, and lunches each morning as we trudged off to school. I would always leave the house carrying it, because I was the biggest. Apparently, as soon as we passed out of sight behind the spruce and alder thicket, I would give the bag to Audrey and she would carry it until the school appeared on the horizon. Then I would retrieve it, and march into the school yard with the schoolbag in my custody. She has never recriminated me for these transgressions.

Sanitary facilities were standard for the day. Two small outhouses, surrounded by high fencing, were provided, one for each gender. The segregation incited curiosity, and some pupils would try to find knot holes in the fences that would enable a peek inside the forbidden enclosure. The fencing was of softwood, and unpainted. However, it was embellished with the graffiti of a dozen decades, and most pupils felt compelled to add small adornments of their own. All this in spite of the teacher's admonishment: Fools' names and monkeys' faces always appear in public places!

Mother always cautioned us not to use the school facilities unless it was a great necessity. Her concern for their cleanliness was well founded, and on the very few occasions that I could not refrain, I was terrified of what dire consequences might ensue.

The heating system was also standard for the thirties and consisted of a pot-bellied stove in each classroom, which had to be stoked constantly by students and teacher. Those who sat too close were unduly heated, while those who occupied seats on the perimeter of the room had to dress very warmly. There were occasions when the teacher would have everyone go to the cloakroom and get their coats from the metal pegs there, and put them on "until the fire got going well."

The Roddick family were the closest neighbours to the school building, and provided a steady infusion of little ones that needed to be educated. Their children were responsible for the task of keeping a fresh bucket of water on the ledge at the back of the classroom. Here an aluminum dipper provided access to a drink, and although the distribution system was casual, the water was always cool and delicious.

The affairs of the school were managed by a group of "trustees," and my mother was one of theses. They met at regular intervals—by lamplight, around the dining room table. There would be grave discussion, thumping of hands on the resonant wood and vocal ejaculations that ranged from whispers to screams. After the meetings, decisions would be circulated as to the "tax" to be levied so that the teachers might be paid and the other expenses met.

One might question the quality of instruction meted out at such a place, but, in retrospect, I would assess it as being remarkably good.

When I started to go to school a young man from the village, William Lent, had just returned from "Normal College" in Truro with a teacher's license. He lived near the school and only a short jaunt down the "Back Lane" would take him home. He knew the families well, and knew what to expect from the children. He used to give the beginners "horsey" rides on his foot, which he swung up and down by pivoting his right leg on his left knee.

He arranged the pupils in rows, according to the grade for which they were working, starting at the east wall. Each year the successful students would move one row west until they reached the final aisle, at which time, the great move to the upstairs classroom would occur.

Each day the beginners were given some guidance with an assignment of seat work in colouring or printing. The teacher then moved west, and repeated the performance with the next row. Today I marvel at the organization required to keep this juggling act in rhythm. Of course, those who readily completed their exercises would listen to the instruction being given to the next aisle, and no small benefit was gained from this activity.

There was always a prayer in the morning and a brief patriotic ritual. ... I pledge allegiance to the flag, and to the country for which it stands – one nation, indivisible...

We sang "O Canada" and "God save the King", but my favorite was "The Maple Leaf Forever." I like the history part of it: "In days of yore, from Britain's shore, Wolfe, the dauntless hero came and planted firm Britannia's flag on Canada's vast domain. Long may it wave...." We often discussed our country and our flag, and there was something that seized the imagination of this wee student and took her soaring on fanciful flights that would give a panoramic (although distorted) view of the whole country.

Some classes were for everyone. The students brought in cocoons and listened, spellbound, to a nature lesson on the stages in the development of a butterfly, or the building of a wasps' nest. There was a large pan of tadpoles to watch in the spring and bean seeds to examine in the fall. We planted bulbs and grated apple trees, but we never talked about "safe sex" or condoms.

There were lessons on the art treasures found in the National Gallery, and each chose a miniature which was "framed" with passé partout tape. There were singing sessions in which we learned about Stephen Foster, and Gilbert and Sullivan, and English folk songs, and Christmas carols. On Friday afternoons there might be a spelling bee, or recitations of memory work, and everyone would take part.

The Christmas Concert was an event of great moment. Every child had a part to play. The village hall would be decorated and crowded to capacity for the performance. I never was given a starring role, but remember watching my friends, Stuart, as Christopher Robin, and Douglas, as Eeyore, on a stage studded with little spruce trees. They were holding balloons into which they stuck pins – my introduction to A.A. Milne.

I was usually one of the pupils who would have to hold a cardboard letter (which we would have covered with sparkles at school) and recite a little verse. All the cardboard letters together would spell something timely such as "MERRY CHRISTMAS," AND SOMEONE WOULD INEVITABLY HOLD ONE UPSIDEDOWN. On one occasion, two little girls sang "The Maple on The Hill," and I thought it was the most elegant music I had ever heard. I could never elicit my mother's concurrence.

After one such concert, the class was divided into groups, each to write a skit of its own, to be performed on a certain Friday afternoon. Each group was given time to rehearse, and there was to be a prize. Always eager to participate, I provided the first lines for our play: "O Mother dear what shall we do. Here come the Indians!" We discussed the possibilities at length, but no one ended up with an absolute script. The play started out with promise, but degenerated into a classroom chase, which the teacher had to interrupt. Even though we had three little Indian boys in the classroom, no one seemed to be concerned with offending them.

The Indian boys always smelled of wood smoke. During the summertime they lived in a teepee on the Tusket Falls Road, but when the weather chilled, the family moved into a tarpaper shelter. They lived in our village in abject poverty, with no government assistance and very little local support.

I fell in love with Stevie. He was the oldest, tall and straight, with sleek black hair and dark brown eyes. I liked to walk to school with Stevie. He knew of a shortcut through the woods, and how to cross over a wide babbling brook without getting wet. He showed me how to make snowballs that were lethal. We dipped them into the bubbling water until they saturated, then left them to freeze on the stone wall until after school. Those snowballs were had and hurtful. Stevie was a good friend to have!

He died when he was sixteen – of tuberculosis, a disease that also claimed his sister. Two little brothers also met a sad end. One day, when they were crossing the railway trestle on their way to school, the train came before they had reached the safety of the other side. They fell into the swirling river and were drowned. I am told that their father searched and searched along the river bank to find his little ones.

The multiplication tables would be written on the board and would remain there for several weeks. Everyone would recite them together several times each day until they were thoroughly learned. When we could say them while the answers were covered with the Hershey's Chocolate Map, it was time to move to the next table.

One day I took it upon myself to assist the teacher with my wisdom. "You're stupid to write in the answers on the tables," I stated, as he was preparing the latest version. Apparently he took a dim view of my allusions to his mental prowess, and popped me over his knee for a couple smacks. I was terrified that my sister would tell our mother and that she might decide on the same treatment.

When I reached Grade II there were only two children ready for those lessons. The teacher decided to place us in Grade III, with extra work on Grade II Spelling, standard procedure for a country school.

In 1938 the children were saddened to learn that Mr. Lent was moving on and was to be replaced by Miss Green. This lady, however, soon won everyone's hearts with her Friday afternoon recitations of verses by Robert Service and by William Drummond, spoken with an assumed French accent. She often conferred with the principal, who taught up-stairs, and at recess they would both go into the cloak room and close the door. Some of the older boys peeked in through the window, and said that they were "kissing." We smaller ones were unhappy that we couldn't get up high enough to see through the window too.

Discipline never seemed to be a problem in that crowded, multi-grade classroom. There was always plenty of copy work to be done, lessons to be read, projects to be completed. Disorderly conduct never occurred until the year that I graduated to the upstairs department.

We had a "lady" principal for the first time. Matilda was her name – Matilda, the Terrible. Her offence was to scowl; her defence was to holler. The upper class boys decided that they did not like her, and they made her life quite horrible. She, in turn, vented her frustration on the classroom door, which she would slam with vicious ferocity, as a means of getting attention. It became a little game to see who could get her to perform the slam routine.

One day she executed her swing with such vigour that the hinges cracked and the door flew across the room and crashed to the floor. The incident amazed the timid and delighted the brash. Matilda dissolved into a flood of tears and ran off to her boarding house.

I was frustrated by the disorderly conduct in the upstairs classroom, and found it hard to enjoy the sessions. Then, one day, my parents told us that we were moving to the town, and we were packed up and whisked away before the apples were harvested or the gardens ploughed for winter.

My education in a country school came to an unceremonious end, and that phase of my life was over.

In 1949 a new school was built on the same property, and after it was opened the old two-story building was demolished.

The "new" three-room Tusket School built in 1949.

This "new school", though a modern building, pre-dated the local consolidation of schools by about a decade. This was never a "consolidated" school, but remained a village school throughout the years that it remained in operation.

191

Pupils of Tusket School – class of 1952

1) Charles Wood, son of Harry & Shirley 2) Gordon Wood, son of James & Bessie 3) Abel Doucet, son of Roger & Gertrude 4) Marion Amirault, daughter of Martin & Mary 5) Karen Hamilton, daughter of Harry & Velma 6) Patricia "Patty" Wood, daughter of Harry & Shirley 7) Dale Hurlburt, daughter of Wallace & Helen 8) Hubert Muise, son of John & Regina 9) Maynard Wood, son of Gerald & Mildred 10) Basil Marlyn, son of Colby & Guytha 11) Teacher 12) Paul Bourque, son of Raymond & Bernadine 13) Gerald Hurlburt, son of Wallace & Helen 14) Jerry Muise, son of Felix & Louise 15) Phyllis Nickerson, daughter of Milledge & Frances 16) Norma Lee Dulong, daughter of Norman & Helena 17) Doreen Bourque, daughter of Raymond & Bernadine 18) Cecile Muise, daughter of Henry & Antoinette 19) Joan Thibeau, daughter of Edward & Irene 20) Brenda Stewart, daughter of Foster & Grace 21) Joyce Muise, daughter of Henry & Antoinette 22) Ron Raynard, son of Alan & Naomi 23) Carl Pottier, son of Benoit & Julia 24) Raymond Bourque (twin), son of Raymond & Bernadine 25) Andrew Jeffery, son of Andy & Margaret 26) Roger Muise, son of John & Regina 27) Ross Jeffery, son of Andy & Margaret 28) Darrell Wood, son of Kenneth & Margaret 29) Roger Thibeau, son of Joe & Lizzie 30) Randolph Bourque (twin), son of Raymond & Bernadine.

The Sainte-Anne-du-Ruisseau Consolidated School, some three miles away in Sainte-Anne-du-Ruisseau was constructed and opened in 1959. At that time some of the students from the Tusket school were transferred to the new school. The minute books for the Argyle Municipal School Board show that a steady stream of requests to have students transferred from the Tusket School to the new SAR School were dealt with between 1963 and 1966. These requests probably peaked around 1966, when additions to the SAR school and new facilities there made it much more attractive to both parents and students. The final year of classes for the Tusket school was in 1968-69. Cecilia Burns of Arcadia was Principal during this last year. She is now a retired teacher and says that her two years in Tusket were the best years of her teaching career. She says: "The kids were just wonderful." It was Cecilia Burns who attended to the closure of the school at the end of the school term in June 1969.

The Tusket School, which was still a relatively new building, remained the property of the Municipality of Argyle. It sat empty and unused for a few years. Occasionally such things as the election polls were held in the building. In 1976 Municipal Council decided to transform the building into their new Municipal Offices and removed their offices from the old Court House, just down the street. The building still serves as Argyle's Municipal Offices in 2005, although it has undergone many renovations over the years.

In 1970, the SAR school became the "new" school for all remaining Tusket children, except on rare occasions when special requests were granted to attend high school in Yarmouth. A few parents of elementary students also chose to send their children to Plymouth School. The SAR school taught courses in both French and English. The SAR school closed in June 2001. In the fall of 2001, a new junior and senior French high school known as École Secondaire de Par-en-Bas was built in Tusket to provide total French education to the students of French communities (or with French parents) in the Municipality of Argyle. The teaching and other staff positions at this school account for another forty-one jobs in the community. (2005 figures) So after a gap of thirty years Tusket once again has a school in the village.

CHAPTER 7

POSTAL SERVICE

CHAPTER 7
POSTAL SERVICE

Postal service in the village of Tusket during early times was served by what was termed a "Way Office." I am not sure who was responsible for this office. Tusket obtained its first proper Post Office around 1865. An article in the *Yarmouth Tribune*, June 1, 1864, notes, "We were pleased to hear that [the] old Way Office at Tusket is at last, to be superseded by a Post Office, and that the change takes effect on the first of July next, a concession to the wants of the business people there which ought to have been made four or five years since."

Post Office, Tusket 1908.

The first Post Office was located in the southern part of the village on the property of James M. Lent (previously described on page 41). Col. James M. Lent was the first Postmaster and he held this position until his death in 1883. Although he held the official "post" it is likely that a number of family members assisted in the running of the post office. After James Lent's death, his son, Adolphus S. Lent, was appointed the new postmaster on 20 August 1883. He held the position for some thirty years, or until his own death in 1913. On 15 April 1913, Miss Cecilia P. Lent was appointed postmaster. She was a sister to Adolphus, and of course a daughter of James M. Lent. Both she and her brother Adolphus were single people. She held this position for seven years, or until her death in 1920. On 23 November 1920 her brother, Thomas K. Lent was appointed postmaster. He died prior to 1925, and was the last of the "Lent" postmasters. The Lent family ran the Tusket Post Office for a total of sixty years.

Dr. James H. Bingay writes, "In my early youth the Post Office was the daily gathering place of the youth of the community when the evening mail came in. In the daytime, I can see the postmaster, Dolph [Adolphus] Lent sitting in his chair at the open door, chewing and spitting tobacco."

On the 28 February 1925 Alfred "Fred" Babin was appointed postmaster, and the Post Office for Tusket moved to the centre of the village. It was located in a small addition on the southern side of the old W.T. Lent Store. The Post Office was located here from 1925 until about 1953.

Tusket's second Post Office ... 1925 – 1953.

The William T. Lent store at Tusket ca. 1890 – 1900. The sign on the store reads: "DRYGOODS – W.T. LENT – GROCERIES." The man standing behind the wagon is W.T. Lent. The Post Office is the "false front' addition to the left on the W.T. Lent store.

In 1952 Daniel Armstrong purchased the old Elmer Hatfield store immediately to the south of the old W. T. Lent store. A small addition was built onto the north end of Armstrong's store in 1953 and the Post Office moved into these new premises. Dr. James Bingay says in 1955, "The new Post Office is a neat little wart attached to the north side of Dan Armstrong's store." In the early 1950s, the old W.T. Lent Store was demolished.

Tusket's third Post Office ... 1953 – 1965.

The photo was taken the day I started to demolish the Elmer Hatfield store. The persons working on the roof are, left to right: my father-in-law, the late Octavien Bourque and my brother-in-law, Kenneth Bourque. The small addition in the foreground was the Post Office operated by Dan Armstrong until they moved to the new building shown in the photograph below.

Fred Babin retired as postmaster 5 December 1956. The new postmaster, Daniel Webster Armstrong, took up the job on the following day, 6 December 1956. For just over a hundred years, 1865-1960s, the Tusket Post Office was always located in premises owned by the various postmasters. In 1965 Canada Post built its own building in the village. This is a small brick-faced building, located a short distance from the main road on Court Street. Dan Armstrong was still serving as postmaster when this took place. He remained the postmaster until 1981.

The present Post Office,
built in 1965.

Pauline "Polly" Patten became the new Post Mistress in 1981 and held the position during the next five years, until her retirement in 1986. Her daughter-in-law, Joan Patten became the next Post Mistress and still holds that position today.

Many rural communities in Yarmouth County have lost their post offices over the years, and are now served by rural route delivery. Tusket's has remained, mainly because it serves a large geographic area. While most residents of the village proper have post office boxes within the building itself, several rural mail drivers also sort their mail and work out of this office. All the villages from Quinan south to Morris Island receive their mail by rural delivery through this office. Residents hope it will remain a fixture in the village for many decades to come.

CHAPTER 8

TRANSPORTATION

TRANSPORTATION

No history of any village would be complete without some reference to transportation. When the first Loyalist settlers arrived here in 1784, there was but one means of transportation, and that was by water. As the "VanTyle account" on page 7 indicates, the settlers came by boat up the Tusket River. The first homes were all built, much as we still seem to do today, facing the highway. That highway in 1784 was the Tusket River. The three oldest surviving houses in Tusket, the Abraham Lent House, the Abigail Price House and the Jacob Lyon Hatfield House, in their unique locations, all provide graphic illustrations of where the road was at that time.

The first settlers were not here for long before they began to contemplate other roadways overland that would connect them with other communities. Yarmouth had been settled in 1761, as had the community of Argyle, one on each side of Tusket. As early as 1789, when the first minutes of the Court of General Sessions are recorded, the building of roads to connect these places was a serious business. In the case of a community such as Tusket, roads were an important consideration - but so too were bridges, since one had to cross the Tusket River in order to proceed in either direction.

Bridges

The Tusket River Bridge, looking west, was constructed around 1892-93.

Prior to a first bridge over the Tusket River, the common place to reach the village from the west side was by crossing the river above the village of Plymouth, by boat in the summer and on the ice in the winter.

An Act was passed in 1796 enabling the inhabitants of Argyle and Yarmouth to build a bridge over the Tusket River, near Tusket village, the Act reads as follows:

> Whereas a bridge over the Tusket River will greatly facilitate the communication between the Townships of Yarmouth and Argyle and the adjacent county:
> First: Be it enacted by the Lieutenant Governor, Council and Assembly, that it may be lawful for the inhabitants of the said Townships to erect and establish a bridge over the said Tusket River, from Salmon Trout Point, on the east side of the said river, to Titus Hallibus [Hurlburt] the west side.
>
> Second: Provided always, that the said inhabitants of Yarmouth and Argyle shall construct and keep in repair in the most convenient situation in the said bridge, a draw-bridge of sufficient width of the passing and repassing of vessels and other boats up and down the said Tusket River.

Although the first intention of the builders was to build a drawbridge, this was not carried out. According to local historian Robert Blauveldt, the first bridge constructed was a covered bridge, as was the custom at the time.

It would be six years later, however, before the construction of a first bridge would become a reality. According to J. R. Campbell in his *History of the County of Yarmouth* (1876), "The bridge over that river was built under the direction of Col. Bond, who, under commission dated 18th May 1802, was appointed 'Commissioner for superintending and directing the expenditure of two hundred and fifty pounds, which were voted in the last sessions of the General Assembly of this Province, for to aid and assist the inhabitants of Argyle and Yarmouth to erect and complete a bridge over Tusket River.'"

This first bridge served for many years, but was eventually torn down and a second one was erected on the same site, a little south of the present bridge. Its approaches from either side of the river may still be seen today, particularly at low tide. The entrance to these first two bridges from the east side of the river would have been almost directly across from the present home of Gordon and Marlene Wood. Exiting the bridge on the west side of the river would have been slightly to the north of the Dr. Milton and Audrey O'Brien house. Somewhere in this area is where stagecoach owner, Rowland VanNorden's first house burned to the ground on December 8, 1875. James Bingay, in his 1955 letter, refers to this area as "Role's Hill" across the river ...... "I used to hear him, easily, roaring at his oxen, while ploughing on his hill beyond the bridge." The main road went over the hill and would have joined the present highway a short distance prior to the present Nova Scotia Power generating plant.

As of yet, I do not know the exact date for the construction of the second bridge. It is known however, that Captain John Murphy moved his barn from Tusket to Collins Street in Yarmouth on August 30, 1882, causing much speculation from the onlookers as to the stability and strength of the bridge under such a heavy load, but it withstood the test admirably. This probably indicates that the bridge was old enough to cause people to think it might be weakening.

The third and final bridge, to date, was constructed in 1892-93. Its only drawback is that it is a one-lane bridge and, since the advent of the automobile, the vehicle that arrives first is given the right-of-way to cross first.

My great-great grandfather, Léon Potier of Belleville, was well known for his excellent knowledge and skills regarding the construction of bridges in Yarmouth County. George S. Brown in his *History of Yarmouth: a sequel to Campbell's History*, on page 155, says "Leon Pothier, of Eel Lake, stands pre-eminent for the construction of bridges and county roads. Tusket Bridge and its approaches bear testimony to his excellent judgment and mechanical ingenuity; and often, when an alteration in a main post-road requiring more than ordinary engineering ability has been decided on, the services of Leon Pothier have been deemed essential."

Both the early roads and bridges were crude entities. They accommodated those riding on horseback and carts and other implements drawn by oxen. As the roads improved, which probably means stumps were gradually cleared, or rotted away, more sophisticated vehicles were able to make use of them.

Rowland "Role" VanNorden's Stagecoach Business

Roads did continue to improve, making communications between distant villages much more accessible. Tusket, being somewhat of a hub, created an ideal opportunity for Rowland "Role" VanNorden of Tusket to open the famous VanNorden stagecoach line. Later, his son William "Will" VanNorden joined his father in the business. Will lived next-door to his father (in the house where Roland Bourque lives in 2005), and in later years continued to operate the business from his own property. Rowland VanNorden placed a daily stage on the route between Yarmouth and Tusket on July 11, 1866. Business soon became so popular that Mr. VanNorden extended his services as far as the distant villages of Argyle and the Pubnicos along the south shore.

DAILY COACH

BETWEEN—
Yarmouth, Tusket, Eel Brook, Argyle and Pubnico.

VANNORDEN, of Tusket, thankful to the patrons who supported him last Fall and Winter in his Daily Route of Coaches between Pubnico and Yarmouth, intends now to resume

DAILY TRIPS

between the above points, viz :—Leaving Carland's, Pubnico, at 5 o'clock, a. m., changing horses at Tusket at 9 a. m., and arrive at Yarmouth at 10.30 a. m., daily. RETURN TRIP.—Leaving Yarmouth about 4 p. m., change horses at Tusket at 6, and arrive at Pubnico at 9 p. m., making the round trip (after allowing passengers about six hours in Town), in sixteen hours,—commencing Thursday morning, the 16th inst.

Small Freight taken at moderate charges. Every comfort and attention to passengers. Orders may be left at John Shehan's, Globe Hotel, Yarmouth; and John Carland's, Esq., Pubnico.

ROWLAND VANNORDEN.

Daily coach schedule: between Yarmouth, Tusket, Eel Brook, Argyle and Pubnico.

As road conditions changed with the seasons, the long rides and weather conditions often meant less than ideal comfort on the coaches, yet Mr. VanNorden's coaches were well used and appreciated; it was considered "riding in style" at the time. As difficult as it may seem for us today, to take ten hours to make a return trip from Yarmouth to Pubnico, this was a great advance for the people of that era, when compared to walking or using ox teams.

As mentioned on our walking tour of the village, Rowland VanNorden lived in the Arthur Wathen house, which was demolished in 2000. Now the new Coastal Financial Credit Union building is located on that property. Arthur Wathen's wife, Gertrude "Gertie", was Rowland VanNorden's granddaughter. It is to her that I owe a debt of gratitude for the pictures and information relating to her grandfather's famous stagecoach enterprise. Gertie lived in the old VanNorden home until 1985. Here, "Role" VanNorden had a large barn complex, well suited for his required storage space. Rowland was not a big man, but apparently had a tremendous voice and could easily be heard from a distance; a valuable asset for a stagecoach driver. He always wore a top hat. He started the stagecoach business with the smaller, locally built coach that can presently be seen in the Yarmouth Museum on Collins Street.

VanNorden's famous stagecoach, the "Deligence," built by Downing and Abbott of Concord, New Hampshire.

The coach most seniors remembered however, when I first began this history, was Rowland VanNorden's larger, second acquisition to the VanNorden coach line. It was the most luxurious coach obtainable at the time. Built by the famous Downing and Abbott Stagecoach Manufacturing Company of Concord, New Hampshire, it carried nine passengers inside, and another five or six outside.

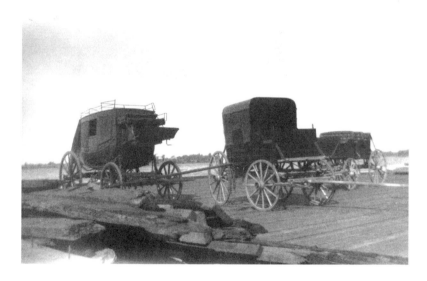

The three stagecoaches used by Rowland VanNorden, photographed here at a wharf in Yarmouth on the day the coaches were sold. The coach to the left was the famous Concord coach; fortunately, it has recently been returned to the Yarmouth County Museum in Yarmouth. The one in the centre is believed to have been built locally and was in service for many years; it is preserved in the Yarmouth County Museum. The smaller, uncovered coach on the right was used when weather permitted.

The opening of the railroad, in February 1896, dealt a severe blow to the VanNorden's stagecoach business. The Coast Railway became the preferred means of transportation and stage coaches gradually became outdated. Although the new railroad had a negative impact, Will VanNorden, Rowland's son, continued to operate the Tusket to Yarmouth route until the advent of the automobile in the early 1920s.

Catherine Farish Ray (born in 1889), a granddaughter of James M. Lent, wrote a brief account for the *Yarmouth Light* newspaper in the 1950s that has been reprinted in *The Argus* (vol.8 no.4, Winter 1996). Of the stagecoach she wrote, "My earliest recollection of travelling to Tusket was of being wrapped in a large plaid shawl and placed by my father, in the care of Mr. Will VanNorden, driver of the Yarmouth Tusket stage coach. 'Mr. Will' sang and whistled lustily all the way to Tusket; there he delivered me along with the mail bags to my uncle, Mr. A. S. Lent, Postmaster."

The Railroad

Tusket River – Railway Bridge – Tusket N.S.

The "old" steam engine approaches the bridge on its way from Yarmouth. The bridge construction was altered several years ago; it no longer has the overhead steel spans. In 1976 the railroad was dismantled; the bridge is still standing ... and rusting away.

A railroad had been in existence along the western shore of the province since 1874 and there were increasing demands to have a railroad built along the south shore as well. It would be nearly twenty years later, however, before the construction of a railroad along the south shore would begin to be realized. Ironically, it appears that two influential groups of individuals became seriously interested in constructing such a railroad at approximately the same time. One group from the Shelburne area was headed by a gentleman by the name of Thomas Robertson of Barrington Passage, and another group from the Yarmouth area was headed by a Mr. Franklin Clements.

Thomas Robertson was a member of the governing Liberal party for the Shelburne area at the time. In the summer of 1883, he became acquainted with a Mr. Leonard Atwood, also originally from Shelburne County, who had worked in the State of Maine and gained experience at constructing narrow-gauge railroads. Together, "they appear to have lost no time in forming a scheme for a local railway," according to the late Herbert Banks in an article in the *Nova Scotia Historical Review*. Being the local Liberal Member of the Legislative Assembly, Thomas Robertson attended to the local and government business; he obtained a charter from the provincial government and the right-of-ways from the various municipalities to clear the way for construction of a narrow-gauge railroad to begin.

Meanwhile, Leonard Atwood, who apparently had made very influential contacts while working in the United States, arranged to have an engineer by the name of L. H. Wheaton come and survey a route from Yarmouth to Barrington Passage. Mr. Wheaton was originally from Nova Scotia but apparently the two men had met while constructing railroads in Maine. Leonard Atwood also managed to gain the confidence of some very influential businessmen from Philadelphia to fund the capital money to build such a railroad. Herbert Banks writes that, "In the fall of 1893, a company was organized in Yarmouth, under the name of the Coast Railway Company of Nova Scotia, with Thomas Robertson as president and L. H. Wheaton as superintendent and chief engineer. The charter which Mr Robertson had obtained from the provincial government permitted the construction of a narrow-gauge line from Yarmouth to Lockport".

Mr. Frank Clements of Yarmouth meanwhile, had already successfully obtained a charter from the provincial government on April 30, 1892, to build a broad-gauge (standard) railroad from Yarmouth to Shelburne. The Act required that work proceed on this new railroad within two years of being incorporated. No right-of-ways had been purchased however, causing potential difficulties since land would have to be purchased as construction went along. It appears that Mr Frank Clements then approached L. H. Wheaton of the newly formed Coast Railway Company in an attempt to sell them his company's charter for a broad gauge railroad, "… but Wheaton, taking the advice of others, refused to deal with him. Clements and some of his friends then actively began to discourage the construction of a narrow-gauge line as less satisfactory, from a commercial standpoint, than their projected standard-gauge road." With a great deal of encouragement to build a broad-gauge railroad, Frank Clements proceeded to somehow gain the support of some large New York industrial firms as well as local support from the two highly influential Yarmouth business firms of E. K. Spinney and Parker-Eakins. A new company was quickly incorporated under the name of the South Shore Railway Company.

It appears that construction began in earnest along the proposed routes for both the narrow-gauge Coast Railway and the broad-gauge South Shore Railway in the fall of 1894 (maybe 1893). Although this was the great event of the year, it was marred by continuous arguments and disagreements as to where the railroad should pass. Naturally, most residents wanted it to pass through their villages - both as a convenience and as an economic boost. The fact that there were two railroads competing simultaneously also caused many divisions among the local people, some favouring one over the other and often forcing families to take sides.

Construction on the narrow-gauge Coast Railway was deemed much more inferior at the time, due to the lack of equipment and a large-scale work force; consequently, it was labelled in the *Halifax Herald* as "Tom Robertson's Wheelbarrow Railroad." Despite these obstacles, work progressed relatively well as far as Tusket.

Railroad construction crew

This photograph (taken by Siffroi Pottier) illustrates construction along the narrow-gauge railroad; it is believed to be somewhere in the Belleville area.

Jackson Ricker in his *Historical Sketches of Glenwood and the Argyles* indicates that construction also got underway for the broad-gauge South Shore Railway Company in the autumn of 1894. On September 28, Yarmouth saw the arrival from Baltimore of the steamer *Bowden*; it was loaded with 76 mules and horses, 35 wagons, 60 wheel scrapers, 40 carts, 3 blacksmiths' outfits, 90 sets of harnesses and 25 ploughs. There were also approximately one hundred labourers, most of whom were black labourers and Italian labourers.

J. Murray Lawson in *Yarmouth Past and Present* explains that the *Bowden* returned to the United States only to return, on Sunday, October 7, 1894, with a second load; this time it carried 110 mules, 40 wagons and gear, 40 scrapers and 15 cart bodies, all for work on the rival railway. Upon the arrival of the equipment from the United States, work was begun immediately and a large amount of grading was done between Yarmouth and Glenwood.

Herbert Banks writes that, "By 1894, a relatively violent contest began to take shape, the project soon developing into a straight political fight between a narrow-gauge line – the

Coast Railway – organized by Liberals … and a standard-gauge promotion – the South Shore Railway – which was supported by the Conservative opposition elements."

The most controversial issue, however, came to a head in the Argyle area when the survey line of the South Shore Railway crossed the proposed path of the Coast Railway. At this point the South Shore Railway refused to allow the Coast Railway to proceed past its line, their objective being that this would stop the construction of the narrow-gauge railway. But Thomas Robertson somehow managed to obtain an option to purchase the necessary land to go around the South Shore Railway at that point.

This prompted the most bitterly divisive and controversial issue during the entire construction of these two rival railroads. It became a highly political issue, with the Liberals in power at the provincial level and the Conservatives holding power in Ottawa. At this point, the South Shore Railway Company of Mr. Clements retaliated by trying to obtain a new charter from the Federal Government in Ottawa. The Coast Railway Company of Mr. Thomas Robertson sent its own representative to Ottawa to oppose this move. An investigation into the matter revealed that the South Shore Railway Company did not have sufficient funds or the necessary legal organization and were therefore denied a new charter. This decision dealt a severe blow to the South Shore Railway Company. Although the company had accomplished much work and spent large sums of money in the county, they were eventually forced into liquidation. The departure of the South Shore mules, horses, labourers, etc. took place on the 9 of May, 1895, when they boarded a special train bound for Boston. Jackson Ricker writes, "Thus ended the operations of the company whose coming had brought much hope and satisfaction to many people between Yarmouth and Lockeport."

The remnants of this abandoned broad-gauge railroad may still be traced throughout the local area to this day. In fact, part of it runs through the swamp on our own property. It was years after we built our homes here that Gordon Wood and I discovered that this old broad-gauge railway bed ran right through our properties. It was all grown in with trees, bushes and alders; after years of clearing it out, it now provides us with an excellent place to go for a walk in the woods in our own back yard.

The Coast Railway train and construction crew.

The Coast Railway Company was now clear to proceed on its own with the construction of its narrow-gauge railroad. Public sentiment, however, was strongly in favour of a broad-gauge railroad. Ultimately, it was deemed in the best interest to build a broad-gauge (standard) railroad; eventually they obtained a new charter and widened their railroad beds to provide for the construction of a broad-gauge railroad. When the provincial government granted this charter in 1901, it stipulated that this railroad was to operate from Yarmouth to Halifax, therefore, changing the name to the Halifax and Yarmouth Railway Company. It later became known as the Halifax and South Western until 1919 when it was taken over by the newly formed Canadian National Railways system.

Tusket River ... Coast Railway train stopped on bridge.

J. Murray Lawson in his history, *Yarmouth Past and Present,* writes, "The first carload of freight over the Coast Railway from Yarmouth was shipped on the 17th February, 1896, by William Law & Co. to the Tusket River Lumber Co. The first carload inwards was received by Parker, Eakins & Co. on the 21st February – a car of pine lumber – shipped by the Tusket River Lumber Co. The first excursion train over this road left Yarmouth about 10 o'clock on Friday, February 28th, 1896. It ran as far as Belleville, where it was met at the station seemingly by every resident of the place. Next day an excursion train was run into Yarmouth from Belleville, carrying about 500 persons, on the return about 300 Yarmouthians joined the party, making 800 in all."

Lawson also indicates that, "The Coast Railway was opened for traffic on Thursday, July 29th, 1897, between Yarmouth and Pubnico. The day was observed as a public holiday, the town being dressed in bunting, and the settlements along the line being decked with flags."

The railway through Tusket, which, on its early inception and operation, caused great interest, has long since fallen into the ranks of things that interest us for a time and then become commonplace. Sadly, all railway lines from the Town of Yarmouth, including the south shore rail through Tusket have become a thing of the past.

The Tusket railway station in the process of being demolished in 1976.

The Tusket railway station was demolished in July and August, 1976, and the rails themselves were removed shortly afterwards. Ironically, the railroad in this area has suffered the same fate that its predecessor, the stagecoach, endured nearly a century earlier, only this time to highway transport trucking.

The Bicycle

It may seem somewhat frivolous to mention the bicycle in the transportation history of a village such as Tusket, but some mention of this vehicle must be made. There are many sources one can go to for a full history of the bicycle, whose earliest appearance, in its most primitive form was around 1817. The 1890s however were the golden age of the bicycle - and the widespread popularity of this "new vehicle" throughout North America is easy to overlook, especially since its importance was so soon overtaken by the arrival of the automobile. In Yarmouth County, from about 1890 to 1910, the popularity of the bicycle as a new means of transportation was quite truly an amazing phenomenon. Even small villages, as remote as Kemptville, some 35 miles inland in Yarmouth County, saw dealers in this new mode of transportation establish themselves - and sales were brisk.

It is easy today for us to forget what an amazing freedom the bicycle presented. Prior to its arrival, you either "walked" or found your way from one place to another by means of horse-drawn vehicles, the ox-cart, or rode on horseback. The ability to simply climb onto this new vehicle and be able to travel wherever the roads would permit, on "your own steam" and at your own leisure must have seemed truly revolutionary at the time. What freedom! Women embraced this new invention along with the men - and although it was considered in many ways the "vehicle of the young," its impact on local life was a major one for a period of some twenty years. Able-bodied seniors in many cases also embraced this new invention.

It was during this period that my grandfather, Albanie Pottier, and Fred Babin, both originally from North Belleville, opened the "Tusket Cycle Company" in the centre of Tusket. The *Yarmouth Light*, reported on 26 April 1906, "Mr. Albani Pottier of Belleville has opened a bicycle shop in this place." They did a brisk business here for a few years. One assumes their business, like so many others, was overtaken by the arrival of the "horseless carriage."

Election Day in Tusket

The small building protruding next to the Court House bears the sign "Tusket Cycle Company" operated by Albanie Pottier and Fred Babin. Two men with bicycles are in the middle of the road.

As late as September 9, 1961, in a column in the *Yarmouth Light,* Guy C. Pelton recalled, "In the gay 90s Tusket was the favorite bicycle ride for Yarmouth bicycle parties … Just ten miles from Yarmouth it was ... not too long a bicycle ride." How times have changed!

The Automobile

The First Automobile in Nova Scotia

According to the Halifax Daily Echo, 11 September 1899, "The first automobile ever seen in Nova Scotia, arrived on the Allan liner Siberian from Liverpool [England] this morning. It is a gasoline horseless carriage, owned by William Exshaw, son-in-law of Sir Sanford Fleming. It was built in France and has been run by Mr. Exshaw since the first of the year. The propelling motor is operated by gasoline. The automobile is boxed up, but Mr. Exshaw expects to be driving it around the streets in a few days."
It seems possible that Yarmouth County, with its steamship connections to New England, may have just beaten Halifax to the finish line in claiming to have imported the first autombile. J. Murray Lawson's Yarmouth Past & Present (1902), records, "Mr. Charles W. Murphy imported a motor carriage from Boston, in June 1899. It was the first seen in Nova Scotia, and possibly in the Maritime Provinces."

Although Charles W. Murphy lived in Yarmouth, Tusket can claim some vicarious connections to this first automobile in the County. Charles Murphy had spent some of his early years in Tusket. His father, Capt. John Murphy, had married Lois Hatfield of Tusket, and they lived in the village for a number of years before moving to Yarmouth in the 1880s. Charles Murphy himself had married a Tusket girl, Mary Elvira Hatfield, a daughter of Isaac S. Hatfield and Sarah (Cochran) (Harding) Hatfield. Having family in the village, they were frequent visitors to Tusket and may well have influenced the first purchase of automobiles here.

First Cars *Sold* in Nova Scotia – 1904

William H. MacCurdy in his history of the MacKay car produced in Nova Scotia tells of the first cars in the Province. "In the spring of 1904 Archie Pelton along with Mr. Porter of Kentville, a successful businessman went to the first automobile show in New York city. Here they bought two Curved Dash Oldsmobiles and had them shipped to Nova Scotia. These were the first two cars in the province for resale. In 1904 there were 15 other cars in the Province, but these had been bought by their owners in the United States."

First Automobile in Tusket

It may be of interest to readers to know how difficult it has been trying to determine who had the first automobile in Tusket. This is a most interesting example of how history slips away from us. Several people whom I spoke to about this could not recall who the first car owner was – and yet this was information they knew thirty years ago. Such things were a common topic of discussion at places like Andy Jeffery's garage.
My friend, Gordon Wood, who was very much involved in antique cars in his younger days, recalls having been told who owned the first car in the village. He believes that it was a very early vehicle. He is quite confident that it was some time before 1910 and

thinks it may even have been steered with a "stick" instead of a steering wheel as we know vehicles today.

Freda (McGrath) Bullerwell, a granddaughter of Thomas N. McGrath, recalls that members of her family always understood that her grandfather was the owner of the first car in Tusket. Jerry Titus, a local researcher, has supplied me with the following reference from from the Yarmouth Light, May 7, 1906, "A fine large automobile came on the steamer Prince George yesterday, billed to Dickie & McGrath, Tusket." We know that Alfred Dickie lived in Stewiacke; obviously the car was meant for Thomas McGrath. The year 1906 would have been a very prosperous time for Dickie & McGrath and in turn for the McGrath family. Thomas McGrath may have started something of a family tradition, as his sons were later well-known for having the fastest cars in the village. After 1906 many cars began to appear in the village. Tracy Hatfield, one of Tusket's leading merchants, lived on the property presently (2005) owned by Margaret d'Entremont. The Yarmouth Light, 28 June 1917, reported that, "Mr. Tracey Hatfield is having a garage built. He recently purchased a Buick car."

Automobile Fever – 1907

By 1907 several newspapers around the province began to speak of the purchase of automobiles as becoming a "fever" among the population. Although by today's standard this may seem a bit of an overstatement, interest had become sufficient to prompt the Province to enact the first Motor Vehicle Law. This law came into effect April 28, 1907, and provided for "the registration of motor vehicles, the licencing of mechanics and employee-drivers as chauffeurs, and the registration of auto dealers. The one-time fee for auto registration was five dollars."By 1923 there were about 18,000 automobiles in the province. It may be of interest to the reader to note the number automobiles present in Tusket at the unveiling of the War Memorial in 1924 (see photo page 286).

The Paving of the Highway

The first paving of local highways through the rural villages in the county took place in 1936/37. In both Yarmouth Municipality and Argyle Municipality this major paving project involved paving what we know today as Highway #3, from the Yarmouth town limits, through Arcadia, Pleasant Lake and Tusket. This paving project extended all the way through the county to Lower East Pubnico at the Yarmouth-Shelburne County line. This was a government project that not only drastically improved road conditions, it provided much needed employment for the area during the Depression years.
In a number of places this project resulted in road alterations. In Tusket the major road alteration involved surveying and cutting a new more direct section of road over the top of the hill leading into the centre of the village. Previously Highway #3 "snaked" around the shoreline. What we know today as the "John White Road" was a section of Highway #3 prior to the paving project.

Before Highway #3 was paved the roadbeds were built up considerably. Deeper ditches to provide proper drainage were also made at this time, considerably changing the appearance of the roadside throughout the villages.

It was many years after this that the other road in Tusket, 308 North, was paved. This section of road began at VanCortlandt Square and passed the former railway station on its way north towards Belleville and Quinan. This paving took place in the early 1960s.

The 103 Highway

The 103 Highway was constructed through Tusket, and other local villages, in 1974-75. This was happening as the railway lines out of Yarmouth were clearly becoming a thing of the past.

In the early "tour" of the village, I mentioned how the route of the highway, for very obvious reasons, was planned to cross the Tusket River at "the Narrows." For strictly practical reasons, in terms of a new highway, this was quite a logical decision. Today we can only be grateful that opposition to such a plan saved Tusket's oldest house, which still stands today at "the Narrows."

The route that the 103 did take has had a major influence on the subsequent commercial development in Tusket. In my chapter "Tusket Thirty Years Later," I have outlined much of what has taken place since that time. Some of that has been positive in terms of the commercial viability of the village. That it has resulted in the loss of many of our older buildings and some important pieces of our local heritage will only be judged fully over a longer period of time.

What is clear, in terms of transportation, is that today the motor vehicle is supreme. During those earliest days when the first settlers arrived, the Tusket River was the only means in and out of this remote place. Roads were rapidly built, providing some communication with other places through alternate means. The rider on horseback progressed to the stagecoach - which was left behind by the railway when it came into being. The bicycle enjoyed a brief lifespan as the vehicle of choice for the able bodied. That vehicle, and the railroad as well, have now been left behind. Today the motor vehicle rules. This is especially evident in Tusket, where in recent decades the prosperity of this small village has been led by such businesses as Tusket Sales & Service (the local Ford dealership) and until recently, Tusket Toyota. How could we possibly hope to predict what the next 100 years will bring?

CHAPTER 9

HOTELS & INNS

CHAPTER 9
HOTELS & INNS

Tusket is a village that has been the home of many hotels and inns. The earliest such establishment that we have any knowledge of is an inn that was operated by Tunis Blauvelt and his wife, on the lot of land to the south of the Court House in the centre of the village. As Tunis Blauvelt was one of the original Loyalist settlers it seems likely that this was the first such establishment in the village. Even in the earliest times people who arrived by river to do business in the community needed a place to stay. As the early roads were developed these inns became even more important. Travel was slow, on horseback or on foot, and the distances between settled villages were sometimes great. Usually these early inns also sold liquor, so they were popular stopping places for the weary traveler.

As Tusket developed and roads improved, these inns became even more important. The stagecoaches stopped at these establishments, and though their passengers may not have always spent the night, usually meals were taken, and horses were refreshed and sometimes changed at these points.

"Gilman's, also known as the "American House" was a regular scheduled stagecoach stop in Tusket. The photograph is dated November 15, 1883, and shows several people waiting to board the coaches. The stagecoach to the left was owned and operated by Rowland "Role" VanNorden and is now in the Yarmouth County Museum on Collins Street, Yarmouth; it is painted red. Unfortunately, this photograph has been exposed to sunlight for too long and fading has obscured many of the details.

Shipbuilding brought many new people into the village, often in need of places to stay for a short time, if not for the duration of their work term. The Supreme Court circuit judges who presided at the Court House also required accommodations. When ship launchings took place, the village filled with outsiders. They inevitably dined at these establishments, and many probably stayed over.

Many of these inns were more on the scale of what we would term a "Bed & Breakfast" today. The owners and their families occupied much of the building while a set number of rooms were set aside for the accommodation of guests. One or two of Tusket's hotels were operated on a grander scale than this - and one - "Gilmans" or the "American House" was by all reports, the finest hostelry in Yarmouth County for at least 20 years. Its sheer size and its elegance during the peak of its operations have caused it to remain large in the imaginations of Tusket people. Many remember this building, for it was only demolished in the early 1970s after sitting vacant and abandoned for an extended period of time.

This hotel was located on the eastern side of the road leading north out of the village (Route 308 North) and sat on the same property occupied in 2005 by a seniors apartment complex known as "Nova Apartments."

This impressive hotel was built sometime between 1863 and 1869, by William H. Gilman, a native of New Hampshire. His reason for establishing himself in Tusket was clearly his wife's connections to the place. His wife, Araminta D. Gavel, was born and brought up in the community of Gavelton, to the north of Tusket. She was the daughter of John and Ann S. (Hatfield) Gavel of that community. She must have gone to the United States in the late 1850s and there, met and married William Gilman. In the 1860 U.S. census return they are found living in Rollinsford, New Hampshire. They had one child at that time, and William H. Gilman's occupation was given as "spinner." He was probably employed in a textile mill at that time. They came to Tusket a short time after this, for with the exception of their oldest two children all the others were born in Nova Scotia.

William H. Gilman

Araminta D. (Gavel) Gilman

Araminta (Gavel) Gilman's connections with the village of Tusket were strong ones, and she would have been well aware of the business opportunities here during the 1860s and 1870s when Tusket's shipyards were booming. Her mother, Ann S. (Hatfield) Gavel was a daughter of James and Elizabeth (Lent) Gavel of Gavelton. Araminta's maternal uncles and aunts were among the most prominent of Tusket's citizens during this time and have been mentioned elsewhere in this history. Some of those uncles and aunts were James Adolphus Hatfield (shipbuilder), Peter Lent Hatfield (surveyor), Isaac S. Hatfield (merchant and M.L.A.), Forman Hatfield (merchant), Caroline (Hatfield), wife of Rev. Charles Knowles and Mary (Hatfield) Bingay, wife of Dr. John M. Bingay. She was well connected to the place.

In the late 1860s William and Araminta Gilman decided to turn their home at Tusket into a hotel. They may, in fact have intended this from the beginning, for they certainly built a home much larger than their family would have required. In December, 1869, William H. Gilman announced the opening of his business with the following advertisement in the *Yarmouth Herald.*

NEW HOTEL AT TUSKET.

THE "American House," situated at Tusket, No. 4, Parade street, is ready, and will be opened on the first day of January next, for the accommodation of Travellers and permanent Boarders.

The Subscriber has very recently fitted up his House, and has spared no *pains* to make it as convenient and commodious as possible for a country Hotel, and in soliciting a share of the public patronage he does not hesitate to promise that all those who will give him a call, will not go away dissatisfied.

W. H. GILMAN.

N. B. Stabling in connection with the above establishment, and a Groom always in attendance.

W. H. G.

Tusket, Dec 23, 1869.

In the 1871 census return William Gilman lists his occupation as "house joiner," so he clearly had the skills to build this home. He may have initially continued to work as a carpenter while his wife attended to the hotel. Certainly with the shipbuilding yards nearby, there was plenty of work for carpenters. By the time of the 1881 census he refers to himself as "hotel keeper." Gilmans was a large rambling structure with many ells and attachments. If any of these attachments were later additions to a smaller original house, they had been added before 1883. One photograph, dated in that year, shows people gathered outside of Gilmans, with stagecoaches and passengers in the yard. A large sign on the left roof of the house announces this as "The American House."

Reports of the time make it clear that the "The American House" was considered the most elegant and hospitable hotel in the entire county. The interior decorations at Gilmans captured the imagination of many. Their furnishings were elegant - and a huge ballroom ensured that they were able to entertain on a scale that could not be matched by other hotels in Yarmouth at the time. Not until 1894, and the construction of the Grand

Hotel in Yarmouth, was there anything that rivalled what this hotel in Tusket had to offer. Excursions from the town of Yarmouth to stay or dine here were the rage of the day as the following account reported in the *Yarmouth Times* on February 21, 1885 testifies to:

> Milton Steam Fire Engine Company had a sleigh ride … attracting much attention as they passed through the streets. The weather was bright and pleasant, the sleighing excellent, and everyone in good spirits so that the drive to Tusket was heartily enjoyed. On arriving at Tusket, they passed through the streets of the village with band and then went on to Gilman's American House. There the company was reinforced by private teams till nearly a hundred were present, but the spacious house gave room for all, and dancing, singing, etc., was kept up till tea time. The spread was one highly credible to the host and hostess, and worthy the company. It was generally remarked that few village hotels in the province could have rivalled it. Everything was of the best quality and in abundance. After supper the band played several choice selections, calling forth many warm encomium [a formal expression of high praise]. Dancing and other amusements were carried on till about 10 o'clock, when the teams were started and came to town by torchlight. Everyone seemed to thoroughly enjoy himself, and all speak in high terms of the drive as one of the best the company has had.

Luxury, gaiety, and gentility reigned there for many years. The clientele was select, the balls and other social events dignified and definitely restricted. Many of Yarmouth's elite were frequent guests who came to be entertained. On 21 February 1885 the *Yarmouth Times* reported, "Lieut. Governor Richey, with Mrs. Richey and daughter … Friday, September 11th, 1885 … dined at Gilman's, Tusket, and were entertained at the Lorne Hotel in Yarmouth. A party of gentlemen went over to escort them into town."

The entire Gilman family was engaged in the running of this establishment and the business clearly consumed most of their energies. Araminta Gilman and all of her daughters are mentioned in various accounts for their charm and hospitality at this hotel. The Gilman children married quite late in life, or not at all, and one presumes the operation of the hotel played a part in this. The most prosperous times for this hotel, however, did not extend much beyond a period of twenty years, probably from about 1875 until 1895.

In the 1891 census William Gilman (age 59) is still listed a hotel keeper. His wife, Araminta (Gavel) was 52 years old. By this time their eldest child, John J. Gilman, who was a carpenter, was no longer living with them. He died two years later in Boston of pneumonia on 14 November, 1893. It is believed that he was still single. In 1891, still living with them were their children Emma (30), Annie (29), Mary (25), Frank (22) and Laura (20). All of these children were still single at this time, and one presumes engaged with their parents in running this large and successful establishment.

As has been indicated above, the Grand Hotel was built in Yarmouth in 1894. For the first time, The American House had serious competition. This situation was further complicated by the fact that by this time, William H. Gilman was unwell. He died at Tusket at the age of 63 on 9 April, 1896. He and his wife had journeyed to Boston to seek medical assistance, only to learn that his condition could not be treated.

It is thought that his wife, Araminta, continued to operate the American House for a time after his death. However, in the 1901 census return she lists herself as "retired" and the only other person living in the household was her daughter, Mary G. Gilman, who was 35 and single. It seems likely that Araminta Gilman and her daughter, Mary, continued to operate their hotel as best they could, but on a much diminished scale during this time period. On 17 August, 1905 the *Yarmouth Light*, reported that, "Mrs. Gilman has completed a beautiful tennis ground for the accommodation of tourists at her house." In 1912, the Yarmouth newspapers mention visitors to Tusket staying at Gilmans. Tradition has it that Supreme Court judges continued to be accommodated here up into the 1920s. Around 1925, Araminta Gilman suffered a stroke, and afterwards she lived at Yarmouth, at the home of her daughter, Annie (Gilman) Law in Milton. She died at her daughter's home at the age of 91 on May 27, 1929. Some reports during this time suggest that her unmarried daughter, Mary G. Gilman, lived in Yarmouth as well and helped care for her mother, and at other times lived in the Tusket home.

During this period, in the 1920s, the youngest daughter of the family, Laura Gilman, who had married Charles E. Cowan in the United States, returned to Tusket. The old Gilman hotel had fallen into a state of disrepair. She and her husband refurbished the old home and for a time reopened the establishment as "Cowans." This must have been for a very brief period.

Charles and Laura Cowan, with the exception of a year or two, did not live here year-round, as William Bourque of South Belleville (father of the late Nelson Burke), was engaged as the caretaker for the property when the Cowans were not present, and attended to the reopening of the property whenever they were to arrive in the spring or summer. Older residents of the village recall the impressive car driven by Mr. Cowan, a greenish coloured McLaughlin Buick.

Laura (Gilman) Cowan died at Brookline, Massachusetts on 23 September, 1932. Her obituary offers the following details on one of the last family members to try and maintain the once glorious family property in Tusket. "Mrs. Cowan's passing at her home in Brookline, Mass., on Friday morning after an illness of six months duration closes a life at the height of its usefulness. Mrs. Cowan was President of the Women's Auxiliary of the Canadian Club of Boston … The Soldiers Monument at Tusket was one of her cherished interests. In 1923 she formulated the plan, and in conjunction with friends far and near, the project was brought to a successful issue in 1924 and was formally dedicated. Mrs. Cowan was President of the Tusket War Memorial Association, and the flag at the monument was half-masted when the report of her death arrived." At the time of her death she left a brother, Dr. Frank M. Gilman of Cambridge, Massachusetts, and two sisters, Mrs. William Law and Miss Mary Gilman of Yarmouth.

Less than a year later, her unmarried sister, Mary G. Gilman died at Yarmouth, NS on 13 March, 1933. Charles E. Cowan remarried after his wife's death, but appears not to have lived in Tusket afterwards. He died in Yarmouth on 14 November, 1948.

"Gilmans" sat empty for many years. There were a few heirs to the property, but there seems to have been some dispute as to the ownership, and clearly no one in the family was willing to take on the care of the large and deteriorating home in Tusket. The obituaries for the family make it clear that the only descendants of William and Araminta Gilman were through their son, Dr. Frank M. Gilman of Massachusetts, who had one daughter.

Several Tusket residents and residents of nearby communities recall touring through "Gilmans" in its final abandoned state. In the early years white sheets covered the furniture and other fixtures which remained intact. Carol (Nickerson) Jacquard, and her sister, Phyllis (Nickerson) Hayes recall the old ballroom. The windows were "huge" allowing light to flood the room, and between the windows, mounted on the walls were half-models of ships, one presumes ships built in some of the old Tusket shipyards. Carol recalls her grandmother telling her to take note of the many items inset into the masonry of the fireplace. Included among other items were a thimble and a set of eye-glasses of Araminta (Gavel) Gilman, put there years before when the fireplace was built.

James H. Bingay in his 1955 letter writes, "And then comes Gilman's. William Gilman, the builder and owner, was a Yankee … Here he opened his noteworthy hostel, where were, at times, high jinks, where wife and daughters took adequate part. The daughters were Emma … who died young and unmarried; and Annie, who eventually married the Hon. Wm. Law, founder of the firm Wm-Law and Co… And lastly Laura, who, after certain vicissitudes, married Charlie Cowan, a retired Uranian broker, who brought her back to Tusket, and more than rehabilitated the decaying property. Laura died. Charles married again, unhappily; he died; and the place, with a disputed title, is again degenerating …"

In the *Yarmouth Light,* 9 September, 1961, Guy C. Pelton, a regular columnist and contributor to the newspaper wrote, "Time was when the Gilman House was THE high class place to eat of Yarmouth County. The Gilman girls had a lot of personality and unlimited ability. One of them became Mrs. William Law. Last year the Gilman House was for sale and I imagine still is."

Standing in a dilapidated state, Gilmans was finally torn down in 1972. I remember Gordon Wood and I, a few years before it was demolished, walking through this grand old building. It was in very poor condition by this time, roofs were leaking, windows were broken and one had to walk carefully so as not to go through the floors in some areas; even then however, one could still appreciate the magnitude and grandeur that once existed within these walls. All the intricate items were still imbedded in the large stone fireplace. The beautiful, well-constructed stonewall that was built during the time the Cowans owned on the property, fortunately, was saved. This wall was built by "François Xavier" Muise of Quinan.

In 1976 Nova Apartments, a Seniors Apartment building was constructed on this lot. The old stone wall still stands in front of the new apartment building, a reminder of Gilman's and the past.

J. L. White's "Riverside Inn"

The Riverside Inn owned and operated by John and Fannie White is presented here after Gilman's, not because it rivaled that business in its prosperity, but because its sheer size indicates that the ambitions of its owners were similar in scope. This property was located on what is now known as the "John L. White Road," a clear indication that their short time on this property, and their ambitions, captured the imagination of Tusket. This property consisted of a large main house, connected by a series of ells with barns and other outbuildings on the property. It boasted a magnificent view of the Tusket River, and was certainly an ideal location to attempt to establish a hotel.

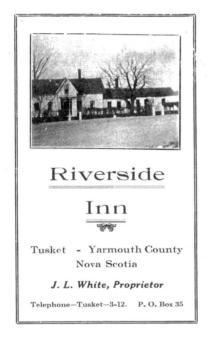

SITUATED on the banks of the charming Tusket River, just at the bend of the road as you enter the village, on the main or Provincial Highway extending around the South Shore from Yarmouth to Halifax.

Only nine miles from Yarmouth, where the train connects with steamers for Boston and New York.

Within easy access are many beautiful drives along the banks of the Tusket River with its numerous picturesque lakes, falls, wooded hills and islands, with a wealth of gorgeous scenery.

Boating, Fishing, Bathing and Camping facilities.

A delightful home for permanent or transient guests, with good home cooking. Milk, eggs and vegetables are raised on the farm.

Invigorating climate, with warm summer days and cool nights.

Special dinner parties accommodated at short notice. Telephone connection.

Rates $2.50 per day. Special rates by the week or season.

Address all requests for information to

J. L. WHITE,
Tusket, Yarmouth Co.,
Nova Scotia.

A brochure for the Riverside Inn.

This was formerly an old Hatfield property, and was purchased by John and Fannie White in the 1930s from W. Chase and Florence Hatfield, a couple that moved to Massachusetts after the closure of the Dickie & McGrath Mill. John and Fannie were an Acadian couple (surname originally "LeBlanc"), who had lived for a number of years in the U.S., where they operated a flower shop. This business failed during the Depression of the 1930s and this is one of the reasons they returned to Tusket.

They opened an inn in this large rambling house, and hoped to attract tourists to Tusket. Unfortunately the hey-day for hotels in Tusket had passed – and the business did not do very well. This was not only the Depression, but many hotel establishments in Yarmouth offered stiff competition. Their hotel here, though ambitious, never captured the imagination of the travelling public, and had a short life. John White died of cancer a relatively young man, leaving Fannie, his widow, the owner of this property. This property was not run as an inn after that time.

The Riverside Inn at "the Narrows"

Tusket's oldest house, the Abraham Lent house at "the Narrows" also operated as an inn for a short time. It too was called the "Riverside Inn", but pre-dated the above-mentioned establishment by a number of years, and had closed by the time John and Fannie White adopted the name for their hotel.

The Abraham Lent house viewed from the river. Mrs. George ("Annie") Hatfield is standing next to the Dutch door.

George A. Hatfield (son of J. Adolphus Hatfield), became the owner of the Tusket's oldest house at "the Narrows" around 1874. After his death in 1896, his widow, Annie (Churchill) Hatfield, continued to live here with her children. It was during this time period that she ran a very popular bed and breakfast style inn from the property, and called it "Riverside Inn." In 1909, a small bungalow was also built on the property to accommodate surplus guests. The *Yarmouth Light* reported on its construction on 16 May, 1907, as follows: "Mrs. Anne Hatfield is having a bungalow built in readiness for her summer boarders. It is situated near her house and the view is charming." Mrs. Annie Hatfield's "Riverside Inn" only operated for a few years after this date. The subsequent fate of this bungalow, which still exists, is discussed near the beginning of the "Walking Tour" in this history.

The Bungalow at Riverside Inn at "the Narrows" in 1908.

The house owned in recent times by the late John & Phyllis (Hatfield) Young, and owned in 2005 by their daughter, Susan Young, was another of Tusket's early inns. Israel Harding, who moved onto this property in the late 1840s, was a shoemaker and tanner, and a Justice of the Peace, and he and his wife also ran an inn from their home for many years.

Harding's Inn (The Swan Hotel)

During at least part of that time the inn was known as "The Swan." The following account reprinted in the *Argus vol.14 no.1,* from the *Yarmouth Herald,* 25 August 1859, is an example of the excellent service and fine meals offered here during the 1850s.

> Having reached the south end of the village … somewhere about dinner time … before the cheerful inn of Squire Harding … We were just in time; a splendid salmon, right from the river, had just been brought in; it was soon head and shoulders under boiling water. The salmon and a capital blueberry fungee pudding made us a hardy dinner, which, having washed down with a few glasses of the skipper's ginger pop … To any one traveling eastward I can recommend Squire Harding's pretty little inn. His horse will be well cared for, he will get a good dinner and a comfortable bed. He may have a patch put on his boot, his harness mended, or a writ for refractory debtor, should he be on a collecting

expedition; and all on the very best terms and shortest notice should he be in a hurry.

Harding's inn was a well-known stagecoach stop; the business and commercial men who operated the coaches on the south shore of the province enjoyed the warm hospitality extended to them whenever they happened to stop for a rest.

The exact period of time that this inn operated is not known, but it was probably for a period of some twenty years, from the 1850s well into the 1870s. Israel Harding died on 17 July, 1880. His, widow, Elizabeth (Flint) Harding died in 1892 at the age of 80. Their son, Smith Harding continued make this his home for a number of years, but did not operate an inn from the house.

Kilby Lodge

Another inn that was located in the southern part of the village was Kilby Lodge. This house was originally the palatial home of Irish-born Dr. Thomas Kirby, who was one of the county's leading medical practitioners during his lifetime. This was his home, and his medical offices were located here. His wife was Lydia Lent, a daughter of Rev. James Lent, and this house was built on Lent lands.

Dr. Kirby's home (later known as Kilby Lodge) on the left, looking east.

After the death of Dr. Thomas Kirby, the family members sold this large house to Mr. and Mrs. Ernest Hayes, who ran an inn from this property. The Kirbys were quite adamant that the doctor's name was not to be capitalized on, but the owners managed to find a loophole by merely modifying the name of their establishment to "Kilby Lodge," all the time complying with the imposed conditions as they were set forth. The Hayes, by all reports, ran a highly successful business here. The *Yarmouth Telegram*, 3 June, 1904, reported, "Kirby house at Tusket is being fitted as hotel by Mr. E. R. Hayes of Boston." This hotel was not operated for much more than five years by the Hayes family. The *Yarmouth Light,* 23 December 1909, reported that "Capt. George Tuffs of Gloucester,

Mass. recently purchased the Kirby house from Mrs. C. W. Hatfield." Many Tusket residents today will remember this house as the home of Alvin Trefry.

The Killam Hotel

The house that became known as "Killam Hotel" in the centre of the village was a home originally built in the mid 1850s by Benjamin Richards, and sold to Nathaniel Churchill, Jr. in 1858. Churchill was one of Tusket's prominent shipbuilders. He lived here until the decline of the shipbuilding industry, and then moved to Caledonia, in Queens County. In 1909 this property was purchased by Mr. Luther Killam, who came to Tusket from New Brunswick. The *Yarmouth Light*, 23 December 1909, reported that, "Mr. Luther Killam of New Brunswick has bought the old Churchill house owned by Mrs. Stephen Jeffery of East Boston and is having it thoroughly renovated. Mr. Killam has moved his family here." One of the earliest pieces of evidence of the arrival of the Killam family in Tusket is the inclusion of their son, Scott Killam, in the photograph of Tusket's baseball champions of 1912. (See page 321).

The Killam Hotel circa 1920s.

By 1915, when Martin Luther Killam deeded this property to his wife, Jennie (Fairweather) Killam, Jennie is identified in the deed as "hotel keeper." Her granddaughter, Phyllis K. Abell, writes in 2005, "She used the eight-bedroom house as a hotel and was the hotel keeper for over 20 years … She died in 1945." This was always known as the "Killam Hotel" during this period. Phyllis Abell also states that many people "remembered her as a kind and religious woman, who listened to church broadcasts every Sunday. She also gave food to some needy people in Tusket, sometimes feeding them in the kitchen or taking dishes to them."

The Killams eventually moved to Yarmouth. Scott Killam, a son, who lived in Yarmouth, gave me a picture taken from the front porch of this house in Tusket, showing the construction of the *Susan Cameron,* the last ship ever built in Tusket. As a boy, he remembered the event well. Since 1960, the old Killam property has been owned by Geraldine Rhyno.

W.H. Lent's "Kilby Lodge"

The Kilby Lodge house in later years. An earlier view of it is shown in the photograph on page 99 .

A few houses north of the "Killam Hotel" was a house built by the master shipwright, Benjamin Richards, this one around 1867. This was his own home. Sadly, he died in 1869, less than two years after building the house. His widow, Bethia Richards, ran a popular and prosperous hotel from this house for many years. I am not aware of her establishment having any official name. She sold the property in 1891. The *Yarmouth Light,* reported on 28 October, 1890, that, "Mrs. B. Richards has given up the hotel business here for the position of Matron of the Old Ladies Home in Yarmouth." In 1894 the house was purchased by William H. and Mary E. Lent and they may have bought the property because of its established reputation, for they too ran a hotel here. For at least a portion of the time that they ran an inn from this house, they called it "Kilby Lodge." How this name related to the other "Kilby Lodge", already dealt with in the southern part of the village remains a mystery.

The Pine Grove Hotel

The handsome home on Court Street built for Job Lyons Hatfield, served as a hotel that was advertised as the "Pine Grove Hotel" for a very brief period (perhaps a matter of months) sometime between 1874-1890, when the house was owned by Calvin Hurlbert. Malcolm Patterson, the current owner, is a direct descendant of Calvin Hurlbert. He is very knowledgeable about this property's history, and does not recall anyone in the family ever mentioning such an enterprise in relation to this house. So "Pine Grove Hotel" must have been operated for a very short period of time.

VanNorden's "Scotia Lodge"

"Scotia Lodge" was another of Tusket's inns. We know very little about it. It was owned and operated by Rowland VanNorden, or his son, William VanNorden, on the property later known at the Arthur and Gertrude Wathen property. The VanNordens operated the highly successful stagecoach line from Yarmouth to Pubnico over a period of more than three decades. One presumes that at some point in time they decided to capitalize on this situation and rather than give business to other inns in the village and established one in their own home. It seems likely that this establishment was run for only a few years, as so little has been recorded about it.

The HP Motel ... on the way to Sainte Anne-du-Ruisseau

After the closure of John and Fannie White's "The Riverside Inn", in the 1930s, and the closure of the "Killam Hotel" during the same time period, Tusket remained without a hotel or bed & breakfast of any kind for some two decades. In the early 1950s, two ambitious women, natives of New Jersey, established Tusket's only modern motel. These two women were Hilda Zellers and Mildred ("Pat") Harper.

They purchased the old Pierre Melanson house on 8 October 1952. "Hilda and Pat" became well known in the area. I remember them well; for a long time they drove a lime green Dodge car. Hilda, had silver-grey hair, always had a pleasant smile and talked to everyone. The old Melanson house remained in their possession for the next thirty years.

They were both ambitious and eager to establish a business in the village. They had the HP Motel (HP standing for "Hilda & Pat") constructed directly across from their house. This was built for them by Abel Surette, a contractor from nearby Sainte-Anne-du-Ruisseau.

Hilda Zellers (left) and "Pat" Harper, proud owners of their "new motel."

The motel was built and opened for business in 1953. It had 12 rooms or units, and these two women did a brisk business here. A separate building was hauled onto the property and became the motel's office. This building had been previously located in nearby Sainte-Anne-du-Ruisseau, just to the south of the present home of Elsie and the late Jacob LeBlanc. On its original site it had been operated as the "Beau Lac" restaurant. This building served as the HP Motel office, but was also where they served breakfast to the motel customers. They also devoted an area in the building to a display of seashells and other curiosities, and they sold shells, as well as other souvenirs.

Hilda and Pat were hard-working women, and did almost all the work connected with the motel themselves. Raymond LeBlanc, a young man who lived nearby, was hired sometimes to mow lawns, and his uncle, Charlie LeBlanc was occasionally hired to do jobs like painting. But there were no regular employees other than the owners themselves. Loretta Warner of nearby Abram's River would sometimes fill in for them on those rare occasions when both Hilda and Pat had to be away on business – but she did not work very often.

The HP Motel with the "Office and Tearoom" on the right.

The property was a well-kept and well-run establishment during the years it was owned and operated by these two women. The two of them had obviously worked at other professions prior to setting up the motel. In 1952 when they purchased this property their occupations are given as Bank Teller and Insurance Office Clerk, of Hillside New Jersey.

"Pat" Harper died in 1968. Hilda Zellers did not continue to operate the motel long after Pat's death, but she did remain living in the house across the road for a number of years. Hilda Zellers, when she became ill at the end of her life, went to New Jersey where she had family members. She died there on 14 March, 1983. Both women were real contributors to the community while they lived here and were well-liked.

Both properties eventually passed into other hands. The motel property was purchased by David Smith, and has since become the property of Wayne Smeltzer. The property has not been operated as a motel since about 1968. The motel property now consists of rental units. The former "office building" is gone.

The Plum Tree
"Bed & Breakfast"

In 2005 the Plum Tree Bed & Breakfast is the only such establishment being run in Tusket. This is owned and operated by Jill and Larry Trask. Jill is a descendant of the Tusket Hatfield family. Their property is one of Tusket's old heritage homes that has retained it original features and integrity, thanks to their thoughtful work on the property. They have operated their B&B since 1994.

CHAPTER 10

INDUSTRIES

CHAPTER 10
INDUSTRIES

The Fishing Industry on the Tusket River

The abundance of fish in the Tusket River became evident to the early settlers shortly after their arrival here in 1784. It is well documented that the Tusket River was far superior in fish stocks to any other river in Yarmouth County. Rev. Campbell for example, in his *History of Yarmouth County* published in 1876, on page 197, says "The Tusket was so full of salmon that the only way the fish could get up the river, was over each other's back" and Brown in his Sequel to Campbell (1888) on page 97, states that "the Tusket River was the natural and favourite habitat of salmon, alewives, chad, and other valuable food-fishes".

Almost immediately upon settlement in the 1780s, a fish trading commerce was established with the West Indies. We may recall Mrs. VanTyle's detailed account of their arrival to Tusket in which she ends her testimony by saying: "The River abounded with fish, salmon, and herring; and there was a large business carried on exporting them to the West Indies." Another source mentions that "the first settlers were induced to come here from the quantity of gasperaux caught in the river" (Argus, winter 2002, "A Summer-Day's Ramble"). This lucrative river fishery quickly became a major contributor to the local economy of the village.

Due to the impossibility of producing materials such as molasses, salt, sugar, and rum, trading with the West Indies became both feasible and profitable. Squire James Lent and Col. Job Hatfield seem to have been among the first to engage in the West Indies trade. Squire Lent's Fish House, which was a local landmark for more than a century, was obviously named for its role in this mercantile activity. Who captained those earliest vessels remains more obscure. According to Jerry Titus, in a 2001 issue of *The Argus,* "As early as the 1830s the brigantine *Hatfield* "was employed in the West Indies trade direct from Tusket, under the command of Capt. Blauvelt, carrying out fish and lumber and bringing back sugar, salt and molasses." The fish was pickled, dried or salted prior to shipping to the West Indies where it would be used on the slave plantations as food for the workers.

As soon as steamship service was established between Yarmouth and Boston a very profitable business of exporting salmon was realized. As early as 1859 a writer in the *Yarmouth Herald, wrote,* "I believe the salmon arrives earlier in this River [the Tusket] than in any other in North America – at least I know the earliest caught bring fabulous prices in the Boston Market – about $7,000 worth were shipped in the steamer during the spring and summer. They are too great a luxury to eat at home …"

Nearly one hundred years later, in the early 1950s, Adolphus Wood (Gordon Wood's grandfather,) was still exporting salmon to Boston.

Sport fishing on the Tusket River was also extremely popular and was highly promoted to the tourists by Tusket hotels. Rev. J.R. Campbell (page 3) has the following to say: "The Tusket River is worthy of the Tourist's time; for it is as varied and picturesque in its surroundings, as it is well known for its Trout, Salmon, and Alewive fisheries. Any one in search of the beautiful in Nature, who overlooks or despises the Tusket, with its pleasing falls and continuous, yet ever varying chain of lakes will be very likely to go further and fare worse."

The J. L. White brochure from the 1930s published within this text on page 227 boasts of the sport fishing activities on the Tusket River at that time.

Unfortunately, over-fishing and the decline of fish stock was a major concern as early as the 1860s. The following statement by J. R. Campbell in 1876 reveals that new regulations and enforcements at that time greatly enhanced the fish stock on the Tusket River for several years afterward. "There is no doubt that carelessness and other causes have very greatly injured many of the river fisheries. Under the new act of 1868, there is however a very marked improvement already. In the one article of salmon yield … in 1873 having been about 20,000 lbs."

A major decline of fish stock on the Tusket River, however, arrived with the construction of the Nova Scotia Power generating plant and dam in the Tusket Falls area in 1928-29. Although a fish ladder was installed for the salmon and other fish, it never did perform up to expectations and gradually spelled the demise of the once lucrative salmon fishery along the Tusket River. Other fish stock such as trout, cod, herring and shad eventually suffered the same fate as well.

Unlike the lobster fishery and other deep sea fishing enterprises, Tusket is a river fishing community; the village is located approximately ten miles inland from the mouth of the river and the open sea.

Harris "Pat" Gavel using a dip-net to scoop kiack on the Tusket River, 1939.

One fish species that has managed to survive to this day is the alewife. Locally, this fish has three adapted names; the English name alewife, as mentioned above; the French name *gaspereaux*; and to the Indians it was known as the *kiack*. The Indian version has prevailed and today most people refer to this fish as a kiack. The kiack fishery remains a very profitable business every spring; it has become the main source of fish bait for the lobster fishermen. It is also a good eating fresh fish, and continues to be a delicacy when smoked. The traditional method of kiack fishing has been to use a large dip-net to scoop the fish from the water. This is done at selected areas where the riverbanks are narrow and the water is shallow. Another popular method of catching kiacks is by setting nets along the river channel. It is a spectacular sight every spring during the kiack fishing season to watch the fishermen in their small boats as they pull their nets, often with lights in the dark to coincide with the tides, the lights giving a semblance of a tiny village lit up at night as the reflections often glitter upon the calm waters of the Tusket River.

Although perhaps not as prosperous as in years past, smelt fishing is still very popular on the Tusket River during the winter months whenever the ice on the river permits this fishery to take place.

Smelt fishing on the Tusket River. Shelters are used as protection against the cold winds.

In 2005 it is the kiack fishery alone that remains as a commercial entity. Many fish eaters will be aware of the term "Digby chicks." This is a common term used in the Digby, NS area to describe smoked herring. The term apparently came into use due to the fact that in early times this fish replaced chicken for Christmas dinner for many of the impoverished early settlers of that place. The late Oscar F. Nauss, first Municipal Historian for the Municipality of Argyle, in a humorous vein, used to refer to kiack as "Tusket turkey."

Although some still sport fish along the river, the catch is modest. Salmon is a thing of the past. A few smelts and frostfish are still taken. Tusket, because of its geographical location on the river is not really a lobster or deep-sea fishing community. Although various Tusket men may be employed in the lobster or other fisheries, they fish on the boats of people from other communities like Surette's Island or Sluice Point, closer to the fishing grounds.

Asa Robbins's Tannery and Shoe Making Business

Asa Robbins homestead and business enterprise, Tusket, N.S.

Left to right: the Asa Robbins house (former Harold Allen house, presently owned by Norman Pottier); the next two buildings were the shoe factory and the large tannery buildings; next is the James "Jim" and Bessie Wood house. It is quite likely that the last two buildings in the distance were the house and barn of John Murphy. Both were hauled to Yarmouth.

Another once prosperous industry in the village of Tusket that is little talked about these days was the large and prosperous tannery and shoemaking enterprise of Asa Robbins. This business was located just north of the public well, almost across from the present home of Carl and Audrey Pottier. Asa Robbins was born and raised at Chebogue Point in Yarmouth County and was a son of "Deacon" Joseph Robbins. He grew up learning how to make shoes and became a successful cobbler, also learning the leather tanning trade as well. In 1843, he realized a business opportunity in the village of Tusket and purchased the existing tannery and shoemaking business of James Sterritt at the north end of the village. This business must have been fairly new because James Sterritt lived in Tusket a very short time. Asa Robbins obviously expanded the business. He became very prosperous and prominent within the community. Records show that he owned a number of buildings in the village. He became a member of the Free Baptist Church in Tusket and served as a Deacon there for fifty years. Shipbuilding was on the rise in the village at the time and Asa Robbins quickly became affiliated with the industry. He had a large family. Several of his sons were employed in the shipyards throughout the village. Misfortunate also struck the Asa Robbins family on the high seas; four of his sons perished at sea.

Asa S. Robbins 1812-1896

Being a tanner and shoemaker by profession, Asa Robbins concentrated most of his efforts towards expanding and promoting his shoemaking and tannery business. The Heritage Inventory Site form for the Asa Robbins property states, "He supplied many ships' crews with footwear during Tusket's prosperous shipping years, and this same shipping industry opened wider markets for his work." Several workers were employed in Mr. Robbins's shoe making business, from apprentices to skilled craftsmen. It was widely known that several of the shoemakers throughout Yarmouth County and the surrounding areas had learned their trade at Asa Robbins shoe factory in Tusket. In a *Yarmouth Herald* newspaper advertisement of 1876, Mr. Robbins was promoting himself as the inventor of "Robbins Process for Tanning and Waterproofing Leather."

Asa Robbins may have sold his shoemaking business later in life. James Bingay writes in 1955, "The story of Uncle Ase's business is an epitome of the Maritimes' economic history since the decline of wooden shipbuilding in the 80's of the last century, particularly in manufacturing. Local tanneries and shoe-making establishments were bought out by big Central Canada concerns, and suppressed or transferred to Montreal or Toronto."

If this was the case with the Asa Robbins establishment, the proceeds did not make him a rich man. After his death in 1896 at the age of 84, his house and any remaining buildings were sold at a Sheriff Sale to the lumber firm of Dickie & McGrath. But during much of his life he was one of the leading businessmen in Tusket and a major employer of local people.

Shipbuilding

The history of shipbuilding in Tusket merits a book of its own. Jerry Titus of Yarmouth, NS, has compiled the most comprehensive research on the shipbuilding industry of Tusket and the surrounding areas to date. Although he will be quoted within this brief sketch as it relates to the history of this village, I strongly recommend anyone wishing to delve deeper into the local shipbuilding industry to read his complete articles as they have appeared in several issues of *The Argus*, the quarterly newsletter of the Argyle Municipality Historical & Genealogical Society. Unless otherwise stated all quotes here can be attributed to Jerry Titus.

In this history, I shall endeavour to give an overview of the industry that for over half a century produced many of the largest ships ever built in the province. This was an amazing feat and perhaps the most impressive part of the history of this small rural village. The shipbuilding industry in Tusket began gradually during the 1820s-30s. By the 1840s an increase in demand for bigger and better ships was beginning to emerge - and by the mid 1850s a trend was being established. Tusket was becoming increasingly recognized as a major shipbuilding centre - and that decade witnessed the first serious building on a large scale.

During the next three decades, the shipbuilding industry in Tusket flourished and continuously ranked among the best in the province. New shipbuilders established themselves within the village quickly acquired excellent reputations. "The shipyards in the small community of Tusket were at one time leading the province and often the Atlantic region in size and design of the great sailing ships." It is worth mentioning a few of the major shipyards and the master shipwrights who played leading roles in shaping the tremendous shipbuilding economy in this tiny village on the south western tip of Nova Scotia.

As early as the 1850s, Tusket had gained fame as a port "of wooden ships and iron men," and its shipyards were already taking the lead in turning out large vessels. "The first such ship of 1,000 tons, or more, owned by a Yarmouthian, was the *GRACE*, built by Benjamin Richards at Tusket for E. W. B. Moody and J. W. Moody in 1854." (George Brown, page 152)

From the mid 1850s into the late 1860s, Nathaniel & Enos Gardner (N. & E. Gardner) had the largest shipyard in the village, located on the west side of the main road, directly in line with VanCortland Square. The remaining slips of this shipyard are still visible at low tide to this day and are identified with the #10 on page 144. Nathaniel Gardner lived across the road in the house where Dr. Renier van Aardt presently lives and his brother, Enos Gardner, lived in the Margaret d'Entremont house. In 1863, they built the ship *N. & E. GARDNER* for Samuel Killam of Yarmouth. This was the largest ship built in Nova Scotia during the 1860s; it registered at 1,465 tons, measuring 187 feet in length and 36 feet wide. The ship saw some fifteen years of service for its owners. "On Jan. 31, 1878, the ship *N. & E. GARDNER*, with Capt. John Kinney as master, sailed from Galveston, Texas with 5299 bales of cotton. This was the largest cargo of cotton ever shipped from that place up to that time and was valued at $290,000. On the passage to Liverpool, England the ship encountered very stormy weather and sprang a leak. The cotton became saturated and by March 9, she lay on her broadside with eight feet of water in the 23-foot hold. On March 14, the crew hailed a passing steamer and abandoned ship, setting her on fire as they left, to prevent her becoming a hazard to navigation."

Unfortunately, in the late 1860s, the N. & E. Gardner firm ran into financial difficulties and were forced into receivership. Samuel Killam of Yarmouth, for whom the *N. & E. GARDNER* had been built, took over what remained of the Gardner business. Nathaniel moved to the United States. Enos remained in Tusket, was a merchant in the village, and eventually became the Municipal Clerk for the Municipality of Argyle. He was a capable manager for the Municipality, and continued in this position from 1880 until his death in 1898.

During the late 1860s, a gentleman by the name of Nathaniel Churchill Jr. moved from the village of Kemptville to Tusket (and lived in the present Geraldine Rhyno house). He came from a very influential family in his home village. He quickly established himself in the shipbuilding business and became one of the most influential shipbuilders in Tusket during the 1870s. His father, Nathaniel Churchill Sr., also moved to Tusket from Kemptville around this time. Nathaniel Sr. was one of the more prominent and prosperous citizens of Kemptville, and at one time was the owner of a sawmill there. He may well have provided much of the financing that enabled Nathaniel Jr. to establish himself as a shipbuilder. "The largest vessel built in Nova Scotia in 1870 was the *ROYAL CHARTER*, 1,247 tons. It was launched from the shipyard of Nathaniel Churchill Jr. … The *ROYAL CHARTER* was 187.6 ft. in length and 38.3 ft. in width … The ship went ashore at Anticosti Island, Quebec on May 15, 1872 and became a total wreck."

In 1873 the Nathaniel Churchill Jr. shipyard launched another ship bearing the name *ROYAL CHARTER*, this one even larger than the previous one built in 1870. It weighed in at 1,304 tons and measured 200.6 feet in length and was 38 feet wide. "The second *ROYAL CHARTER* was abandoned in the North Atlantic six years later on Oct. 29, 1879. The ship was insured for $20,000."

This thriving shipyard continued to be the leader in ship production in Tusket throughout the 1860s. By the mid 1870s, however, the new steamships cruising the oceans were rapidly replacing the wooden vessels. Nathaniel Churchill Jr. was "suffering financial losses from wrecked ships and the general decline of the industry. He was heavily in debt and was forced to sell his business holdings to clear his name." He later moved to Caledonia in Queens County.

Of all the shipyards in Tusket, perhaps the one with the longest lifespan and deserving of the most recognition is that of J. Adolphus Hatfield. This shipyard was located at the extreme southern end of the village, where we initially started our tour through the village.

Tusket village in 1869, looking north

To the immediate right, a large ship is under construction at the Adolphus Hatfield shipyard. Directly over the ship, on the hill-top at Lent's corner, one can see the house of pioneer Squire James Lent, built in 1785. A rare view of J. Lyons Hatfield's house at the entrance to his wharf complex is clearly visible in the centre of the picture.

This shipyard began operation in 1860 and had an astonishing career in the shipbuilding industry. During the next twenty-six years this shipyard averaged one ship per year; an astounding feat. Most ships required well in excess of a year to build. At least nine of the ships built at this shipyard are in the top one hundred largest ships ever built in the province. "He was no doubt the leading ship building contractor in Yarmouth County and likely the province." James Bingay indicates, "Here is where Uncle Dolph made his fortune … And then he lost it all in the flick of a pen, by endorsing notes for his wife's nephew."

J. Adolphus Hatfield
1821 - 1902

"On Sept. 18, [1872] the largest ship built in Nova Scotia up to that date was launched at Tusket. The ship *ROSSIGNOL*, 1,509 tons, was 203.6 ft. in length and 38.8 ft. in width. The ship was built by James Adolphus Hatfield under the supervision of Denis Surette … The *ROSSIGNOL* sailed for 20 years but finally went ashore at Port Greville, N.S. on Oct.1, 1892."

In 1883, the shipyard of Adolphus Hatfield built the largest ship ever built in Yarmouth County, the *FRED B. TAYLOR*. The launching of this ship was a major event in the village and I quote part of the account of the launch written in the Spring 2000, vol.12 no.1 issue of *The Argus* by Jerry Titus.

"On Tuesday 9 May 1883, many people in the town of Yarmouth stirred early and got their teams ready to make the voyage to Tusket. For on that day a historic and gala event was going to take place. The Milton brass band was going to be on hand and so was Mr. F. B. Taylor of Boston. At 9:00 a.m. several teams started. Everyone hoped the rain would hold off.

"The ways in the shipyard were greased early and there was a high tide. Shortly before 11:00 a.m. only six blocks remained under the huge vessel. Then suddenly she trembled, moved and swept majestically down the greased ways into the water, churning the blocks which remained, into splinters. The cheers could be heard at the other end of the village, where many were a little late for the grand sight.

"The new ship was christened the *FRED B. TAYLOR*. She was 236 feet long, 42 feet wide and 1799 tons register, the largest ship ever built in Yarmouth County and, at that time, the largest ship owned in Nova Scotia. It was the twelfth largest wooden sailing vessel ever built in Nova Scotia. It took 16 months to build her and cost $80,000."

In 1886, the J. Adolphus Hatfield shipyard was again the scene of another major ship launching, the *LOUISE M. FULLER*. This great ship registered 1,760 tons, 220 feet long and 41 feet wide. The master shipbuilder was the well-known Stephen Jeffery. Unfortunately, the launching of this grand ship was not a successful event.

On Saturday morning, April 17, 1886, in the presence of a large number of visitors from the town and county, the blocks were knocked away and the ship kept moving and had gone about her length when the ways broke. The ship careened to one side, then to the other, and finally slammed into the river. Her stern was in eleven feet of water and her bow was dry.

For the next three weeks a gang of men dug a trench nine feet deep under the bow and the vessel was blocked up. At high tide on May 7, the blocks were tripped, letting the bow drop into the trench and thus raising the stern. She immediately went across the river and ground on the flats. Two steam boats freed her and towed her to Yarmouth for her sails and rigging.

Before the end of the year, the glorious ship *LOUISE M. FULLER*, with all her mishaps, would meet its final fate. On Dec.1, 1886, only two days after leaving New York for Liverpool, England, she sprang a leak. After seven days of desperately trying to salvage the ship, in order to save their lives the crew abandoned the ship, and set it on fire so that it wouldn't cause a navigation problem for other ships.

The ship CHARLES built at Tusket in 1879

Other prominent shipyards were also established throughout the village. In 1879 the shipyard of John Murphy launched the eight largest ship built in the province during the 1870s, the *CHARLES*. This great ship registered at 1,500 tons and measured 211.8 feet long by 39.3 feet wide. The master shipwright was Gabriel Servant. "The ship was owned by John Murphy and his son Charles W. Murphy, for whom the ship was named." A ship's portrait of the *CHARLES* is presently owned by my friend, Gordon Wood of Tusket.

The year 1890 saw the last great ship built in Tusket launched from the shipyard of Forman Hatfield. Denis Surette of Eel Brook was the master shipwright.

Lyons wharf looking north, 1891

Viewed from the narrows, tall ships such as the JOHN Y. ROBBINS anchored at Lyons Hatfield's wharf demonstrate the prosperity of the village at the time. Mr. Lyons's house stands tall to the right of his mill next to the wharf. With the Baptist church to the right, sights such as this panoramic view along the Tusket waterfront were common.

This was the ship *J.Y. ROBBINS*. This huge ship was built for John Y. Robbins and others; it was registered at 1,708 tons, measuring 229 feet long and 42 feet wide.

"On Thursday 3 July 1890, the largest crowd ever gathered at Tusket, estimated at 2,000 people and 500 carriages, to watch the launch of this great ship … The launch of the fine ship *J.Y. ROBBINS* was a perfect success."

This grand ship, like many of her predecessors, had a short lifetime on the sea. The ship *J.Y. ROBBINS* with Capt. Charles W. Crosby, master, bound to Hakodate, Japan, went ashore in the Tsuguru Strait, seven miles from her destination, Dec.14, 1893 and became a total wreck." So she served her owners only three years.

These are but a sample of the many Tusket built ships built prior to 1900.

Although shipbuilding had clearly become a part of the past for Tusket, it took many years for the village to accept that an industry that had been so vital to its prosperity would not return. In fact, as late as 1918-19, the Tusket Shipbuilding Company undertook the task of building what was to be the very last wooden ship ever to be launched from the Tusket shipyards. One has to wonder about the reasoning behind such a venture when clearly, by this time, the glory days of wooden ships on the high seas were a thing of the past. Nevertheless, the company went ahead with the construction of a large, four masted ship. After more than two years of various setbacks; including lawsuits and bankruptcies, the *SUSAN CAMERON* set sail for New York laden with lumber on January 23, 1920, with Captain MacLean at the helm.

The *SUSAN CAMERON* was built on land just to the south of the site where the Harold

Floyd sawmill used to be located, more or less in the same location where the N. & E. Gardner shipyards had flourished some sixty years earlier. More details on the construction of this ship are offered under Floyd's Mill in the section on Lumber Mills.

After I completed my original manuscript thirty years ago, I was invited to give a presentation, in the form of slides made from old photographs of Tusket to the Yarmouth Historical Society. After my presentation, a pleasant, older gentleman with pure white hair introduced himself to me. His name was Scott Killam. He had grown up in Tusket and remembered the construction and launch of the *SUSAN CAMERON* as a boy. He was thrilled to have seen pictures of Tusket from the past. He told me that his mother had taken a picture of the ship from the front veranda of their home in Tusket while it was being constructed. After seeing my presentation he wanted me to have the picture. I still cherish it to this day and it is shown below.

The ship SUSAN CAMERON under construction at Tusket. Photograph was taken on October 18, 1918, from the Killam Hotel. The Floyd Mill (with chimney stack) is visible in the background

The two following photographs have since been added to the Archives collection at the Tusket courthouse and I offer them below. They are the only pictures available to date that illustrate a wooden ship under construction in the village.

The SUSAN CAMERON under construction. The chimney stack from the lumber mill on the far side of the ship is seen in the centre. The Bernard Hurlert house is visible to the far right.

The SUSAN CAMERON in the stocks, near completion.

The Master Shipwrights

The successful operation of the shipyards of Tusket depended a great deal on the master shipbuilder (or master shipwright). A master builder would have been equivalent to a superintendent on a large construction project today. Throughout my research, it became obvious that a good deal of competition existed between the shipyard owners, each of them trying to hire the best master shipwrights available. It is interesting to note that most times the master shipbuilder is mentioned along with the name of the shipyard owner, an indication of their importance in the productivity of the shipyard. Certain master shipbuilders' names appear frequently enough that they deserve a special mention here.

Benjamin Richards: During the early boom days of the shipbuilding industry in Tusket, Benjamin Richards was one of its leading architects. "He had been building vessels at Tusket since 1854 and previous to that he had built vessels at Eel Brook and at Yarmouth. In 1857 he joined the company of William S. Robbins as master shipbuilder …" In 1864 he joined the shipyard firm of Nathaniel Churchill Jr. as master shipbuilder. His name is frequently mentioned as one of the most accomplished builders during his time. After his death, he was replaced in the Nathaniel Churchill Jr. shipyard by Donald Ross.

Donald Ross: The name Donald Ross stands out among the top master shipwrights of his time. He was "a celebrated naval architect, who had gone into private business." His distinguished naval engineering background and training obviously was a great asset to the Tusket shipyards. Prior to his arrival in Tusket, Donald Ross had worked in Meteghan, and prior to that in Saint John, New Brunswick. He obviously contributed largely to the successful operations of Nathaniel Churchill Junior's shipyard, where it appears most of his working life in Tusket was spent. He was also the master shipwright during the construction of the ship *N. & E. GARDNER.* "Mr. Ross built ten large vessels at Tusket during his career then retired from shipping. He died at his home in Yarmouth on 28 July 1890, in his 69th year."

Donald Ross likely rented the house where Ruth Wood has lived in recent years. Since this is the only Ross family known to have lived in Tusket, it is likely that Donald Ross was the father of Charles Sarsfield Ross whom I mentioned earlier as having written a popular Mother's Day poem.

Denis Surette: Another master shipwright in high demand was Denis Surette from the nearby community of Eel Brook (now Sainte-Anne-du-Ruisseau). His name often appears as master shipbuilder for James Adolphus Hatfield who operated the largest shipyard at the southern end of the village.

Denis Surette
1826 -1897

"Denis Surette had a long career in shipbuilding, covering three decades … He was master builder of at least four large three-masted ships at Tusket." He spent some time working in the Boston area, returning home after a serious work accident. Denis Surette is probably best remembered as master shipwright for the record setting ship *ROSSIGNOL* in 1872. He also has the distinction of being master shipwright for the last of the great ships to be built at Tusket, the *J. Y. ROBBINS* in 1890.

Stephen Jeffery: Another master shipwright worthy of mentioning was Stephen Jeffrey. He worked as a master shipbuilder in various shipyards for approximately twenty years in Tusket. "In 1886 he was the master builder for the great ship *LOUISE M. FULLER* built at the famous J. Adolphus Hatfield shipyard. He had worked in the different shipyards in Tusket since 1867. He had a long career in the shipbuilding business." He lived in Hubbard's point on what is known as the "Back Road."

The Common Carpenter & Labourer

Besides the shipyard owners and the master shipwrights, there were also the often forgotten common workers who contributed so much and deserve to be mentioned. Jerry Titus, in his accounts of the local shipbuilding industry sums it up in this way: "One final note about these builders of wooden ships. Most of the financing came from Yarmouth town and overseas, but the greatest part of the labour was supplied by the workmen and skilful shipwrights of the Acadian people of Argyle Township. A credit to their skill and ability, in all of the hundreds of men and thousands of hours spent putting these ships together …"

The End of an Era

"By the end of the 1880s the shipbuilding industry was in its final days; the shipyards in Tusket lay in silence."

Although several factors played a role in the decline and ultimately the end of the tall ships, probably the most significant factor was the advent of iron and steel ships powered by steam. The industry which had for so many years been the mainstay of life in Tusket suddenly became history.

As has been mentioned above, the last ship built in the village was the *SUSAN CAMERON,* completed in 1919, after many years with no vessels being built in the village at all. Although this was a significant event at the time, its impact for the village probably lies more in the establishment of "Floyd's Mill" which continued for many years afterward. It will be discussed more fully under "Sawmills."

That wooden shipbuilding should come to an end in Tusket was inevitable. When steel ships and steam-powered vessels replaced the older technology, locations such as Tusket were left behind. The village geographically was not located near any of the raw materials needed to sustain such an industry. When the wooden ship was supreme Tusket was in the ideal location. Located on the Tusket River, timber and lumber could be rafted down the river from the inland communities. Villages such as Kemptville, some thirty five miles inland, and many other communities along the river were able to prosper as well, supplying the hungry Tusket shipyards with their needed materials.

Tusket, in its time, was one of the most important shipbuilding centres in the entire province. It is a part of our history that we can all take pride in.

Lumber Mills

Sawmills and the lumber industry have had an important role in Tusket's history. In the early years of Tusket's settlement, I have found no indication that sawmills of any size existed within the village proper. The sawmills which supplied the lumber that built Tusket's early homes were probably located in communities to the north, namely at Gavelton and Tusket Falls. The "falls" located in those communities made them a natural choice for the location of the very first mills. Although small mills may have existed within the village in its early history they appear not to have been very large enterprises. In the early years of shipbuilding in the village, it is quite possible that temporary mills were set up in different shipyards to take care of their own needs.

The Job Lyons Hatfield Mill

The Job Lyons Hatfield mill appears to have been the earliest mill of any size in the village. "Lyons" inherited the extensive property of his father, John V.N. Hatfield, in the southern part of the village. John V.N. Hatfield had been one of the leading mercantile figures in the village during his time. He was involved in shipbuilding, was a merchant, and developed an extensive commercial property along the banks of the Tusket River. He established a store there, and also the most extensive wharf in the village, built well out into the channel of the river. This extensive wharf is shown clearly on the surveyed plan of Tusket drawn by Peter Lent Hatfield and dated 1862. Even today the rotted pilings of this wharf remain visible in the river. By 1862 this would have been Job Lyons Hatfield's property. On the riverbank, located near the wharf, Lyons built a house, continued to operate his father's former store, and also built a saw-mill. He too was heavily involved at different times in shipbuilding and owned shares in a number of vessels.

Looking north at the large wharf complex of Job Lyons Hatfield. His house was near the road and his lumber mill was adjacent to the house.

Exactly when Lyons built his sawmill remains somewhat unclear. The A.F. Church Map of 1866 shows no mill here at that time. Yet, in 1880, Lyon's mill is referred to as the "Old Mill" clearly suggesting that it pre-dated that of Andrew Mack built in 1871. Also in the Industrial Returns of Tusket in the 1871 census return, no sawmills are enumerated. It is possible that Lyons Mill existed at this time but was not in operation.

This was an ideal location for a mill in many ways, for the extensive wharves meant that vessels up to about 500 tons could anchor here and load lumber. This mill, like so many others, eventually burned - and there are no family members to question about this man's enterprises. Some mentions of the business in local newspapers provide us with the little knowledge we have of this business, so I will offer that information here.

Looking southeast towards Lyons' wharf, 1908. A three-masted vessel is tied up at the wharf loading lumber.

Yarmouth Herald, 4 March 1880 - "Nothing as yet has been done towards the erection of a new sawmill to replace the old one burned [this refers to Mack's Mill]. The 'Old Mill', adjacent to the store of J. Lyons Hatfield is however, occasionally in operation."

Yarmouth Herald, 29 April 1880 - "J. Lyons Hatfield has contracted with Burrell-Johnson to construct a boiler to drive his steam sawmill, planning and gristmill. It is expected the mill will be in operation in a few weeks."

Yarmouth Herald, 3 March 1881 - "The mill of J. Lyons Hatfield is almost in daily operation and considerable amounts of logs are being brought in for future use."

Yarmouth Herald, 28 July 1881 - "The steam mill of J. Lyons Hatfield is almost constantly running."

Yarmouth Herald, 4 January 1883 - "The mill of J.L. Hatfield Esq., is now confined chiefly to sawing barrel staves. J.H. Porter & Co. of Tusket Wedge is buying all the mill can make."

Yarmouth Herald, 15 April 1885 - "Tusket: There has been an extensive addition to the wharf of J. Lyons Hatfield, in the rear of his steam mill."

Yarmouth Herald, 5 January 1887, "Tusket: J. Lyons Hatfield has put in a new boiler double the size of the old one at a cost of $1000. It was manufactured by the Burrell-Johnson Iron Co. He has also put in a lath machine and a matcher. This year he expects to double his cut of laths, which will be shipped to U.S. markets. This year he shipped 480,000 feet of scantling and lumber for $3360 and 27,000 laths for $27.

Yarmouth Herald, 20 August 1890 - "The valuable steam mill at Tusket owned by J. Lyons Hatfield was destroyed by fire on Saturday night. Mr. Hatfield left the mill about 9:00 P.M. and everything was all right. About an hour later the mill was discovered on fire. It is thought the fire started in the boiler room. The loss is about $6000. There was no insurance."

A good deal of the machinery must have survived this fire, as J. Lyon Hatfield obviously rebuilt within the year.

Yarmouth Herald, 30 September 1891 - "Hatfield's saw mill is operating again and its whistle is the only sound, which breaks the monotony of this place."

Only two years later fire took more than the mill on this property, J. Murray Lawson in his book, *Yarmouth Past & Present*, reports as follows:

> 1893 - The combined dwelling house and store of J. Lyons Hatfield, Tusket, were destroyed by fire on Tuesday night, November 7th. Mr. Hatfield was alone in the house – his wife being in the States – and was awakened about 11:30 by the smoke, which filled his room. The flames spread so rapidly that he could only save two of the books in the safe and the horse in the barn, which was connected with the house. None of the furniture was saved. The building and stock were insured for $3800 in the Imperial and Union Offices. A flour store on the opposite side of the passage way on the wharf, only a few feet distant, was saved with difficulty.

This fire marked the end of Lyons Hatfield's business activities in Tusket. By this time he was just over 60 years of age. He and wife purchased a home in the Town of Yarmouth, and spent their last years there. He died in 1916.

The Mack Mill

The 1871 census return for Yarmouth County, as has been stated previously, enumerated of the business establishments in the county in April of 1871. At that time the largest sawmill in the county was located at Kemptville. A few months later that would change. Probably the largest sawmill ever established in Yarmouth County up to that time was built at Tusket in the same year.

The *Yarmouth Tribune*, 19 July 1871, reported, "Andrew Mack, formerly of Bear River, has recently purchased the old mill site at Gavel Falls, Tusket River, and raised a mill 85 feet long, 47 feet wide and three stories high in which he intends to run a gang saw."

This report seems to be somewhat erroneous. It seems unlikely that Mack really did any building at "Gavel Falls." Or if he did, he must have dismantled the entire building and moved it to Tusket only a short time later. The site where his mill went up was in the village of Tusket proper, on the property that is later better remembered as the site of the "Dickie & McGrath Mill." Today the home of Hubert and Phyllis Pothier occupies much of the former mill property.

J. R. Campbell in his *History of Yarmouth*, (1876), page 193, states: "the double gang steam mill at Tusket, owned by Andrew Mack & Co., deserves mention. This mill, together with the timber lands, cost upwards of fifty thousand dollars; and is capable of producing annually about six million feet of lumber." The Mack Mill was established at a time when large ships were still being built in Tusket, but the mill was obviously established to export lumber as well. The Yarmouth newspapers record in June 1874 that a cargo of deals (a trade name for sawn fir timber) was shipped to England by Andrew Mack & Co., of Tusket. These were shipped on the *ACADIAN* and were the first shipment of deals to leave Tusket.

On July 10, 1876, according to Yarmouth newspapers, a boarding house connected with this company's steam mill was engulfed in flames. There is no question that Andrew Mack's mill was a large enterprise, the largest piece of evidence for that, which survived for many years, was the huge eighty-foot chimney that had been constructed in connection with the property. Unfortunately Andrew Mack's business did not enjoy a long life

Constructing the eighty-foot lumber mill chimney, Tusket, N.S.

The huge eighty-foot brick chimney, surrounded by staging, is nearing completion; workers are visible on top. It remains unclear if the photograph was taken at the time of original construction or during the rebuilding process after the first one fell down. Ownership of the mill at the time this picture was taken is not clear, although most sources indicate it was likely the Andrew Mack & Company mill.

In November 1877, Andrew Mack retired from the company. He was a native of Queen's County but lived in Yarmouth for several years, and he died September 4, 1894. After November 1877 the remaining partners continued to operate the lumber mill under the new name of N.W. Blethen & Company, Mr. Blethen being one of the partners in the former business. During the next few years this company appears to have been plagued by major disasters and did not survive long. On June 28, 1878, a fire in the mill house caused a considerable amount of damage. Two months later, the huge 80-foot high chimney fell down. The following account appeared in the *Yarmouth Herald*, on September 5: "About 4:00 P.M. last Thursday the lining of the steam chimney of Blethen & Co.'s saw mill at Tusket tumbled down, bursting the chimney, 80 feet high, which fell in the direction of the river and across the engine and boiler house, cutting through the roof of the latter and setting the building on fire. Two men, Norman Earle of Riverdale and Daniel Bristow of Yarmouth were severely injured. The damage to the mill is estimated to be $3000. There is insurance. Had the chimney fallen in the opposite direction, where most of the men were working, the consequences would have been very serious." The chimney was immediately rebuilt and the Blethen & Co. lumber mill showed tremendous growth over a short period of time. During the winter of 1878-79 the mill underwent a major overhaul and among other improvements the *Yarmouth Herald* reported that, "a new rotary mill was added." Approximately 100 men were employed in the woods cutting lumber and another 80 men worked on the river drive in the spring. The same newspaper also reported, "N.W. Blethen & Co.'s drive containing 4 to 5 million feet of logs arrived at Tusket on June 2nd after one of the best runs they ever had." Another million feet of dry lumber sat ready for shipment in the lumberyard.

The glory days of this prosperous mill, however, would be short lived. J. Murray Lawson writes that on September 9, 1879, "The extensive steam saw mill at Tusket, owned by N.W. Blethen & Co., of Yarmouth, was totally destroyed by fire … together with about a million and a half feet of lumber … origin of the fire unknown." This dealt the fatal blow to the N.W. Blethen & Co. lumber mill. The following March, in 1880, the *Yarmouth Herald* reported: "Nothing as yet has been done towards the erection of a new sawmill to replace the one burned."

In September 1880, the entire mill site and timberlands were sold to an American firm from Colorado.

James H. Bingay, who was born in 1878, had the following to say about this mill property in his youth: "In my young days, it [the mill property] was all desolation, as it is today, except for a big 80' chimney, which you must remember. It belonged to a mill before my time, called 'Mack's Mill.' Who 'Mack' was (perhaps the word is 'Mac' something), I don't know."

Although Bingay makes it clear that nothing remained on this property but the large chimney by about 1884-85, in 1891 and 1892 the entire property was purchased by parties who intended to establish a new sawmill on the old site.

Tusket River Lumber Company

Yarmouth Light, 9 June 1891 - "A new company to be called the Tusket River Lumber Co. has applied for incorporation. The company will carry on lumbering, general trading and shipbuilding at Tusket. Composed of John C. Blackadar, Albert Blackadar, E. E. Archibald, David Wetmore, E. K. Spinney, John H. Mahon, J. Archibald Blackadar and Joseph N. Lane." Another prominent figure with this company was Nathaniel Ellenwood Butler. His name is not mentioned among the initial owners, but it is believed he soon joined and became one the leading men in this business.

The book *Butlers and Kinsfolk* states that in1892 a prominent businessman from Weymouth, in Digby County, by the name of Nathaniel E. Butler "with others he formed a company and incorporated as the Tusket River Lumber Company, buying a mill site at Tusket and 15,000 acres of timberland on the Tusket and its tributaries. He opened a general store at Tusket in connection with the mill business, sold his Weymouth farm and built a home in Tusket." This is the same Nathaniel Butler who we find as having built the house that Vivien and Roy Sweeney's son Murray, continued to live in until recently.

Thus, after more than a decade of lying idle, the huge 80-foot chimney on this once thriving mill-site would once again be bellowing steam for this new lumbering venture. Construction of the mill was brisk in the spring of 1892 as the company strove to complete the mill in time for a large drive of logs that was scheduled to arrive from up the Tusket River. By mid-summer, the *Yarmouth Light* reports: "The shrill of the mill is once again heard at the old place known as Macks Mill after a silence of fifteen years. The Tusket River Lumber Company now owns the property and have several new buildings erected so that end of the village has quite a business air." By the end of the summer, thirty men were employed, and the mill was "… working day and night to meet the demand." The mill usually closed during the winter months due to the inability to move the logs down the frozen river to the mill-site.

Loading lumber at the Tusket River Lumber Company wharf at Tusket

Although some sources list this photograph as the Dickie & McGrath Lumber Mill, it was more likely taken prior to the Dickie and McGrath ownership. The main mill building and the surrounding area in the last two photographs bear common similarities. Later pictures during the ownership of Dickie and McGrath reveal major differences in the main buildings structure. St. Stephen's Anglican Church is seen to the right.

Although the Tusket River Lumber Company prospered, it doesn't appear to have achieved the magnitude of its predecessor, the N. W. Blethen & Company mill, and in

1896, after being in operation for only four years the Tusket River Lumber Company sold its mill and lands to Mr. Alfred Dickie of Lower Stewiacke, Colchester County. September 4, 1894, the *Yarmouth Telegram* reports: "Thomas McGrath, former manager of Dickie's mill at Truro will go to Yarmouth to take charge of the mill."

Dickie & McGrath

After the decline of the shipbuilding industry, one of the few remaining industries in the village was the Tusket River Lumber Mill at the north end of the village. Alfred Dickie, a native of Stewiacke, Nova Scotia, was a very prominent and rich businessman. He was an industrialist, and perhaps was to Nova Scotia, in his day, what K. C. Irving has been to New Brunswick. He had built a huge empire in the lumbering business, stretching throughout the Maritime Provinces and as far north as Labrador and Newfoundland. In 1901 the *Chronicle Herald* reports: "Alfred Dickie of the firm (Dickie & McGrath, Tusket) of Lower Stewiacke will handle the largest output of lumber this season that has ever been shipped from Nova Scotia in one year. He ships lumber to England, Scotland, Ireland, France, Spain, Baltimore, New York, Boston and South America." The *Yarmouth Light* reported: "He can safely be styled 'The Lumber King of Nova Scotia.'"

Apparently, on a trip to Yarmouth, he realized the potential of the lumber industry which lay in Tusket. He persuaded a clever worker of his, Thomas N. McGrath, to enter a partnership with him and move to Tusket in order to manage the newly acquired holdings. The month of August, 1896 marked for Tusket the beginning of a changing era with regard to lumber mills. The Tusket River Lumber Company's mills and lands at Tusket were sold to Dickie & McGrath for the sum of $40,000. The Dickie & McGrath Company soon became a huge and prosperous corporation and certainly the largest of its kind in the area. During the next decade and a half this lumber mill generated one of the biggest economic booms in the history of the village.

Thomas N. McGrath's kind personality soon became known to all Tusket residents. He was regarded highly not only as an astute business manager, but as an honest man, and a good person to work for. During the years he managed the mill he was obviously one of the richest men in the village. He and his family were generous, and supported many community organizations.

The properties of the Dickie & McGrath Lumber Company extended along the north side of the highway from St. Stephen's Anglican Church as far as the former Nathanial Blauvelt homestead (now the Henry Muise – Doug & Joyce Sisco property). On the west side of the main road, along the waterfront, their property covered practically the entire north end of the village along the shores of the Tusket River.

The Dickie & McGrath Lumber Company – Tusket, N.S.

The Henry Muise house is to the extreme left; next is McGrath's large general store. The Free Baptist Church on Parade Hill is visible slightly to the right of the lumber mill. The large, dark building (cookhouse) just below and to the right of this church is the exact site of my carriage shed. St. Stephen's Anglican Church is to the right. The lumber mill was located where the homestead of Hubert & Phyllis Pothier is today.

Dickie and McGrath wasted no time in expanding the lumber mill, and soon the entire area became a beehive of activity. Modern equipment and extra large cutting saws were installed to equip the mill for mass production. Within their first year of operation the *Yarmouth Light* reported: "The Dickie & McGrath firm … made some very important improvements in the property. They have put in new furnaces, new box machines, a 1,128 ft long chain, 'live' rollers for delivering the sawn lumber to the pile in the yard, and other improvements. They are now sawing daily 40,000 ft. of long stuff, 30,000 laths, 400 boxes … Their annual cut is about 8,000,000 feet of logs."

A new, much larger trough and conveyor belt was constructed from the mill to carry the left-over bark and scrap slab-wood overhead all the way to the west side of the main road. A wooden trough of this size would have been a rare sight at any lumber mill during those days. Other smaller troughs were added to the sides of the mill and the large trough from the mill to the river was also enlarged to increase productivity. A railroad siding was constructed on a corduroy road and connected directly to the Coast Railway from the lumber yard. As smoke from the steam-operated mill bellowed from the huge 80-foot high chimney, a second smaller chimney was added to the mill to further increase production.

By 1900, the *Yarmouth Daily Globe* had this to say: "Dickie & McGrath are building a large addition to their mill in Tusket and are setting up modern machinery. One of the new saws will cut several logs at a time." By the end of the summer, "Dickie & McGrath will have electric lights in the yard and riverfront adjoining their mill and are now working day and night. The steam whistle sounds the lunch hour at midnight …" Fire hoses hung from the ceiling as a fire protection measure; a rare sight in those days. I have been told that this was the first such fire prevention equipment in any lumber mill in this part of Nova Scotia at the time. The standard earlier procedure was to set up a row of water barrels on top of the roof so that the water would help to extinguish the flames in case of a fire.

Working crew inside the Dickie & McGrath lumber mill

Fire hoses hanging from the ceiling as a means of fire protection was an unusual precautionary measure in those days. Pictures inside lumber mills such as this one are very rare. The young man with the pee-vee to the right is John "Tiga" Doucette. He lived where James & Barbara Pottier live in 2005.

The magnitude of the Dickie & McGrath Lumber Co. drew attention from the media, both positive and negative. The *Yarmouth Times* reported: "Alfred Dickie of Lower Stewiacke will manufacture an enormous quantity of lumber this year. His largest operation will be at Tusket … The total amount of lumber [for the province] to be produced is 32,000,000 feet."

While the Dickie and McGrath enterprise was a huge economic boost to the village, it also brought with it obvious negative impacts on the forest. Numerous concerns were expressed regarding clear-cutting and the eventual destruction of the forest, causing anxiety among many people. One news report stated: "The question arises how long our limited Nova Scotia forest can stand this enormous demand upon them."

This was an extremely prosperous time for the lumbering industry. Several smaller mills were also established along the inland reaches of the Tusket River and surrounding communities. As the demand for lumber increased, those who resented the forest destruction were often blamed for the numerous lumber mills that were being set on fire.

On January 8, 1900, the *Yarmouth Daily Times* reported: "The steam mill at Tusket, owned by Forman Hatfield, was destroyed by fire early Sunday morning …" The following week it reported: "A reward of $950.00 is offered for the arrest of the wretches who set fire to Forman Hatfield's mill in Tusket."

Eight years earlier, in 1892, the *Yarmouth Light* reported the following from Belleville: "About 11:00 Sunday morning the sawmill on the Fork Road, owned by Lezin V. Potier … was burnt to the ground. Also the Babin Mill about ¼ of a mile distant was on fire at the same time … Neither mill had been in operation for several days and it is undoubtedly the work of an incendiary."

On May 27, 1903, the *Yarmouth Light* reported: "the new planing mill of Dickie & McGrath was destroyed by fire …". Jerry Titus, a Yarmouth historian, who has provided a great deal of information on this industry writes, "I think they built and burnt more mills in Tusket than anywhere else in the world." These are but examples of the local lumber mills that were obviously thought to have been deliberately set on fire during those times.

Nevertheless, the Dickie & McGrath lumber mill continued to grow at an enormous pace.

Thomas McGrath & others in front of his general store

Thomas N. McGrath is sitting in the foreground; he had an artificial right leg from the knee down which is noticeable in the photograph. Sitting, left to right: Mr. Towner, a man from the West Indies; Jack McCarthy, book-keeper for the Dickie & McGrath firm. W. Chase Hatfield (also a book-keeper) is sitting to the right. Standing, left to right: Arthur McGrath, Thomas' eldest son, who became an employee of the firm, and John D. Armstrong.

Thomas N. McGrath also operated a large country store just to the north of the mill, almost directly across from the Henry Muise property. This was likely the same general store established years earlier by Andrew Mack. All general goods were sold here and it also provided a great gathering place for the workers as well as other community residents. The store was located on the site where the Golden Pheasant Restaurant was situated prior to its burning in 1972.

While some outbuildings that served as storage and utility sheds already existed on the property, Dickie & McGrath constructed many others throughout the lumberyards. Several large cookhouses were also included as part of the mill complex, where local women would be employed as cooks and cleaning ladies. The lumberyards were buzzing with workers. Horses and wagons were used to haul the sawn lumber to where the yard workers would sort and stockpile it. While much of the lumber was stockpiled in the traditional manner with wooden cleats making rectangular piles, photographs indicate that large stockpiles along the river were also laid to dry in the shape of Indian tee-pees; this was obviously made for a faster drying time.

One can only imagine what it would have been like to work in these lumberyards at certain times of the year, particularly under wet and muddy conditions. During the summer months several children of a young age would be employed as "water boys," going around the lumberyards offering drinking water to the workers.

Spring was always the busiest time of the year at the Dickie and McGrath mill. Thomas McGrath would travel as far as Saint John, New Brunswick in search of extra labourers for the annual early spring rush of log drives from far up the river. During peak season, the rush gave employment to several hundred, including some from Tusket Wedge (now Wedgeport) and from the Clare district. Everyone benefited, directly or indirectly, from these operations. During the long winter months, various small communities all along the Tusket River as far inland as Kemptville would cut logs and haul them to the river, waiting for the ice to thaw in the spring. Thus would begin the long river drives by the many skilled lumbermen needed to move the logs down the river, eventually reaching the Dickie & McGrath Lumber Mill at Tusket.

In June 1897, the *Yarmouth Times* reported: "The drive of logs for Dickie & McGrath now coming down the Tusket River with a small army of men working all spring numbers 70,000 logs. The largest drive ever on that river."

Often, these men would wear special boots with sharply pointed nails or cleats protruding through the soles in order to provide a better grip, for stability while on the log drives. These log drives were generally contracted out to the various lumbermen who had established businesses and had their own hired men. One of the best known in the lumbering industry at the time was John Armstrong from Bell Neck. John Armstrong was a highly respected man and a friend of Tom McGrath. His services were frequently called upon to deliver large quantities of lumber to the McGrath mill. The text of a signed agreement below by John D. Armstrong and the Dickie & McGrath firm serves as testimony to this. It is interesting to note that as the river became less treacherous, the price paid to Mr. Armstrong would decrease accordingly.

"Stream drive" signed agreement between John D. Armstrong and Dickie & McGrath Lumber Mills.

It is mutually agreed between John D. Armstrong of Belle Nek, Yarmouth County, Nova Scotia, Lumberman, and Dickie & McGrath Limited, a body corporate, incorporated under the "Companies Act" of Nova Scotia, of Tusket [Yarmouth] County, and Province aforesaid. That the said John D. Armstrong is to stream drive all the logs on the Main Branch of the Tusket River, in the spring of 1911, beginning in Borrio and driving all the logs to the mouth of the Rockingham River for the sum of Two Dollars ($2.00) per thousand, and from the mouth of the Rockingham River to East River Bridge, for the sum of One Dollar and twenty five cents per thousand ($1.25) and the logs from East River Bridge to Belle Nek for the sum of Sixty Cents (60) per thousand, and from Belle Nek to Tusket for the sum of Fifty cents (50) per thousand Superficial Feet. All the above logs to be delivered at the head of Hurlburt's Falls securely fastened to the satisfaction of Dickie & McGrath Limited or their agent. And it is further agreed that Dickie & McGrath Limited have the right to enter upon, and drive these logs, at the expense of the said John D. Armstrong at any time during the spring that the work is not being carried on to the satisfaction of Dickie and McGrath Limited, or their agent.

Dated in Tusket, N. S.
this 6th day of April 1911.
Signed, sealed, and delivered,
in the presence of:

A Dickie & McGrath log driving crew taking a rest along the Tusket River.

Supplying food to the river or stream drive crews also had to be carefully planned. Before the crew got underway in the morning, cooks would be told approximately where the stream drivers were expected to be by lunchtime; the cooks would then proceed to that location, dig a large hole (like a pit) in the ground, and build a huge fire. After a bed of hot coals was achieved, large pots of food, often beans, were cooked over the hot fire to be ready for when the river drivers arrived. Although some locations became regular stops, sometimes the river drives would not go quite as planned, therefore it was always necessary to keep in touch with each other and the meals were cooked wherever necessary.

When these floated logs would finally reach the Dickie & McGrath mill, they were secured in a "pier boom line" while waiting to be sawn at the lumber mill. The boom line extended all the way to the Tusket River Bridge and was secured in the middle of the river by large, hand made stone pylons that can still be seen at low tide to this day. I am frequently asked by people the purpose of the large stone piles in the river.

Log boom taken from the Tusket bridge, looking southeast. The large building to the far left was Thomas McGrath's general store.

Tugboats played a major part in the movement of ships and cargo along the waterfront. The Tusket river channel, being relatively narrow and shallow, particularly at low tide, required skilled seamen to manoeuvre ships up and down the river. George S. Brown in his *Yarmouth, N.S.: a sequel to Campbell's History* (1888), writes, "The navigation of the Tusket River from the village to the sea is very intricate, and in some parts dangerous. … a skilful and experienced pilot is an absolute necessity; and Solon Doucette of Tusket Hill has for many years been one of the few men who could be relied upon to conduct the largest ship safely through the shoals and ledges of the Tusket River …" In most cases, this was done with the aid of tugboats that would tow the loaded ships further out to deeper waters. In fact, Dickie & McGrath owned their own tugboat bearing the name of Thomas McGrath's wife, *Alice Maud*.

A tugboat manoeuvres a ship loaded with lumber from the Dickie & McGrath Mill through the river channels.

The wharf at the Dickie & McGrath firm became one of largest in the entire area during the mill's busiest years. Commerce with foreign countries, particularly the West Indies flourished, with wood exporting being at the top of the list.

Nevertheless, it soon became evident to Dickie & McGrath that the wharf facilities at their newly renovated high-production mill were not sufficient to meet their exporting demands. The shallow channels of the Tusket River were a major concern, as the captains of these large ships were reluctant to bring the ships up the river as far as McGrath's mill. The *Yarmouth* Light, 9 September 1897, carried an extensive report on McGraths ambitious plans to establish a wharf at Wedgeport. The article reported that before this time vessels would "anchor in an exposed position at the mouth of the Tusket River [Wedgeport area] while the cargo was being lightered [a term used in the lumbering industry meaning to haul the lumber on barges with tug boats] down to them." A large quantity of lumber was also being freighted nine miles to Yarmouth on the newly opened Coast Railway while some was carted by ox-team. Thomas McGrath quickly realized that freighting the lumber "… absorbed a large percentage of the profits." Thus the energetic mill manager set about to find a more economical way of getting his lumber to market in order to "… increase the margin between the cost of production and the market price of their commodity."

Information supplied to him by some helpful residents of Tusket Wedge [Wedgeport], along with other information gathered, led him to believe that there was a strong possibility of a harbour deep enough in the area to accommodate large ships. An extensive shipping business operated by J.H. Porter [Pothier] was already well established in the Wedgeport area and they were very accommodating to Dickie & McGrath. In 1897, merely one year after purchasing the mill, the *Yarmouth Times* reports: "Dickie & McGrath intends to build a wharf at Tusket Wedge."

The *Yarmouth Light,* 9 September 1897, mentioned above, indicated that as a first step, Thomas McGrath hired the 1361-ton ship *RUBY* out of Yarmouth, with Capt. S.B. Robbins in command. He then hired Capt. Hilaire T. LeBlanc of Wedgeport, who was known as one of the best local navigators, with his tug, the *Ida Lou* "to take soundings and make a survey of certain deep waters outside the regular channel which serves the Wedge traffic." A large channel with a depth of six to seven fathoms at low tide "which led to a pool of five phantoms" was discovered near Corporon's Cape and Birch Island. Capt. Robbins was thrilled when he easily managed to manoeuvre and anchor the *Ruby* in all directions without any difficulties. Other large ships were soon brought in to test the new waters and all met with approval.

Dickie & McGrath soon "secured a privilege along the water front" and immediately began construction of a new wharf. A large well, similar to the two in Tusket village, was also dug above the wharf to supply the necessary fresh water for the vessels prior to setting sail on the open seas. Large vessels could dock at the new facilities at low tide on a year-round basis. Dickie & McGrath "chartered the Norwegian ship *LANSING* to load lumber at Tusket Wedge for Buenos Aires. The *LANSING* was 2600 tons, a four-masted ship and was the largest vessel ever to load lumber at a port in Eastern Canada." Now they could lighter huge piles of sawn lumber from the mill-site at Tusket to the new wharf at Tusket Wedge during summer and fall, and loading and shipping was now possible during winter months as well as summertime.

Some smaller ships leaving the Dickie & McGrath wharf in Tusket would be towed by tugboats as far as Plymouth and to the deeper waters where they would set sail for the high seas.

The Dickie & McGrath wharf, Tusket Wedge, N.S.

A continuous relationship with other businessmen from other areas of the province within the lumber industry was of vital importance. In 1903, an association was formed among the leading lumber producers from the counties of Lunenburg, Queens, Shelburne,

Yarmouth, Digby, Annapolis, Kings, Hants, and Colchester. The association was known as the Lumberman's Association of Western Nova Scotia. On May 30 and 31, 1907, the Association members met in Yarmouth. Ironically, "the theme of the meeting was forest protection, and there were talks about conservation, preservation and re-forestation." It is obvious from this that the voices of the people were being heard. Several high-ranking dignitaries were in attendance and the subject matter was given serious attention. The press gave a clear message that it was the duty of these lumber producers to take positive steps toward eliminating the destruction of the forests, and that their actions would be carefully monitored and that positive results were to be expected. A thorough survey of the forested lands was conducted and when it was completed it became clear "that the days were gone when they could without question believe that the forest was inexhaustible." During the two-day meeting in Yarmouth, time was taken to visit the Dickie & McGrath Lumber mill at Tusket, at which time the following photograph was taken.

Lumbermen's Association of Western Nova Scotia, Tusket May 30, 1907

The persons identified are numbered, left to right, as follows: # 1– Thomas McGrath; # 2 – Alfred Dickie; # 3 – Member for Yarmouth County, E.H. Armstrong, (Premier of Nova Scotia: 1923-25); # 4 – Arthur Eakins, born and raised in Tusket; a partner in the Yarmouth firm of Parker-Eakins; # 5 – Yarmouth Mayor, Willard Kelley.

The Dickie & McGrath Lumber Company did extremely well during the early 1900s. By the end of 1908, however, the first indication of trouble began to surface and a major shake-up in the company took place. On December 29, several newspaper reports confirmed it. The *Yarmouth Times* headlines read, "The Alfred Dickie Company Sells To English Syndicate." A Halifax paper reported: "The big N.S. lumber concern, Alfred Dickie Co. has been sold to an English syndicate headed by Sir Thomas Trowbridge, the chief promoter of the Blackpod Steamship Enterprise from Ireland to Canada." *The*

Yarmouth Herald also reported, "The Alfred Dickie Lumber Company of N.S. has been sold ... for $1,567,500. It was negotiated by the Royal Bank of Canada, which had a claim against the Dickie Company of one million. The sale includes 8 properties, 7 east of Halifax and one in the western part of the province." The property in the western part of the province was obviously the Tusket mill operation. Thomas McGrath was appointed manager of the new company at a salary of $10,000 per year. His ability to oversee a profitable enterprise such as this one was clearly still held in very high regard. Although the name Dickie & McGrath continued to be used on the Tusket mill, it appears unlikely that Alfred Dickie was involved in the Tusket operations after this time.

A few months later, the company suffered another major setback. On the evening of May 27, 1909, the mill burned to the ground. The following appeared in the *Yarmouth Light*:

BIG LUMBER MILL BURNED

TUSKET, N.S., May 27 - One of the finest lumber mills in the province, owned by Dickie & McGrath, was burned during the night, but the company store and residence near and about 2,000,000 feet of lumber were saved. The loss will amount to about $50,000. A new and larger mill will be put up immediately. About 200 men were thrown temporarily out of employment by the fire.

The machine shop, blacksmith shop, and old barn were also destroyed. The summer production was a total loss and it was the following December before the *Yarmouth Light* reported: "Dickie & McGrath have commenced the erection of a new large mill at Tusket to replace the one destroyed by fire some months ago." The mill was rebuilt and for the next three years it was business as usual; they had one of the best-equipped mills in eastern Canada.

In December 1912, however, the unthinkable was announced. The *Yarmouth Times* headlines: "Dickie & McGrath Limited in Liquidation. Tenders will be received by Eastern Trust Co., liquidators of clothing, hardware etc., contained in the warehouse and store in Tusket." It had been only three years since most newspapers had reported the first signs of trouble for the company.

The entire liquidation of the mill and site appears to have taken a considerable amount of time to finalize. More than two years later, in May 1915, the following appeared in the *Yarmouth Times*: " Eastern Trust, liquidators of Dickie and McGrath Ltd. sold 50,000 acres of land near the Tusket River; also the saw mills, steam tug, scows, lumber, general store, blacksmith shop to James Stewart of Halifax for $14,000, representing the Bank of Canada."

It remains somewhat uncertain as to the exact cause of the collapse of this once "giant" enterprise in the village. According to the late Yarmouth historian, and Tusket native, Robert B. Blauveldt, whom I have quoted several times in this history, Dickie & McGrath were heavily financed for the spring rush of logs. McGrath ran into difficulties when a late spring kept all the logs frozen in the ice up the Tusket River. His creditors pressured him until he finally had to liquidate the company and declare bankruptcy in order to pay the debts. Reports indicate that there had been no justifiable reason to force the company out of business, that it had been merely a move on the part of greedy creditors to get rich, and in fact, they did get rich. When the ice finally thawed, the lumber was sawed and sold. This dealt a severe blow to the prosperity of the area. Much of this information in regard to the final demise of the company is anecdotal, and I can not vouch for its accuracy. Clearly the bankruptcy of such a large operation was probably a complicated legal and business matter, and probably not many people outside of the firm understood the full details.

In 1922, the last traces of the mill disappeared. The *Yarmouth Herald*, 15 August of that year reported:

> The present owners of the extensive milling property at Tusket, formerly controlled by Dickie & McGrath Ltd., have a number of men there cleaning up the property and as a consequence Tusket will lose a landmark of many years standing when all is done. The tall brick chimney, which for over 40 years has withstood the blasts of many storms, is to be taken down. It was originally erected by the firm of Andrew Mack & Co., lumber manufacturers ...

Thomas McGrath was left with little means of support other than his general store, which he had obviously been able to acquire during the liquidation of the business. To add to the discomfort of the times, as we saw earlier, his lovely home also burned down during these difficult times. Mr. McGrath died suddenly on July 8 1923, of heart failure at the age of sixty nine; he was buried in Mountain Cemetery in Yarmouth.

The magnitude of the Dickie & McGrath Lumber Company obviously impressed professional and amateur photographers alike; consequently several outstanding pictures are available of this huge lumber mill. Much of the information and photos in the above text, and many of the pictures on the following pages are originals given to me by Thomas N. McGrath's son, Dr. Percy McGrath of Kentville, as mentioned earlier in this history.

Following is a photographic tour of the Dickie & McGrath Lumber Mill.

A view looking north, from the lumberyard, shows a different perspective and the enormous length of the Dickie & McGrath Mill.

Sawn lumber ready for exporting at the Dickie & McGrath Mill.

Ship timbers are stock piled for drying in this 1906 photograph. The location of most of the piled lumber is today behind the homestead of Carl and Audrey Pottier. Slightly left of centre, in the background, is Asa Robbins' shoe factory and tannery.

A view from the northeast. This is the present site of the home of Hubert and Phyllis Pothier.

*A view from the southeast. Thomas McGrath's general store is to the right,
beyond the overhead wooden trough.*

Mill workers in front of the Dickie & McGrath store, Tusket, N.S. The sign on the store front reads Dickie & McGrath Limited. The gentleman with the light coloured shirt, centre of third row (in the rear) is John D. Armstrong.

A Dickie and McGrath "mill crew." The gentleman with a suit, on the right, back row, directly in line with the window, is Thomas McGrath. The building in the rear was one of the cookhouses.

A Final Word or Two on the End of Dickie & McGrath

It has been noted by different writers that the horrible Depression of the 1930s was felt less in some ways in Nova Scotia than in other places. Although the 30s was a grim time in the Maritimes, this area had already experienced many such depressions, much of it connected with the ups and downs of the shipbuilding and shipping industries, and in some ways by the redistribution of power and wealth in the country following Confederation in 1867. So when the big "Depression" arrived, many Nova Scotians were already seasoned survivors of such hard times.

Tusket clearly got a very early jump-start on the Depression with the liquidation of Dickie & McGrath in 1915. This large mill enterprise had in many ways replaced the loss of the shipbuilding industry and breathed new economic life into the area. Tusket and the surrounding area were truly devastated by the loss of this industry.

LeBaron Floyd & Harold Floyd's Mill

What followed was a very grim economic period for Tusket. One sawmill however, established a few years prior to 1920, provided the village with at least one industry and employment for a few people. This mill was never an enterprise as large as the Mack Mill, the Tusket River Lumber Company or Dickie & McGrath, but in its own modest way, it continued a sawmill tradition in the village for several decades where there was quite literally no other industry in the village at all.

I am indebted here to Jerry Titus for what information there is available on the beginnings of "The Floyd Mill" at Tusket. It had very complicated beginnings, and those details will be provided here. The best information available on the establishment of this business is found in the pages of the local newspapers of 1917 and 1918, as they have been uncovered by Jerry Titus in his own research. I quote liberally from those excerpts as they have been so generously supplied to me.

The Floyd Mill in 1937-38.

What was later known in Tusket as the "Floyd Mill" was built at Tusket only a few years after the closure of Dickie & McGrath. It was not established here with the intent of creating a permanent business, but was set up specifically to deal with the lumber needs associated with the construction of the *Susan Cameron,* the last substantial tall ship built in the village. One can safely assume that the intention would have been to dismantle the mill when any vessels were completed.

A company, known as the Tusket River Shipbuilding Company, was established to undertake the construction of the *Susan Cameron.* Louis N. Fuller of New Glasgow, Nova Scotia was closely involved with these operations for a time. He worked for the Central Realty Company of New Glasgow and was also a business partner with Walter P. McNeil, President of W.P. McNeil & Co. Ltd. of New Glasgow. That firm was involved in many business enterprises and in fact was the company hired to engineer and complete the installation of the Sluice Point-Surette's Island Bridge in 1909.

Apparently Louis Fuller was active in Yarmouth County on various business enterprises as early as 1912. He was certainly a central business figure in the plans to build the *Susan Cameron* at Tusket. "Fuller had big plans for Tusket. The keel for the *Susan Cameron* was laid in mid-September 1917." LeBaron Floyd was hired and brought into Tusket as the manager of the sawmill set up to saw the lumber needed for the construction of this vessel. The *Susan Cameron* was built right in the centre of the village, in the same location where the N. & E. Gardner shipyards had been located in the 1860s. Robie McLeod of Liverpool was master builder.

The *Yarmouth Herald,* on 3 July 1917 reported, "*The Telegram*, an issue or two past, announced that work had commenced on the first schooner to be built at Tusket by the Tusket River Shipbuilding Company. This may have been a little premature for we find that the actual work at shipbuilding has not really started. This company has, however, commenced building a mill on the property on the north corner of Charles K. Hurlbert's store, where the large ship John Y. Robbins was built 27 years ago. When the mill is completed the company will equip it with modern machinery that will permit them to build and launch vessels with the quickest possible dispatch. LeBaron Floyd will be in charge of the mill. The company now have men in the woods surveying timber and also holds an option on some valuable timber property."

Yarmouth Light, 12 July 1917 - "Tusket Shipbuilding Company. Reports from Tusket go to show that fast progress is being made by the Tusket Shipbuilding Company. The mill is nearly completed. The company has purchased the mill and 700 acres of timberland of Lycett & Prosser at Kemptville. The company has also purchased the Allen Mill at Brazil Lake and will move the steam plant into the woods at Kempt. The other equipment is to be taken to the Tusket Mill. It is rumoured the company has purchased two or more woodlots near Tusket. Ship timber and machinery are arriving daily at the yards in Tusket and report has it that two keels of the 500 ton schooners will be laid at once. It would seem the company intends building on a large scale, owning and operating three saw mills and large tracts of timberland. Ship timber is arriving from the Carleton river way and the management says they have no difficulty securing labourers."

Digby Courier, 10 Aug. 1917 - "The Tusket River Shipbuilding Co. have completed their mill at Tusket and about all the machinery installed. They are experiencing some delay in the shipment of belting and after the arrival will be ready for operation. The building is 40 feet by 90 feet."

The business of building this vessel seems to have been very complicated indeed, and it seems a miracle that it was ever completed. By the spring of 1918, things had obviously gone very wrong between the parties involved in building this ship. Both Robie McLeod and LeBaron Floyd sued the Tusket River Shipbuilding Company and won. They went their own ways and soon after the Tusket River Shipbuilding company went bankrupt. It seems likely that these two men would have been suing for wages or salaries owed to them.

"In May of 1918 the company was re-organized and renamed The Argyle Shipbuilding Company. Captain W.B Butler, W.L Harding, J. Archibald Blackadar, D.B Stoneman and Mayor Grant of Yarmouth put $25,000 of their own money into the company. Victor Hatfield of Yarmouth took charge of the mill and Jacob Langille of New Glasgow became master shipbuilder."

It appears that this group, too, went bankrupt in October 1918. The company involved in building the *Susan Cameron* was afterwards referred to as the Tusket Shipbuilding Company. Walter P. McNeil of New Glasgow (who had been involved earlier) stepped in one day before the place was to be auctioned off and paid the debts. By this time it appears that Louis P. Fuller, who has been mentioned earlier, was out of the picture.

Yarmouth Light, 2 Sept. 1918 - "The yard of the Tusket Shipbuilding Company Limited presents a very busy appearance. About twenty men are employed in the mill and yard and the vessel is more then two thirds framed out. Jacob Langille of Pictou is the builder and his son and several other men from Pictou are working with him. Miss J. Hatfield of Springhaven is bookkeeper."

Yarmouth Herald, 26 November 1918 reported on yet more troubles. There was a Sheriff's Sale held, selling various equipment of the Tusket Shipbuilding Company in order to satisfy the demands of yet another lawsuit. Some of the items listed as being for sale offer a few details on some of the equipment held in the mill at that time. The list includes the following pieces of equipment and machinery: One 75 hp engine; one 24 Cown jointer with knives and counter shaft; one split saw; Eclipse planer; post borer; rotary saw; drill; treenail machine; wood lathes; rotary band saws and other saws; trimmer saw; etc.

In 1919, the Tusket Shipbuilding Company launched the four-masted schooner *Susan Cameron*, official number 138,656,601 tons gross, 163.7 feet long, 36.3 feet wide and 13.1 feet depth of hold. The owners at that time were the Susan Cameron Shipping Company, Pictou, Nova Scotia.

The various parties involved in the building of the *Susan Cameron* did not attempt to build another vessel in Tusket.

LeBaron Floyd, who had been brought here in connection with this sawmill, seems to have been able to purchase the mill sometime after the launch of the *Susan Cameron*. Any details connected with his acquisition of the mill cannot be cited here.

What is known is that LeBaron Floyd must have liked Tusket as a community, for he chose to remain here. He eventually owned and operated the sawmill originally established for the construction of the *Susan Cameron*. He was clearly a good mill manager, for he operated this business for many years, and eventually the mill became the property of his son, Harold Floyd.

Although this mill was a much more modest operation than the larger and more impressive enterprises described in this history, its operations were obviously on a more sustainable scale. It operated for a longer period of time than any of the previous mills. As late as 1955, James H. Bingay, in speaking of the untidiness of the mill property, writes, "But as it is now Tusket's sole industrial plant, we should do anything but complain about it."

The Floyd family worked here and owned the mill and also provided employment for some men of the area. The well-known "Toots" Hatfield worked here for a number of years before establishing his business in the town of Yarmouth. Some others that are recalled as having been employed here are Remi LeFave (sawyer), Martin Amirault, Toussaint Muise, Charlie Muise, Fred Doucette (Hubbard's Point), Eddie Landry (Amirault's Hill), and Roger Surette (Lower Eel Brook). Harris "Pat" Gavel worked at Floyd's mill through much of the 1940s. His wages were set at $17.25 per week.

The Floyd Mill finally closed its doors in the mid 1950s. There has not been a sawmill in the village since that time.

Uncle Ben Pottier's Lobster Plug Business: One of Tusket's Last Industries

Another small industry that existed in the village during the 1960s and 70s, and deserves mention, was the lobster plug manufacturing business that was established by my Uncle Benoit Pottier. "N'oncle Benoit", as we always called him, was a very special man. Although he was an automotive mechanic by trade, he was something of a mechanical genius, and seemed capable of engineering machines or parts for almost any purpose. Most people in my generation will always remember him as the man who invented the lobster plug machines. In terms of employment, this was a small family operated business, but one which paid high dividends.

Uncle Ben developed a system of machines that mass-produced the tiny wooden plugs (or pegs) that for many years were used as wedges in the lobster claws to prevent the lobsters from biting. This process included a series of four intricately designed machines, each performing a specific task in achieving the end product. The first machine was like a large drum in which pine boards were placed all around it in a vertical position and as the drum rotated, a saw would cut off pieces to exact length. These pieces were then stacked into another machine that had two saw blades parallel to each other and would cut the wood pieces further into three thinner pieces. These pieces were then stacked into a third machine that would taper them on one side. The same pieces were then stacked in a fourth machine that produced the final product. This was an incredible machine to watch at work; it was like a human hand "spitting out" these tiny wooden pegs ... made to perfection! Two identical machines produced this final product, each throwing out at least one peg per second – something that the lobster fishermen used to sit and carve out by hand! The entire process was like watching a robot at work.

Maintenance and adjustments were required on a regular basis to keep the machines in top working condition. Special cutters were made and had to be maintained razor-sharp. Uncle Ben was a master at this type of work. Occasionally, whenever my brothers or I would visit our cousins at my Uncle Ben's, we considered it both an honour and a privilege to be able to help in filling the machines with wood, considering that no one (except a very few personal friends) was allowed to see the machines at work. Uncle Ben had spent countless hours developing his own designs for these machines and he made sure that no one would copy them; the doors were always kept locked and whenever someone came to see him, he would talk to them outside the shop, never inside.

The business was first established in the barn which still sits today behind his son Carl Pottier's house. As the business developed, Aunt Julia, (Uncle Ben's wife) and their two sons, Carl and Mike all joined in with a helping hand as much as possible. As time passed, other careers took Carl and Mike away from home; Uncle Ben eventually retired from his regular job and he and Aunt Julia continued to operate the business on their own. As the business expanded, more space was required to store dry lumber. A large building was constructed to serve as a new shop to manufacture the lobster plugs and as storage space for the large amounts of wood required for them. At the north end of the building on a lower floor was Uncle Ben's machine shop where he spent most of his time, especially after he sold the lobster peg business. This is the long white building that still stands there today, just to the north of the old barn.

The packaging of these "wooden pegs" was also time consuming and very meticulously carried out. The bags, stamped with the "Benoit Pottier Lobster Plugs" logo, were then filled with 1000 pegs per bag and sealed. Each bag was then carefully packed in large cardboard boxes; each box containing 50 bags, (or 50,000 pegs per box). All boxes were also stamped with the same logo. The "wooden pegs" were then shipped throughout the Maritimes and to several places along the New England seaboard.

On March 2, 1975, N'oncle Benoit sold this business to Vernon D'Eon of West Pubnico. Thus the business name Vernon D'Eon Lobster Plugs is still in existence to this day, although the wooden lobster plug was replaced by a large rubber band several years ago. N'Oncle Benoit spent most of his retired life working in his machine shop, continually inventing something new. He was known as the person you would always go to when you were stuck with a mechanical problem. He was a very charitable and generous man, always doing something for others and never charging what it was worth. His enthusiasm and love for his work lasted his entire life. Sadly, in 2000, Uncle Ben passed away at the age of eighty three.

Uncle Ben at work in his machine shop duplicating the spire for my barn cupola.

As an example of Uncle Ben's varied capabilities, I share below with the reader two photographs of him duplicating the spire for the cupola on my barn during the time of reconstruction. This solid piece of cedar wood was more than five feet long by five inches square. The length presented him with a challenge of safely securing such a large piece of wood in his metal lathe; but as usual, Uncle Ben made an adaptor to hold the piece solidly into place and soon got the job underway. Although this was a minor challenge to him, there was no other place locally that would even attempt to turn such a large piece of wood in a lathe. This is just an example of how blessed we were to have Uncle Ben around for so many years.

The finished product.

CHAPTER 11

THE MILITARY

CHAPTER 11
THE MILITARY

Tusket's settlement in 1784 was, as has been stated earlier, closely connected with war and the military of that time. All of the original settlers to the village were United Empire Loyalists who had fought on the side of the British during the American Revolutionary War. At the end of the war these people became refugees, were forced to give up their properties in the United States and make a new home in British territory. The Tusket settlers arrived first in Shelburne, Nova Scotia, and afterwards made their way to the Tusket area.

The local militia was an established entity in Argyle Township when the Loyalists arrived here in 1784. This militia had been raised largely due to the Revolutionary War, and Jackson Ricker's *Historical Sketches of Glenwood and the Argyles* (1940) and Edmund Duval Poole's *Annals of Yarmouth and Barrington (Nova Scotia) In the Revolutionary War* (1899) make it clear that this militia had been a very active one. Tensions had been very real even within the local population during the War, as many of the New England Planters in both Yarmouth and Argyle, only some ten years removed from their former homeland, sympathized with their American friends, while the local militia was raised to protect British interests.

The Loyalists were fortunate, after settling here, to live through a prolonged time of peace. The memories of the war were fresh, however, and the militia remained an active force for many years to come. Many of the Loyalists, having clearly shown their loyalties, quickly became part of the local militia. Jackson Ricker in his *Historical Sketches of Glenwood and the Argyles* provides a list of the local officers of the militia as taken from the provincial "Commission Book" for 1793-1796. We list them here with an indication of whether the person in question was Loyalist, New England Planter from Argyle or Acadian:

Names	Rank	Date of Commission	Local group
Lewis Blanchard	Lieut.Col.	24 July 1793	Tusket Loyalist
Job Hatfield	2nd Lieut.Col.	24 July 1793	Tusket Loyalist
Joseph Bell	Major	24 July 1793	?
Tennis[sic] Blauvelt	Captain	21 July 1794	Tusket Loyalist
Paul Surat	Captain	22 July 1794	Acadian
Nathaniel Ricker	Captain	23 July 1794	Argyle Planter
Paul D'Entremont	Captain	24 July 1794	Acadian
Jacob Hatfield	Lieut.	21 July 1794	Tusket Loyalist
Peter Porter	Lieut.	22 July 1794	Acadian [surname Pottier/Pothier]
Lemuel Hobbes	Lieut.	23 July 1794	Argyle Planter
William Andrews	Lieut.	24 July 1794	Tusket Loyalist

Through years of peace the need for the militia would wane, and so would its activities.

The War of 1812 was the next in local history that made the formation of the local militia a necessity once again. At the end of this war a long period of peace and inactivity followed. In the 1860s the Fenian Raids saw local militias again formed and practicing military manoeuvres on their parade grounds in various villages, including Tusket. In the 1880s the distant Riel Rebellion in the Canadian west elicited a similar response.

The Old Parade Ground

On the main road (Route 308 North), proceeding north out of Tusket, and on the eastern side of the road, is a parcel of land that was used as the Parade Ground for the local militia. The railroad passed through this area in the 1890s and altered the appearance of the land here considerably. This portion of the road was at one time referred to as "Parade Street" and the hill, as "Parade Hill." Tusket had its own unit in the local militia during the 1800s. James Bingay, in his 1955 letter, reminisced with the following comments regarding the militia training grounds after the opening of the railroad in 1896. [The railroad] "… has almost obliterated the actual Parade, where the men of Tusket, including your father [Forman Hatfield] and mine, [Dr. John Bingay] marched and countermarched (under the command of Col. Lent, postmaster), 'ready, aye, ready' to plunge into the western wilds (no railways there, then), and help put down Riel's Rebellion."

A remarkable photograph of Lt. Col. James M. Lent, Commanding Officer of the 5th Regiment Militia of Tusket in 1871, in full dress uniform, is shown below.

Lt. Col. James M. Lent, Commanding Officer of the 5th Regiment Militia of Tusket. This is the same photograph so vividly described on page 43 by James "Jimmie" Lent as hanging on the wall in the James M. Lent house at the southern end of the village.

After the Riel Rebellion in the West in 1880s, local militias and military activity of any kind became largely dormant, until the time of World War I, the "Great War."

Tusket and World War I

Many more sophisticated histories than this one have been written in regard to Canada's great contributions to the military effort against Germany during the First World War. Tusket's great claim to fame, and it may have been unique in this regard, was that 100% of her eligible young men enlisted as soldiers in this struggle. This was an unusual show of patriotism, and one of which the village was justifiably proud. Tusket became one of the earliest villages to erect a monument to its soldiers following the War.

VanCortlandt Square and the War Memorial Monument

VanCortlandt Square, as it is now known, is a triangular park in the centre of the village. This piece of public land was first used as a small park around 1923 when the Tusket War Memorial Association decided to erect a monument in recognition of all those local men who had fought in the War, as well as those who had died in the conflict. The work by this group commenced in 1923. The monument, a large piece of local granite, was erected and dedicated in 1924. Although it was a sad occasion for some, the unveiling of the Tusket War Memorial, dedicated to the local men who lost their lives in World War I, as well as those who had returned, marked a day of celebration in August of 1924. Newspaper accounts of the unveiling make it clear that never before had such a large group of people ever congregated in the village – not even at the launchings of the great ships of old.

Tusket War Memorial Monument – 1924

Unveiling the War Memorial Monument, August 1924.

The following is inscribed on the west side of the War Memorial:

1914 - 1918

**IN HONOUR AND LOVING MEMORY
OF OUR HEROES
WHO MET DEATH TO SAVE LIFE**

CORP. JOSEPH B. JEFFERY
Aged 25 years

PTE. CLEMENT JEFFERY
Aged 31 years

PTE. FELIX DOUCETTE
Aged 27 years

PTE. SIMON DOUCETTE
Aged 22 years

PTE. JOSEPH E. KING
Aged 23 years

PTE. ANTHONY DOUCETTE
Aged 24 years

THE PATHS OF GLORY LEAD BUT TO THE GRAVE

A separate plaque under the above one bears the following:

1939 - R. A. F. - 1945
40474 PILOT OFFICER
JACK ELMER HATFIELD
MISSING IN ACTION MAY 28, 1940
AGE 27 YEARS

The following is inscribed on the east side of the War Memorial:

1914 - 1918
TUSKET
ANSWERED THE EMPIRE'S CALL
IN THE GREAT WAR
100%
IN GRATITUDE TO OUR LIVING HEROES
AND IN THANKSGIVING TO GOD
WE SUBSCRIBE THE NAMES OF THOSE
WHO SURVIVED

BARTLETT, SIMON	**HUBBARD, LIBOIRE**
BENT, GODFREY D.	**HUBBARD, REUBIN**
BLAUVELT, HUGH O.	**HURLBERT, BERNARD H.**
BLAUVELT, ROBERT B.	**JEFFERY, JOHN**
BRAYNE, GERALD	**KILLAM, A. MAUD**
COLEMAN, ERNEST	**KILLAM, KENNETH A.**
DOUCETTE, ADOLPHE E.	**KILLAM, SCOTT B.**
DOUCETTE, ALFRED J.	**LENT, WILLIAM H.**
DOUCETTE, CHARLES	**LITTLE, BARNEY**
DOUCETTE, EUGENE A.	**MACK, ROBERT T.**
DOUCETTE, JOHN	**McGRATH, ARTHUR**
DOUCETTE, LOUIS A.	**McGRATH, FRANK**
DOUCETTE, LOUIS F.	**McGRATH, J. PERCY**
FLOYD, HAROLD	**MUISE, LOUIS**
GAVEL, EDGAR	**PATTERSON, SHERIDAN L.**
GILMAN, FRANK M.	**RAYNARD, ALTON**
GLODE, STEPHEN	**RAYNARD, CLARENCE**
HAMILTON, PERCY M.	**RAYNARD, STANLEY**
HATFIELD, ALLAN I.	**ROBBINS, WILLARD**
HATFIELD, JAMES A.	**SHUPE, BERNARD**
HATFIELD, P. LENT	**SHUPE, ROBERT**
HEWEY, TALMAGE	**STEWART, BAZIL**
HUBBARD, FRANK G.	**VEINOT, MURRAY**
HUBBARD, G. EDWARD	**WOOD, LOUIS E.**
	WOOD JAMES A.

Although the memorial is specific to the village of Tusket, the names suggest that it also includes a number of men from what is now known as the village of Hubbard's Point, just to the south of the village. The Acadian names of Doucette, Hubbard and Muise include both communities. Two names, those of Simon Bartlett and Stephen Glode are Mi'kmaq members of the local community. A. Maud Killam stands out as the only woman represented on the monument. The Tusket War Memorial is unique in that it acknowledges the contributions of both the living and the dead.

Barney Little

James Adolphus Wood

Joseph Alphé Doucette

Louie Albanie Doucette

Peter Lent Hatfield

Robert Thornton Mack

"R. T." Mack deserves a special mention here. His name appears on the list of Tusket men who served in World War I. He first came to Tusket around 1904, in which year he married Ida Hatfield. He worked mainly as a schoolteacher throughout his life, in Bridgewater, Tusket and Yarmouth. He served in World War I, but afterwards maintained a strong interest and involvement military concerns in his civilian life as well. He died in April 1950, and I quote here from his obituary which appeared in the Yarmouth newspapers, which offers some information on his life and activities.

> The funeral of the late R. T. Mack, soldier, educator and good citizen, took place at Tusket, with full honours by the Canadian Legion. Members of the Yarmouth branch of the Legion, of which he served as Treasurer for a long period of years, attended the funeral in a body. John Bushell sounded the "Last Post."

> The late Mr. Mack, always prominent in Cadet activities enlisted with the 219th Battalion early in 1916, attained the rank of Sergeant, and was later transferred to the 85th Battalion, of the Nova Scotia Highland Brigade. He was wounded at the Battle of Vimy Ridge, which has gone down in Canadian history as one of the greatest battles in which the Canadian Army ever took part. Returning to Canada after the war … he resumed his civilian endeavours and was one of those vitally interested in the organization and maintenance of the Canadian Legion as the organized voice of those who served the Nation in time of war.

All of the other men listed on the monument for World War I made important contributions. A history of their military service in this War could almost constitute a book in its own right, but lies beyond the scope of a general history of the village.

World War II, 1939-1945

Like most other Canadian communities, Tusket sent many men overseas during World War II. The War memorial indicates that the only loss of life was that of Jack Elmer Hatfield. He was a son of Elmer Hatfield, one the village merchants and was in the Royal Air Force. He was killed in air combat on May 28, 1940. He was 27 years old.

I regret that there has been no easily available source for a list of the men and women of the Tusket area who served in World War II. Roland Bourque, Charlie Muise and Tracy Hatfield are all veterans of World War II, and have been extremely helpful in finding as many names as possible of all those men and women who served in this conflict. All were enlisted in the military, some serving overseas, and some at home.

I list below the names of those I have been able to obtain by speaking with people in the village, but regret the incompleteness of the list, and apologize to the families of those who may not be included. No one has been overlooked intentionally. The following list of Tusket area men and women who served in World War II includes a number of people who were natives of nearby villages, but later settled in Tusket and have lived here for most of their lives. Some, on the other hand, grew up in Tusket and moved elsewhere later in life. All of the names that I have been able to obtain are included here.

Amirault, Arthur "Portagee"(Army)
Blauvelt, Franklyn (Air Force)
Bourque, Frederick (Army)
Bourque, Richard (Army)
Bourque, Roland (Artillery)
Campbell, Claire E. (Roddick) (Air Force)
Corporon, Edmund (Army)
Crosby, Carl (Army-paratrooper)
Crosby, St. Clair (Army)
Doucet, Roger (Army)
Dulong, Adolphe (Air Force)
Dulong, Otis (Army)
Gaudet, Anthony (Army)
Gaudet, Joseph "Joe" (Army)
Goldring, Charles (Army – Sergeant Major)
Goldring, Jean (W.R.E.N.S.) (Navy)
Hamilton, Harry (Army)
Hatfield, Jack Elmer (Air Force)
Hatfield, Roger (Merchant Navy)
Hatfield, Tracy (Air Force)
Hubbard, Raymond "Peege" (Army)
LeBlanc, Anthony (Army)

Little, Donald (Navy)
Little, Frank (Air Force)
Muise, Charles "Charlie" (Army)
Muise, Henry (Army)
Nauss, Oscar (Army)
Pottier, Alphonse (Air Force)
Pottier, Benoit (Navy)
Robbins, Earle (Air Force)
Roddick, Morton G. (Army)
Roddick, Stanley B. (Army)
Sweeney, Edwin (Army)
Sweeney, Borden (Army)
Sweeney, Roy (Army)
Thibeau, Edward "Eddie" (Army)
Thibeau, Joseph "Joe" (Army
Wathen, Arthur (Army)
White, Trafton (Army)
Wood, Harry (Air Force)
Wood, Gerald (Army)
Wood, Kenneth (Army)
Wood, Whitfield (Army)
Young, John (Air Force)
Young, Phyllis (Air Force)

As with "R.T. Mack", a veteran of World War I, I have included some information on two of our World War II veterans. They represent a sampling only, of the stories that could be told. Unfortunately, Frank Little passed away a few years ago, before I was able to talk with him personally. However, I feel privileged to be able to relate Tracy Hatfield's story as he personally related it to me in January through March of 2005.

TUSKET MAN DECORATED FOR LEADERSHIP AND SKILL

Frank B. Little

October 1941 – Travelled at own expense to England and enlisted in the R. A. F. Took wireless course to qualify, six months before war commenced.

One of Yarmouth County's most popular young men, Sgt. Frank B. Little, son of Mr. and Mrs. Barney Little of Tusket, has been awarded the distinguished Flying Medal. The 28 year-old Tusket flier is the first Yarmouth County man to be decorated for bravery during the present war. He was awarded the medal for gallantry, leadership and initiative shown during bombing raids in the Grecian campaign.

Sgt. Little joined the R.A.F. about six months before the outbreak of war following a radio-wireless course taken at Toronto. He sailed to England at his own expense and enlisted in the R.A.F. He was one of the first to take part in bombing raids over Germany. During the early months of the war he and crew members made at least three flights weekly over German territory. On their last flight they narrowly escaped disaster when their ship was struck by anti-aircraft fire over the French Coast, while returning from a foray into German territory. The pilot managed to make the English coast but Little and fellow crewmen were forced to bail out at 1,000 feet. All escaped uninjured while the bomber crashed.

Sgt. Little and his crew were then transferred to Egypt where they saw extensive action in the Egyptian and Greek campaign for several months. Sgt. Little was then transferred back to England on furlough as instructor at one of the English training schools. About two months ago his parents received a letter stating that he found these duties "dull." He expressed the hope that he would soon be on active service. Sgt. Little was born in Tusket and received his schooling in that community. Following this he worked on his parents' farm for some time. He is well known throughout Yarmouth County and is very popular. His father, Barney Little, is a world war veteran.

November 1942 – Word has been received by Mrs. Lloyd Cann of Dayton, that her brother, Pilot Officer Frank B. Little had a part in the recent Investiture service at Buckingham Palace where he was presented with the Distinguished Flying Medal by the King. Frank is the son of Mr. and Mrs. Barney Little of Tusket and is well known throughout the county.

Tracy G. Hatfield (P.O.W.)

Tracy G. Hatfield
1920 - 2005

On June 18, 1942, Mr. and Mrs. Elmer Hatfield of Tusket were notified that their son, Flight Sergeant Tracy Hatfield "formerly announced as missing, is now officially reported to be a prisoner of war in enemy territory. He is slightly injured … the Hatfield family are overjoyed to learn of Flight Sergeant Hatfield's safety." It was only two years earlier, on May 28, 1940 that another son, Jack Elmer, had died in air combat over Europe.

On August 19, 1942, a Yarmouth newspaper reported: "Two Yarmouth airmen are in the same German war prison camp, according to a card received by Mr. and Mrs. G. R. Nickerson, from their son, Sergeant Jack Nickerson. The card said Sgt. Tracy Hatfield, son of Mr. and Mrs. Elmer Hatfield of nearby Tusket, "breezed in last night (July10th). Been down six weeks. Bailed out. Had stiff neck but 100 per cent now."

I feel privileged to be able to share with the reader Tracy's long ordeal as a prisoner of war during the next three years as he related it to me during recent visits at his home (January – March 2005).

We begin his story as he and his fellow comrades were on their way as part of the very first massive air-bombing raid over Europe to include a force of 1000 airplanes or more. In the darkness of the night, he remembers a fellow comrade asking what the lights below were; the pilot replied that it was the city of Cologne. At that precise moment, they were caught in enemy aircraft fire. The first hit must have caught the tail section, because the pilot could no longer control the aircraft with his control sticks; the airplane went into a spiral motion like a corkscrew. "Suddenly there was a second hit and the aircraft was rapidly filling with flames" recalls Tracy. "There was very little time left … it was extremely difficult to remain oriented as the plane spun around in circles." He recalls how difficult it was to parachute out. Tracy pauses, with his head down, then slowly looks up to me and says "I looked through the escape hatch … I had to go … there was not much choice." (Of the six crew members, three died and three survived).

The next thing Tracy remembers is regaining consciousness a couple of days later from raindrops hitting his face. He was in a large wheat field … the grass was about four feet high. The first sound he heard was someone sharpening a scythe with a stone; as he slowly got up, he saw an old man in the distance cutting hay in this huge field. Tracy had a very sore neck and his face was badly bruised; his eyes were nearly closed from swelling and when he tried to move on, he realized how terribly weak he was. In his tiny survival kit was a cigarette with some type of dope (probably opium, although they were never told what the substance was) to use if necessary under such circumstances, "to give you a charge," he says. Tracy made use of it and soon managed to drag himself into a large haystack in the field. Suddenly he felt someone kicking at him through the hay. As he looked up, a gun was pointed directly in his face; he was sure he had met his final fate. He then realized this man was not in military uniform. Shortly afterwards, however, two military men arrived and Tracy was brought to a small country town where he was introduced to the mayor. Here two Gustapo soldiers appeared on the scene. The first two soldiers told Tracy to stay close to them. He realized what they were trying to tell him. The last thing Tracy wanted was to be under the hands of the Gustapo. He was pleased and relieved however, at the way he was treated.

Arrangements were made to transfer him to a hospital in Cologne for his injuries. After being treated, he was transferred to another prison in Frankfurt where he was interrogated for the next two weeks. He recalls some tense moments during this interrogation process. When Tracy was told that they had ways to make him talk, he knew perfectly well what they meant. "It sent shrills through your body," recalls Tracy … "one of the more common practices was pulling out fingernails." But Tracy recalls that the most tense moments came when he was told that he apparently did not wish to see his parents again. After thirteen days of interrogation, this same interrogator reached out, shook Tracy's hand and said, "Mr. Hatfield, you're a fine soldier." Tracy replied "Thank you, sir."

"I walked through that door and never saw the man again." To this day, Tracy feels that this man was a gentleman and his parting words made Tracy feel very good. "I never forgot him," says Tracy. He felt fortunate, realizing that he could have fared much worse.

Tracy was then transferred to a prisoner of war camp in Sagan (Zegan) Poland, just over the German border. The camp was located approximately 100 miles southeast of Berlin and was known as Stalag Luft III (Air Camp 3). He recalls, "It was a huge camp … when I walked through those gates, I was sure that we had lost the war. There were thousands of prisoners … it seemed like as far as you could see there were prisoners. They were from all over the world. It was difficult to believe there could be enough soldiers left out there to fight the war. This place was so big!" Tracy was a prisoner of war here for approximately a year and a half and was then transferred to another camp in Latvia, near the Russian border. This camp was known as Stalag Luft VI (Air Camp 6).

When Tracy arrived at Stalag Luft III, a risky escape plan was already underway by a large of group of inmates. The plan was to dig a long, deep, underground tunnel leading to the edge of the woods outside of the prison walls and escape at night. The ground was very sandy and made for easy digging, but also made it easy to collapse. To discourage such attempts, the Germans often used bulldozers to go back and forth to cause vibrations that would collapse such tunnels. For this reason, the tunnel had to be very deep. Although some shovels were smuggled into the tunnels, most of the digging was done with large, empty milk tin cans that were shaped into digging utensils. Three tunnels were being dug simultaneously; although the Germans did discover one, the main one was kept a secret to the end.

The labour involved an undertaking was enormous … and done at great risk. Everyone had to work together to make things work. Professional engineers, now prisoners, would continually be working on designing makeshift systems (bellows to pump air) for importing oxygen into the tunnel. This was always a priority in order for the escape plan to work … they had to have oxygen to dig into the tunnel! Inmates had their own guards posted throughout the compound and were strategically positioned to relay any suspicion of being discovered.

The entrance to the tunnel was located inside one of the washrooms. Small "pot belly" cast iron stoves were installed within the washrooms for "some heat" during the winter months. Under a stove was the entrance to the tunnel. A stove could be removed and re-installed within seconds," says Tracy. Two wood planks were positioned under the "overhang lip" and it could very quickly be moved. Everything had to be "timed to perfection" so as not to get caught: "the stove was removed, the guys dropped through the hole. Underneath was a fairly large dug out area … like a room … and the tunnel led from here." The tunnel was only a crawl space and often had to be shored up; usually with boards removed from parts of the beds that would be inconspicuous to the guards. Tracy recalls that the beds got to be horribly uncomfortable.

A major concern was always what to do with all the sand that was being dug from underground, especially when the digging got to be very deep and the sand became a different shade, making it difficult to hide. Shower towels were often rolled up with sand in them and slowly "shaken", allowing the sand to be dropped around the complex. Another common method used was to roll up sand into the bottom of their pant legs and slowly let it drop on the ground as they walked around the courtyards, rubbing their feet in the sand in order to mix it together as it fell from their pant legs. This was slow however, and a faster and more practical method was devised. Long, narrow cloth bags were hand stitched with a flap in the bottom that could easily be opened with a simple tug from a short string that led into the pant pockets. Another longer string was attached to each bag, hung around the neck and inside their shirts, down inside their pant legs. Each bag was then filled with sand and "dropped out" wherever it was convenient. Ironically, the inmates were provided with shovels and rakes and permitted to try and grow small gardens. Of course nothing would grow in such sandy soil, but these gardens became the practical place to empty the sand bags. As the sand was dropped, the "gardeners" would quickly rake and mix the sand together so that the colour variations went unnoticed. This method meant that much more digging could be accomplished in less time.

After more than a year of digging, they finally reached outside the compound. Unfortunately, they came up approximately twenty feet short from the edge of the forest. Being so close, the decision was made that a successful escape could still be accomplished. The order of who would go first was determined by who had been a prisoner and working on the tunnel the longest – in other words – by seniority. On the night of the planned escape, Tracy was near the end of the line due to less seniority.

The plan was that one by one they would come out and crawl on their stomachs to the nearby woods. As this was taking place, bad timing spoiled the plan … one of the guards, apparently needing to urinate, in order to be "out of sight", ended up not too far from the escape hole. Tracy says the story was that the guard thought he saw an unusual tree stump in the distance; then it was gone. As he started walking towards that direction, it suddenly appeared again. Realizing it was a person, the guard (in German) shouted "hands up" … shots were fired; other guards quickly arrived on the scene.

With the commotion and excitement going on outside, Tracy and others in the tunnel managed to return to their barracks before being apprehended and were spared their lives. How many made it outside or to the woods, Tracy doesn't really know. What is known, however, is that a group of fifty escapees were eventually rounded up, loaded in the back of a truck, driven to a field outside the prison camp, lined up and machine gunned down. Today, near the entrance to the former Stalag Luft III prisoner of war camp in Poland, the names of these fifty men are enshrined in stone.

In 1963, a full feature movie called "The Great Escape", starring Steve McQueen was based on this attempted escape. According to Tracy, except for the usual "Hollywood drama," the story was quite accurately portrayed. The movie ends with three escapees making it to freedom through the help of the "underground forces." Tracy cannot verify if this is fact or fictional. His personal story, however, doesn't end here.

Under the Geneva Convention Agreement, prisoners of war were supposed to be moved to another camp approximately every six months, but Tracy says this hardly ever happened. Approximately a year and a half after being imprisoned at Stalag Luft III, Tracy was transferred to Stalag Luft VI in Latvia, near the Russian border. This was further north and much colder. Tracy recalls that the worst about both camps was the food. He says that during most of his captivity, the meal of the day was cabbage soup and one eighth of a loaf of what they called "sawdust bread." It was some sort of brown bread that crumbled apart when you barely touched it. Eventually, Tracy gradually began to realize that he was losing stamina and always felt weak. For a long time he didn't know what was wrong. One day during a soccer game, he couldn't run from a severe chest pain. He brought the matter to a doctor, was examined and told nothing was wrong. Two days later Tracy suffered a haemorrhage and was soon diagnosed with TB (Tuberculosis). Arrangements were made to take him to a hospital in Riga, Latvia's capital city.

Ironically, at this point, Tracy recalls one of the most beautiful experiences in his life. He asked me if I had ever seen the movie Dr. Zhivago, to which I replied "yes." He proceeded to tell me that they left the prison camp in the darkness of the night in a horse drawn sleigh. "It was a cold and clear winter night" he recalls. "It was so calm, the stars were very bright and the beautiful sounds of the sleigh bells were just ringing into the distance. The sleigh simply 'glided' along as the snow glistened against the moonlit sky and into the pink sunrise as we approached our destination. It was so peaceful and beautiful ... I never forgot it. Later in life when I saw the movie Dr. Zhivago ... that famous sleigh ride in the movie was exactly what I had experienced so many years ago," says Tracy.

After a brief pause, we come back to the present. Tracy recalls his feelings when told he had tuberculosis. "During those times it was like a death sentence," he recalls. After being reassured that new developments for a full recovery were more promising for the disease, he was returned to Stalag Luft III prison camp in Latvia. He remained a prisoner there until three months prior to the end of the war. When asked about the daily life within the prison camp, Tracy says the food was the worst, and he attributes his failing health largely to malnutrition. When first captured, Tracy was a very healthy and physically fit young man, weighing 165 pounds. When released almost three years later, he weighed 108 pounds.

With regards to being mistreated in general, he says, "not really ... it could have been much worse." They were allowed to play various sports games, like soccer, etc. and were often given various chores to do. He recalls "having my knuckles rapped a few times," for peeling the potatoes too thick. Although the prisoners here were from various fighting divisions, it should be pointed out that Stalag Lufts (Air Camps) were primarily intended for Air Force prisoners. Consequently, no Air Force prisoner was allowed to go outside the camp to work for the farmers in the fields. Tracy recalls that often several "other" prisoners from the camp were allowed to work (under guards) for the local farmers and fared far better for food because the farmers would often give them fruits and vegetables from the fields.

Most of the guards were German soldiers who had been wounded in previous battles but were now well enough to perform guard duties at these prison camps. Most doctors within the camp were Allied soldiers who were doctors by profession and had joined the war and been captured. The German doctors were used on the front lines to look after their own soldiers. "Hitler was a horrible man, but there were still a lot of good people in Germany," says Tracy.

Still suffering health problems, Tracy was finally released as an "exchange prisoner" of war (repatriated) just three months prior to the end of the War. Sweden being a neutral country, he was boarded on a huge ocean liner ship and docked at Malmo, Sweden. Tracy appeared quite surprised when I told him I knew where Malmo was because my great aunt had worked there for the Canadian Red Cross during the war. He proceeded with his story, recalling how wonderful it was to hear the cheering crowds on the dock. Suddenly, a loud voice from the dockside asked if there were any Canadian soldiers aboard the ship, to which Tracy hollered "yes." "From what part of Canada?" the voice replied. "Nova Scotia" said Tracy. "What part of Nova Scotia?" the voice replied. "Tusket" said Tracy, to which the raised voice again replied "Tusket! I'm from Belleville!" When they were finally allowed to disembark, Tracy recalls how they embraced each other with open arms and what a wonderful moment of rejoicing it was, to hold onto someone from home once again. Ironically, her name was Dorothy "Dora" (Pottier) Dohrman … she was my great aunt. Tante Dora, as we always called her. She had married in Sweden but was now a widow. She had enlisted in the Canadian Army and spent much time working for the Canadian Red Cross in Malmo, Sweden toward the end of the war, helping with former prisoners of war. Before she passed away, she shared several horror stories about survivors with me … but this one had a very happy ending.

Although Tracy was a "lucky survivor" of the war, he says that his health was never quite the same afterwards; he was never able to regain most of the weight that he had lost. I have known Tracy since the early 1960s; he is a special person and always a pleasure to talk with. The time spent with him, and the stories that we shared during these past few months will always remain cherished moments for me.

I know full well that many of the other Tusket veterans of World War II have equally dramatic stories to tell. I hope those stories, not included in this history, will be recorded for future generations. All are stories that need to be told. What has been offered here must be regarded as a sampling only of the stories brought back from this horrible War by our local men.

April 6, 2005: Today I have lost a good friend. Tracy Hatfield passed away at the age of eighty five.

The (R.C.A.F.) Radar Station at Tusket

(No. 3 radar detachment – Tusket, Nova Scotia)
(Later known as Camp Montebello)

A piece of Tusket's military history that is often overlooked is the history of the radar station that was established here during World War II. The road entrance to the radar station was located just slightly to the north of the present Tusket Industrial Park entrance. Traveling northwest on this side road for a distance of approximately one mile brought you directly to the radar station, which was located on top of "Blueberry Hill", so-called by the local people at that time. Information about the station was very sketchy and becoming difficult to find until the recent publication of a book called *R.C.A.F. Radar 1941-1945 SECRET* by William "Bill" McLachlan who was stationed here during the War. This book deals with all established radar stations on both the east and west coasts of Canada and provides an interesting insight into the value of these stations at a time of critical need. With Bill McLachlan's permission, I have taken much of the information found here from his book. He provides many details on the once thriving and "secret" Air Force Radar Station at Tusket.

During World War II "as a precaution against any eventuality … the government decided to build a chain of early warning stations along the Eastern seaboard and other strategic locations." Beginning in 1941, thirty units were gradually built along the east coast of Canada. "Personnel were recruited from all over Canada; they came from every walk of life. There were teachers, clerks, engineers, students and of course many radio amateurs 'hams.'"

A basic requirement for station location was high land. This was essential for proper station-spacing in order to provide suitable transmitting coverage and overlapping between stations. The map below "East Coast Air Defence Radar Coverage" illustrates how effective this series of radar stations were in providing a solid barrier for the entire east coast as their signals overlapped each other.

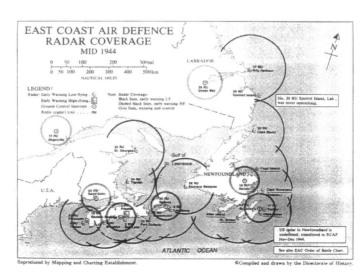

East Coast Air Defence Radar Coverage – 1944.

While some sites were in civilized areas, the majority were located in isolated and inaccessible places. Many of these locations demanded individuals with an aptitude for enduring isolation and adverse conditions. The entire area at each station was fenced in and guards were on duty at all times.

One of the basic criteria for site selection being a high point of land, the Tusket site was chosen for the high ground at "Blueberry Hill" and it's proximity to the coastline. Geographically, the Tusket station provided easy access, and being located only two miles to the north from the village centre, it was one of the stations that personnel generally welcomed being posted to. "Frequently, those fortunate enough to be posted to Tusket arrived from Halifax on the "Blue-Berry Special", a train that actually stopped at times to allow passengers en-route to engage in the picking of the 'blue fruit' which grew in abundance on the railway right-of-way."

A new recruit from Regina recalls his arrival at Tusket: "one fellow … came up to us and said 'Welcome to Tusket fellows!' It seemed we'd be one big-happy family here on this station and so far it has been so."

Some of the married personnel stationed at Tusket brought their families with them and rented homes in the village, traveling to and from the base for work. Some of their children were even born here. Tusket was considered one of the more civilized postings.

Overlooking the Tusket River and Lake Vaughn to the north, high upon the top of Blueberry Hill, the Tusket radar station served as a sub-base of the Yarmouth air base, although it operated entirely on its own. "It had its own cooks, security, male nurse and of course, radar personnel." The radar operating equipment was installed here in August, 1942. The area was fenced in and guards were on full-time duty. The telephone centre was operated by Cecil Goodwin, a local gentleman from Argyle Sound. "Cecil owned a very handy 1923 Buick car which was used for night time adventure."

In order to maintain morale at a high level and avoid monotony, various recreation activities were quickly organized at the Tusket station. Most stations published a newsletter of some sort. The Tusket station was no exception, and the name given to the newsletter was "The Tuscan;" it was published monthly. Articles which appeared in this newsletter provide much insight as to the various activities at the Tusket radar station.

"Each of the four shifts supplied information to the station paper, relating the events of their crews." With the assistance of an educational promoter, courses were made available through the Royal Canadian Legion for anyone wishing to enroll. Various sports activities: i.e.; basketball, floor hockey and bowling were established and competed against their counterparts from the Yarmouth station. During the summer months, it was common practice to go clam-digging for an "all you can eat" gathering. With the Tusket River (and Lake Vaughn) in their back yard, swimming was a most popular pastime for many "as the local beauties in their scanty suits displayed their figures at the canal bridge." [Raynardton Bridge]. During the fall hunting season, deer hunting was very popular and the deer meat was a much-welcomed treat back at the station. Transportation for these hunting expeditions was usually supplied by Cecil Goodwin's 1923 Buick and the successful hunting party was rewarded with a two day pass. The radar technicians kept the electronics in top working order for the radar operators who were constantly kept busy plotting aircrafts … the main reason for their being here. Diesel mechanical engineers made sure that the electrical generators for the station were well maintained and fully operational at all times. Movies were shown in the mess hall twice a week and full uniforms were a must on Sundays "when friends and relatives were invited." Wednesday nights, however, were "just for the guys." All accounts attest to excellent meals prepared by the cooking staff and "the place ran like a well-oiled machine."

Documents also indicate that if the airmen from the radar station were called upon during an emergency in the village, their prompt assistance was much welcomed. The following account can attest to this fact: "One night after a thunder and lightning storm we received a phone call from the town of Tusket that lightning had struck the church, and started a fire in the belfry, would we come to put it out? A group of us … sped to Tusket … climbed into the belfry with a fire extinguisher and put the fire out. [The] wooden structure was well on its way, and the wooden church would have been consumed." This would have been the Methodist Church in the centre of the village.

The following is but an example of the fond memories that were left with the personnel who served at this station during the 1940s: "Looking back after spending a year and a half at this location I remember it as a very good place to be stationed; it had a strength of about seventy-five men and everybody got along fine. We had very good relations with the people in the area; the girls would invite us to strawberry socials. I remember skating on a pond; it was reminiscent of a Currier and Ives Christmas card".

Undoubtedly, these are but a few examples of what life was like during those few years that the Tusket radar station was in existence.

The Radar station also provided an economic boost to the village and the entire area during this time. The Tusket station "… provided a valuable contribution to the defense of Yarmouth area while, at the same time, providing working conditions and comradeship of which it can be proud. Very few stations are as well geographically situated, which perhaps is a factor."

It should be mentioned in closing here, that the Radar Station also made some additional lasting contributions to the area. In every location where such military establishments were set up during World War II, it was inevitable that some of the service people would meet and marry local women. A few would choose to settle in the area permanently.

Bill McLachlan of Ottawa, Ontario, married Phyllis Raynard of Raynardton. Although not a permanent resident, they have returned to the Tusket area during the summer months for several years. Jacob LeBlanc of Scoudouc, N.B. married Elsie Deveau of Sainte Anne-du-Ruisseau and lived here the remainder of his life.

Emilien "Ted" Surette of Sainte Anne-du-Ruisseau and Cecil Goodwin of Argyle Sound were both local men who served at the Tusket Radar Station. It was Cecil Goodwin in fact, who was one of the leading young men from the radar station who performed the heroic task of extinguishing the fire in the belfry of the Methodist Church steeple mentioned above.

The radar station was established on the site that my generation remembers as Camp Montebello. In 1948 St. Ambrose Parish of Yarmouth, under the direction of Father William A. Penny, purchased the property and set up a youth summer camp on the site, making use of the existing buildings. There were fourteen buildings in all and it was given the name of Camp Montebello. A large piece of land at the bottom of the hill was purchased separately to build a ball field. (The piece of land is still owned by St. Ambrose Parish to this day). The summer youth camp became very popular, drawing youths from as far away as Shelburne and Annapolis.(My wife attended summer camp here in the early 1960s). It continued to operate until 1966, when vandalism became a factor in its closure. It was eventually sold to Sonny Hill from Dayton for $2300.00; he used the lumber from the buildings to build the Honey Hill Motel which still exists today as the Lighthouse Lakeside Inn in Dayton. Some of the lumber was also used to construct part of the large building next to St. Ambrose Cathedral in Yarmouth which today houses the administration offices for the diocese. There are two residential homes on the former radar property at Tusket today, and the road is privately owned. Today it bears the name "Camp Montebello Road."

Being one of the highest points of land in Tusket, the former radar site on top of "Blueberry Hill" is presently used for a modern telecommunications tower. It can easily be identified at night by the bright light on its peak.

Since World War II

Since World War II we have been blessed to live in a time of extended peace. The local militia is still a reality, but is stationed solely in Yarmouth. Many young people throughout Yarmouth County have been involved over the years as members of Sea, Air or Army Cadets. Various local people have entered the Canadian Forces and chosen military careers, but there has been no need in this country to call forth the civilian population for military service since 1945. May we continue to live in times of peace.

CHAPTER 12

ACADIANS IN TUSKET

CHAPTER 12
ACADIANS IN TUSKET

The First 90 Years

As time passed, and I came closer to the end of this history project, it became obvious to me that no clear mention had been made of the major population shift that has taken place in Tusket over the years. This change mainly centres on the influx of Acadians to the village over a long period of time. Some of these changes I have witnessed since I first settled in Tusket in 1965.

Tusket has long been regarded as a Loyalist and an Anglophone community, and those are certainly the historical roots of this village. Nothing has been found in the records to indicate that any Acadian people lived within the bounds of the village in the 1780s or 1790s . Today however, the village is largely populated by Acadian families.

There are several histories of the Acadians in Argyle that readers can turn to for a more detailed history of this cultural group. But it is probably appropriate even in a community history such as this one, to provide some historical background. Acadians were settled in Argyle Municipality prior to the Deportation, and 1653, the date acknowledged as the settlement of the Pubnico area by the d'Entremont family, probably marks the first permanent French settlers in this part of Yarmouth County. They were established in East Pubnico. In the years after 1653, other settlements also took place. By the time of the Deportation in the 1750s, substantial communities existed at Argyle, Argyle Head, and Roberts Island. The remnants of the Acadian dykes in communities such as Argyle Head and Roberts Island are evidence of their years spent there and the agricultural development of their lands. All of these families had their properties confiscated and destroyed by the British government in Halifax in the 1750s. These families were then sent into exile.

Starting in the year 1763, a number of Acadian families who had been exiled to Massachusetts, began to make their way back to Nova Scotia. There were one or two families, like the d'Entremonts and Amiraults, who had lived in this area prior to the Deportation, and they re-settled at West Pubnico. The majority of the other Acadian families who settled in Argyle after the Deportation had previously lived in other parts of Nova Scotia and New Brunswick. Of all the Acadian families to settle in Argyle after the Deportation, only the Moulaison family is believed to have avoided deportation and lived in hiding until it was safe to once again show themselves. The late Acadian historian, Rev. Fr. Clarence J. d'Entremont, maintained that every other family can be found living in Massachusetts, or elsewhere, during the years of exile.

Shortly after 1763 a number of other Acadian families began to arrive in Argyle as well, and settlements like Wedgeport, Sainte-Anne-du-Ruisseau, Sluice Point, Amirault's Hill and Hubbard's Point were all settled during this time. These families were not returning to previously cultivated land, but faced the task of clearing forested land and establishing farms that would sustain them in the wilderness. Settling in coastal areas, their livelihoods were often taken from the sea as much as the land. In Argyle Municipality, these Acadian communities tended to be located on points of land jutting out into the ocean. The development of neighbouring areas by New England Planters and Loyalists meant that these French communities were often separated by English communities situated between them.

A number of Acadian families had arrived in the area south of Tusket before the arrival of the first Loyalist settlers in 1784. In the earliest account of Loyalist settlement quoted elsewhere in this history, Deborah (VanTyle) states of the first settlement, "On the 20th of March they left the family, and with thirteen others set sail for Yarmouth, Joshua Trefry, pilot. There they found the land all taken up; were recommended to Tusket. Found the land there looked more favourable, returned to Shelburne, took the family on board, and arrived at Tusket 11th of May, 1784. At this time there was no one settled on the river, but the French."

The Acadian settlers certainly arrived in post-Deportation Argyle with little but their ingenuity and a willingness to rebuild their lives. This was not always the case with the Loyalist settlers. Although all the Loyalists had suffered tremendous losses in the Revolutionary War, many were able to salvage a good deal from their properties, and did not arrive penniless in Nova Scotia. Some came with their black slaves, which certainly would have given them an advantage in establishing new lives in what was an undeveloped wilderness. Most were compensated for their losses in the War, either through land grants, cash settlements or both.

Language and religion were both cultural barriers that created divisions between these two groups during early times, and of those two barriers, religion may well have been the more important of the two. All of the Acadians were Roman Catholic while the Anglophone population belonged to one Protestant denomination or another. Mingling for religious worship during these early times simply did not happen. Marriage between the two groups was rare, and frowned upon by both groups.

The Acadians were also held back locally due to a very high level of illiteracy during this time. This was clearly a result of their earlier history, both prior to, and during the Deportation. Overall, the ability to read and write does not appear to have factored importantly in their lives previous to this time. Early petitions in the 1780s and the early 1800s make it clear that only a handful of Acadians in Argyle were able to read and write. This meant that most of them were excluded from holding public positions such as "Justice of the Peace," as literacy was one of the conditions of these offices. As late as 1801, when the land grants were confirmed to the Acadians living south of Tusket, Benoni d'Entremont, from the then distant community of West Pubnico, is also included in the grant. This is clearly because his ability to read and write enabled him to transact the government business associated with the grant on behalf of this group, and he in turn received land in exchange for these services. He was also a Justice of the Peace.

There were a few Acadian people (usually men) who through the efforts of Rev. Father Jean Mandé Sigogne, and the Church, were able to learn to read and write - but these people were the exception, rather than the rule. As late as 1824 there were still no public schools in the Municipality of Argyle, for either the English or the French. Later in the 1820s and the 1830s this began to change as schools were established. It took several decades, however, for the literacy level among Acadians to rise. They were also handicapped by the fact that they needed to become literate in English as well as French, if they wished to conduct business with their neighbouring English communities. Although there were no public schools in the area before 1824, illiteracy was not nearly as common in English communities. Clearly, these English families who were literate made some effort to pass some degree of education on to their children.

Although Acadian families were settled along the Tusket River when the first Loyalists arrived here in 1784, they were living on land along the banks of the river in what we know today as the communities of Hubbard's Point, Amirault's Hill and Sluice Point. There is no record of Acadian families living in "Tusket proper" at this time. Acadians, in fact, would not settle in Tusket until some ninety years later.

The A.F. Church Map which dates to the year 1866 in the village of Tusket, marks every house within the community, and places the owner or occupant's name beside the property. In that year there were still no Acadian families shown in the village of Tusket. If any were living here they must have been "renters," but it seems likely that no Acadians owned property here at that time.

The 1860s, and the two decades that followed, saw an unprecedented boom in shipbuilding in this village. Those activities have been discussed elsewhere in this history. These activities had a direct impact on the nearby Acadian population. These shipyards not only required the skills of master shipwrights and blacksmiths, they could not survive and prosper without a large work force of general carpenters and labourers. Many of these labourers came from the neighbouring Acadian communities, especially Hubbard's Point, which was close enough to enable workers to walk to and from their homes to the nearby shipyards. There were prosperous Acadian families in the community of Hubbard's Point, and their surviving homes are much like the Tusket homes of the same era. There were, however, a large number of poor and uneducated families in that community as well. Those families supplied a large part of the labour force in the shipyards. These were difficult times and many of the workers were exploited in a number of ways by their employers. They worked for wages, but were also encouraged to take a good part of their pay in goods from the company store which almost every shipyard operated. Tradition has it that their wives, who were managing households in need, were also encouraged to take any provisions they needed, and more, on account. It was not unusual for many of these labourers to end their season of employment in debt to their employer.

James Adolphus Hatfield, who operated one of the largest shipyards, was also the shipbuilder located closest to Hubbard's Point. James H. Bingay in his 1955 letter has the following to say about his operations: "Uncle Dolph was anything but a brilliant businessman. Like the saintly Quaker cotton manufacturers of Manchester in the early 19th century he grew up in the development period of his business: and like them he exploited (quite unintentionally and non-understandingly) the poor French devils who worked for him and fed from his shop a double profit."

Adolphus Hatfield was not the only shipbuilder to take advantage of this readily available supply of cheap labour, hungry for employment. These activities had a long-lasting impact on the community of Hubbard's Point, which remained a noticeably poor community well up into the 1960s. Although there were Acadian labourers in the Tusket shipyards from more distant communities, it is clear from the history of communities like Sainte-Anne-du-Ruisseau, Belleville, Amirault's Hill and Sluice Point - that as an Acadian, the further away you were from Tusket during these times, the better off you were.

Lest I paint a picture that is too black and white here, it must also be stated that there were families from Hubbard's Point and other Acadian communities who did prosper from these same business operations. Solen Doucette of Hubbard's Point was the most sought-after river pilot in the area. Knowing all the intricacies of the hazardous route up the Tusket River for tall ships, he was depended upon to guide these large vessels up and down the river, and did very well for himself. Théophile Doucette of Hubbard's Point was also one of the most skilled stevedores in the county. He was depended on to load and ballast the large ships leaving Tusket, and often travelled with them to perform the same duties in their various ports of call. Denis Surette of nearby Eel Brook (now Sainte-Anne-du-Ruisseau) was a master shipwright and was well paid for his role as the architect of several of the finest vessels built in Tusket. But for every Acadian family in this district that prospered during this era, many others struggled to provide for their families under these conditions.

James H. Bingay in his 1955 letter relates the following incident that he recalled from the launching of the ship *Louise M. Fuller* in 1885 or 1886. "Just before she reached the water, she [the ship] spraddled the ways, and settled gracefully in the mud. It was weeks before she could be raised. The 'ways', you know, were heavily greased with lard for a launching. There I saw a long train of women and girls from Hubbard's Point, armed with tin receptacles and old kitchen knives, eagerly scraping the foul lard from the ways, and depositing it in their cans, to carry home to boil down for cooking, and perhaps for making inferior tallow candles."

The First Acadians to Settle in Tusket Proper

Returning to the A.F. Church Map of 1866, it should be pointed out that one Acadian household is noted, that of Peter (Pierre) Melanson on Highway #3. This house is located across the road from the old HP Motel. Today, due to the current location of road signs, this is considered to be part of Tusket. Seniors within the village maintain that this was never considered Tusket in times past, but was considered part of the Acadian community of Sainte-Anne-du-Ruisseau. This dwelling's location, a half mile from the nearest English household in Tusket, in 1866, suggests that they are correct.

It was certainly not many years after 1866 that the first Acadian families from nearby communities began to settle in Tusket. James H. Bingay, whose 1955 letter has been quoted throughout this history, offers some important information on the earliest Acadian families to establish themselves in Tusket. James H. Bingay was born on 14 August 1878, so it seems safe to state that his clear recollections of the village would date from 1888 at the very latest.

One of the earliest Acadian families to settle in the village, as shown by the research generated by the Heritage Property Inventory of the village, was that of Cyrille Doucette. In the 1871 census return of Tusket, Cyrille Doucette is found living in the household of Ephraim C. Simonson on Court Street. At that time he was nineteen years old and was obviously learning his trade as a blacksmith under Simonson. On 1 October 1878 Cyrille Doucette purchased the Simonson home and blacksmith shop. This is the home known in more recent times at the Toussaint and Exilda Muise house. Cyrille appears to have broken the cultural barrier in purchasing this property in Tusket. Many other Acadians would follow in the years afterward.

Cyrille Doucette, one of Tusket's earliest Acadian home owners, was a native of either Hubbard's Point or Amirault's Hill.

Sometime in the 1870s or 1880s, Moïse Muise and his family built a small house at the eastern end of Court Street. This house, which would have been one of the early Acadian dwellings in Tusket, was later owned by Vincent Muise, and then his son "Tommy." The old house was demolished in 1987.

James Bingay mentions another Acadian family that purchased property within the village two years later. He speaks of the house on what is now known as the "Frank Doucette Road," which has in recent decades been known as the Melanie Hubbard house, as follows: "When I first remember it, the house was occupied by one of the very few Frenchmen then living in Tusket. I've forgotten his name, but he was universally known as 'Old Soldier', as he claimed to have served in the British Army during the Indian Mutiny." According to Yarmouth County deeds this property was purchased on 19 July 1880, from the original owner (Thomas Phillips) by Julian Doucette, Sr.

Around 1885 James Bingay also recalls a French family (though not by name) living in a dilapidated house across from the Tusket School on Court Street. The head of this household was a sailor working on vessels that traded with the West Indies. One of the sons of this man, about James Bingay's age, offered him his first taste of raw sugar cane. It seems likely that this family was renting this property.

James Bingay also states that in the house more recently known as the Remi LeFave House on Highway #3, "dwelt one of the few French Tusketers of my youth - 'old Chris' Doucette." Chris Doucette was obviously renting this property in the 1880s. His son, Peter Doucette, purchased this house in 1906. The property passed from Peter Doucette to Remi LeFave in 1941. Peter Doucette had a brother, Reuben (Urbain) Doucette, who owned the former Felix Muise house a short distance away.

Simon Doucette, a brother of Cyril Doucette, mentioned above, also established himself in Tusket in the 1880s. The Heritage Property Inventory research on Simon's house, on what is now known as VanNorden's Road, suggests that he put together his property by a complicated series of land purchases that involved no less than six different deeds. He then moved a house onto this property and used that as the main part of his dwelling. Simon Doucette was a fisherman, and later, after the construction of the railroad through Tusket, was a "railway section foreman." This house has been known in recent decades as the Roger and Ruth Hatfield house.

It should be noted that in 1866 (A.F. Church Map) the area on what is now known as the "John White Road," was owned exclusively by members of the Hatfield family, all of them probably descendants of Jacob Lyon Hatfield, who built one of Tusket's earliest homes there. Sometime after this date (1866) this entire area, which is also known as "the Cove," became an "Acadian" section of the village. Gordon Hatfield, the photographer, was instrumental in moving Mark "Maco" Hubbard onto the property next to the old Jacob Lyon Hatfield house. John and Fannie White ("LeBlanc") in the 1930s became the owners of the former W. Chase Hatfield property which they ran as the "Riverside Inn" for a few years. Other residents of this section, as have been mentioned elsewhere in this history, were Mary Boucher, Reuben Doucette, Felix Muise, Peter and Louise LeBlanc and others.

Further along on Highway #3, approximately where Hubert Pothier's "old Body Shop" is located, was the home of William Doucette. His family was living here as early as the 1920s. Who the house belonged to previously is not known. The house has been gone for many years.

The house owned in 2005 by Cleve and Lisa Muise on the road leading north out of the village (Route 308 North), was purchased by Zacharie Doucette in 1901, and has been owned primarily by Acadian families since that time. Zacharie would have been among the early Acadian property owners in the village. Zacharie Doucette was a brother to both Peter and Reuben (Urbain) Doucette mentioned earlier.

This is but a sampling of the earliest Acadian families to make the village their permanent home. They were the first of many such families that would settle in the village in the decades that followed.

It should be noted here that from the 1860s up until the 1930s, Yarmouth County, and other parts of Nova Scotia, saw a tremendous exodus of people move from this area to the New England states. The industrial revolution in more populated centres along the

American eastern seaboard offered employment opportunities that were simply not available in Nova Scotia. Both Acadian and English communities experienced this loss of local residents. This exodus of local people did not affect Tusket in the same way it did surrounding communities. The presence here of the many shipbuilding enterprises and the availability of work for a wide range of people meant families in Tusket did not leave the area until much later. When shipbuilding came to an end the large lumber mills in the village offered new employment opportunities for another decade or two. The closure of the Dickie & McGrath sawmill in 1912 resulted in many of the original English families finally selling their properties and moving to the United States or elsewhere permanently. Some of the early Loyalist surnames that had been in the village since the 1780s began to disappear. Many Acadian families from neighbouring communities purchased Tusket properties and began to move into the village during this time.

These were difficult times for the Tusket area. The so-called "Great Depression" of the 1930s arrived some 15 years early in Tusket. There were very few employment opportunities here at this time. Many of those families that remained in Tusket suffered through these dismal economic times – the French and English alike.

Changing Times

It was in the 1930s that the American government, due to the Depression, took steps to limit immigration. Previously it had been very easy for Nova Scotians to move freely to the New England states permanently, or for temporary employment. This was no longer the case. The effect this had on both the English and French population of the county was not totally negative. James H. Bingay has the following to say about this era:

> In my youth, or early middle age, our Frenchmen sailed fishing out of Gloucester, Mass. living home only in the winter. Their little farms went uncultivated, their houses were mean. (Some also went carpentering in the States with the same results.
>
> But when the USA put an embargo on 'foreign' workmen they were perforce compelled to cultivate their neglected properties, and found that their natural mechanical ingenuity brought them ready cash over and above their mere living from their farms. The result, in a quarter of a century, was prosperity and security on a modest scale. Extreme poverty and squalor has almost disappeared. Their houses, built by themselves, are neat and comfortable without and within.

During the early decades of Tusket's history, and well up into the 1950s, it was common for Acadian women, especially the younger women, to be employed in the households of Tusket as servants. A few actually lived in these homes, but more often they travelled home at the end of the day to their homes in Hubbard's Point or elsewhere in the village itself. Many Acadian men were employed in similar positions as gardeners and farm hands. This was simply the accepted way of life for many. After the end of shipbuilding, and the closure of the Dickie & McGrath sawmills, employment of any kind was difficult to secure.

James H. Bingay in his 1955 letter makes it clear that by 1955, all of this was changing. It would change even more quickly in the years ahead. These changes were brought about largely through education. Schools throughout this area changed drastically in the 1950s and 1960s. Many of these changes were brought about due to the work of a local Acadian, Vincent J. Pottier, a native of Belleville, who would eventually become "Judge Vincent Pottier." He was commissioned, with others, to undertake a review of the state of public education in Nova Scotia. In 1954 he delivered his *Report of the Royal Commission on Public School Finance in Nova Scotia*. This was an extensive and highly critical report on the status of education throughout the province. It held many important recommendations for improving the situation. The government took the report very seriously and acted upon many of the recommendations.

The events that followed this report were far-reaching in their impact. Teachers' salaries were increased substantially, and qualifications for filling these positions were also raised. The closure of one-room schools began to take place and the creation of Consolidated Schools with higher standards followed. A Vocational School had also been established in Yarmouth, and offered opportunities for many young people to learn a trade and enter the work force with qualifications. While this improved the opportunities for everyone, the Acadian population appear to have seized these new opportunities with a real enthusiasm.

Acadians in Tusket Today

Tusket, with its solidly Anglophone and Loyalist roots, is today largely populated by Acadian families. This is nothing more than an instance of changing demographics, some of the causes of which have been cited above.

Today, the majority of the large businesses in Tusket providing employment to local people are owned by Acadians. Their contribution to the present prosperity of the place is enormous. The village has always been the seat of local government, and the present Municipal Office for the Municipality of Argyle offers (with minor exceptions) a fully bilingual staff. The Argyle Township Court House & Archives, which is the centre-piece of heritage and cultural concerns in the village, is widely acknowledged for its enlightened and even-handed efforts to preserve the history of every community within the Municipality, be they Acadian, Planter or Loyalist in origin.

Many of the Acadian senior citizens of Tusket, who have lived here for decades, have interesting stories to tell about the early attitudes they encountered in the village. Most of these stories are related with amusement, rather than bitterness - and also with some astonishment at how the village has changed.

Tusket is a community today, where little thought is given as to whether one is "English" or "French." Marriage between the two cultures is so common today that it is difficult to find a household in the community that is purely "English" or "Acadian." We have come to a very comfortable place in our history in this regard. Perhaps the only lingering confusion in this regard comes from the Acadian community itself. Many surrounding "purely" Acadian communities in the Municipality, sometimes continue to regard Tusket as an Anglophone community. Those of us who live here know otherwise.

This is a wonderful place to live, regardless of your ethnic background, language or culture. Many of us feel grateful to be living in this most historic village at this time in its history.

CHAPTER 13

ODDS & ENDS

CHAPTER 13
ODDS & ENDS

Telephone, Electricity, Fire Department, Baseball, Musical Band, Medical Doctors, etc.

This brief chapter is offered here to touch on some general historical facts that I have uncovered about Tusket in the course of writing this manuscript that do not fit into any of the other categories of information presented in the history. These are often interesting tidbits that do not merit a chapter of their own, but will, I think, be of interest to the reader.

Telegraph

Telegraph was the first "modern" form of communication to arrive in North America. J. Murray Lawson's *Yarmouth Past and Present* states that, "The telegraph poles through town were erected on the 22 September 1851, via the Digby route. The office was first opened in the Queen's Row on 8 June 1852 with A. Lawson as manager and operator."

Although we do not have an exact date for the arrival of telegraph in Tusket, it could not have been many years after Yarmouth received this new mode of communication. Some of the earlier photographs in Tusket used in this history show poles carrying wires through the village. In many instances what we are seeing is telegraph, not telephone wires.

Telephone Service in Tusket

The Yarmouth Telephone Company was organized on June 1, 1882, and its lines were opened to Tusket on June 17 of that year.

Christina ("Chrissie") Hatfield operated the first local telephone office, or switchboard, from her house on the John White Road. The switchboard was installed there as early as 1932 and she remained the operator well into old age. She retired from the position in 1959. Most local people referred to these telephone offices as "Central." During her last years as the telephone operator Chrissie was assisted by Frances Blackburn, an adopted daughter of Capt. George P. Tuff.

Margaret d'Entremont was the next telephone operator for the area. She took over the office and the switchboard in 1959 and continued to hold the position until 1964. Like Chrissie Hatfield, she had "Central" set up in her own home.

Doris Trefry took over the telephone office in 1964 from Margaret, and operated it from her home (the Forman Hatfield house) until 1969 when Maritime Tel & Tel set up their own dial-up network connecting directly to Yarmouth. This "sub-unit" was established in a trailer on Court Street, a short distance past the Municipal Offices, on the southern side of the road. It continues to serve the same function to this day.

Electricity

The Yarmouth newspapers announced the fact that electricity had been installed at Tusket at the Dickie & McGrath sawmill in 1900. All indications are that this electricity was produced by generators installed by this firm, rather than by electrical lines being run through the village.

Electricity, for the general public, first found its way to Tusket around 1929. Cecelia "Sis" Crosby remembers her parents discussing whether or not to have their house wired for electricity as it was "going through" the village. The price quoted to wire their house at the time was $200.00, she recalls. Although her father wanted to have it wired, her mother thought it was too expensive … "consequently we did not have it done at that time," she says. Her sister was born on August 25, 1929 and Sis vividly remembers the discussions regarding the installation during this time.

It is believed that the first house to receive electricity in the village was the old Thomas Coleman house. It would have been owned and occupied by William H. Raynard at the time, a butcher by trade. Alfred ("Fred") Babin was the person who did the wiring of the house. This is the home that has been owned since 1946 by Charles and Annie Muise.

Although not in the village proper, a few miles north in the community of Tusket Falls, Nova Scotia Power constructed a dam and a power generating plant in 1928-29. This was a major capital project and provided employment to many people from different parts of county. In 1971 Nova Scotia Power built another facility in Tusket proper.

Tusket Combustion Turbine Generating Plant

The Tusket Turbine Plant was built for and by Nova Scotia Power Corporation in 1971. The purpose of this plant is of course to produce electricity, which feeds into the Nova Scotia Power Corporation grid for the province. Although this plant is considered a "stand-by" unit, needed at peak times of demand, mainly during winter months, it does feed 25,000 kilowatts of electricity into the grid as required throughout the year. While many of Nova Scotia Power's plants are connected with "hydro," this plant is operated by a turbo jet engine, fuelled by diesel. This is a Pratt & Whitney jet engine – equivalent to the engines found in a DC-8 aircraft. The Tusket plant is somewhat unique in that it is a one-man operation. When additional assistance is required it usually comes from the NS Power Hydro Plant a few miles away at Tusket Falls. The operators since the Turbine Plant opened have been as follows: Bruce Marling, Jack Andrews, Jimmy Fox and Gerald Jacquard. Gerald Jacquard, the current operator, has held this position for the last 16 years.

Television

Although today television does not figure very largely in our minds as a modern invention, its first arrival to rural communities in Nova Scotia in the 1950s created quite a stir. The first household in Tusket to enjoy this new marvel was that of Frank Hubbard on the John White Road. A brother of Frank Hubbard, who lived and worked in Massachusetts, had delivered the first television here to his brother's home. This small unassuming household immediately became an important gathering place for those eager to witness the marvels of this new form of entertainment. The homes of Benoit Pottier and Milton and Audrey O'Brien were the next ones to acquire this "latest invention."

Tusket's Early Fire Department – The Mayflower Engine Company

*One of Tusket's early "pumpers."
The photo is taken next to the home of
Gertie & Arthur Wathen. Their son
Douglas is in the photograph.*

Tusket had its first "Fire Pumper" in 1866 which was called "Emerald No. 4." This appears to have been purchased for the village by the Court of General Sessions of the Peace. This Court was the equivalent of municipal government prior to municipal incorporation in 1880. At this time the Court of General Sessions appointed such officers as Fire Wardens and a stipend was paid to those filling this position. One assumes that whoever was appointed Fire Warden for Tusket at this time was in charge of the pumper and responsible for delivering and operating this primitive piece of firefighting equipment to any fire in the village.

In October 1871 the Court of General Sessions approved the following expenditures: $66.58 for a fire bell, $9.88 for duty and freight from Seneca Falls, NY, $37.50 for repairs to the belfry, $3.85 for supplies and labour for painting the belfry, $1.00 for transporting the bell from Yarmouth to Tusket, and $3.40 for 17 feet of rope for the bell.

Around 1879 what more closely resembled an official fire department for the village was formed.

Tusket's first organized fire department was the Mayflower Engine Company, No.1 of Tusket Village. Their first official minute book, which is held at the Argyle Township Court House Archives, begins in March 1879, thirteen years after the village had acquired its first piece of fire-fighting equipment. The first information recorded in the minute books are the by-laws of this organization, and the offices. The leading office of this fire department was the Captain, followed by First and Second Lieutenants, Secretary and Treasurer, and also Foreman of the Suction Hose, and Foreman of the Leading Hose.

The original list of members of the Mayflower Engine Company make it clear that this organization began with 14 members.

1. J. Lyons Hatfield "Hon."
2. Wm. H. Gilman   "
3. E. C. Simonson   "
4. Ansel Kinney   "
5. Barry Bingay   "
6. Abram Lent   "
7. Chas. W. Hatfield
8. Wm. H. Kinney
9. Wm. Jeffery
10. Charles Brown
11. James H. Robbins
12. Smith Harding
13. Stephen Jeffery
14. Jas. McCarthy

The term "Hon." Refers to those holding the offices listed above.

It may be of interest to readers to know the names of the Captains, (today we would probably use the term "Fire Chief") of the Mayflower Engine Company. According to the official minutes they were as follows:

J. Lyons Hatfield, 1879-1881; Ansel Kinney, 1882-1883; Ephraim Simonson, 1884; Ansel Kinney, 1885-1886; Douglas Waters, 1887-1890; Smith Harding, 1891-1893; Ralph Blauvelt, 1894; Douglas Waters, 1895-1897; Charles K. Hurlbert, 1899-1900; Ralph Blauvlet, 1901; W. C. Hatfield, 1903-1905; Simon Doucette, 1906; W. H. Lent, 1907-1912; Norman B. Hatfield, 1913-1914; William H. Raynard, 1915- ?; and Andrew Jeffery, 1921-1922.

The official minutes of this organization cease in 1923, and it seems likely that this marked the end of any sort of fire department in Tusket as an officially incorporated and functioning body. It is clear that the Mayflower Engine Company's property was retained, and perhaps used sporadically, without a fire department, for another ten years.

Early in the history of the Mayflower Engine Company a building had been constructed to house their fire engine, while the second floor of the building was used to hold their meetings and for other purposes. This building was located directly behind the Court House in the centre of the village. A lattice-work tower (referred in the records as a "belfry") had been built earlier in 1871 and a fire-bell placed on top. This was rung in order to alert members of the department and others in the village of a fire. This tower, with its bell, can be seen at the rear of the Court House in the photograph on page 59.

Members of the Mayflower Engine Company paid annual dues, and the records also indicate that they paid fines to the company as well, for not attending meetings. In the 1880s and 1890s a significant source of income for the company was also the "watering of ships." These activities are recorded many times in their records. This involved using the pumper to draw water from wells and then pump it into barrels and other receptacles on ships.

Some eleven years after the minutes of the Mayflower Engine Company cease, in 1934, steps were taken by the Municipality of Argyle to dispose of their property. By this time the Municipality seems to have reverted to appointing Fire Wardens as the Court of General Session had done prior to 1879. On 14 March 1934, the Fire Wardens (L.S. Floyd, A.C. Jeffery & B.H. Hurlbert) hired a Mr. E. Fleet to cut a door in the rear of the Court House in Tusket in order to have a space to store the fire engine. By June 1, 1934, the old Engine House was to be removed from the Court House property.

It was moved north at this time to the lot it occupies today, where it became a private dwelling. Through the years, several additions and alterations have been made to the original small building. At the same time that this building was moved the old fire tower with its bell was also dismantled, and the bell was installed in the cupola on the Court House. The bell remained there for approximately fifty years. During the restoration of the Court House in the early 1980s it was necessary to carry out extensive repairs to the cupola. In doing so the old fire bell was lifted by crane and placed on the ground to the rear of the Court House. During these operations the old bell cracked. It now sits inside the Court House, at the foot of the spiral staircase in the entrance, with appropriate signage indicating its illustrious history.

After 1934 the village of Tusket remained without a fire department or any effective firefighting equipment for about twenty years. It should be noted that for a brief period at least, during the Second World War, that the Radar Station in Tusket extended its firefighting equipment and abilities to help out with emergencies in the village. In 1952 the Eel Brook Fire Department was incorporated and it has since provided the village with fire protection.

The old pumper, which had become an antique, was stored for a number of years in the Court House, and eventually was moved to the Eel Brook Fire Department building. In 1969 it was finally transferred to the Yarmouth Fire Fighters Museum in Yarmouth where it is still on display.

The Dickie & McGrath pumper.

It should be noted here that during the 1870s and at different times afterwards the Mayflower Engine Company was depended on heavily to attend to emergencies at the fire-prone sawmills in the village. In the 1870s this was the Andrew Mack Mill. At later times it was the Blethen sawmill, then the mills of the Tusket River Lumber Company and finally Dickie & McGrath. These establishments were important commercial enterprises in the village, and were at the same time "tinder boxes." The Mayflower Engine Company's success in dealing with these disasters was not always viewed favourably. As such, at times, the mills themselves took efforts to provide their own firefighting equipment on site. The Dickie & McGrath sawmill purchased their own fire pumper for their business in 1906. This pumper had originally been purchased by the city of Fredericton, New Brunswick, from the Silsby Company, Seneca Falls, New York. While owned in New Brunswick this pump had been known as "The City of Fredericton."

One of Tusket's Early Baseball Teams

In the early 1900s, the village of Tusket had a very prominent baseball team, winning the Yarmouth County league championship in 1912. The championship team photograph shown below, was taken by the side of the Tusket Community Hall. The Tusket ball field was located on this same site, just to the south of the Community Hall. This was when the Community Hall was still located on it original site on the eastern side of the road (Rte. 308 North). I recall that a few years after I came to work in Tusket around 1961, the grass and brush in this same field was cleared and it was once again used to play baseball. This field was located between the present Bernard "Bernie" Doucette and James Pottier houses.

Tusket baseball team – 1912; Yarmouth County Champions

Standing, left to right: Towner from the West Indies, unknown, unknown, Steve Glode, Clyde Gilmore. In the centre with trophy: Arthur McGrath. Sitting, left to right: Bernard Hurlbert, Percy McGrath, Murray Veinot, Scott Killam and Allan Hatfield.

The Dickie and McGrath sawmill paid for the uniforms for this team and it is believed this is why Arthur McGrath is holding the cup. A few notes of interest on some of the individual players: Towner, from the West Indies was an excellent baseball player. He was employed at the Dickie & McGrath lumber mill firm and he is also seen in another photograph in this history, sitting with others on the steps of the Dickie & McGrath general store. Steve Glode was a native Mi'kmaq and was considered one of the best on the team. Claude Gilmore was not a player on the team and it is unknown how or why he got into the picture. Bernard Hurlbert became a very successful businessman operating his general store in the village centre for many years. Percy McGrath (son of Thomas McGrath) became a distinguished medical Doctor, practicing in Kentville and worked diligently to promote youth baseball in his community. Murray Veinot became perhaps the best-known baseball player ever from Yarmouth County; his name continues to be mentioned to this day. Scott Killam moved to Yarmouth. Allan Hatfield moved to Massachusetts and became a very successful businessman. He died quite young and it was his widow, the late Mildred Hatfield, who provided me with most of the information on this photograph.

During the late 1940s Sheridan "Pat" Patterson allowed the young men of community to use a piece of property to the west of his home on Court Street to play baseball. This spot was used as a ball field well into the 1950s.

In 1974-1976 a new ball field was built on the southern side of Court Street, just east of the Harold and Eileen Tatton home. This ball field was created on land that had been donated by Harold Allen for this purpose. Although the creation of this field was the work of the Argyle Recreation Committee, most of the work was carried out on a volunteer basis. It was mainly Malcolm Sweeney of Tusket, and me who worked on this project. Malcolm "Mac" did all the bulldozing work. This ball field has not been used for a number of years now, and was recently expropriated by the Municipality of Argyle as land needed to accommodate the new sewer system that is to be installed in the village in 2005.

A new ball field was built in 1989 beyond the 103 overpass and very close to the northern boundaries of the village on the Gavel Road. This ball field was built by an organization that was formed for this purpose, called the Argyle Municipal Ball Field Society. Although several people were involved in this project, most of the work needed to make this new ball field a reality was carried out by Marcel Muise of Tusket and Donald Nelson of Plymouth.

Music & the Arts

Tusket does not appear to have been a great centre for music and the arts, or at least little of an outstanding nature seems to have survived in the memories of the local residents in relation to such activities. Like all rural communities, music of a sacred nature was always a part of church life here, in all four of the village churches. The pump organ was a common instrument in the Victorian parlours of the village, and many families indulged in the old fashioned sing-song as a form of evening entertainment.

During the 1890s and the early years of the 1900s Tusket artist Jacob Blauvelt played a leading role in cultural activities in the village. He not only served as organist at the Anglican Church, but staged regular theatrical performances in the community hall, with the young people of the village taking part. He composed some music himself, and was well known locally as a talented artist. He painted several religious paintings in the local churches and painted portraits as well. The late Phyllis (Hatfield) Young collected Blauvelt paintings. After Jacob Blauvelt's death in 1917, most activities of a cultural nature seem to have been those offered by the village school in the form of Christmas concerts and other activities of that nature staged by the teachers and students of the school.

In the 1890s Tusket also had an excellent band for a short time. It was known as the "Tusket Concert Band."

Tusket Concert Band

The identified members of the "Tusket Concert Band" shown in this photograph are: # 1 – Thomas Coleman; # 2 – Mr. _____ Cleveland; # 3 – Chase Hatfield and # 4 – Gordon Hatfield. The band conductor was a Mr. Adams; his picture is superimposed on the face of the drum. This photograph is believed to have been taken in front of the Methodist Church.

Tusket's Medical Doctors

Tusket has had a number of medical doctors over the years, who served the village and the surrounding area. Although this list may not include every physician who has ever worked and lived in the village, I believe it includes the majority of them.

Dr. Thomas Kirby Dr. Thomas Kirby is the earliest known physician who practiced in Tusket, settling here about 1846. He married Lydia Lent, a daughter of Rev. James Lent. His palatial home in the southern part of the village has been discussed in our village tour. He died at Tusket on 4 January 1897. At the time of his death the *Yarmouth Herald* carried the following obituary: "Thomas Kirby, Esq., M. D., died at Tusket yesterday. Dr. Kirby was born in Cork, Ireland, on May 30th, 1812. He was the son of Lieut.-Col. Thomas Cox Kirby. He came to Ontario in 1836, and went to Columbus, Ohio where he lived 10 years, practicing his profession. Dr. Kirby came to Tusket in Sept. 1846, where he has enjoyed the esteem of the public for 50 years. His field of practice for many years was a large one, there being no other physicians between Yarmouth and Barrington. Dr. Kirby was twice married, his last wife, a daughter of the late Rev. James Lent, survives him."

Dr. John M. Bingay John Moody Bingay was born 30 November 1836, the son of James and Mary (Moody) Bingay of Tusket. As a young man he attended medical school and afterwards set up his practice in Tusket. His offices were located in the centre of the village in a building that sat where the parking lot for Carl's Store is located in 2005. The exact years of his practice are not known – but he was married in 1877 and had set up shop at least nine years previous to that. His medical office is shown on the A.F. Church Map of 1866. His large elegant home was located on Court Street and is owned in 2005 by Abel Warner. John M. Bingay died on 31 March 1922, and had probably been retired a few years before his death.

The above two men are believed to have been Tusket's first physicians. The following is a list of known doctors who afterwards worked and lived in the village. Although I cannot give the exact years of service of each - I have noted what is known from property deeds concerning when these men owned property in the village. This should provide at least some indication of the time period each worked in the area.

Dr. John W. Pennington He practiced in the village and owned the "Bernard Hurlbert" house from 11 July 1892 to 29 October 1906.

Dr. Vernon L. Miller He practiced in the village and owned the "Bernard Hurlbert" house from 29 October 1906 to 11 February 1914.

Dr. Roderick O. Bethune He practiced in the village and owned the "Bernard Hurlbert" house from 11 February 1914 to 1 October 1922.

Dr. Lewis M. Morton He practiced in the village and owned the "Bernard Hurlbert" house 1 October 1922 to 22 September 1923.

Dr. Harold Trefry He practiced in the village and owned the "Bernard Hurlbert" house from 22 September 1923 to 6 July 1925.

Dr. Donald Roderick Sutherland He practiced in the village and owned the "Bernard Hurlbert" house from 6 July 1925 to 26 August 1927.

Dr. Milton O'Brien He practiced first (1955-1958) from the former May Stephenson property in the southern part of the village. From 1961-1963, he practiced from the home later owned and occupied by Dr. H. J. Fulde. Milton O'Brien afterwards moved his medical offices to Yarmouth. He and his wife lived for a number of years in Yarmouth, but returned to Tusket in 1981 and built a new home high on the crest of "VanNorden's Hill" or "Lents Hill" on the western side of the river, not far from the Tusket Bridge.

Dr. Gerald Belliveau He practiced medicine briefly in Tusket in the 1960s at the same time that Milton O'Brien had a practice here. He was located in the house owned by Geraldine Rhyno in 2005. He worked for a year or two from this location.

Dr. William Francis Mason He practiced from the "Fulde" house from 7 November 1963 to 11 June 1964.

Dr. Allan Lupin He practiced from the "Fulde" house from 11 June 1964 to 16 June 1966.

Dr. Ronald R. Charwood He practiced from the "Fulde" house from 16 June 1966 to 6 March 1967.

Dr. H. J. Fulde He came to Tusket in the 1960s. He purchased the property where Ronald Charwood practiced on 6 March 1967. He continued with his practice in the village and had one of the few pharmaceutical dispensing practices remaining in the province. He died tragically in an automobile accident on March 9, 1999. After the death of Dr. H. J. Fulde, Tusket was without a resident physician for some time.

Dr. Renier vanAardt The former Bernard Hurlbert house (the Oscar Nauss house during my time) has once again become a Doctor's residence. Dr. Renier vanAardt arrived in Tusket in October 1997 and officially opened his office doors on November 3, 1997. He established a much-welcomed medical clinic with three doctors to serve the community. In 2005, Dr. vanAardt moved his practice to Truro, but two physicians, Dr. Ognian I. Pelov and Dr. Maria Pelova, husband and wife, continue to practice from the clinic established here.

Eel Brook Physicians There are periods of time when there may have been no resident physician in Tusket. It is possible during some of these periods that the physicians of nearby Eel Brook or Sainte-Anne-du-Ruisseau handled the medical needs of Tusket. Some of those physicians were Alexandre Pierre Landry (1887-1905), Amedée Raymond Melanson (1905-1930), Bernard L. Chiasson (1931-1937), Flavien Melanson (1939-1973) and Emile Melanson (1950-1959).

Note: The 1930s and 1940s are not covered by the above list. It is possible physicians practiced here during that time that I have not been able to obtain information on. If not, clearly the physicians of nearby Sainte-Anne-du-Ruisseau took care of the medical needs of Tusket.

CHAPTER 14

TUSKET THIRTY YEARS LATER
(2005)

CHAPTER 14
TUSKET THIRTY YEARS LATER (2005)

When I decided to embark on a revised edition of this manuscript in the fall of 2004, it was with shock and disbelief that I realized thirty years had elapsed since I had first written my pictorial essay of Tusket's past. When I dusted off the document I was amazed at the changes that had taken place in the village during this time.

Looking over the years covered by this history, 1784-2005, one thing becomes very obvious; Tusket's days as a community of industry seem to have passed. Although the village has a vibrant economy today, it has little to do with industries that produce goods. In times past, Tusket produced an impressive number of the largest ships ever built in the province. Concurrently, it also was the home of a major tannery and shoemaking shop. Afterwards, it was one of the largest lumber producing communities in Nova Scotia.

Today, though the village thrives, its economic base has little to do with primary industry. The economy of the place is based on service industries, such as car dealerships, construction firms, accounting firms, service stations, banking facilities, schools, and government offices.

Although several small businesses have established themselves within the village, there are a few large businesses that have played important roles in the new economic era that we experience in the village today. They are Tusket Sales & Service, the former N.A. Pottier Building Supplies Store and woodworking mill, Carl's Store, our local Credit Union and Garian Construction. Today four of these businesses remain and employ approximately 125 people.

Hubert Pothier's Businesses at Tusket

The business establishment of Tusket Sales & Service is situated on the southwest corner as we arrive at the Tusket exit off Highway 103. Tusket Sales is by far the largest business enterprise that the village has enjoyed since the Dickie & McGrath Lumber Company nearly a century ago. Since Tusket Sales has provided such an economic boost to the community, it is worth delving into the history of this expansive business.

In 1959, my brother, Hubert Pothier, opened a small body shop in an old country store in Belleville North. When this shop burned to the ground in the fall of 1960, our uncle, Benoit Pottier, gave Hubert a small lot of land to the north of his house in Tusket to rebuild the body shop with the idea that being on the main highway would generate more business - and indeed it did. During the winter of 1961, Hubert's Body Shop opened its doors in Tusket for the first time. We were all totally unaware of what the business would grow into. As the business prospered, the body shop was expanded a number of times. During the early1960s, Hubert purchased all the former lands of the Dickie & McGrath Lumber Company in Tusket, situated to the north of the body shop, on the western side of Highway #3. In 1966 a Texaco Service Station was built next to the body shop. By this time Hubert was deeply involved in buying and selling used automobiles. In 1969 the Tusket Toyota dealership was established at this service station, prompting a major addition to the existing building. The year 1975 saw the addition of the Ford dealership on the same premises.

In 1974-75 the construction of the new 103 Highway through the north end of the village was completed. Hubert seized the opportunity and purchased most of the land on the southwest corner of the Tusket interchange, and in 1977, transferred the Ford Dealership to that location. Expansion to the dealership continued to grow at a steady pace in the years afterward. The present Ultra Mart Service Station was soon built, and shortly afterwards Hubert purchased the Gerald Wood property, located immediately to the south of the new service station. He renovated the house, turned it into a restaurant, and leased it as the "Riverside Restaurant." Eventually this building was torn down as more space was required for the service station and Hubert built the present Marcos Restaurant, nearby. He also leases that property. As the Ford dealership prospered, the main building was almost doubled in size. In 1998, a new state of the art auto body shop was constructed to the west of the Ford dealership. Thus, after thirty-seven years, the doors to the original small body shop in the village on Highway #3 were closed. Today, Tusket Sales & Service alone has approximately seventy employees.

Tusket Toyota remained at its original location on Highway #3 until December 22, 2003. Although this dealership has moved to Yarmouth, it continues to operate under the same name, "Tusket Toyota" and with most of the same employees.

N. A. Pottier Building Supplies

In 1968 my brother Norman Pottier, who had been employed as a carpenter in Halifax, purchased a lot of land in Tusket on the eastern side of Highway #3, directly across the road from Hubert Pothier's auto body shop. Here he opened a woodworking mill which was known as N.A. Pottier Building Supplies. This was not a lumber mill, but a mill that made windows, door casings and all types of wood dressing that customers required. There was also a store where he sold lumber, doors, windows and a range of other building supplies. It was a growing business and one that was a welcome addition to the community. Unfortunately, only five years after being established, on the night of November 23, 1974, fire engulfed this entire woodworking business.

After my brother Norman's woodworking shop and store burned, he purchased the former Elmer Little and the Russell d'Entremont properties across from Tusket Sales & Service near the 103 Highway and established a construction business and building supplies store, as well as a woodworking mill. This business was also known as N.A. Pottier Building Supplies Ltd. and was established in 1975-76. He had several employees at the height of his operations in the 1980s. It was a much larger business enterprise than his former establishment on Highway #3.

Norman Pottier's first woodworking mill and store.

In developing this property for his business, the Elmer Little-Budd Gavel house was hauled in 1977 to the rear of the property and for a few years it was used as a storage-shed for the woodworking mill. It has since been demolished. A short time after 1987 the Russell d'Entremont house, a bit to the south, was torn down to make room for more expansion. Unfortunately, during the recession in the late 1980s, the business failed, and the buildings were eventually sold. The demise of this business, however, has led to the opening of two more businesses in these buildings. They will be dealt with elsewhere in this chapter.

Garian Construction

North of the 103 overpass, an old barn stood for many years on the property now occupied by Garian Construction. The barn was demolished around 1995. A young ambitious contractor by the name of Ian McNicol in partnership with Gary Dixon (thus the name "Garian") constructed a substantial mini-mall on this property. This houses Garian Construction's own offices, a restaurant known as the "Hickory Hut," an accounting firm operated by Susan Hubbard and Tusket Motor Sports. The motor sports business is also owned and operated by Ian McNicol and Gary Dixon and employs five people. Garian Construction itself employs twenty-five people.

One of this company's more recent jobs was the construction of our new Coastal Financial Credit Union in Tusket in 2004.

Carl's Store

In the centre of the village, Carl's store has been the scene of several expansions and major changes to the original "Bernard Hurlbert store" since Carl and his wife Audrey purchased it in 1983. Carl knew the retail trade well and immediately set out to promote and expand the business. Carl and Audrey devote a great deal of effort toward maintaining customer satisfaction. They have expanded the building on three different occasions; in fact, the original store has all but disappeared in the modern additions that have been constructed around it. The expansions, however, have created several new employment opportunities for local residents; consequently, they currently have eighteen employees working at the store, making Carl's Store one of the larger employers in the village. This is a highly successful general and hardware store. It is certainly unique in Yarmouth County - being the only "general store" outside of the Town of Yarmouth that has capitalized on its location and managed to maintain a share of the market. In an economic climate where large conglomerates dominate the market, Carl's Store is unique.

The Credit Union

The new Credit Union building, 2005.

Another large employer in the village today is our local credit union. This credit union was first established in 1949 under the name of St. Anne Parish Credit Union Ltd. At that time it serviced the villages of Sainte-Anne-du-Ruisseau, Lower Eel Brook, Rocco Point, Tusket, Hubbard's Point, Belleville, Bell Neck and Abram's River. These were the same villages then encompassed by Sainte Anne's Catholic parish. One of the principle organizers in the establishment of this Credit Union was Rev. Father Clarence Thibeau, who was the parish priest at Sainte Anne's Church at the time.

Clarence Thibeau informs me that one of the major obstacles to establishing a credit union was the fear of local people that they would no longer enjoy any privacy where their financial business was concerned. He recalls a meeting where these concerns were the major topic of discussion. Those of us who have been involved in such community organizations can often recall pivotal moments in such meetings where suddenly one person speaks out who sets the tone for the decision that follows. Father Clarence Thibeau recalls that at this meeting Mack Saulnier of Abram's River spoke up at one point and said, "If the priest says its okay, it has to be the right thing to do." Everyone finally agreed; the rest is history.

The early meetings of the credit union were held in what was formerly an old abandoned country store located on the northern side of the main road just at the curve before the Eel Brook Bridge. Father Clarence Thibeau had organized a youth club in the area, called "Sainte Anne's Athletic Club," and this building was being used as their club house. The Credit Union originally had twenty five members and the first Treasurer-Clerk was [Peter Pothier] Pierre Pottier from Belleville. Of the twenty-five original members, only three are still living in 2005. They are Rev. Clarence Thibeau, Avite Pottier and his brother Pierre, the first Treasurer.

The old country store was eventually demolished and for several years most of the business transactions were conducted from the home of David and Pearl Madden in Belleville. In 1966 the first official Credit Union building was constructed at Sainte Anne-du-Ruisseau. This was a small, square building located on the property of Edmund d'Entremont. The building sat almost directly across the road from his garage, presently owned and operated by his grandson, Malcolm Madden.

In November 1970, a special meeting was held to discuss the possibility of expanding the area served by the credit union. It was agreed that those communities served should include the villages of Amirault's Hill, Sluice Point, Surette's Island, Morris Island, Springhaven and Quinan along with the previously mentioned villages. These villages were all outside the boundaries of Sainte Anne's Parish. At the same meeting a motion was passed to rename the institution as St. Anne's Credit Union, dropping the word "parish" from its title.

During the summer of 1974, a special meeting was held to discuss the possibility of relocating the existing building from Sainte-Anne-du-Ruisseau to Tusket, as a more central location from which to do business. This became a very controversial issue, with some members threatening to withdraw their membership if the office building was moved to Tusket. The vote results were 21 in favour and 18 against. In the spring of 1975 the building was hauled to Tusket and situated on the western side of the main road (Highway 308 North), near the corner of the VanNorden Road.

In 1979 the original small building saw its first major expansion. A decade later, in 1989, the building was expanded a second time. In 2001 four local credit unions amalgamated and formed the new Coastal Financial Credit Union. Those four institutions were the credit unions in the communities of Wedgeport, Tusket, Yarmouth and Coastal. (Coastal was an earlier amalgamation of the credit unions from Argyle, East Pubnico and West Pubnico). In 2000, the former Arthur and Gertie Wathen house, located a short distance further north at the corner of the VanNorden Road leading to the public well was purchased and demolished, to make way for a new Credit Union building. This new building was opened in 2004. The continued growth of this successful financial institution means that they presently employ ten people at their Tusket offices.

Other Changes in the Past 30 Years

There have been many changes in Tusket over the past 30 years. While some of those changes have been connected with the businesses listed above, others have had no connection with those enterprises. Looking at the village again, from south to north, I will attempt here to itemize some of the obvious changes that have taken place, following the same route taken in the "Walking Tour" of the village. It is my hope, that when the readers combine this chapter, with the earlier "Walking Tour," that they will find every property within the village of Tusket has been mentioned.

1 – Abraham Lent House: Tusket's oldest house, at "the Narrows," saw the present owners, John Terry and Andrea Doherty, enthusiastically allow the property to be designated a Municipal Heritage Property in 1993 and a Provincial Heritage Property in 1994. This protects this important piece of Tusket's history from demolition or substantial exterior alteration in the future.

2 – William and Cecile Wood House: On the Horatio Wood Road there is one modern house on the southern side of the road between the home of Margaret Wood and the next older dwelling. This is the home of "Billy" (Margaret's son) and Cecile Wood. It was built here, by them in 1979-80.

3 – Roger Doucet Blacksmith shop: Nearby, on the eastern side of the main road (Route 308 South) the old Roger Doucet blacksmith shop remains intact, but has been closed and inactive since his death in 1984.

4 – "Dora's Take Out", Laundromat, etc: On the other (western) side of the road, not far from the blacksmith building is a small commercial building that was built in 1979. It was built originally as a small restaurant called "Dora's Take Out." Later a combination laundromat, video rental outlet and poolroom were located in this building. In 2005 it is owned by Rob Muise and it is presently being renovated into a two unit apartment.

5 – Patsy and Randy Scoville House: Nearby, on the Frank Doucette Road there have been four modern houses built in the past 30 years. The oldest of the four is a home built in 1984-85 for Randy and Patsy Scoville. They still own the property in 2005. Their house is located on the south side of the road a short distance east from Route 308 South.

6 – Robert and Debbie Surette House: A bit further along the road, and still on the same side, is the modern home built in 1985-86 for Robert and Debbie Surette. They still own the property in 2005.

7 – Kenneth and Donna Crane House: A short distance to the north and on the same side of the road is the home built in 1986 by and for Kenneth and Donna Crane. They still live here in 2005.

8 – Gordon and Angie Kerr House: A bit further along, just past the Melanie Hubbard property and on the opposite side of the road, is the home of Gordon and Angie Kerr. It was built here, by them, in 1999.

At the intersection of the Frank Doucette Road with Highway #3, we will proceed eastward to the last buildings in the village, and then return from there to the centre of the village. We will discuss each newer property along the way.

9 – HP Motel: On Highway #3 near the end of village, on the way to Sainte Anne-du-Ruisseau, the once "new and prosperous" HP Motel, which opened in 1953, closed its doors shortly after 1968. The tea-room and office building have been demolished. The motel units built in 1953 are now rental units.

10 – David and Sandra Pothier House: This house was built in 1975 for Terry and Christine Moulaison. After a few different owners, in 1995 David and Sandra Pothier purchased this property and continue to live here in 2005. This house is situated on the north side of Highway #3.

11 – Kevin and Denise Hubbard House: The next newer home along this stretch of road is found on the south side of the highway. It was built here in 1999 for Kevin and Denise Hubbard who still own the property in 2005.

12 – Edwin and Sheila Robicheau House: A short distance west, and also on the south side of the highway, what began as a mobile home was placed on this lot in the mid-1970s for and by Donald and Marjorie Davis. They sold this property in 1980 to Edwin and Sheila Robicheau, who over the years have enlarged the house. They still own the property 2005.

13 – Clarence and Virginia Doucette House: Clarence and Virginia Doucette have an attractive modern home on the south side of Highway #3 a short distance west of the old "Mission House" (John and Erite Frotten house). They built this home in 1984, and still reside here in 2005.

14 – Mark Taylor Rabbit Barn - Huskins Apartment Building: This building is located on the north side of the highway and is owned in 2005 by Terrence Huskins; it is used as rental apartments. This building was built here around 1985 for Mark Taylor, at that time of nearby Pleasant Lake. It was used originally as a barn to house rabbits which he raised and sold. Terry Huskins purchased the property in 1993 and converted the building into apartments.

15 – Dr. Thomas Kirby House: The old Thomas Kirby home (later Kilby Lodge), which in my younger days was the Alvin Trefry house where we used to go for those "good hamburgers", has been demolished. A modern bungalow has been built some distance further back from the main road on the same property. In fact, it was largely built from materials from the old Kirby home. This house was built around 1980 for Jack Jacobsen, who was later killed in the *Ocean Ranger* disaster off Newfoundland on February 15, 1982. This house, too, is on the north side of the highway very near the apartment units. The present owners, Terrence and Debbie Huskins, purchased the property in 1986.

16 – May Stephenson - Joe Blanchard House: The former May Stephenson - Joseph Blanchard house on the south side of the highway sits abandoned. Its demolition seems inevitable.

17 – Peter Lent Hatfield House: The current owners of this home, Michael and Kerry Lawson, insured that this property was declared a Municipal Heritage Property in 1992 and a Provincial Heritage property in 1993-1994. Like the old house at "the Narrows" this property is now protected from demolition or substantial exterior alterations.

18 – Lent Hatfield's Store: At Lent's corner, Susan Young, by appointment, continues to operate the Hanging Oak Antique Shop that her mother Phyllis operated from this building until her death in 1988. Phyllis had a most pleasant personality and it was great news when she opened the antique shop in the old Lent Hatfield store. It was always a treat to receive a phone call from her, or to drop in to see if she had acquired anything "odd" that might enhance my collection of old barn artefacts. Often, the discussions would turn to the subject of "old days in Tusket."

19 – Hanging Oak Tree: Sadly, the legendary hanging oak tree on the bank of the river at this corner has lost another large branch and it appears to be nearing the end of its life.

20 – Terry and Karen Cottreau House: This house, which occupies the former property of "Squire" James Lent, was built here in 1975 for Scott and Roberta Swinimer. They lived here for a few years before selling to the present owners, Terry and Karen Cottreau. This house sits on high land with a breathtaking view of the Tusket River.

21 – Gregory and Denise LeBlanc House: Just to the north of the public cemetery on the eastern side of Highway #3, is a modern home built in 1981 by Wayne and Gerarda LeBlanc. It is owned in 2005 by Gregory and Denise LeBlanc.

22 – Nettie Reed House & Property: The next property to the north, and on the same side of the road, is the former Gordon Hatfield (Nettie Reed) property. This was purchased by Gordon and Evelyn Muise in 1985. The historic house, dating back to 1823, was demolished and in 1986 they built a lovely brick house on top of the hill, just beyond where the former house stood. It is nice to see that they have restored the large barn and saved the attractive, small curved-roof shed by the roadside which has been a landmark on this property for so many years.

23 – Dr. H. J. Fulde House: The medical practice of the late Dr. Heinz Jurgen Fulde closed upon his death on March 9, 1999. His former home is now owned by Edwin and Carmen Coffin as a private dwelling.

24 – Fred Babin House: Lisa Hurlburt is operating a successful beauty salon from their well kept property; the former Alfred Babin home. She and her husband, Scott, have made some very attractive improvements to this property, all of them respecting the architectural integrity of this old home.

25 – Methodist Church: The old Methodist Church, later the Seventh-Day Adventist Church was designated a Municipal Heritage Property in 1991. Significant developments on this property are discussed elsewhere in this history. These improvements are scheduled to take place in 2005.

26 – Harold Floyd House: The old W.T. Lent house (later known as the Harold Floyd and later still, as the Dan Armstrong house), located between the Court House and the former Methodist Church was demolished in March 1990. The lot sits empty and has now become part of the Argyle Municipality property, joining the Court House and the church together as one lot. Although major improvements are about to commence on these properties in 2005, sadly, it has been at the expense of another "older" Tusket home.

27 & 28 – Elmer Hatfield Store & Warehouse: Two Tusket commercial "landmark" buildings have been lost in the centre of the village. In 1983, Carl and Audrey Pottier purchased the two buildings at the southern end of their parking lot; namely the old Elmer Hatfield store and the old warehouse (once known as the Smith Harding store) to the south of Elmer's store. Both of these buildings were demolished shortly after they purchased them. As previously mentioned in this history, Carl resold the Elmer Hatfield store to me; I took it apart and rebuilt it as a barn in my back yard. The "old warehouse" was demolished and Carl then filled in the area and created the present day parking lot for his general store.

29 – Court House: The historical Court House was restored in the 1980s and has created employment in the community since then. Peter Crowell is our full-time archivist and there is now another part time employee, as well as many volunteers. On a year-round basis these people are always ready to assist anyone wishing to carry out historical or genealogical research. Several students are also given employment at the courthouse as tour guides and archival assistants during the summer months. The historical Courthouse was registered as a Provincial Heritage Property in 1986 and a Municipal Heritage Property in 1987.

30 – Daniel Armstrong Trailer: This mobile home is found at the corner of the John White Road and Highway #3, and face onto the highway. This mobile home was moved onto the property in the late 1970s for Daniel and Patsy Armstrong. The current owners are Justin Doucette and Amanda Hubbard.

31 – Neil and Cindy Doucette House: This house which is located on the water side of the John White Road, between the properties of Cecelia Crosby and Freddie White, was built in 1985-86 for Neil and Cindy Doucette. Cindy is a daughter of Freddie and Barbara White. They still live here in 2005.

32 – Raymond Hubbard House: A short distance further north, the Raymond "Peege" Hubbard house has also been demolished. It was taken down shortly after 1975.

33 – A bit further along Highway #3, and on the same side of the road, in 2005, the old "auto body shop" of Hubert Pothier, and the former service station and Toyota dealership buildings sit empty. These businesses have moved to other locations.

34 – St. Stephen's Anglican Church: This Church was designated a Municipal Heritage Property in 1988 and a Provincial Heritage Property in 1990.

35 – Dr. Milton O'Brien House: Just across the Tusket Bridge, on the western side of the river, is the home of Dr. Milton and Audrey O'Brien. They built their new home here in 1981. The new house is situated on what was once known as "VanNorden's Hill," and later as "Lent's Hill." They still live on the property in 2005.

36 – Quick Industries: Also across the Tusket Bridge, and on the north side of Highway #3 is a concrete block building built in 1986 for James Quick. This commercial building was used as a retail tire outlet, and also carried out heavy equipment repair, sandblasting and painting until 1995, when the owner moved his business to Yarmouth. He continues to own this building and rents out parts of the property for different purposes.

37 – Darrell and Bonnie LeBlanc House: A short distance further, driving towards the community of Pleasant Lake, also on the north side of Highway #3 is a new bungalow style home. It was built in 2000 for Darrell and Bonnie LeBlanc, who still own the property in 2005.

38 – Lynn and Ron Comeau House: A bit further along the highway, and still on the north side of the road, is another bungalow. It was built in 1990 for James and Carrie Sweeney and purchased in 1991 by Lynn and Carrie Comeau. They continue to live here in 2005.

39 – Garth and Bernice Hatfield Cottage Driveway: A short distance past the Tusket Power Generating Plant, on the south side of Highway #3 is a long driveway leading to the cottage of the late Garth Hatfield and his widow Bernice. This cottage is located near the site on the west side of the Tusket River where Jacob Tooker and his family established the very first homestead in Tusket in 1784.

40 – Tusket Seafoods: This building, on the north side of Highway #3, a short distance beyond the Turbine Plant, was built as a freezer for herring roe by Fred Churchill of Raynardton around 1983-85. The building was purchased by Jeff d'Entremont in May 1988. In 2005 Jeff is still the owner and uses this as a fish processing plant, mainly for scallops.

41 – Gordon and Mary Hatfield House: Continuing toward Yarmouth, a short distance further, and on the south side of Highway #3 is a small house built in 1991 by Gordon and Mary Hatfield. Gordon is a son of Jim Hatfield of Pleasant Lake. They continue to occupy the house in 2005.

42 – James and Julie Hatfield House: Approximately a quarter of a mile further toward Pleasant Lake, on the northern side of Highway #3 is the home of James and Julie Hatfield; it was built by them in 1981-82 and they still live in the house in 2005. James is another son of Jim Hatfield of Pleasant Lake. This is the last house within the bounds of Tusket in this area of the village.

At this point we will return to the centre of the village and the Court House area, and proceed up Court Street. We will first look at the newer properties on the north side of the street proceeding west to east, and those on the south side as we make our way back to the main road.

43 – Post Office: The village Post Office is still located north of the Court House at the same place that it was thirty years ago. Joan Patten is the Post Mistress and Cecile Doucette is her assistant.

44 – Nate Crosby Mobile Home: Just beyond the old Evelyn Wood house, at the rear of the Municipal Office, is a mobile home. This was brought onto the property in July 1981 by Nate Crosby. It is owned in 2005 by Stephen Babin.

45 – Municipal Office: The Argyle Municipal Council and business offices moved from the old Court House in 1976 to the former Tusket schoolhouse, a short distance east along Court Street. Several departments of municipal government have been established within the Municipal Office creating more jobs over the years. In recent years, major renovations have been made to the Council Chambers.

46 – Moïse Muise House: Almost at the end of Court Street the old Moïse Muise house was demolished in 1987. A new house has been built on the same lot for Moïse Muise's grandson, Tommy Muise. This is the eastern end of Court Street; we will turn around and make our way back to the main road.

47 – Arthur and Donna LeFave House: On the south side of Court Street, a short distance west of the old Edmund LeFave property, is the home of Arthur and Donna LeFave. After their first house was consumed by fire, Arthur and Donna LeFave built this house in 1975. They still own the property in 2005.

48 – Ernie Doucet House: The next house on the south side of the road was built in 1975 by Raymond Muise. It was later purchased by Ernie Doucet from Quinan and in 2005 is occupied by his son and daughter-in-law, Keith and Faye Doucet.

49 – Dulong's PC Repair: The next house, also on the south side of the road, is a mobile home. It was placed on this lot in the mid-1980s for Verna Tatton. She sold the property to the current owner, Peter Dulong. He has made additions to the original home. He has operated his business, "Dulong's PC Repair," from this property since 1996. He provides repair and service to local residents, including handling all of the computer needs for Tusket & Sales Service. Other major customers are Coastal Financial Credit Union, Vaughne Assurance Ltd. and Tusket Ultra Mart.

50 – Forman Hatfield House: Returning to the main road and heading in a northerly direction, the Forman Hatfield house is now a rental property owned by Roger Devine of Yarmouth. It has had a number of small commercial businesses that operated from the front of the building for short periods of time. A small store and lunch counter here was operated by the Yould family, then members of the Burton family and finally by Doris Trefry until about 1973. When I began this history in 1973, it housed the offices of a denturist, but this business did not remain in the village many years. Today Charmaine Smith operates a part of her Teddy's Day Care business from these premises and has done so since about 2001.

51 & 52 – Andrew Jeffery's Garage & Blacksmith Shop: Next to VanCortlandt Square, two more "old" heritage buildings have disappeared. Andy Jeffrey's garage and his father's old historical blacksmith shop have both been demolished.

53 – Bernard Hurlbert House: The former Bernard Hurlbert house, (the Oscar Nauss house during my time) has once again become a Doctor's residence. Two physicians, Dr. Ognian I. Pelov and Dr. Maria Pelova, husband and wife, are practicing here in 2005. A daycare centre known as Teddy's Daycare, (part of the same Daycare business mentioned above) also currently operates from these premises. The house itself has undergone numerous additions, not only in the past few years, but during the years when it was owned by Bernard Hurlbert. The original home of Nathaniel Gardner, shipbuilder lies buried within the many additions.

We will now proceed north along Route 308 North.

54 – Barbara Hubbard House: The driveway for Bernie Doucette's property also leads to another home situated to the rear of Bernie and Linda's house. This is a mobile home that was moved onto this property in 1975 for Raymond "Peege" and Barbara Hubbard.

"Peege" has since passed away. In 2005, his widow Barbara continues to live here with her brother Albert Muise.

55 – Community Hall: Almost directly across the road from the home of Bernie and Linda Doucette, (not far from the Roy & Vivian Sweeney house) stood the old Community Hall when I first moved to Tusket. It burned in the mid 1970s and was not replaced.

56 – Roy & Vivian Sweeney House: In recent years this house has been owned and occupied by Murray Sweeney, a son of Roy and Vivian Sweeney who lived here for many years. Murray has since moved to Yarmouth, and his brother, Rodney Sweeney, now owns the house. May 2005: This house is in the process of being sold to Edward LeBlanc of Sainte Anne-du-Ruisseau and his son Brian LeBlanc of South Belleville. Brian is the owner of Acadian Plumbing & Heating & Electrical Ltd. His plans are to move his business operations into this house and will try to retain as much of the original architectural details as possible. This is welcome news for this old house.

57 – Nova Apartments: A short distance further, on the eastern side of the road, another of Tusket's great landmark buildings, Gilmans, was demolished in 1972. In 1976 a Senior Citizen's Apartment complex (Nova Apartments), was constructed on the same site where the once glorious Gilman Hotel stood. The original stone wall along the road front still remains as an added feature to the property.

58 – William and Sharon Muise House: Just to the north of the Nova Apartments Senior complex is a small bungalow. It was built in 1974 by William and Sharon Muise. Patsy Post Nedimovich moved into this house in 1979 and continues to live here in 2005.

59 – Duck's Garden Centre & Variety: Just north of the Patsy Post Nedimovich house, also on the eastern side of the road, this small garden centre was opened for business in 2003. It is owned and operated by John Duckworth and Arlene Muise of Forest Glen, Yarmouth County.

60 – The "Old" St. Anne's Credit Union Building: A short distance further on the western side of the road was Saint Anne's Credit Union building until last spring (2004) when they moved to their new premises a short distance north. Their former building has since been purchased by Eddie Madden.

61 – Randy and Gail Muise House: There is one new house on the south side of the VanNorden Road; it is located just east of the home of Ruth Hatfield. It is a modern bungalow style house built in 1976 by Randy and Gail Muise and they still live here in 2005. Gail is the daughter of Ruth and the late Roger Hatfield.

62 – Arthur & Gertrude Wathen House: Another Tusket landmark on the corner of the VanNorden Road was the Arthur and Gertrude Wathen home. This was what remained of the old Rowland VanNorden homestead ("Gertie's" grandfather) and was demolished in 2000, to make way for the new St. Anne's Credit Union building (now known as

Coastal Financial Credit Union).

63 – Railroad Station: Almost across Route 308 North from the VanNorden property, the railroad station is no longer in existence. It was demolished in 1976, two years after I wrote my first unpublished document; a few years later the tracks were removed as well.

64 – Tim and Carol Wood House: Arriving at the top of "Parade Hill" on the eastern side of the road is a modern one and a half story Cape Cod style house. This house was built between 1985-87 by Tim and Carol Wood. They still live here in 2005.

65 – The Plum Tree B & B: Just past the crest of the hill, on the west side of the road, Larry and Jill Trask operate a well known bed & breakfast known as the "The Plum Tree." More recently, they have also opened a water pond accessories business known as "The Oasis."

66 – Wheelans White Chartered Accountants: North of Jill and Larry Trask's house is the Chartered Accounting firm of Brenda Wheelans and Jennifer White. This business was originally established by Ulysse Cottreau (of Amirault's Hill) in Tusket around 1971. Initially the business was located in a small building between Bernard Hurlbert's and Elmer Hatfield's stores. The business expanded, and the present building was constructed around 1978-79.

67 – Vaughne Assurance Agency: Immediately next door to the north is the insurance firm of Eddie Madden, known as Vaughne Assurance Agency. Eddie Madden established his business in Tusket in 1980. He has worked diligently over the years and has seen his business expand tremendously. This business has generated several employment opportunities in the community. Part of Eddie's building is also utilized as rental space, generally renting offices to the local elected provincial Member of the Legislative Assembly. Another rental space has been a beauty salon known as "Cheveux Chic", operated by Darlene Amirault for a number of years.

68 – James Adolphus Wood House: This fine old home has sat empty for more than 20 years. Its last owner, Whitfield Wood, a son of J. Adolphus Wood, maintained an apartment elsewhere in the village. Unfortunately, this house seems unlikely to survive much longer.

69 – Shirley and Paul Deveau House: Just to the north of the Adolphus Wood house, on the same side of the road is a small modern bungalow. This house was built in 1977-78 for Lynn West, native of Newfoundland, who was employed as a librarian for Western Counties Regional Library in Yarmouth. In 1984 this property was purchased by Shirley and Paul Deveau; they still live here in 2005. Shirley is a daughter of Cecelia and the late Carl Crosby.

70 & 71 – Norman Kuhn & Gerald Wood Homes: Further north still, on the properties of Tusket Sales & Service on the western side of the road, the former Norman Kuhn (Sterns Blauvelt) house and the Gerald Wood (Gerald Brayne) house have both been demolished.

72 – Norman Kuhn House: In 1976-77 Norm Kuhn built a new hip roofed modern bungalow on his property but closer to the highway, at which time he moved from the old Sterns Blauvelt house mentioned above. This new house is located almost directly across from the present home of Trafton White. In 1987-88 he sold this new house to Hubert Pothier and in 2005 Hubert continues to make use of it as a rental property.

73, 74 & 75 – Budd Gavel, Henry Gaudet & Arnold Gavel Homes: On the eastern side of the road in this same area, the former Budd Gavel (Tommy Robicheau) house, the Henry Gaudet (Russell d'Entremont) house and the home of Arnold Gavel have all disappeared. Arnold Gavel's small home sat very close to the 103 Exit. It was demolished in 1999. As mentioned earlier in this chapter, the first two homes mentioned here were demolished around 1987 by Norman Pottier to expand his business, N.A. Pottier Building Supplies. The properties are now owned by Hubert Pothier and Gordon Wood. They presently rent them out as a furniture store known as Tusket Furniture Plus and the used clothing store known as Frenchies. A small video rental store and a service garage next to the Frenchies store are also part of the Tusket Sales complex.

76 – Collège de l'Acadie: A short distance further north on the opposite side of the road is the Tusket Industrial Park, established by the Municipality of Argyle shortly after 1981. Just off the highway at the entrance to the park is the Collège de l'Acadie building. This building is part of the Nova Scotia Community College and its purpose is to offer courses to French-speaking students wishing to take technological courses in their native language. It was built in 1993.

77 – Technical Horizons T.H.E. Repair Shop: Proceeding a short distance further into the industrial park is an electronic repair shop known as "Technical Horizons". It opened in 1995 and is still owned and operated by Shawn Winters. Originally opened as an electronics and TV repair shop, it has also expanded into an RV trailer parts and service shop. More recently Shawn has also ventured into the Renewable Energy sector, dealing in sales and installation for solar, wind and hydro power.

78 – Department of Fisheries & Oceans Building: A short distance further north in the Industrial Park is the recently constructed Federal Government Department of Fisheries and Oceans Canada building (Fisheries Service Centre); a very welcome addition to the community. It officially opened its doors on November 7, 2003.

79 – Malcolm and Joan Patten House: From the entrance to the Industrial Park is a private road known as Camp Montebello Road. At the extreme end of this road is the home of Mac and Joan Patten. They built this house in 1987 and still live here in 2005.

80 – École Par-en-Bas: Proceeding again along the highway, in the direction of Belleville or Gavelton, we soon arrive at the newly constructed junior and senior French high school known as École Par-en-Bas. Although an educational institution, rather than a business, it should be acknowledged that the teaching and other staff positions at this school account for another 41 jobs in the community. (2005 figures)

81 – Scott & Judy Sweeney House: This house on the western side of Route 308 North was built in 1992 by Scott and Judy Sweeney. They continue to live here in 2005.

82 – Nova Scotia Department of Natural Resources Building: A few hundred yards further to our left is the Nova Scotia Department of Natural Resources regional building. This regional office operates under three separate branches within the same department. It houses Regional Services which deals with the general public. Another branch known as Integrated Resource Management (I.R.M.) deals with forestry issues, and they have their own biologist. A third branch houses a Land Survey Division where a Crown Land surveyor and a team of workers look after all matters relating to Crown Land surveys. The building was constructed in 1991 and eighteen persons are employed at these premises.

83 – Wayne & Hayley Muise House: This house is located a short distance off the main road, on the William Robbins Road. The house sits on the southern side of the William Robbins Road and was built in 1987 for and by George Muise. In 2005 it is owned by Wayne and Hayley Muise, who purchased the property in December 1999.

84 – George Muise House: A little further along the road, also on the south side, is the house of George Muise. It was built by George in 1992. He continues to own and occupy the house in 2005.

85 – Marcel & Kathleen Muise House: Some distance to the west, and still on the south side of the road is the home of Marcel and Kathy Muise. It was built in 1982. They still reside here in 2005.

86 – Norman Pottier's Seniors Apartment Building: A short distance north of the William Robbins Road, on Route 308 North, is a new building presently under construction. This is a four unit seniors' apartment building being built and owned by Norman Pottier. It is scheduled to open later this year.

A short distance further, Route 308 North takes a sharp turn to the east and continues to North Belleville and Quinan. The main road that leads north from this corner, to Gavelton and Kemptville, is called the "Gavel Road."

87 – Alfred & Leota Sweeney House: Alfred and Leota Sweeney built this new home around 1972-1974. The house is owned in 2005 by their son, Jack Sweeney. This house is located on the western side of the Gavel Road a short distance north of the corner leading to Belleville.

88 – Gary Bourque Mobile Home: This mobile home was placed on this property by Timothy Bourque around 1990. His brother, Gary Bourque, owns it in 2005 and uses it as a rental property. This property is on the eastern side of the Gavel Road, directly across the road from the Arthur Bowering house.

Tusket is certainly a much more prosperous centre today than it was thirty years ago. It is gratifying to see the tremendous amount of progress and economic growth that the village has experienced during these past thirty years.

Historically speaking, however, some of these advances have come at a price - the loss of many of our heritage buildings. While some of these properties had simply outlived their usefulness, others were outstanding properties with great historical value to the village. These buildings have not all been victims of expanding business interests. Unfortunately, we have been slow, as a people, in developing an appreciation for many of these buildings. At present, two older homes sit empty in the village; they are in an advanced state of decay, and unless a miracle takes place they seem doomed for demolition.

While these losses are very real, some appreciation for heritage homes and other properties has slowly developed - and we can only hope this trend will continue. The restoration of the Court House in the centre of the village in the early 1980s has provided an important anchor and an example of how new life can be breathed into a building that many thought had outlived its usefulness. The upcoming restoration of the Methodist Church, just south of the Court House and the development of the land between the two buildings as a small park will be a dream come true for many.

Almost all of the properties south of the Methodist Church as far as "Lent's Corner," and including the former Lent Hatfield Store and the home of Susan Young, are vintage heritage homes, whose architectural integrity has been appreciated and maintained by their owners over the years. Tusket's oldest house at "the Narrows", and the Peter Lent Hatfield house have both been designated Provincial Heritage Properties, protecting them from future demolition or "substantial exterior alteration." The Public Cemetery and the former Methodist Church are both Municipal Heritage Properties. The Court House and St. Stephen's Anglican Church are Provincial Heritage Properties as well.

The homes of Malcolm Patterson and Abel Warner on Court Street are superior examples of heritage homes meticulously cared for and appreciated. The former Evelyn Wood house, on School Street, tucked behind the Municipal Office, has received very sympathetic treatment from it recent owners. "The Plum Tree" Bed & Breakfast, the home of Jill and Larry Trask is a splendidly preserved property. All is not lost, and there is every reason to hope that this trend will continue in the future.

CHAPTER 15

FINAL THOUGHTS

CHAPTER 15
FINAL THOUGHTS

Throughout the years since I became interested in the history of the village, and involved in working on this manuscript, I have always been puzzled by the fact that no one had previously written a formal history of Tusket. Scholars such as James H. Bingay, and historians such as Robert B. Blauveldt, were certainly more qualified than I to undertake such a task. Although they did not leave behind any formal histories, I am grateful that they did write articles, letters and some other documents that recorded their knowledge and recollections of the place. They have helped in documenting much of the village's history.

I have outlined my own background in my Preface to this history. I am neither a scholar nor an academic - simply someone with a passionate interest in the past, and someone whose imagination was captivated by the history of my adopted community. This is not the village of my birth.

Another fact that has perplexed me from the beginning of this project is the total lack of photographs illustrating ships under construction at the various shipyards in Tusket. During the glory days of the shipbuilding industry here, these shipyards boasted some astonishing accomplishments for a village of this size. Surely, professional and amateur photographers alike would have flocked to Tusket to take pictures of at least some of these ships being built and launched. From the very beginning of this project more than thirty years ago, I remember Gordon Wood and I would often say, "surely, next week someone is going to come up with a fantastic picture of a tall ship under construction." The years have passed, the Archives have been established, and their outstanding collection of old photographs increases steadily each year. Still no such photographs have surfaced. Last year, in a final attempt, I advertised in the *Argus*, trying to locate such pictures to include in my manuscript, but to no avail.

Peter Crowell and I remain convinced that some family members who have moved on to other areas carried those pictures with them. I still hope that some of those photographs will eventually find their way "home."

As I read my notes and looked back to the times when the Loyalists first undertook the great task of establishing this community, it was with a sense of sadness that I realized that of all the first settlers, only two of the original family surnames remain in the village today, Blauvelt and Hatfield. To my knowledge, there are only four households within the bounds of Tusket where these surnames are still found. Nathaniel Blauvelt lives in the southern part of the village. Ruth Hatfield (widow of the late Roger Hatfield), lives in the central part of Tusket. James Hatfield and Gordon Hatfield, both sons of Jim Hatfield of Pleasant Lake, have modern homes on Highway #3 on the western side of the river. These are the only four households in Tusket in 2005 carrying surnames that are found on the old confirmed land grant of Tusket dated 1809. Although few other households have descendants of original settlers, they do not carry those surnames today. Ironically, this once totally English speaking community is now mostly Acadian and French speaking, a fact that is often overlooked by both the residents of the village and those from outside its borders.

For some reason, even when I was a young boy growing up, I always had an interest in old things. I remember I once asked my mother if someday I could have my great-grandfather's sleigh that was in our barn. Later, the rebuilding of a country store into a barn on my own property was like bringing back a part of my youth for me. In the past three years I have been able to restore that "old sleigh" and it is now one of my prized possessions in my barn in Tusket.

During the past two years, whenever someone asked my wife Barbara what I was doing, she replied, "Don is living in the past." This was quite literally so. It is difficult to describe in words how many times I have paused from certain vantage points throughout the village and found myself drifting into the past, visualizing tall ships rising on the horizon in the various shipyards, listening to the roar of the Dickie & McGrath lumber mill in full operation, walking into the country stores during the cold winter months and seeing a pot-belly stove in the middle of the floor throwing out a special radiant heat, or the sound (and smell) of meeting a horse and buggy clattering along the road and fading into the distance as they would each proceed along their own way.

I hope this history will in some way serve to share my enthusiasm with others. Above all else, I hope this history will be read and enjoyed. No history is ever perfect or complete. Some facts remain elusive, and I have not always been able to find complete answers to my questions. As my chapter entitled "Tusket Thirty Years Later" indicates, history is not a static thing. It continues to unfold before our eyes each day. After many years of research, and more than two years of writing and revising this manuscript, my project has been completed, and some important personal goals reached. It is my sincere hope that this book will be but a beginning, and that others will continue to explore the history of Tusket in even greater detail in the future.

As I reflect on what I first wrote over thirty years ago, I leave the reader with the following quote from my original document: "I cannot fail to wonder what the future holds for Tusket. Human nature being what it is, we always look for better things, regardless of how good things were in the past. At this time (March 1974), construction of a new all weather highway is in progress near what will be Tusket's fourth bridge … Nearly a century ago, people were bursting with excitement over the coming of the railroad; today, the new highway is the general topic of conversation. What is in store for us tomorrow? History will record it for future generations to read."

SOURCES

SOURCES

Chapter One: TUSKET'S BEGINNINGS

Blauveldt, Robert B. *The Blauvelt Family in Nova Scotia - including all the Yarmouth County Lents and Many of the VanNordens and Hatfields; with all These Lines Traced Back to Their Arrival in America in the Early 1600's.* Yarmouth, NS: the author, undated [1972?].

Brown, George S. *Yarmouth, NS: a sequel to Campbell's history.* Boston: Rand Avery Company, 1888.

Byers, Mary & McBurney, Margaret. *Atlantic Hearth: early homes and families of Nova Scotia.* Toronto: University of Toronto Press, 1994.

Campbell, J. R. (Rev.) *History of the County of Yarmouth, Nova Scotia.* Saint John, NB: J. & A. McMillan, 1876.

Elliott, Shirley B. *The Legislative Assembly of Nova Scotia; a biographical directory.* Halifax, NS: Dept. of Government Services Information Division, 1984.

Hatfield, Abraham, F.G.B.S. *Descendants of Matthias Hatfield.* New York: New York Genealogical & Biographical Society, 1954.

Lawson, J. Murray. *Yarmouth Past and Present: a Book of Reminiscences.* Yarmouth, NS: Herald Publishing, 1902.

Lent, Nelson Burton. *History of the Lent (vanLent) Family.* Newburgh, NY, 1903.

Paul, Daniel N. *We Were not the Savages: A Micmac Perspective on the Collision of European and Aboriginal Civilization.* Halifax, NS: Nimbus, 1993.

Robertson, Marion. *King's Bounty: a History of Early Shelburne, Nova Scotia.* Halifax, NS: Nova Scotia Museum, 1978.

Whitehead, Ruth Holmes. *The Old Man Told Us.* Halifax, NS: Nimbus, 1991.

Jacob Mood entry, "Court of General Sessions of the Peace, Shelburne County: Selected Documents," *Nova Scotia Historical Review*, vol.3, no.1, 1983, p.113.

"A Summer-Day's Ramble," *The Argus: the quarterly newsletter of the Argyle Municipality Historical & Genealogical Society,* vol.14 no.4 (Winter 2002), pp.23-32, as reprinted from the *Yarmouth Herald,* Yarmouth, NS, 25 August 1859.

Margeson, Shirley (Prosser), "My Little Red School House: an article on the Tusket School in the 1930s." *The Argus: the quarterly newsletter of the Argyle Municipality Historical & Genealogical Society*, vol.5 no.4 (Winter 1993), pp.27-32.

"Yarmouth Woman Lived to the Age of One Hundred and Six - Days of Slavery Recalled ...," obituary for Hester McKinnon, *Yarmouth Times,* Yarmouth, NS, 29 January 1893.

Charles Alexander Daurie obituary, *The Vanguard,* Yarmouth, NS, 9 February 1990.

Mary Helen (Paul) Daurie obituary, *The Vanguard,* Yarmouth, NS, 7 July 1992.

Bingay, James Harold. "History of Tusket," an unpublished beginning to a history of the village of Tusket, Yarmouth Co., NS, circa 1950-54, 5pp. - photocopy of manuscript held by Argyle Township Court House Archives (ATCHA), Tusket, NS.

Steve Glode burial record, Sweeny's Funeral Records, index & finding aid, compiled by George & Anne (Porter) Sorensen, Springdale, NS, 1990, Ledger 25, page 27 (1957).

Land grant documents & maps for the village of Tusket from the Crown Lands Office, Dept. Natural Resources, Halifax, NS and from the Nova Scotia Archives and Records Management (NSARM), Halifax, NS.

Sorensen, George & Anne (Porter). "Yarmouth County, NS Deeds Excerpts & Index, 1774-1827," Springdale, NS, 1987 [unpublished], printed copy held by ATCHA, Tusket, NS.

"The Mood Family," an unpublished genealogy by Clement V. Doane, Yarmouth, NS, circa 1955-1963. Microfilm copy held by ATCHA, Tusket, NS

"The Servant Family of Nova Scotia," [genealogical chart] compiled by Emerson Flint Servant, Chegoggin, NS, unpublished, circa 1979. Original chart held in 2005 by ATCHA, Tusket, NS (M1994:727).

"Tooker Genealogy," compiled by Jeffrey R. Tooker, Paynes Creek, CA, ca.1994. Manuscript held by ATCHA, Tusket, NS (MG10 Ser.B Tooker Item #2).

Jacob & Margery Tooker gravestones inscriptions, Yarmouth County Gravestone Inventory, Church Hill Cemetery, Yarmouth, NS, Marker number 21. Inventory forms held by ATCHA, Tusket, NS.

James Lent & Bridget Lent gravestone inscriptions, Yarmouth County Gravestone Inventory, Tusket Cemetery, Markers #32 & 31. Forms held by ATCHA, Tusket, NS.

Last will & testament and related documents for Col. Job Hatfield (1745-1825), Yarmouth County, NS Probate Records, 1825. Microfilm copy held by Argyle Township Court House Archives (ATCHA), Tusket, NS, LDS microfilm # 0835729.

Deed from Abraham Lent Esquire of the Town of Orang[sic], Rockland County, New York to James Lent Esquire of Argyle, Nova Scotia, dated 23 May 1804. This a photocopy of an unrecorded deed that has been mounted on board and then laminated. Location of original deed is not known, this copy is held by ATCHA, Tusket, NS (M1992:142).

John Hamilton Gray, 1811-1887 entry, Charlottetown Conference of 1864 website, http://collections.ic.gc.ca/charlottetown/index/html, 12 April 2005.

Christ Church Anglican Records, Shelburne, NS, Christenings, 1783-1944. Records held on microfilm by ATCHA, Tusket, NS.

Peter Lent Hatfield document, circa 1887, concerning Nathaniel Richards, churches of Tusket, etc. This document is clearly a rough draft of a letter being addressed to someone who had written to Peter Lent Hatfield inquiring into the above topics. Original document held by ATCHA, Tusket, NS.

Heritage Property Inventory site form for the Abigail Price property, compiled by Peter Crowell, 12 December 1985. Original site form held by ATCHA, Tusket, NS.

Interviews with Margaret d'Entremont, Cecelia Crosby and Charles Muise, all of Tusket, NS, by the author and Peter Crowell, March 2005, regarding the Glode and Daurie families of Tusket, NS. Notes taken during interviews held by the author, Tusket, NS, 2005.

Interview with the late Phyllis W. (Hatfield) Young (Tusket, NS), by the author, 1974. Notes taken during interview held by the author, Tusket, NS, 2005.

Interviews with the late Robert B. Blauveldt (Yarmouth, NS), by the author, 1968 & 1973. Cassette tapes of interviews now held by ATCHA, Tusket, NS (M2000:41).

Chapter Two: A VILLAGE WALKING TOUR

Brown, George S. "The Harding and Harris Families: Yarmouth Genealogies, no.94." *Yarmouth Herald,* Yarmouth, NS, 25 February 1902.

Burnett, Frederick C. *Biographical Directory of Nova Scotia and New Brunswick Free Baptist Ministers and Preachers.* Hantsport, NS: Lancelot Press for Acadia Divinity College and the Baptist Historical Committee of the United Baptist Convention of the Atlantic Provinces, 1996.

Butler, Elmer Ellsworth. *Butlers and Kinsfolk.* Milford, NJ: Cabinet Press, 1944.

Byers, Mary & McBurney, Margaret. *Atlantic Hearth: early homes and families of Nova Scotia.* Toronto: University of Toronto Press, 1994.

Elliott, Shirley B. *The Legislative Assembly of Nova Scotia; a biographical directory.* Halifax, NS: Dept. of Government Services Information Division, 1984.

Hatfield, Abraham, F.G.B.S. *Descendants of Matthias Hatfield.* New York: New York Genealogical & Biographical Society, 1954.

Lawson, J. Murray. *Yarmouth Past and Present: a Book of Reminiscences.* Yarmouth, NS: Herald Publishing, 1902).

Lent, Nelson Burton. *History of the Lent (vanLent) Family.* Newburgh, NY, 1903.

Macauley, Sheila Hubbard. *The Hubbard Family of Nova Scotia.* Baltimore, MD: Gateway Press, 1996.

Paroisse Sainte-Famille, compiled by the Sainte-Famille Parish Council. [Amirault's Hill, NS: the compilers, 2005].

Seasoned Timbers: a Sampling of Historic Buildings Unique to Western Nova Scotia, vol.1. Halifax, NS: Heritage Trust of Nova Scotia, 1972.

Seasoned Timbers: Some Historic Buildings from Nova Scotia's South Shore, vol.2. Halifax, NS: Heritage Trust of Nova Scotia, 1974.

"The Bingay Letter: Tusket Through the Eyes of Dr. James H. Bingay, 1878-1957," *The Argus: the quarterly newsletter of the Argyle Municipality Historical & Genealogical Society,* vol.3 no.4 (Winter 1992), pp.28-41, vol.4 no.1 (Spring 1993), pp.20-34, vol.4 no.2 (Summer 1993), pp.24-36, vol.4 no.3 (Fall 1993), pp.22-36, and vol.4 no.4 (Winter 1993), pp.16-29.

Crowell, Peter, "The Tusket Meeting House," The Argus: the quarterly newsletter of the Argyle Municipality Historical & Genealogical Society, Tusket, NS, vol.1 nos.1&2 (Spring & Summer 1989), pp.22-24.

Lent, "Jimmy" (James W.) "The Corner – Tusket Nova Scotia," an article published in the Yarmouth Light, Yarmouth, NS, circa 1950s. [Few original or microfilmed copies of the Yarmouth Light for the 1950s have survived. Photocopies of the James W. Lent article available at present are undated.]

George Clements obituary, The Vanguard, Yarmouth, NS, 18 March 2003.

Arnold Gavel obituary, *The Vanguard,* Yarmouth, NS, 29 December 1987.

Lawrence LeFave obituary, *The Vanguard,* Yarmouth, NS, 10 March and 17 March 1998.

Antoinette Muise obituary, *The Vanguard,* Yarmouth, NS, 4 June 2002.

Asa Robbins obituary, *Yarmouth Herald,* Yarmouth, NS, 16 June 1896.

William Halstead house reference, *Yarmouth Light*, Yarmouth, NS, 24 December 1896.

Thomas N. McGrath house fire reference, *Yarmouth Light,* Yarmouth, NS, 17 October 1912.

E. C. Simonson Store reference, *Yarmouth Light*, Yarmouth, NS, 13 Sept. 1894.

Tusket railroad station reference, *Yarmouth Light,* Yarmouth, NS, 21 November 1895.

C.R.K. Allen Nature Preserve, "Gulf of Maine Times," vol.5 no.3 (Fall 2001); website: http://www.gulfofmaine.org/times/fall2001/gulf_voices, 14 April 2005.

Church, Ambrose Finson. *Map of the County of Yarmouth, Nova Scotia* (1871). Commission date on map is 1864, publication year was 1871. Most information contained on the map in relation to houses and their owners was gathered around 1866 in the village of Tusket, NS.

Lent, James M. "Plan of Tusket Village," 20 June 1862, surveyed plan provided by Crown Lands Office, NS Dept. of Lands & Forests, Halifax, NS, 1974.

"Tusket," a pictorial history of Tusket compiled by the Tusket Women's Institute. Unpublished, undated, circa 1954. History consists of a 50-page photograph album, with photo captions serving as the only text. Original held by ATCHA, Tusket, NS, 2005.

Heritage Property Inventory site forms for 71 pre-1914 properties in the village of Tusket, Yarmouth County, NS - researched and compiled by Peter Crowell, 10 December 1985 - 30 January 1986. Original site forms with attached photographs held by ATCHA, Tusket, NS, 2005.

Heritage Property Inventory site forms for 6 pre-1914 properties in the village of Tusket, Yarmouth County, NS - researched and compiled by Jerry Titus, 1 February 1995-
3 March 1995. Original site forms with attached photographs held by ATCHA, Tusket, NS, 2005.

Nova Apartments reference, "Municipality of the District of Argyle fonds, 1926-1987," Administrative History. Archival description held by ATCHA, Tusket, NS, 2005 (RG4).

"Mayflower Engine Company Records, 1879-1923," Municipality of the District of Argyle fond. Original records held by ATCHA, Tusket, NS (RG3, Ser.P, Sub-series 1).

Adolphus Lent burial record, Sweeny's Funeral Records, excerpts and index compiled by George & Ann (Porter) Sorensen, Springdale, NS, 1990, Ledger 7, p.99 (1913). Printed copy held by ATCHA, Tusket, NS.

Polly Lent burial record, Sweeny's Funeral Records, excerpts and index compiled by George & Ann (Porter) Sorensen, Springdale, NS, 1990, Ledger 10, p.63 (1920). Printed copy held by ATCHA, Tusket, NS.

Arabella Theodosia Lent burial record, Sweeny's Funeral Records, excerpts and index compiled by George & Ann (Porter) Sorensen, Springdale, NS, 1990, Ledger 11, p.13 (1923). Printed copy held by ATCHA, Tusket, NS.

Abram Jeffery Lent burial record, Sweeny's Funeral Records, excerpts and index compiled by George & Ann (Porter) Sorensen, Springdale, NS, 1990, Ledger 11, p.177 (1924). Printed copy held by ATCHA, Tusket, NS.

Thomas K. Lent burial record, Sweeny's Funeral Records, excerpts and index compiled by George & Ann (Porter) Sorensen, Springdale, NS, 1990, Ledger 11, p.154 (1924). Printed copy held by ATCHA, Tusket, NS.

Helen "Nell" Theodosia Gillis burial record, Sweeny's Funeral Records, excerpts and index compiled by George & Ann (Porter) Sorensen, Springdale, NS, 1990, Ledger 20, p.317 (1943), printed copy held by ATCHA, Tusket, NS.

Harry Gillis burial record, Sweeny's Funeral Records, excerpts and index compiled by George & Ann (Porter) Sorensen, Springdale, NS, 1990, Ledger 20, p.350 (1943). Printed copy held by ATCHA, Tusket, NS.

Rev. James & Elizabeth (Harding) Lent gravestone inscriptions, Yarmouth County Gravestone Inventory, Tusket Cemetery, Marker #29. Inventory forms held by ATCHA, Tusket, NS.

Lent family members gravestone inscriptions, Yarmouth County Gravestone Inventory, Tusket Cemetery, Marker #28. Inventory forms held by ATCHA, Tusket, NS.

Deeds and title search for Benoit Pottier property, as carried our by Gerald Pottier, Belleville, NS, and the author, March 2005.

Deeds and related documents for Benoit Pottier property as supplied by Carl and Audrey Pottier, Tusket, NS. Copies held by the author in 2005.

Deeds to the George A. Clements property provided by Gerald Saulnier, Abrams River, NS, executor of the last will & testament of George A. Clements, March 2005. Copies held by the author, Tusket, NS, 2005.

Deed from Abraham Lent Esquire of the Town of Orang[sic], Rockland County, New York to James Lent Esquire of Argyle, Nova Scotia, dated 23 May 1804. This is a photocopy of an unrecorded deed that has been mounted on board and then laminated. Location of original deed is not known, this copy is held by ATCHA, Tusket, NS (M1992:142).

Interviews with Cecilia "Sis" (LeBlanc) Crosby, Tusket, NS, by the author, 2004 & 2005. Notes taken during interviews held by the author, Tusket, NS, 2005.

Interviews with Gordon Wood, Tusket, NS, by the author, 2004 & 2005. Notes taken during interviews held by the author, Tusket, NS, 2005.

Interviews with Margaret (Pottier) d'Entremont, Tusket, NS, by the author, March & April 2005. Notes taken during interview held by the author, Tusket, NS

Interviews with Hubert Pothier, Tusket, NS, by the author, March 2005. Notes taken during interviews held in 2005 by the author, Tusket, NS.

Interview with Norman Pottier, Tusket, NS, by the author, March 1975. Notes taken during interview held by the author in 2005.

Interview with Tracy Hatfield, Yarmouth, NS (concerning Andrew Jeffery), by the author, March 2005. Notes taken during interview held by the author, Tusket, NS, 2005.

Interviews with Polly Patten and Joan Patten, Tusket, NS, by the author, March & April 2005. Notes taken during interviews held by the author, Tusket, NS, 2005.

Interviews, email correspondence and photographs from Earle Robbins, Ottawa, Ont., February, March and April 2005. Notes taken during interviews and copies of email correspondence held by the author, Tusket, NS, 2005.

Interviews with Melanie Hubbard and her son, Roy Hubbard, Tusket, NS, by the author, March 2005. Notes taken during interviews held by the author, Tusket, NS, 2005.

Interviews with Laura Butler, Yarmouth, NS, by the author, March & April 2005. Notes taken during interviews held by the author, 2005.

Interview with Alphonse Pottier, Sainte-Anne-du-Ruisseau, NS, by the author, March 2005. Notes taken during interview held by the author, Tusket, NS, 2005.

Interview with Donald Gavel, Pleasant Lake, NS, by Peter Crowell and the author, March 2005. Notes taken during interview held by the author, Tusket, NS, 2005.

Interview with Mac and Karen (Hamilton) Sweeney, Tusket, NS, by Peter Crowell and the author, March 2005. Notes taken during interview held by the author, Tusket, NS, 2005.

Interview with Rosanne Blades, Raynardton, NS, a former MT&T employee regarding the Tusket "switching station," by the author, March 2005. Notes taken during interview held in 2005 by the author, 2005.

Interview with Evelyn Muise, Tusket, NS, by Peter Crowell, March 2005. Notes taken during interview held by the author in 2005.

Interviews with the following people, who unless otherwise indicated are Tusket residents, by the author, March & April 2005: Emma Bourque (Hubbard's Point), Frederick Bourque, Roland Bourque, Timmy Bourque (Amirault's Hill), Fred Churchill (Raynardton), Edwin Coffin, John and Linda Conrad, Marvin Cunningham, Bernard d'Entremont, Arlene (Hubbard) d'Eon (Pubnico), Abel Doucet (Pleasant Lake), Lawrence Dukeshire, Yvonne Eaton, Doris Gaudet (Arcadia), Velma Hamilton, Barbara Hubbard, Bruce Hubbard (Sainte-Anne-du-Ruisseau), Jackie Jacquard, Freddie and Barbara LeBlanc, William and Rose Emma LeFave, Don and Marina Little (Arcadia), Nicole MacNeil, Shirley Margeson (Wolfville), Linda Morris, Albert Muise, Charlie and Annie Muise, Danny Muise (Abram's River), George Muise, Norma Muise, Barbara Nauss (Yarmouth), Doug Nickerson, James Pottier, Josephine Pottier, Doug and Joyce Sisco, Rodney Sweeney, Harold and Eileen Tatton, Kenneth and Carmen Thibeau and Ralph Thibeau (Sainte-Anne-du-Ruisseau). Notes taken during interviews held by the author, Tusket, NS, 2005.

Chapter 3: GENERAL STORES

Hatfield, Abraham, F.G.B.S. *Descendants of Matthias Hatfield.* New York: New York Genealogical & Biographical Society, 1954.

Lawson, J. Murray. *Yarmouth Past and Present: a Book of Reminiscences.* Yarmouth, NS: Herald Publishing, 1902.

Lent, Nelson Burton. *History of the Lent (vanLent) Family.* Newburgh, NY, 1903.

Land grant documents & maps for the village of Tusket from the Crown Lands Office, Dept. Natural Resources, Halifax, NS and from the Nova Scotia Archives and Records Management (NSARM), Halifax, NS.

Last will & testament and related documents for Col. Job Hatfield (1745-1825), Yarmouth County, NS Probate Records, 1825. Microfilm copy held by Argyle Township Court House Archives (ATCHA), Tusket, NS, LDS microfilm # 0835729.

Tracy G. Hatfield store reference, *Yarmouth Light,* Yarmouth, NS, 30 May 1907.

"New Store at Tusket," *Yarmouth Light*, Yarmouth, NS, 14 November 1907, reprinted in *The Argus: the quarterly newsletter of the Argyle Municipality Historical & Genealogical Society,* vol.6 nos.3 & 4 (Fall & Winter 1994), pp.54-55

Margeson, Shirley (Prosser). "Two Tusket Stores in the 1940s," *The Argus: the quarterly newsletter of the Argyle Municipality Historical & Genealogical Society,* vol.7 no.1 (Spring 1995), pp.27-30

"William T. Lent – Municipal Warden – 1911-12," *The Argus: the quarterly newsletter of the Argyle Municipality Historical & Genealogical Society)*, vol.6 no.2 (Summer 1994), pp.16-20.

James Bingay General Store Day Book & Ledger, 1832-1872. Original held by ATCHA, Tusket, NS (MG503 Ser.A).

Church, Ambrose Finson. *Map of the County of Yarmouth, Nova Scotia* (1871). Commission date on map is 1864, publication year was 1871. Most information contained on the map in relation to houses and their owners was gathered around 1866 in the village of Tusket, NS.

Lent, James M. "Plan of Tusket Village," 20 June 1862, surveyed plan provided by Crown Lands Office, NS Dept. of Lands & Forests, Halifax, NS, 1974.

"The Bingay Letter: Tusket Through the Eyes of Dr. James H. Bingay, 1878-1957," *The Argus: the quarterly newsletter of the Argyle Municipality Historical & Genealogical Society,* vol.3 no.4 (Winter 1992), pp.28-41, vol.4 no.1 (Spring 1993), pp.20-34, vol.4 no.2 (Summer 1993), pp.24-36, vol.4 no.3 (Fall 1993), pp.22-36, and vol.4 no.4 (Winter 1993), pp.16-29.

W.T. Lent Store reference, *Yarmouth Light*, Yarmouth, NS, 7 May 1903.

E. C. Simonson Store reference, *Yarmouth Light*, Yarmouth, NS, 13 Sept. 1894.

Smith Harding store references, *Yarmouth Light,* Yarmouth, NS, 29 October 1896 and 10 December 1896.

Chapter 4: THE JEWEL OF TUSKET: The Court House

Brown, George S. *Yarmouth, NS: a sequel to Campbell's history.* Boston: Rand Avery Company, 1888.

Campbell, J. R. (Rev) *History of the County of Yarmouth, Nova Scotia.* Saint John, NB: J. & A. McMillan, 1876.

Carter, Margaret. *Early Canadian Court Houses: Studies in Archaeology, Architecture and History.* Ottawa, Ont.: National Historic Parks & Site Branch, Parks Canada, Environment Canada, 1983.

Hale, C. A. *Canadian Inventory of Historic Building: Former Argyle District Court House.* Ottawa, Ont.: Parks Canada, 1977.

Lawson, J. Murray. *Yarmouth Past and Present: a Book of Reminiscences.* Yarmouth, NS: Herald Publishing, 1902.

Thurston, Arthur. *The Tragedy of Omar Pasha Roberts and Flora Ellen Gray.* Yarmouth, NS: Arthur Thurston Publications, 1991.

"The Bingay Letter: Tusket Through the Eyes of Dr. James H. Bingay, 1878-1957," *The Argus: the quarterly newsletter of the Argyle Municipality Historical & Genealogical Society*, vol.3 no.4 (Winter 1992), pp.28-41, vol.4 no.1 (Spring 1993), pp.20-34, vol.4 no.2 (Summer 1993), pp.24-36, vol.4 no.3 (Fall 1993), pp.22-36, and vol.4 no.4 (Winter 1993), pp.16-29.

Crowell, Peter, "Future Home of the Argyle Township Court House Archives has Interesting History," *The Argus: the quarterly newsletter of the Argyle Municipality Historical & Genealogical Society*, vol.12 no.3 (Fall 2000), pp.32-35.

Court of General Sessions of the Peace for the Districts of Yarmouth & Argyle, NS, 1789-1855, Minutes Books & Jury Books. NSARM microfilm, RG34 - 324 Yarmouth County - Series P - vols.1-4. Microfilm copy held by ATCHA, Tusket, NS.

Heritage Property Inventory Site form for the Argyle Township Court House, Tusket, N.S, compiled by Peter Crowell, 29 January 1986. Original site form and property files held by ATCHA, Tusket, NS.

Minute Books of the Argyle Municipality Historical & Genealogical Society, 1989- , Tusket, NS. Original minute books held by the Society at ATCHA, Tusket, NS, 2005.

Stipendiary Magistrates' Court (Argyle) fonds, 1861-1945, ArchWay, Council of Nova Scotia Archives Descriptive Database, http://webarchives.nsarm.gov.ns.ca/webcat/request, 12 April 2005. Original records held by ATCHA, Tusket, NS.

"The Bingay Letter: Tusket Through the Eyes of Dr. James H. Bingay, 1878-1957," *The Argus: the quarterly newsletter of the Argyle Municipality Historical & Genealogical Society*, vol.3 no.4 (Winter 1992), pp.28-41, vol.4 no.1 (Spring 1993), pp.20-34, vol.4 no.2 (Summer 1993), pp.24-36, vol.4 no.3 (Fall 1993), pp.22-36, and vol.4 no.4 (Winter 1993), pp.16-29.

Supreme Court at Tusket references, *Yarmouth Herald,* Yarmouth, NS, 7 May 1841 and *Yarmouth Telegram,* Yarmouth, NS, 26 September 1924.

"Tusket," a pictorial history of Tusket compiled by the Tusket Women's Institute. Unpublished, undated, circa 1954. History consists of a 50-page photograph album, with photo captions serving as the only text. Original held by ATCHA, Tusket, NS, 2005.

Chapter 5: CHURCHES

Burnett, Frederick C. *Biographical Directory of Nova Scotia and New Brunswick Free Baptist Ministers and Preachers.* Hantsport, NS: Lancelot Press for Acadia Divinity College and the Baptist Historical Committee of the United Baptist Convention of the Atlantic Provinces, 1996.

Campbell, J. R. (Rev) *History of the County of Yarmouth, Nova Scotia.* Saint John, NB: J. & A. McMillan, 1876.

Campbell, Joan Bourque. *Histoire de la Paroisse de Sainte-Anne-du-Ruisseau (Eel Brook).* Yarmouth, NS : Lescarbot, 1985.

d'Entremont, Clarence Joseph (Rev). *Histoire de Sainte-Anne-du-Ruisseau, Belleville, Rivière-Abram (Nouvelle-Écosse).* West Pubnico, NS: the author, 1995.

Hatfield, Abraham, F.G.B.S. *Descendants of Matthias Hatfield.* New York: New York Genealogical & Biographical Society, 1954.

Lawson, J. Murray. *Yarmouth Past and Present: a Book of Reminiscences.* Yarmouth, NS: Herald Publishing, 1902.

Lent, Nelson Burton. *History of the Lent (vanLent) Family.* Newburgh, NY, 1903.

"The Bingay Letter: Tusket Through the Eyes of Dr. James H. Bingay, 1878-1957," *The Argus: the quarterly newsletter of the Argyle Municipality Historical & Genealogical Society,* vol.3 no.4 (Winter 1992), pp.28-41, vol.4 no.1 (Spring 1993), pp.20-34, vol.4 no.2 (Summer 1993), pp.24-36, vol.4 no.3 (Fall 1993), pp.22-36, and vol.4 no.4 (Winter 1993), pp.16-29.

Blauveldt, Robert B. "St. Stephen's Anglican – the Old Loyalist Church at Tusket," *Vanguard,* Yarmouth, NS, 1973.

Crowell, Peter. "The Tusket Meeting House," *The Argus: the quarterly newsletter of the Argyle Municipality Historical & Genealogical Society,* Tusket, NS, vol.1 nos.1&2 (Spring & Summer 1989), pp.22-24.

Crowell, Peter. "St. Stephen's Anglican Church at Tusket – heritage plaque unveiling Sunday," *Vanguard,* Yarmouth, NS, 11 July 1989, page 2C.

Crowell, Peter. "Future Home of the Argyle Township Court House Archives has Interesting History," *The Argus: the quarterly newsletter of the Argyle Municipality Historical & Genealogical Society,* vol.12 no.3 (Fall 2000), pp.32-35.

"Rev. James Lent" [an obituary], *Christian Messenger* [newspaper], Halifax, NS, Friday 13 December 1850.

Methodist Church references, *Yarmouth Light,* Yarmouth, NS, 16 December 1890 and 31 May 1894.

Church, Ambrose Finson. *Map of the County of Yarmouth , Nova Scotia* (1871). Commission date on map is 1864, publication year was 1871. Most information contained on the map in relation to houses and their owners was gathered around 1866 in the village of Tusket, NS.

Lent, James M. "Plan of Tusket Village," 20 June 1862, surveyed plan provided by Crown Lands Office, NS Dept. of Lands & Forests, Halifax, NS, 1974.

"Tusket," a pictorial history of Tusket compiled by the Tusket Women's Institute. Unpublished, undated, circa 1954. History consists of a 50-page photograph album, with photo captions serving as the only text. Original held by ATCHA, Tusket, NS, 2005.

Hatfield, Peter Lent. "Draft Letter." An original document, obviously a rough draft for a more formal letter, written by Peter Lent Hatfield in or around 1887. The document suggests that he was responding to a letter he had received requesting information on early Tusket settler Nathaniel Richards, and on the churches of Tusket. Original document held by ATCHA, Tusket, NS. (M1999:52).

Blauvelt, J. L. *Seven New Tunes to Church Hymns.* [Yarmouth, NS?]: the author, 1913. Original published sheet music held by ATCHA, Tusket, NS.

Rev. James Lent gravestone inscription, Yarmouth Gravestone Inventory, Tusket Cemetery, Marker #29. Inventory forms held by ATCHA, Tusket, NS

Heritage Property Inventory Site Form for the Charles Knowles house, Tusket, NS, compiled by Peter Crowell, 10 December 1985. Original site forms and property file held by ATCHA, Tusket, NS.

Heritage Property Inventory Site form for the Anglican rectory, Tusket, NS, compiled Peter Crowell, 28 December 1985. Original site form and property file held by ATCHA, Tusket, NS.

Heritage Property Inventory Site form for Nathaniel E. Butler house, Tusket, NS, compiled Peter Crowell, 10 January 1986. Original site form and property file held by ATCHA, Tusket, NS.

Heritage Property Inventory Site form for the David McDonald house, Tusket, NS, compiled Peter Crowell, 14 December 1985. Original site form and property file held by ATCHA, Tusket, NS.

Heritage Property Inventory Site form for St. Stephen's Church, Tusket, NS, compiled Peter Crowell, 28 January 1986. Original site form and property file held by ATCHA, Tusket, NS.

Blauveldt, Robert B. "Down Memory Lane," *Vanguard,* Yarmouth, NS, 17 July 1974.

Interviews with the late Robert B. Blauveldt (Yarmouth, NS), by the author, 1968 & 1973. Cassette tapes of interviews now held by ATCHA, Tusket, NS (M2000:41).

Chapter 6: SCHOOLS

Bulletin of the Public Archives of Nova Scotia: A documentary study of early education policy. Halifax, NS: Public Archives of Nova Scotia, 1937, vol.I, no.1, p.37

Lawson, J. Murray. *Yarmouth Past and Present: a Book of Reminiscences.* Yarmouth, NS: Herald Printing, 1902.

"The Bingay Letter: Tusket Through the Eyes of Dr. James H. Bingay, 1878-1957," *The Argus: the quarterly newsletter of the Argyle Municipality Historical & Genealogical Society,* vol.3 no.4 (Winter 1992), pp.28-41, vol.4 no.1 (Spring 1993), pp.20-34, vol.4 no.2 (Summer 1993), pp.24-36, vol.4 no.3 (Fall 1993), pp.22-36, and vol.4 no.4 (Winter 1993), pp.16-29.

Margeson, Shirley (Prosser). "My Little Red School House: an article on the Tusket School in the 1930s," *The Argus: the quarterly newsletter of the Argyle Municipality Historical & Genealogical Society*, vol.5 no.4 (Winter 1993), pp.27-32.

Argyle Municipal School Board Minutes 1949-1969, Municipal School Board of the District of Argyle (Nova Scotia) fonds, 1860-1982, RG10, Ser.A, Sub-series 1, School Board Minutes. Original records held by ATCHA, Tusket, NS.

School return for "Tusket Village no.9," 1831, Nova Scotia Archives & Records Management, Halifax, NS, RG 14, vol. 1-54, 56-61.

"Tusket," a pictorial history of Tusket compiled by the Tusket Women's Institute. Unpublished, undated, circa 1954. History consists of a 50-page photograph album, with photo captions serving as the only text. Original held by ATCHA, Tusket, NS, 2005.

Lent, James M. "Plan of Tusket Village," 20 June 1862, surveyed plan provided by Crown Lands Office, NS Dept. of Lands & Forests, Halifax, NS, 1974.

Church, Ambrose Finson. *Map of the County of Yarmouth , Nova Scotia* (1871). Commission date on map is 1864, publication year was 1871. Most information contained on the map in relation to houses and their owners was gathered around 1866 in the village of Tusket, NS.

Interviews with the late Robert B. Blauveldt (Yarmouth, NS), by the author, 1968 & 1973. Cassette tapes of interviews now held by ATCHA, Tusket, NS (M2000:41).

Chapter 7: POSTAL SERVICE

"A Summer-Day's Ramble," *The Argus: the quarterly newsletter of the Argyle Municipality Historical & Genealogical Society,* vol.14 no.4 (Winter 2002), pp.23-32, as reprinted from the *Yarmouth Herald,* Yarmouth, NS, 25 August 1859.

"Post Offices and Post Masters," entry for Tusket, NS, Library & Archives Canada website, http://www.collectionscanada.ca/archivianet/02010902_e.html, 14 April 2005.

"The Bingay Letter: Tusket Through the Eyes of Dr. James H. Bingay, 1878-1957," *The Argus: the quarterly newsletter of the Argyle Municipality Historical & Genealogical Society*, vol.3 no.4 (Winter 1992), pp.28-41, vol.4 no.1 (Spring 1993), pp.20-34, vol.4 no.2 (Summer 1993), pp.24-36, vol.4 no.3 (Fall 1993), pp.22-36, and vol.4 no.4 (Winter 1993), pp.16-29.

"Tusket," a pictorial history of Tusket compiled by the Tusket Women's Institute. Unpublished, undated, circa 1954. History consists of a 50-page photograph album, with photo captions serving as the only text. Original held by ATCHA, Tusket, NS, 2005.

Interviews with Polly Patten and Joan (Muise) Patten, Tusket NS by the author, February and March 2005. Notes taken during interviews held by the author, Tusket, NS, 2005.

Chapter 8: TRANSPORTATION

Brown, George S. *Yarmouth, N.S.: a sequel to Campbell's History.* Boston: Rand Avery Company, 1880.

Campbell, J. R. (Rev) *History of the County of Yarmouth, Nova Scotia.* Saint John, NB: J. & A. McMillan, 1876.

Lawson, J. Murray. *Yarmouth Past and Present: a Book of Reminiscences.* Yarmouth, NS: Herald Publishing, 1902.

Ricker, Jackson. *Historical Sketches of Glenwood and the Argyles.* Truro, NS: Truro Printing & Publishing Co., 1941.

Banks, Herbert R. "The Coast Railway: 'Tom Robertson's Wheelbarrow Railroad,'" *Nova Scotia Historical Review*, vol.6 no.2 (1986), pp.11-16.

Rowland VanNorden stagecoach advertisement, *Yarmouth Herald,* Yarmouth, NS, 19 July 1866.

Ray, Catherine Farish. "Sentimental Journey - Tusket, Nova Scotia," *Yarmouth Light*, Yarmouth, NS, 17 Sept. 1953, Section 3, p.17.

Pelton, Guy C. Untitled column, *Yarmouth Light,* Yarmouth, NS, 9 September 1961.

Railroad references, *Yarmouth Herald,* Yarmouth, NS, 18 February 1896 and 3 March 1896.

Albanie Pottier Bicycle Shop reference, *Yarmouth Light*, Yarmouth, NS, 26 April 1906.

Thomas N. McGrath autmobile reference, *Yarmouth Light*, Yarmouth, NS, 7 May 1906.

Tracy Hatfield automobile reference, *Yarmouth Light,* Yarmouth, NS, 28 June 1917.

"Tusket," a pictorial history of Tusket compiled by the Tusket Women's Institute. Unpublished, undated, circa 1954. History consists of a 50-page photograph album, with photo captions serving as the only text. Original held by ATCHA, Tusket, NS, 2005.

"Paving Highway #3," a series of 37 photographs, probably taken by the NS Dept. of Highways, 1936-1937, before and after the paving of the #3 Highway. Original photographs held by ATCHA, Tusket, NS, 2005.

"History of Automobiles - The Early Days in Nova, 1899-1949," website, http://www.littletechshoppe.com/ns1625/automobiles.html, 14 April 2005.

Interviews with the late Robert B. Blauveldt (Yarmouth, NS), by the author, 1968 & 1973. Cassette tapes of interviews now held by ATCHA, Tusket, NS (M2000:41).

Interviews with Gertrude Wathen, Tusket, NS, by the author, 1968 & 1973. Notes taken during interviews held by the author, Tusket, NS, 2005.

Interviews on the subject of Tusket's first automobile, with Gordon Wood (Tusket), Freda (McGrath) Bullerwell (Brooklyn, Yar.Co.), Tracy Hatfield (Yarmouth) and Charles Muise (Tusket), March 2005. Notes taken during interviews held by the author, Tusket, NS, 2005.

Chapter 9: HOTELS & INNS

Blauveldt, Robert B. *The Blauvelt Family in Nova Scotia - including all the Yarmouth County Lents and Many of the VanNordens and Hatfields; with all These Lines Traced Back to Their Arrival in America in the Early 1600's.* Yarmouth, NS: the author, undated [1972?].

Hatfield, Abraham, F.G.B.S. *Descendants of Matthias Hatfield.* New York: New York Genealogical & Biographical Society, 1954.

"The Bingay Letter: Tusket Through the Eyes of Dr. James H. Bingay, 1878-1957," *The Argus: the quarterly newsletter of the Argyle Municipality Historical & Genealogical Society*, vol.3 no.4 (Winter 1992), pp.28-41, vol.4 no.1 (Spring 1993), pp.20-34, vol.4 no.2 (Summer 1993), pp.24-36, vol.4 no.3 (Fall 1993), pp.22-36, and vol.4 no.4 (Winter 1993), pp.16-29.

John & Ann S. (Hatfield) Gavel Family Bible Record, *The Argus: the quarterly newsletter of the Argyle Municipality Historical & Genealogical Society*, vol.3 no.3 (Fall 1991), pp.13-14.

Wm. H. "Gillman" household, 1860 US Census, New Hampshire, Strafford County, Rollinsford (Salmon Falls Post Office), page 247. Microfilm & CDROM #M653-680. Record downloaded and printed from http://www.ancestry.com, 15 April 2005.

William Gilman household, 1871 Canada Census, Nova Scotia, Yarmouth County, Sub-district h-1 Tusket, p.4, household no.12, family no.15. NAC (National Archives of Canada) microfilm no.C-10546.

William Gilman household, 1881 Canada Census, Nova Scotia, Yarmouth County, Sub-district h-1 Tusket, pp.40-41, household no.158 family no.167. NAC microfilm no.C-13171.

William Gilman household, 1891 Canada Census, Nova Scotia, Yarmouth County, Sub-district u-Tusket, p.4, household no.15. NAC microfilm no.T-6322.

Araminta Gilman household, 1901 Canada Census, Nova Scotia, Yarmouth County, Sub-district s-Tusket, p.3. NAC microfilm no.T-6456.

John J. Gilman obituary, *Yarmouth Light*, Yarmouth, NS, 16 November 1893.

American House advertisement, *Yarmouth Herald,* Yarmouth, NS, 23 December 1869, page 3, col.2.

American House/Gilmans reference, *Yarmouth Times,* Yarmouth, NS, 21 February 1885; *Yarmouth Herald*, Yarmouth, NS, 16 September 1885; *Yarmouth Light,* Yarmouth, NS, 17 October 1912 (Tusket community news column), 9 September 1961 (Guy Pelton column).

Adolphus Lent burial record, Sweeny's Funeral Records, excerpts and index compiled by George & Ann (Porter) Sorensen, Springdale, NS, 1990, Ledger 7, p.99 (1913). Printed copy held by ATCHA. Tusket, NS.

John J. Gilman burial record, Sweeny's Funeral Records, excerpts and index compiled by George & Ann (Porter) Sorensen, Springdale, NS, 1890, Ledger 1, p.146 (1893).

William H. Gilman burial record, Sweeny's Funeral Records, excerpts and index compiled by George & Ann (Porter) Sorensen, Springdale, NS, 1890 Ledger 2, page 58 (1896).

William Gilman obituary, *Yarmouth Light*, Yarmouth, NS, 16 April 1896 (Tusket community news column).

Araminta Gilman burial record, Sweeny's Funeral Records, excerpts and index compiled by George & Ann (Porter) Sorensen, Springdale, NS, 1890, Ledger 13, p.141 (1929).
Araminta Gilman obituary, *Yarmouth Herald,* Yarmouth, NS, 28 May 1929, p.1.

Laura (Gilman) Cowan burial record, Sweeny Funeral Records, excerpts and index compiled by George & Ann (Porter) Sorensen, Springdale, NS, 1890, Ledger 15, p.32 (1932).

Laura (Gilman) Cowan obituary, *Yarmouth Herald*, Yarmouth, NS, 27 September 1932.

Mary Gardner Gilman, burial record, Sweeny's Funeral Records, excerpts and index compiled by George & Ann (Porter) Sorensen, Springdale, NS, 1890, Ledger 15, p.134 (1933).

Mary Gardner Gilman obituary, *Yarmouth Herald,* Yarmouth, NS, 14 March 1933.

Interview with Carol (Nickerson) Jacquard, Tusket Falls, NS, by the author, March 2005. Notes taken during interview held by the author in 2005.

François Xavier Muise information, from an interview with Adolph Doucette, Villa St. Joseph du Lac, Dayton, NS, by Phyllis Pothier, Tusket, N.S., 2000. Notes taken during interview held by Phyllis Pothier, Tusket, NS, 2005.

"Riverside Inn, Tusket – Yarmouth County, Nova Scotia, J. L. White, Proprietor," original printed brochure, undated. Original given to the author by the late Gertrude Wathen, Tusket, NS, 1968.

Riverside Inn and Mrs. Anne Hatfield reference, *Yarmouth Light*, Yarmouth, NS, 16 May 1907.

"A Summer-Day's Ramble," *The Argus: the quarterly newsletter of the Argyle Municipality Historical & Genealogical Society,* vol.14 no.4 (Winter 2002), pp.23-32, as reprinted from the *Yarmouth Herald,* Yarmouth, NS, 25 August 1859.

Kilby Lodge references, *Yarmouth Telegram*, Yarmouth, NS, 3 June 1904 and *Yarmouth Light*, Yarmouth, NS, 23 December 1909.

Killiam Hotel references, *Yarmouth Light*, Yarmouth, NS, 23 December 1909.

Mildred "Pat" Harper death notice, *Light-Herald,* Yarmouth, NS, 11 July 1968, sect.2, page 4, col.3.

Church, Ambrose Finson. *Map of the County of Yarmouth , Nova Scotia* (1871). Commission date on map is 1864, publication year was 1871. Most information contained on the map in relation to houses and their owners was gathered around 1866 in the village of Tusket, NS.

"Tusket," a pictorial history of Tusket compiled by the Tusket Women's Institute. Unpublished, undated, circa 1954. History consists of a 50-page photograph album, with photo captions serving as the only text. Original held by ATCHA, Tusket, NS, 2005.

Bethia Richard's hotel reference, *Yarmouth Light*, Yarmouth, NS, 28 October 1890.

Email letter from Phyllis Killam Abell, Portsmouth, NH, to the author, 6 December 2001. Printed copy of email held by the author, Tusket, NS, 2001.

Interview with Adeline Doucet, Quinan, NS, by the author, March 2005. Notes taken during interview held by the author, Tusket, NS, 2005.

Interviews with the late Robert B. Blauveldt (Yarmouth, NS), by the author, 1968 & 1973. Cassette tapes of interviews now held by ATCHA, Tusket, NS (M2000:41).

Interviews with Cecilia "Sis Crosby, Tusket, NS, by the author, February 2004 and March 2005. Notes taken during interviews held by the author, Tusket, NS, 2005.

Interview with Raymond LeBlanc, Sainte-Anne-du-Ruisseau, NS, by Peter Crowell, Tusket, NS, March 2005. Notes taken during interview held by the author, Tusket, NS, 2005. Loretta Warner, Gordon Wood, etc.

Interview with Loretta Warner, Abrams River, NS, by Peter Crowell, Tusket, NS, March 2005. Notes taken during interview held by the author, Tusket, NS, 2005.

Interview with Gordon Wood, Tusket, NS, by the author, March 2005. Notes taken during interview held by the author, Tusket, NS, 2005.

Chapter 10: INDUSTRIES

Brown, George S. *Yarmouth, NS: a sequel to Campbell's history.* Boston: Rand Avery Company, 1888.

Butler, Elmer Ellsworth. *Butlers and Kinsfolk.* Milford, NG: Cabinet Press, 1944.

Campbell, J. R. (Rev) *History of the County of Yarmouth, Nova Scotia.* Saint John, NB: J. & A. McMillan, 1876.

Lawson, J. Murray. *Yarmouth Past and Present: a Book of Reminiscences.* Yarmouth, NS: Herald Publishing, 1902.

Robertson, Barbara R. *Sawpower: making lumber in the sawmills of Nova Scotia.* Halifax, NS: Nova Scotia Museum & Nimbus, 1986.

"A Summer-Day's Ramble," *The Argus: the quarterly newsletter of the Argyle Municipality Historical & Genealogical Society,* vol.14 no.4 (Winter 2002), pp.23-32, as reprinted from the *Yarmouth Herald,* Yarmouth, NS, 25 August 1859.

Crowell, Peter. "Skill and Craftmanship of Yarmouth County's Early Builders in Tusket," an article on the Adolphus Wood house, Tusket, NS, *The Vanguard,* Yarmouth, NS, 9 June 1987, p.B12.

"The Bingay Letter: Tusket Through the Eyes of Dr. James H. Bingay, 1878-1957," *The Argus: the quarterly newsletter of the Argyle Municipality Historical & Genealogical Society,* vol.3 no.4 (Winter 1992), pp.28-41, vol.4 no.1 (Spring 1993), pp.20-34, vol.4 no.2 (Summer 1993), pp.24-36, vol.4 no.3 (Fall 1993), pp.22-36, and vol.4 no.4 (Winter 1993), pp.16-29.

Asa Robbins obituary, *Yarmouth Herald,* Yarmouth, NS, 16 June 1896.

Heritage Property Inventory Site Form for the Asa Robbins house, Tusket, NS, compiled by Peter Crowell, 16 December 1985. Original site form and property file held by ATCHA, Tusket, NS, 2005.

Church, Ambrose Finson. *Map of the County of Yarmouth , Nova Scotia* (1871). Commission date on map is 1864, publication year was 1871. Most information contained on the map in relation to houses and their owners was gathered around 1866 in the village of Tusket, NS.

Lent, James M. "Plan of Tusket Village," 20 June 1862, surveyed plan provided by Crown Lands Office, NS Dept. of Lands & Forests, Halifax, NS, 1974.

Asa Robbins advertisement, "Robbins Process for Tanning and Waterproofing Leather," *Yarmouth Herald,* Yarmouth, NS, 28 September 1876, p.4, col.5.

Titus, Jerry. "Ships and Shipbuilders of Argyle: Early Development," *The Argus: the quarterly newsletter of the Argyle Municipality Historical & Genealogical Society,* vol.13 no.2 (Summer 2001), pp.35-40.

Titus, Jerry. "Ships and Shipbuilders of Argyle: The 1840's," *The Argus: the quarterly newsletter of the Argyle Municipality Historical & Genealogical Society,* vol.13 no.4 (Winter 2001), pp.21-26.

Titus, Jerry. "Ships and Shipbuilders - The 1850's," *The Argus: the quarterly newsletter of the Argyle Municipality Historical & Genealogical Society,* vol.14 no.2 (Summer 2002), pp.21-28.

Titus, Jerry. "Ships and Shipbuilders of Argyle - Sails of the Seventies," *The Argus: the quarterly newsletter of the Argyle Municipality Historical & Genealogical Society,* vol.16 no.3 (Fall 2004), pp.23-31

Titus, Jerry. "Tusket Ships and Their Builders 1860-1870," *The Argus: the quarterly newsletter of the Argyle Municipality Historical & Genealogical Society,* vol.11 no.2 (Summer 1999), pp.13-25.

Titus, Jerry. "Tusket Ships and Their Builders 1870-1880," *The Argus: the quarterly newsletter of the Argyle Municipality Historical & Genealogical Society,* vol.10 no.3 (Fall 1998), pp.25-33.

Titus, Jerry. "Tusket Ships and Their Builders 1880-1890," *The Argus: the quarterly newsletter of the Argyle Municipality Historical & Genealogical Society,* vol.12 no.1 (Spring 2000), pp.36-46.

J. Lyons Hatfield mill references, *Yarmouth Herald,* Yarmouth, NS, 4 March 1880, 29 April 1880, 3 March 1881, 28 July 1881, 4 January 1883, 15 April 1885, 5 January 1887, 20 August 1890 and 30 September 1891.

Andrew Mack Mill references, *Yarmouth Tribune,* Yarmouth, NS, 9 July 1871 and *Yarmouth Herald,* Yarmouth, NS, 28 February 1878.

N.W. Bethen & Co. sawmill references, *Yarmouth Tribune,* Yarmouth, NS, 10 July 1878, *Yarmouth Herald,* Yarmouth, NS, 5 September 1878, 5 June 1879, 13 November 1879, 4 March 1880 and 30 September 1880.

Tusket River Lumber Company references, *Yarmouth Light,* Yarmouth, NS, 9 June 1891, 21 April 1892, 26 May 1892, 21 July 1892, 25 August 1892, 28 December 1892, 2 March 1893, *Yarmouth Herald,* Yarmouth, NS, 9 January 1894; *Yarmouth Telegram,* Yarmouth, NS, 4 September 1896.

Dickie & McGrath sawmill references, *Yarmouth Daily Globe,* Yarmouth, NS, 27 May 1909; *Yarmouth Daily Times,* Yarmouth, NS, 13 January 1900, 29 December 1908, 31 December 1908; *Yarmouth Herald,* Yarmouth, NS, 29 December 1908, 3 December 1912, 15 August 1922, 10 July 1923; *Yarmouth Light,* Yarmouth, NS, 9 June 1891, 9 September 1897, 11 June 1901, 28 May 1903, 24 December 1903, 18 March 1909, 27 May 1909, 9 December 1909; *Yarmouth Telegram,* Yarmouth, NS, 4 September 1894; *Yarmouth Times*, Yarmouth, NS, 20 November 1896, 13 April 1897, 11 June 1897, 29 September 1900, 10 December 1912, 3 January 1913, 28 May 1915.

LeBaron & Harold Floyd mill references, *Digby Courrier,* Digby, NS, 10 August 1917; *Yarmouth Herald,* Yarmouth, NS, 3 July 1917, 26 November 1918; *Yarmouth Light*, 12 July 1917, 2 September 1918.

Thomas N. McGrath burial record, Sweeny's Funeral Records, excerpts and index compiled by George & Ann (Porter) Sorensen, Springdale, NS, 1990, Ledger 11, p.154 (1924). Printed copy held by ATCHA. Tusket, NS

Interview with Dr. Percy McGrath, Kentville, NS, by the author, 1968. Notes taken during interview held by the author, Tusket, NS, 2005.

Interview with Carl Pottier, Tusket, NS, by the author, March 2005. Notes taken during interview held by the author, Tusket, NS, 2005.

Chapter 10: THE MILITARY

Brown, George S. *Yarmouth, NS: a sequel to Campbell's history.* Boston: Rand Avery Company, 1888.

Campbell, J. R. (Rev) *History of the County of Yarmouth, Nova Scotia.* Saint John, NB: J. & A. McMillan, 1876.

McLachlan, William W. "Canadians on Radar in Canada*." Canadians on Radar – Royal Canadian Air Force, 1940-1945.* Comp. George K. Grande, Sheila M. Linden & Horace R. Macauley. Ottawa: Canadian Radar History Project, 2000.

McLachlan, William W. *Royal Canadian Air Force Personnel on Radar in Canada During World War II.* Ottawa: the author, 2003.

Poole, Edmund Duval. *Annals of Yarmouth and Barrington (Nova Scotia) In the Revolutionary War.* Yarmouth, NS: Lawson Publishing, 1899.

Ricker, Jackson. *Historical Sketches of Glenwood and the Argyles.* Truro, NS: Truro Printing & Publishing, 1941.

Robertson, Marion. *King's Bounty: a History of Early Shelburne, Nova Scotia.* Halifax, NS: Nova Scotia Museum, 1978.

Thurston, Arthur. *A Monument Speaks.* Yarmouth, NS: Arthur Thurston Publications, 1989.

"The Bingay Letter: Tusket Through the Eyes of Dr. James H. Bingay, 1878-1957," *The Argus: the quarterly newsletter of the Argyle Municipality Historical & Genealogical Society,* vol.3 no.4 (Winter 1992), pp.28-41, vol.4 no.1 (Spring 1993), pp.20-34, vol.4 no.2 (Summer 1993), pp.24-36, vol.4 no.3 (Fall 1993), pp.22-36, and vol.4 no.4 (Winter 1993), pp.16-29.

Minute Books of the Tusket War Memorial Association,1923 -1945. Original minute books held by ATCHA, Tusket, NS, 2005 (TMS-36E 212).

Tusket War Memorial inscriptions, photographed and transcribed by the author, February 2004.

Robert Thornton Mack obituary, undated clipping from and unnamed Nova Scotia newspaper, 1950. Original clipping held by ATCHA, Tusket, NS (M1995:318).

Crowell, Peter, ed. "Jack Elmer Hatfield of Tusket, NS - A Casualty of World War II," *The Argus: the quarterly newsletter of the Argyle Municipality Historical & Genealogical Society,* vol.1 no.4 (Winter 1989), pp.15-18.

"Tusket Man Decorated for Leadership and Skill - Frank B. Little." Scrapbook of Yarmouth County, NS World II Military Newspaper Articles compiled by Deanne McArthur, Yarmouth, NS, circa 1998. Scrapbooks held by ATCHA, Tusket, NS, 2005.

Interviews with Tracy Hatfield, Yarmouth, NS, by the author, January – April 2005. Notes taken during interviews held by the author, Tusket, NS, 2005.

Interviews with Roland Bourque, Tusket, NS, by the author, March and April 2005. Roland Bourque, a veteran of World War II, contributed in a major way in compiling the list of local men who served in the War. Notes taken during interviews held by the author, Tusket, NS, 2005.

Interviews with Charlie Muise, Tusket, NS, by the author, March and April 2005. Charlie Muise, a veteran of World War II, contributed in a major way in compiling the list of local men who served in the War. Notes taken during interviews held by the author, Tusket, NS, 2005.

Interview with John Muise and Leslie Muise, Hubbards Point, NS, by the author, March 2005. Notes taken during interview held by the author, Tusket, NS, 2005.

Interview with Jean Goldring, Yarmouth, NS, by the author, March 2005. Notes taken during interview held by the author, Tusket, NS, 2005.

Chapter 11: ACADIANS IN TUSKET

Brown, George S. *Yarmouth, NS: a sequel to Campbell's history.* Boston: Rand Avery Company, 1888.

Campbell, J. R. (Rev) *History of the County of Yarmouth, Nova Scotia.* Saint John, NB: J. & A. McMillan, 1876.

Campbell, Joan Bourque. *Histoire de la Paroisse de Sainte-Anne-du-Ruisseau (Eel Brook.)* Yarmouth, NS : Lescarbot, 1985.

d'Entremont, Clarence Joseph (Rev) *Histoire du Cap-Sable de l'an Mil au Traité de Paris, 1763.* Eunice, Louisiana: Herbert Publications, 1981, 5 vols.

Pottier, Vincent J. *Report of the Royal Commission on Public School Finance in Nova Scotia.* Halifax, NS: Province of NS, 1954.

Church, Ambrose Finson. *Map of the County of Yarmouth, Nova Scotia* (1871). Commission date on map is 1864, publication year was 1871. Most information contained on the map in relation to houses and their owners was gathered around 1866 in the village of Tusket, NS.

"The Bingay Letter: Tusket Through the Eyes of Dr. James H. Bingay, 1878-1957," *The Argus: the quarterly newsletter of the Argyle Municipality Historical & Genealogical Society*, vol.3 no.4 (Winter 1992), pp.28-41, vol.4 no.1 (Spring 1993), pp.20-34, vol.4 no.2 (Summer 1993), pp.24-36, vol.4 no.3 (Fall 1993), pp.22-36, and vol.4 no.4 (Winter 1993), pp.16-29.

Petitions in Benjamin Muise Papers, Université de Moncton, Moncton, NB, photocopies held by ATCHA, Tusket, NS.

Court of General Sessions of the Peace for the Districts of Yarmouth & Argyle, NS, 1789-1855, Minutes Books & Jury Books. NSARM microfilm, RG34 - 324 Yarmouth County - Series P - vols.1-4. Microfilm copy held by ATCHA, Tusket, NS

E. C. Simonson household, 1871 Canada Census, Nova Scotia, Yarmouth County, Sub-district h-1 Tusket, p.10, household no.36, family no.42. National Archives of Canada microfilm #C-10546.

Heritage Property Inventory site form for the property of Cyril Doucette, Tusket, NS, compiled by Peter Crowell, 14 December 1985. Original site forms held by ATCHA, Tusket, NS.

Heritage Property Inventory site form for the property of Moïse Muise, Tusket, NS, compiled by Peter Crowell, 12 April 1986 & 2 May 1988. Original site forms held by ATCHA, Tusket, NS.

Heritage Property Inventory site form for the property of Peter Doucette (son of Christopher), Tusket, NS, compiled by Peter Crowell, 25 January 1986. Original site forms held by ATCHA, Tusket, NS.

Heritage Property Inventory site form for the property of Mark "Maco" Hubbard, Tusket, NS, compiled by Peter Crowell, 29 August 1987. Original site forms held by ATCHA, Tusket, NS.

Heritage Property Inventory site form for the property of Julien Doucette, Tusket, NS, compiled by Peter Crowell, 28 January 1986. Original site forms held by ATCHA, Tusket, NS.

Heritage Property Inventory site form for the property of Simon Doucette, Tusket, NS, compiled by Peter Crowell, 14 January 1986. Original site forms held by ATCHA, Tusket, NS.

Heritage Property Inventory site form for the property of Zacharie "Harry" Doucette, Tusket, NS, compiled by Peter Crowell, 8 January 1986. Original site forms held by ATCHA, Tusket, NS.

Heritage Property Inventory site form for the property of John "Tiga" Doucette and Charles Doucette, Tusket, NS, compiled by Peter Crowell, 14 December 1985. Original site forms held by ATCHA, Tusket, NS.

Baptismal and Marriage Registers, Sainte-Anne's Catholic Church, 1799-1920, Sainte-Anne-du-Ruisseau, NS. Microfilm copies held by ATCHA, Tusket, NS, 2005.

Chapter 12: ODDS & ENDS

Campbell, Joan Bourque. *Histoire de la Paroisse de Sainte-Anne-du-Ruisseau (Eel Brook).* Yarmouth, NS : Lescarbot, 1985.

Lawson, J. Murray. *Yarmouth Past and Present: a Book of Reminiscences.* Yarmouth, NS: Herald Publishing, 1902.

McLachlan, William W. *Royal Canadian Air Force Personnel on Radar in Canada During World War II.* Ottawa: the author, 2003

"The Bingay Letter: Tusket Through the Eyes of Dr. James H. Bingay, 1878-1957," *The Argus: the quarterly newsletter of the Argyle Municipality Historical & Genealogical Society,* vol.3 no.4 (Winter 1992), pp.28-41, vol.4 no.1 (Spring 1993), pp.20-34, vol.4 no.2 (Summer 1993), pp.24-36, vol.4 no.3 (Fall 1993), pp.22-36, and vol.4 no.4 (Winter 1993), pp.16-29.

"The Victorious Tusket Baseball Team, 1912," Argyle Township Court House & Archives 1996 Calendar, Tusket, NS: Argyle Municipality Historical & Genealogical Society, 1996.

Dr. Thomas Kirby obituary, *Yarmouth Herald,* Yarmouth, NS, 4 January 1897.

Blauvelt, J. L. *Seven New Tunes to Church Hymns.* [Yarmouth, NS?]: the author, 1913. Original published sheet music held by ATCHA, Tusket, NS.

James & Mary T. R. (Moody) Bingay (married 29 July 1824) Family Bible Record. *The Argus: the quarterly newsletter of the Argyle Municipality Historical & Genealogical Society,* vol.8 no.2 (Summer 1996), pp.12-18. Original Bible held by ATCHA, Tusket, NS.

Church, Ambrose Finson. *Map of the County of Yarmouth , Nova Scotia* (1871). Commission date on map is 1864, publication year was 1871. Most information contained on the map in relation to houses and their owners was gathered around 1866 in the village of Tusket, NS.

Court of General Sessions of the Peace for the Districts of Yarmouth & Argyle, NS, 1789-1855, Minutes Books & Jury Books. NSARM microfilm, RG34 - 324 Yarmouth County - Series P - vols.1-4. Microfilm copy held by ATCHA, Tusket, NS.

Court of General Sessions of the Peace for the District of Argyle, 1856-1879. Original minute books held by ATCHA, Tusket, NS, 2005.

Mayflower Engine Company Records, 1879-1923, Municipality of the District of Argyle fonds, RG3, Ser.P (Fire Prevention), Sub-series 1. Original records held by ATCHA, Tusket, NS.

Heritage Property Inventory Site Form for the Nathaniel Gardner house, Tusket, NS, compiled by Peter Crowell, 6 January 1986. Original site form and property file held by ATCHA, Tusket, NS, 2005.

Heritage Property Inventory Site Form for the James Langille house, Tusket, NS, compiled by Peter Crowell, 13 December 1985. Original site form and property file held by ATCHA, Tusket, NS, 2005.

Heritage Property Inventory site forms for Charles Knowles house, Tusket, NS, compiled by Peter Crowell, 10 December 1985. Original site form and property file held by ATCHA, Tusket, NS, 2005.

Interviews with Cecelia "Sis" Crosby, Tusket, NS, by the author, 2004 & 2005. Notes taken during interviews held by the author, Tusket, NS, 2005.

Interviews with Charles Muise, Tusket, NS, by the author, 2004 & 2005. Notes taken during interviews held by the author, Tusket, NS, 2005.

Interview with Gerald Jacquard, operator of the Tusket Combustion Turbine Generating Plant, by the author, March 2005. Notes taken during interview held by the author, Tusket, NS, 2005.

Interviews with Margaret (Pottier) d'Entremont, Tusket, NS, by the author, March 2005. Notes taken during interviews held by the author, Tusket, NS, 2005.

Interview with Marcel Muise, Tusket, NS, by the author, March 2005. Notes taken during interview held by the author, Tusket, NS, 2005.

Interview with Gordon Wood, Tusket, NS, by the author, March 2005. Notes taken during interview held by the author, Tusket, NS, 2005.

Chapter 13: TUSKET THIRTY YEARS LATER (2005)

Note: Information on modern businesses, houses and other buildings has been gathered primarily through interviews conducted with local residents of Tusket in March and April 2005. Extensive interviews are listed separately, while those involving information on only one property or piece of information are found in a multiple listing.

Interview with Ian McNicol, Tusket, NS, by the author, April 2005. Notes taken during interview held by the author, Tusket, NS, 2005.

Interviews with Hubert Pothier & Norman Pottier, Tusket, NS, by the author, March & April 2005. Notes taken during interviews held by the author, Tusket, NS, 2005.

Interviews with Carl & Audrey Pottier, Tusket, NS, by the author, March & April 2005. Notes taken during interviews held by the author, Tusket, NS, 2005.

Interview with Irving Surette, Sainte-Anne-du-Ruisseau, NS, by the author, April 2005. Notes taken during interview held by the author, Tusket, NS, 2005.

Interview with Rev. Clarence Thibeau, Yarmouth, NS, by the author, March 2005. Notes taken during interview held by the author, Tusket, NS, 2005.

Interview with Eddie Madden, Surette's Island, NS, by the author, March 2005. Notes taken during interview held by the author, Tusket, NS, 2005.

Interviews with Doreen Bain, Coastal Financial Credit Union, Tusket, NS, April 2005. Notes taken during interviews held by the author, Tusket, NS, 2005.

Interview with Charlotte Muise, Abrams River, NS by the author, April 2005. Notes taken during interview held by the author, Tusket, NS, 2005.

St. Anne's Credit Union Scrapbook-Album, held by Coastal Financial Credit Union, Tusket, NS, 2005.

Minutes of St. Anne's Credit Union, held by Coastal Financial Credit Union, Tusket, NS, 2005.

Interviews by Don R. Pothier, the author, Tusket, NS, with the following people, March & April 2005, all residents of Tusket, unless otherwise indicated: Marco Albright, Gary Bourque (Belleville), Fred Churchill (Raynardton), Edwin Coffin, Lynn Comeau, Ulysse Cottreau (Amirault's Hill), Kenneth Crane, Cecilia "Sis" Crosby, Nate Crosby (Dayton), Marvin Cunningham, Alice d'Entremont (Dept. of Fisheries), Jeff d'Entremont (Arcadia), Abel Doucet (Pleasant Lake), Cindy Doucette, John Duckworth (Forest Glen), Peter Dulong, Yvonne Eaton, David Gordon (Dept. Natural Resources), Gordon Hatfield, James Hatfield, Amanda Hubbard, Barbara Hubbard, Kevin Hubbard, Terrence Huskins, Angie Kerr, Leslie Kuhn (Yarmouth), Brian LeBlanc (South Belleville), Carol LeBlanc (Arcadia), Darrell LeBlanc, Elsie LeBlanc (Sainte Anne-du-Ruisseau) (HP Motel property), Denise LeBlanc, Donna LeFave, Eddie Madden, Linda Morris, Gail Muise, George Muise, Hayley Muise, Kaye Muise (École Secondaire de Par-en-Bas), Marcel Muise, William and Sharon Muise, Dr. Milton & Audrey O'Brien, Joan Patten, Polly Patten, David Pothier, Hubert Pothier, Audrey & Carl Pottier, Josephine Pottier, Norman Pottier, James Quick (Yarmouth), Geraldine "Gerry" Rhyno, Edwin Robichaud, Debbie Surette, Raymond Surette (Sainte Anne-du-

Ruisseau) (HP Motel property), Judy Sweeney, Malcolm Sweeney, Rodney Sweeney, Brenda Taylor (Yarmouth), Shawn Winters, Billy Wood and Tim Wood. Notes taken during interviews held by the author, Tusket, NS, 2005.

Interviews by Peter Crowell, the editor, Yarmouth, NS, with the following people, March & April 2005, all residents of Tusket, unless otherwise indicated: Patsy Scoville, Barbara Muise, Clarence Doucette, Roberta Swinimer (Argyle), Evelyn Muise, Karen Sweeney, Ernest Doucet and Don Gavel (Pleasant Lake). Notes taken during interviews held by the author, Don R. Pothier, Tusket, NS, 2005.

PHOTOGRAPH SOURCES

PHOTOGRAPH SOURCES

Note: The origin or source for many of the photographs used in this history is somewhat complicated. Even before I began the history in 1973 Gordon Wood and I were collecting historic photographs of Tusket. In most cases we borrowed original photographs from the owners, had negatives and copies made, and returned the originals to the owners. In some cases originals were given to me. After the establishment of the Argyle Township Court House Archives (ATCHA) in 1982 I donated many prints of these images to the archives, or loaned negatives so that they might have prints made. The archives itself has also received many donations of original photographs over the years since 1982. In many cases, the originals, from which my prints were made, are now owned by the archives. In citing my sources for photographs, I have endeavored to give credit to all those people who owned the original images at the time. In any case where the Argyle Township Court House now holds a print of the same image, I have cited their call number for the photograph as well. This will enable readers who might wish to do so to obtain prints from the archives of individual photographs.

Chapter 2 – A VILLAGE WALKING TOUR

p. 25   Aerial photo of Tusket by Don R. Pothier, June 1975.

p. 26   "The Point, Tusket, NS." Photo by Gordon S. Hatfield. Original loaned to the archives for copying by Mrs. Frances Nickerson, Tusket Falls, NS. ATCHA Photo # P1993:210.

p. 27   "River View Farm." Photo by Gordon S. Hatfield, ATCHA Photo #P1991:584.

p. 27   Abraham Lent. Photo courtesy of Susan Young, from the collection of the late Phyllis (Hatfield) Young. ATCHA Photo #P1991:420.

p. 29   Wilbur and Margaret Wood house. Photo by Don R. Pothier, 2005.

p. 29   Adolphus Hatfield house. ATCHA Heritage Property Inventory photo, Film#27, photo 26A.

p. 31   Roger Doucet blacksmith shop. Photo by Don R. Pothier, 2005.

p. 31   Abel Doucet with oxen. Photo courtesy of Abel Doucet, Pleasant Lake, NS.

p. 32   Melanie Hubbard house. Photo by Don R. Pothier, 2005.

p. 32   Roy Hubbard. Photo by Don R. Pothier, 2003.

p. 33   Pierre Melanson house. Photo by Don R. Pothier, 2005.

p. 34   "Mission House." ATCHA Photo #P1998:334.

p. 35   Joseph Blanchard house. Photo by Don R. Pothier, 2005.

p. 36   Dr. Thomas Kirby house. ATCHA Photo #P1998:335.

p. 36   Peter Lent Hatfield house. Photo by Don R. Pothier, 2005.

p. 37   Peter Lent Hatfield. Photo courtesy of Susan Young, from the collection of the late Phyllis (Hatfield) Young. ATCHA Photo #P1991:566.

p. 57	Methodist Church and W.T. Lent house. Photo by Gordon S. Hatfield. Photo courtesy of Susan Young, Tusket, NS, from the collection of the late Phyllis (Hatfield) Young. ATCHA Photo #P1992: 212.
p. 57	Old W.T. Lent house. Don R. Pothier collection. Original loaned for copying by the late Mildred (Lent) Hatfield, Tusket, NS. ATCHA Photo #P1987: 90.
p. 58	Centre of Tusket. Don R. Pothier collection. Original loaned for copying by the late Gertrude Wathen, Tusket, NS. ATCHA Photo #P1989: 652.
p. 59	"Tusket, N.S." Village centre. Photo by Gordon S. Hatfield. Don R. Pothier collection. Original print supplied by the late Phyllis (Hatfield) Young, Tusket, NS. ATCHA Photo #P1983: 55.
p. 60	"May 24th Horse & Buggy Trip." Don R. Pothier collection. Original loaned for copying by the late Mildred (Lent) Hatfield, Tusket, NS. ATCHA Photo #P1992: 473.
p. 61	"Paving Highway #3." ATCHA Photo #P1994: 689.
p. 61	Aerial photo of the John White Road. Photo by Don R. Pothier, June 1975.
p. 62	Chrissie Hatfield house. Original photo loaned to the archives for copying by Mrs. George Lortz, Raleigh, NC. ATCHA photo P1988: 638.
p. 63	Frank Hubbard house. Photo by Don R. Pothier, 2005.
p. 63	Hauling of a building. Photo courtesy of Susan Young, Tusket, NS, from the collection of the late Phyllis (Hatfield) Young. ATCHA Photo #P1991: 425.
p. 65	John and Fannie White house. Photo loaned to the archives for copying by B. Malcolm Patterson, Tusket, NS. ATCHA Photo #P1986: 26.
p. 65	Felix Muise house. ATCHA Heritage Property Inventory photo, Film #13, photo 19A.
p. 66	Raymond "Peege" Hubbard house. Photo courtesy of Diane & David Muise, Hubbards Point, NS.
p. 68	Remi LeFave house. ATCHA Heritage Property Inventory photo, Film #13, photo 14A.
p. 69	"Gingerbread House." ATCHA Photo #P1995:161.
p. 69	"Gingerbread House - north gable end." ATCHA Photo #P1995:162.
p. 70	Mr. & Mrs. Thomas N. McGrath in front of their home. Don R. Pothier collection. Original given to the author by the late Dr. Percy McGrath, Kentville, NS, 1968. ATCHA photo #P1992:465.
p. 71	Interior photograph of the Thomas N. McGrath house (dining room), by an unknown professional photographer. Don R. Pothier collection. Original given to the author by the late Dr. Percy McGrath, Kentville, NS, 1968. ATCHA Photo # P1987:131.
p. 72	Interior photograph of the Thomas N. McGrath house (reading room), by an unknown professional photographer. Don R. Pothier. Original given to the author by the late Dr. Percy McGrath, Kentville, NS, 1968. ATCHA Photo # P1987:130.

Chapter 6 – SCHOOLS

Chapter 7 – POSTAL SERVICE

Chapter 8 – TRANSPORTATION

Chapter 11 – THE MILITARY

Chapter 12 – ACADIANS IN TUSKET

Chapter 13 – ODDS & ENDS

Chapter 14 – TUSKET THIRTY YEARS LATER (2005)

Back cover: Photo by Gerry Green, 2004.

INDEX

396

NOTES